America's Geisha Ally

Naoko Shibusawa

America's Geisha Ally

REIMAGINING THE JAPANESE ENEMY

HARVARD UNIVERSITY PRESS

CAMBRIDGE, MASSACHUSETTS

LONDON, ENGLAND

2006

Library of Congress Cataloging-in-Publication Data
Shibusawa, Naoko.
America's geisha ally :
reimagining the Japanese enemy /
Naoko Shibusawa.
p.   cm.
Includes bibliographical references.
ISBN-13: 978-0-674-02348-2 (alk. paper)
ISBN-10: 0-674-02348-X (alk. paper)
1. United States—Relations—Japan.
2. Japan—Relations—United States.
3. Japan—Foreign public opinion, American.
4. Public opinion—United States.
5. Japan—Civilization—1945–
6. National characteristics, Japanese.
I. Title.

E183.8.J3S52 2006
303.48′27305209045—dc22   2006043556

Designed by Gwen Nefsky Frankfeldt

For Andy, Arisa, and Miya

CONTENTS

Note on Japanese Names

I have followed the Japanese convention of placing surnames before given names and using macrons to denote long vowel sounds (for example, Tōjō Hideki). I make an exception to this either when the Japanese name is given in a quotation (for example, Tojo) or when I am describing the actions of a Japanese individual in the United States. In the American context, I have written the Japanese names in the western convention, with given names first and surnames last (for example, Kiyoshi Tanimoto). If there is any doubt about whether a name is a given name or a surname, the reader can consult the index, where the names are listed alphabetically according to surname. Japanese place names (for example, Tōkyō, Ōsaka) appear without macrons for ease of reading.

The Japanese attack on Pearl Harbor on December 7, 1941, shocked and disturbed Americans. *Time* magazine captured popular sentiment when it called the attack "premeditated murder masked by a toothy smile." Caught unguarded and literally sleeping, "tens of thousands" of now rudely awakened Americans cried, "the yellow bastards!" At once amazed and outraged that the Japanese pilots were able to cross the Pacific and successfully launch a surprise attack, Americans demanded vengeance. In Norfolk, Virginia, the first man to show up at a military recruiting center declared: "I want to beat them Japs with my own hands!" A misguided patriot in Washington, D.C., "frustrated that he couldn't get at the real Japanese," chopped down four Japanese cherry trees along the Washington tidal basin. And in Nashville, Tennessee, the Department of Conservation reportedly denied a requisition for 6 million two-dollar licenses to hunt "Japs." It explained the refusal with a note: "Open season on 'Japs'—no license required."[1] The war in the Pacific unleashed a racial hatred that sometimes bordered on genocidal rage, which continued throughout the conflict.[2]

As Americans waged a "war without mercy," they were influenced by pre-existing fears of the "yellow peril"—the thrifty, industrious, imitative, and clever Japanese immigrants in the United States. The Japanese were allegedly an unassimilable people who could survive on rice alone and who threatened to undermine the livelihoods of Euroamerican workers and farmers.[3] Many Americans believed that the inscrutable "Japs" used sneaky methods to gain an unfair advantage, and the attack on Pearl Harbor confirmed their suspicions that the Japanese were a uniquely treacherous people. Because so many Americans believed that this treachery was an inherent, racial characteristic, Japanese immigrants and their American-born children came to be categorized as enemies just like those in Japan. Under the false, wrong-headed guise of military necessity, the federal government rounded up and interned the entire west coast Japanese American population—babies, children, and teenagers as well as adults—as potential saboteurs.

Toward the end of the war, Time-Life publisher Henry Luce observed: "Americans had to learn to hate Germans, but hating Japs comes natural—as natural as fighting Indians once was."[4] To him and other Americans at mid-century, racial animosity and cultural incompatibility were "natural" or commonsensical.[5] In their eyes, both the Native Americans and the Japanese were "savages" who adhered to strange, irrational beliefs and failed to abide by the laws of the "civilized" western tradition. The brutal treatment of Allied prisoners of war by the Japanese and their alleged suicidal devotion to the emperor made them, Americans believed, more outrageous foes than the Germans, and fighting in the Pacific was thus more vicious. Because of their cultural affinity with Germans, most Americans differentiated "good Germans" from the Nazis, but they tended to condemn all Japanese as fanatics who sought to glorify their "son of heaven."[6]

After the war's end many American public figures and private citizens still saw the Japanese as the enemy. In fact, a Gallup poll showed that a majority of Americans regretted that there were not more atomic bombs to drop on Japan. At a dinner celebrating the return of the Third Fleet to San Francisco, Admiral William Halsey declared that a policy of "leniency" to the Japanese would be an insult to the sacrifice and horrors that American fighting men endured to secure the "total defeat of a ruthless foe."[7] Articulated at a time when newspaper front pages carried testimonies by former POWs about Japanese atrocities, Halsey's argument made sense to a larger public disinclined to look upon the Japanese with kindness.

Clearly many Americans continued to despise the "Japs" after the war, but as the Cold War intensified shortly thereafter, Japan became America's most important ally in Asia. Although American bombardiers devastated nearly all of its cities during the war, Japan remained an industrialized nation with financial institutions, a transportation and communications infrastructure, and an educated, disciplined workforce. Because it retained the necessary components of a successful capitalist society and was strategically located off the Asian mainland, Japan became America's "bulwark" against communism in the Far East. As U.S. policymakers increasingly worried about communism spreading throughout Asia, they focused on their former enemy's economic revitalization in an attempt to make Japan a model of capitalism in Asia.[8] Thus American policymakers had to abandon their earlier Occupation priorities of democratizing Japan and holding it accountable for its aggressive war against its Asian neighbors. After 1947 and 1948 the military government in Japan, SCAP (the Supreme Commander for the Allied Powers), embarked on what historians now call the "reverse course." SCAP rolled back many of its ambitious reforms such as land redistribution, canceling plans to make Japan a more democratic, equitable nation. Intent on strengthening the Japanese economy, the United States also stopped Japan's reparations to its Asian victims and coerced Asian nations to serve once again as Japan's quasi-colonial source of raw materials. Adding insult to injury, the United States refused to have Hirohito tried as a war criminal, thereby protecting the man in whose name Japan had waged a horribly destructive war that brought death and misery to millions of Asians.[9] Thus Japan, the predominant Asian aggressor of World War II, became the region's greatest beneficiary of the Cold War. To further its Cold War objectives, the United States protected and fostered the Japanese economy, laying the groundwork for Japan's "economic miracle" of the 1950s and 1960s.[10]

We know why U.S. policymakers decided to make Japan such an important ally so quickly after a brutal war, but much less is known about how they were able to get Americans' support for their policies regarding postwar Japan. How was the American public able to accept an alliance with Japan when not so long ago the "Japs" had been thoroughly vilified as subhuman, buck-toothed apes with Coke-bottle glasses? Elite policymakers may have decided to make Japan a bulwark against communism, but how did the public come to accept this policy so soon after World War II?

This remarkable reversal from hated racial enemy to valuable ally can best be understood by tracing the shifts in attitudes toward the Japanese in American public discourse. The postwar public discourse assumed two "natural" or universally recognized hierarchical relationships—man over woman and adult over child—and compared them to the relationship between the United States, a "white" nation, and Japan, a "nonwhite" nation. Portraying Japan as a woman made its political subjugation appear as natural as a geisha's subservience to a male client, while picturing Japan as a child emphasized its potential to "grow up" into a democracy. After the war, Americans began to view the U.S.-Japan relationship through these commonly accepted, pre-existing ideologies about gender and maturity. By conceiving the bilateral relationship in the mutually reinforcing frameworks of gender and maturity, many Americans began seeing the Japanese not as savages but as dependents that needed U.S. guidance and benevolence. In other words, the ideologies of gender and maturity helped to minimize racial hostility. Feminizing the hated enemy or regarding them as immature youths made it easier to humanize the Japanese and to recast them as an American responsibility.

The ideology of maturity, like those of race and gender, has helped to rationalize power hierarchies. Analogies derived from the natural life cycle have long been used as conceptual devices to justify political privileges and dominance. "Maturity," which white Americans believed nonwhites had not attained, signified ability, wisdom, and self-control—characteristics that supposedly entitled adult white men to status and power. Unlike gender or race, however, immaturity was not a permanent fate, but a transitional stage. Prior to World War II, American policymakers had emphasized that this notion of immaturity implied that a nation could potentially grow into "responsibility." They used this thinking to argue for the "temporary" subjugation of another people until they were "ready" for autonomy, but often did so without sincerity. After the war, however, policymakers became more earnest about their pronouncements that nonwhite nations could "grow up" into modern, liberal capitalist democracies. This belief undergirded what became known as the modernization theory.[11] With its focus on the potential of nonwhite nations to "develop" toward modernity, the ideology of maturity permitted postwar commentators to claim they were rejecting the existence of biological racial differences while in fact they continued to promote an international racial hierarchy.[12]

These ideologies of race, gender, and maturity overlapped and buttressed one another. At the same time, they were characterized by a degree of fluidity and conditioned by historical context and circumstances. Ideology, in the useful definition of diplomatic historian Michael H. Hunt, is "an interrelated set of convictions or assumptions that reduces the complexities of a particular slice of reality to easily comprehensible terms and suggests appropriate ways of dealing with that reality."[13] Ideologies are both ways of viewing the world and calls for particular actions at specific moments. At different times in U.S. history, American racial ideology has called for the noblesse oblige of the "white man's burden" and for genocidal warfare against Native Americans. Of course, not all beliefs or assumptions that comprise an ideology stay fixed over time. Late-nineteenth-century scholarship told Americans that immutable biological differences made nonwhites inferior to whites. By the mid-twentieth century, research about deviance and "abnormal" psychosocial development was reinforcing American beliefs about the inferiority of nonwhites in a more subtle way. Thus to understand the reversal in the American public perception of Japan, we must examine the historical context in which these ideologies operated.

How Americans reframed Japan after the war was influenced both by the way Americans came to grips with their new role as global leaders and by the way they viewed the meaning of democracy in a changing world where old hierarchies were being challenged. At home, the changes most tangible to Americans involved gender and race relations. Women were poised to challenge the established economic and political dominance of Euro-american men and to sustain the greater authority, opportunity, and pay they had enjoyed during the war. Although an organized challenge by women did not gain momentum until a couple of decades later, the potential for disrupting the traditional gender order was evident in postwar public discourse. Indeed, the way Americans depicted Japanese women as exemplars of femininity in the Cold War culture can be seen as a defense against this new attitude. African Americans, on the other hand, were better organized and prepared to demand social and political equality now that the fight for democracy abroad had been victorious. Their plight and the fact of racial discrimination in American society heightened the discussion about the need for "tolerance" of minorities in a democratic society. The way Americans treated racial minorities—including the recently interned Japanese Americans—became not just a matter of moral conscience, but one of foreign policy and national prestige as the United States sought to win over newly decolonized nations into its orbit.[14]

The postwar images of the Japanese, therefore, were the product of transformations in American thought resulting from changes in race and gender relations domestically as well as the emergence of the United States as a global power confronting the Soviet Union and the Communist bloc. Although the Japanese certainly participated in the process of altering their image by trying to present their nation as a peaceful, reliable friend of the United States, my focus here is on American discourse and culture as they concerned Japan and the way internationally-minded Americans understood their responsibilities as world leaders in the middle of the twentieth century.

The reimaging of the Japanese in American public discourse engaged a broad range of governmental and nongovernmental actors, including General Douglas MacArthur, California Superior Court Judge William Mathes, and State Department officials, as well as journalists, writers, Hollywood filmmakers, and private citizens. Particularly important in this process were the Americans who went to Japan during the Occupation; they were the vanguard of the shifts that took place stateside. In addition to MacArthur and other SCAP officials, ordinary soldiers like Hugh O'Reilly, Elliott Chaze, and Martin Bronfenbrenner reported their perceptions to their fellow Americans back home. Similarly, journalists like Clark Lee, Frank Kelley, Cornelius Ryan, and John LaCerda wrote extensively about their experiences in Occupied Japan, as did other writers and memoirists including Lucy Herndon Crockett, Helen Mears, and Margery Brown. The resulting new portrayal of Japan became a standard way to understand the Japanese in American media, film, and academic works during the Cold War.

Although a broad range of individuals were involved in the changing discourse about the Japanese, the majority of them can be identified as postwar, consensus, or Cold War liberals. While they differed in status, political affiliation, and degree of sensitivity or affinity toward the Japanese, theirs were among the dominant voices of the era that sustained a broad discussion about racial tolerance and its importance to U.S. credibility as a champion of human freedom and dignity. The postwar liberals' engagement with race and international relations made them, as a group, vital to the reimaging of the nonwhite Japanese enemy. Tending to be more affluent and better educated than other Americans, these individuals—the Occupation memoirists, the writers of the *Saturday Review of Literature*, the editors of *Senior Scholastic*, Hollywood filmmakers, and even lawyers and judges involved in courtroom battles—were bound by a similar stake in American society. These postwar liberals, influenced by a common cultural tradition, trusted that an enlightened use of government power could safeguard individual liberties while preserving a commitment to the common good and "universal," humanistic values. Cold War consensus liberals believed that the combination of political rights, material wealth, and educational attainment could bring about a vibrant democratic society that would be resistant to totalitarianism. While they were generally optimistic about their state's and their citizenry's ability to bring about and guarantee these conditions, they often believed that other states and peoples lacked the maturity to do this competently. Thus, in addition to the openness and desire for international goodwill that postwar liberals displayed, there was an arrogance and faith in American exceptionalism that often undercut their efforts to be antiracist.

As the images of the Japanese changed, this altered view profoundly affected many lives. In this book we will encounter the stories of GIs who married Japanese wives, postwar Japanese college students living in the United States, a Japanese American accused of treason, and the Hiroshima Maidens and Moral Adoptees. All of these narratives go beyond perceptions to reveal the real-life impact of ideologies. But at the same time, as we will see, all these individuals—willingly or unwillingly—participated in shifting the American discourse about the Japanese.

Transforming the Japanese enemy into an acceptable ally in American culture was a complex and uneven process, sometimes involving various branches of the government—either directly as in SCAP's orientation materials for Occupation personnel, or indirectly through its support of efforts by private entities. The government, by and large, did not orchestrate the postwar shift in popular perceptions about the Japanese. Independently and sometimes unknowingly, Americans tended to spread views that supported government objectives. Together with U.S. government officials, American writers and filmmakers put forth a remarkably cohesive message about the Japanese and about the proper relationship between the United States and its former enemies. Although many of these historical actors seemed to realize that they were participating in a process to bring about greater amity between Americans and Japanese, they were not always conscious of *how* they were doing this. Because these Cold War liberals shared commonly accepted attitudes about American greatness as well as race, gender, and maturity, their statements about Japanese childishness or naiveté appeared self-evident to them; they did not consciously employ ideologies of gender and maturity.

The shift in American perceptions of Japan, especially in cultural outlets such as periodicals, films, and newspapers, occurred unevenly, moving irregularly and fitfully toward a greater acceptance of the Japanese as friendly allies. Nor did these cultural changes necessarily proceed in lockstep with political events occurring at the state level. In other words, there was rarely a unidirectional movement from policy objectives to popular culture. Instead, political goals and popular culture existed in a complex interplay—a symbiosis that allowed for some differences and contradictions. This meant that the various elements within American public discourse and culture generally validated but sometimes opposed the goals of the policymakers, who themselves often disagreed on the particulars of policy. Nor did all Americans accept this changed perception of Japan. While many readers of *Life* magazine or viewers of a Hollywood movie were receptive to the lessons about racial tolerance and the Japanese, numerous others rejected them. Even today in America one can encounter confessions about still not trusting the Japanese, or anecdotes about how an older relative continues to hate the Japanese because of Pearl Harbor. Negative stereotypes of Japan remain embedded in American culture, ready to be pulled out as the political and economic situation changes.

This book is not an examination of how Occupation officials formulated policy; rather, it is a cultural history that seeks to understand how ideologies in the United States supported American foreign policy. While many historians of U.S. foreign relations have been influenced by the "cultural turn" in the last decade, most continue to focus on policymaking and build arguments that try to show how cultural constructs like gender shaped policy.[15] Others have studied American or western images of Japan, but have not explicitly connected these images to the expression of American or western power at home and abroad.[16] Some scholars, however, have sought to understand how American culture has supported the extension of U.S. power abroad.[17] Edward Said's theory of Orientalism demonstrated how seemingly innocuous European texts of literature or academic scholarship helped maintain unequal and often exploitive relations between imperial European powers and their subject Middle Eastern colonies by depicting the "oriental Other" as incapable of self-control, hence of self-rule.[18] Thus the ideology of Orientalism provided imperialists with a justification for keeping colonized peoples subjugated. To be sure, the United States never exploited resource-poor Japan as a formal colony; instead, the U.S. helped make Japan a model of capitalism so that it became, in Chalmers Johnson's words, the "richest prize in the American empire."[19] Nevertheless, Said's theory does allow us to appreciate how the citizens of a powerful nation can unwittingly or subconsciously perpetuate their nation's foreign policy.

Despite the title of this book, it has very little to do with actual geishas. But the notion of the geisha—a very marginal cultural institution in Japanese society—was central to postwar America's vision of Japan. How that came to be is the subject of this book.

CHAPTER ONE

Women and Children First

On a gray December day in 1945, Lucy Herndon Crockett arrived in Japan to begin a stint as a Red Cross worker for the Occupation. Her attitude toward the Japanese was grim as the winter sky that day: the "Japs," she believed, were a nation of fanatical die-hards who deserved the thorough punishment they had received from the Allied Forces, not least from the B-29 bombers that made all Japanese cities resemble Hiroshima and Nagasaki. As she was driven from Atsugi Airfield to Tokyo, however, she was surprised to find the Japanese landscape vaguely familiar. The tile and straw-hatched roofs, fallow rice paddies, and neatly manicured trees she had seen "all before"—on paper fans, chinaware, and textiles. "Each scenic feature," Crockett later wrote in her Occupation memoir, "was already as familiar as a Fujiyama trademark."[1]

After marveling at the familiarity of the Japanese countryside, Crockett found herself deposited at the Dai Iti Hotel, her billet. After she dumped her bags in the lobby, she "scatter[ed] no smiles among any of the little people who scurried and bowed and hissed." Her resolve to remain cold toward "the little people" was shared by many, if not most, Americans at this time. Mainstream media statements attested to the widespread belief that the Japanese were predestined, born enemies; it was common to find matter-of-fact observations such as "We Americans find it easy to hate the Japanese" or "hating Japs comes natural—as natural as fighting Indians once was."[2] After the war, the testimonies of freed POWs detailing the deprivations and brutalities inflicted on white Allied prisoners in "Jap prison camps" reinforced the racial enmity toward the Japanese. In September 1945, the *Honolulu Advertiser* editorialized that "self-respecting Americans" would not be able to use the term "friend" to describe the Japanese for some time. Japan, after all, was "a land of treachery and unspeakable horror whose people hardly without exception are fiendish and cruel."[3] Although "the most fantastically nationalistic people on earth" surprised Americans by peaceably accepting the presence of the American conquerors, early reports of the Occupation told Americans to remain on guard against further treachery because "down in their hearts the conquered people of Japan [were] bitterly hostile."[4]

Aware of these latest reports, Crockett went to Japan determined to be frosty toward the former enemy—until one morning when the hotel maid timidly knocked at her door. She entered Crockett's room, bowing over and over. "American ladies very nice-u," Crockett recalled, trying to mimic the maid's Japanese accent. The woman shyly proffered a vase of flowers as a "present-o," touching Crockett and softening her defenses. "How could I help but be won over?" she asked. "Such ingenuously friendly overtures serve[d] to disarm the most coldly skeptical newcomer, as cordial hospitality [was] extended the conqueror on all sides."[5] Japanese women, like Crockett's hotel maid, helped to chip away at the wartime stereotype of brutal Japanese soldiers by exhibiting humility rather than arrogance, consideration rather than cruelty, and loyal service instead of treachery. The Japanese women, especially those in service positions, seemed to redeem their people in the eyes of many Americans. The supposed servility and hyper-femininity of Japanese women facilitated American amity toward an enemy race.

Even more than Japanese women, it was the Japanese children, Crockett wrote, who constituted "the strongest sympathetic Japanese element in breaking down the barrier between conqueror and ex-enemy." At the start of the Occupation the Americans encountered tense and aloof adults in Tokyo, and fearful and defeated adults throughout the rest of Japan. The vanquished people had been told to expect the very worst from American soldiers.[6] The Americans, however, discovered that few barriers existed with the Japanese children. A Marine Corps sergeant told Lucy Crockett that when he and his group came into a Nagasaki neighborhood, the streets were nearly deserted because the residents were hiding in their homes. As they went through town, however, the GIs spied some curious children peeking out around a corner, and soon, more children. They paused to hand out candy. "Before we knew it we were surrounded," the sergeant recalled. "When the older people watching our every movement saw that we weren't bayoneting their kids and tearing them apart, but instead were treating them with kindness, they realized we weren't quite the monsters they had expected. Soon the panels began sliding open."[7] *Newsweek* reported in September 1945 that the GIs had fraternized very little with the Japanese, but could not resist giving candy or food to the "especially cute" and "wide-eyed Jap kids, who often show far less hatred toward Americans than their war-conscious parents."[8] By the time Crockett arrived in December, the children pleading for "chocoretto" or "chuingamu" from big American soldiers had emerged as archetypal figures of the U.S. Occupation of Japan, remembered by all who lived through it.⁹

Crockett noticed that by far the most popular leisure-time activity among Americans upon arrival in Japan was shopping. In addition to the pleasing women and cute kids who helped persuade Americans to resume friendly interactions with the defeated enemy, consumer items encouraged them to restart a commercial relationship with the Japanese. "Yanks Start Kimono Hunt, Learn What Geisha Doesn't," announced *Newsweek* in its first report of Americans in Occupied Japan.¹⁰ The Americans went on such a frantic search for souvenirs that several correspondents and memoirists wryly noted that buying things Japanese must be "the primary object of the Japanese occupation." Important missions to Kyoto from Washington or General Headquarters in Tokyo, Crockett observed, tended to collapse "into hectic shopping tours" to buy "cheap white silk kimonos embroidered with flamboyant dragons and flowers . . . white silk scarves, handkerchiefs, pajamas, and doilies similarly embroidered or brightly painted with pictures of Fuji-yama, geisha girls, cherry blossoms, and torii gates," as well as other products made, once again, for "foreign consumption."¹¹

Tourism provided another way for the American conquerors to become familiar with Japan. Amidst the everyday business of the Occupation, stated Crockett, the American conquerors "dispassionately and systematically surveyed" Japan for their pleasure and entertainment. It seemed to Crockett that the "most colorful sights that fifteen hundred miles of beauty-packed archipelago and a thousand or more years of culture have to offer has been neatly processed and packed for the benefit of Allied personnel." She acknowledged the extensive damage inflicted by American B-29s and described the Japanese landscape as "the face of a still-beautiful woman pockmarked by ugly scars." The pockmarks, however, did not unduly diminish her or other Americans' enjoyment of scenic Japan—pagodas, rice paddies, geishas, and babies carried on the backs of their mothers.[12] The Occupation forces shot so many photographs in Japan, Crockett observed, that part of every American's "uniform" was not pistols in holsters but Kodaks, Leicas, or Speed Graphics in leather cases with shoulder straps.[13]

The U.S. Occupation government knew that many Americans, like Lucy Crockett, had arrived in Japan still deeply hostile and suspicious of their recent enemy. SCAP (Supreme Commander for the Allied Powers) carried the added burden of reducing the antagonism of its personnel in order to help reintegrate Japan into the liberal capitalist order. One strategy SCAP used to cope with this challenge was emphasizing the Americans' historic responsibility. "Here's where we can clinch our victory or muff it," warned *Our Job in Japan,* the War Department film that was required viewing for American troops throughout Japan, Okinawa, and Korea. Lasting peace could be had if Americans could "solve the problem of 70 million people" who had been "trained to follow blindly wherever their leaders led them." This problem originated with the Japanese brain, which was, the film stressed, not physically different from an American brain—an indication that SCAP rejected scientific racism. Cutting to a picture of Japanese babies, the camera focused on one: "This kid starts life as any other kid. None of them was born with dangerous ideas." It was SCAP's job to re-educate the Japanese brain which had been warped by the "militarists" to think that Japan could rule the world. Now it was time to teach and allow the Japanese to think, read, speak, and hear "the truth" about the folly of their old ways and embrace "a form of government we know will work for peace."[14]

Our Job in Japan underscored the Americans' pedagogical role in Japan: teaching the wayward Japanese pupils to give up adolescent dreams to "lick the whole cockeyed world" and embrace peace instead. This meant GIs had to learn that a "conquering-hero complex isn't going to help anybody," as the U.S. Army's pamphlet *A Pocket Guide to Japan* intoned. The *Pocket Guide* reminded GIs that "even in occupied Japan, the hero role doesn't fit. We're trying to teach [an] authority-ridden people the meaning of democracy. It isn't going to help if the occupation simply means a change in bullies. It's up to us to teach them that 'kicking around' is not the normal scheme of things." Since proper authorities would be punishing the Japanese war criminals in courts of law, the *Pocket Guide* admonished, "it is not your job to decide on the spur of the moment that you want to 'punish' the Japanese by molesting them." The GIs should not treat people as if "they belong to an inferior race or group." "Respect strange customs and traditions." The guide reminded them that as members of the Occupation, they were to be "unofficial ambassadors of the United States" and exhorted them to act with the civility that they would exhibit at home.[15] The "Orientation Pamphlet for New Personnel" of SCAP's Civil Information and Education (CIE) section stated that "the Japanese people cannot be expected to accept the new ideas which are being brought to them if the American whom they observe daily makes no effort to understand Japanese society." The pamphlet therefore urged the CIE personnel to get out and try to know the Japanese better through sympathetic observation and polite questioning.[16]

Likewise, SCAP had the GIs learn more about Japanese customs in order to foster empathy and respect toward a people who a few months earlier "were being described in Army propaganda," journalist John LaCerda noted, "as split-toed apemen who deserved a death as brutal as . . . they inflicted." All soldiers now had to receive an hour's worth of instruction in "combat subjects [such] as Japanese flower arrangement, incense burning, marriage, dress, tea ceremonies, and fishing with cormorants."[17] The *Pocket Guide to Japan* not only explained that the servicemen's purpose in going to Japan was to protect a defenseless nation, but also tried to foster respect for the Japanese by praising their "beautiful work in woodcarving, lacquer, and cloisonné." The guide briefly sketched Japanese history, giving the impression that while the Japanese were talented in the arts, they were dangerous and incompetent in worldly, manly affairs. Not surprisingly, the guide depicted on its cover two young Japanese girls in kimonos flying a kite.[18]

SCAP's strategies to remake the Americans' image of the Japanese thus dovetailed with the Occupation personnel's warm response to Japanese women and children. SCAP's orientation materials promoted a traditional view of women's and children's dependence and helplessness and called for Occupation forces to bestow strong, manly protection, intervention, and guidance. The focus on Japanese femininity and childishness—as well as on actual Japanese women and children—thus allowed Americans to downplay the supposed barbarism of the Japanese soldier and to display a form of liberal paternalism toward the Japanese. Different from colonial paternalism, this liberal paternalism tried to foster quicker growth and development from a "backward" state toward a democratic political economy. By seeing themselves as mentors and protectors of a Japan that was as vulnerable and helpless as a woman or a child, liberal Americans softened their perceptions about Japan. This framework made the temporary protection and tutelage of Japan seem logical and necessary.[19] It was a narrative that even stateside Americans could eventually agree to, if grudgingly, because it appeared commonsensical.

But it was the Americans in Occupied Japan who first accepted this view and who, moreover, saw their mentoring role as consistent with their enjoyment of Japan's commercialized attractions and service economy. SCAP encouraged tourism, believing it would provide a wholesome recreational activity for the servicemen and a way for them to mingle with the Japanese in a friendly manner. That the relations would be mostly unequal was unquestioned, for this fit within the mentoring framework. Thoroughly defeated in war, the Japanese were now apprenticed to the Americans.

Telling this story of racial enmity transformed into Cold War alliance would be incomplete without relating the experiences of Americans in Occupied Japan. It was they who first underwent this change and reported the transformation back to stateside audiences.

"Jap Dolls" and the Victorian "Japan Craze"

Lucy Crockett and other Americans in postwar Japan were surprised at how "familiar" Japan seemed and how quickly Americans began to see Occupied Japan as an exotic tourist locale and a souvenir-hunter's paradise. Kindly feelings toward the women and children of a defeated enemy could be expected after any conquest, but just weeks after dropping two atomic bombs on Japan, Americans began viewing the country and its people as an entertaining spectacle. Americans were primed to see Japan as a "still beautiful woman pockmarked with ugly scars" because of a nineteenth-century western precedent that emphasized a cherry-blossom Japan. Travelogues, tales by missionaries, and the accounts of wealthy European and American travelers depicted Japan as small, childlike, and feminized—a dainty place of apple-cheeked children, kimonoed women in jinrikisha, and peasants in straw hats working in rice paddies. This notion was reinforced by the late-nineteenth and early-twentieth-century image of the Japanese as producers of trifling bric-a-brac and other consumer products for the domestic sphere. Most Americans in Occupied Japan could not help seeing—indeed strove to see—Japan in the way the nineteenth-century American and European visitors had framed the country: a place to tour and to shop for artwork and curios.

The Americans waged "war without mercy on a treacherous foe" during World War II, but their attitudes toward the Japanese cannot be completely reduced to genocidal or contemptuous racism.[20] Inspired by French *japonisme* to take notice of Japanese arts and culture in the last quarter of the nineteenth century, Americans had admired Japanese aesthetics and art as much as they found Japanese society "queer" or backward. The hugely popular Japanese exhibits visited by hundreds of thousands of Americans at the Philadelphia Centennial Exposition (1876), Chicago (1893), and St. Louis (1904) sparked and helped sustain a "Japan craze" in the United States through the first decades of the twentieth century. The craze rested on an Orientalist vision of Japan as an antidote to modern industrialized society with its smoke-belching factories, mass-produced items, corrupt politics, labor disputes, and uppity "New Women."[21] Sentimental Victorian Orientalists saw Japan as an enchanted, conflict-free land of verdant rice paddies, pagodas set in tall, ancient forests, clever artisans handcrafting goods in small, family-owned shops, adorable "wee ones" toddling about, and attentive "rosy-lipped, black-eyed damsels" serving refreshments and smoothing troubled brows.[22] These images of a picturesque "Oriental Eden" were reinforced by an astonishing range and number of literary and theatrical treatments of Japan in the United States and Europe: travel guides, travelogues, missionary newsletters, magazine articles, novels, short stories, poems, songs, silent movies, and stage productions such as Gilbert and Sullivan's *The Mikado* and, of course, Puccini's *Madame Butterfly*.[23] Most westerners—with the significant exception of those in California decrying the "yellow peril"—chose to frame the Japanese in a romanticized manner, and often stubbornly refused to alter their view even after more accurate and realistic information about a modernizing Japan became widely available.[24]

Orientalist visions that feminized Japan as a dainty "land of fans and flowers" and "a realised fairyland" helped support a growing international and feminized consumer market in western industrialized nations.[25] While upper- and middle-class Americans found a new intellectual and cultural interest in Japan, nearly all classes of Americans began to purchase consumer items made in Japan or Japanese-inspired objects made elsewhere.[26] Japanese and Japanese-inspired products became so commonplace in both Europe and the United States that the nineteenth-century traveler Isabella Bird commented, as Lucy Crockett would in 1945, that the scenery and the people reminded her of "pictures on trays, fans, and tea-pots."[27] American importers and other businesses exploited notions of a feminized Japan as a marketing tool—not only to sell decorative Japanese items for the home, but also to advertise household products to be used by female consumers in their role as homemakers.[28] The American consumer market associated Japan so strongly with the domestic sphere that Pear's Soap, Bissell Carpet Sweepers, Quaker Puffed

Rice, and other companies with no connection to Japanese imports used images of Japanese women to sell their products.[29]

The product that Americans and Europeans most associated with the Japanese was probably the handcrafted Japanese doll. Presumably intended for girls, the dolls were frequently purchased by or for western women as their decorative plaything. Often called the "Jap doll" or the "Jappie" with affectionate condescension in the United States, the dolls were also familiar characters in advertisements, magazine illustrations, sheet music, postcards, and children's books.[30] The ubiquity of "Jap dolls" inspired westerners to objectify actual Japanese as "dolls." In the semi-autobiographical novel that inspired *Madame Butterfly*, for example, Pierre Loti frequently describes the Japanese bride as a "doll," a real-life version of "one of the figures of porcelain or silk that fill up our market stalls at the moment."[31] In this famous story, the western sojourner purchases and enjoys his Japanese bride, discarding her when he no longer has use for her. Thus calling Japanese women "dolls" not only objectified them as temporary and easily manipulated playthings, but also implied that they were naive and childlike.

This impression extended to the Japanese people as a whole, whose relatively diminutive size led westerners to diminish their achievements and capabilities. Henry Adams described Japan as a "toy-world" with people living in "doll-house[s] with paper windows and matted floors." Thoroughly unimpressed with the "toy" temples of Nikko, Adams wrote to a friend, "I am still in search of something serious in this country, but with little hope of success."[32] Rudyard Kipling claimed he could not help laughing when he saw a Japanese sentry who wore an ill-fitting western-style uniform and carried weapons that were much too big for him. "The Japanese makes a trim little blue-jacket, but he does not understand soldiering," Kipling contended. "Fans and dainty tea-sets do not go with one's notions of a barrack." Comparing the Japanese to the Japan-inspired consumer products in the west, both Kipling and Adams insisted on seeing their abilities as inconsequential and trifling.[33] Similarly, upon their arrival in defeated Japan, most Americans were struck, as *Newsweek* reported in September 1945, by how everything in Japan, including the "broken and blasted cities and factories," had a miniature, "toylike appearance." Witnessing Japan's utter defeat, many wondered: How did "those people ever get up the nerve to throw a Pearl Harbor punch at us"?[34] How did their soldiers manage to sweep over eastern Asia? "They were so small!" exclaimed British journalist Honor Tracy. "One marvelled at their impudence."[35]

Like the Victorians, mid-twentieth-century westerners perceived the Japanese character through overlapping frames of reference about gender and maturity. Within these frames, they determined what they thought the Japanese were capable of doing, what privileges the Japanese deserved, and what their relationship with the Japanese should be. As in the past, they could not help relating the diminutive size of Japan and its people to concepts of capability and entitlement. Thus they interpreted Japan's attempt to build an Asian-Pacific empire as insolent, as if the Japanese were acting too big for their britches—like boys playing at war with toy weapons.

Despite this prewar western view of Japanese infantilism as a more or less permanent state—the idea that the Japanese lived in a perpetual "toy-world"—there could be little romanticizing about Japan's delicacy after the brutal and powerful war fought by the Japanese military. Postwar observers found it difficult to recapture a pristine, premodern Japan in the wake of the Japanese military and industrial might that had waged war so impressively. Therefore, they stretched the pre-existing frame of reference about Japanese immaturity to accommodate a picture of a nation needing a political education and the Americans as teachers of democracy to young Japanese students. As *Senior Scholastic* explained to American high school students in mid-September 1945, the warrior Uncle Sam was now "Schoolmaster Uncle Sam," faced with the task of re-educating a classroom of "some 73 million hard-to-handle pupils—the entire Japanese nation." Or, as the *New York Herald Tribune*'s Frank Kelley and *Time* magazine's Cornelius Ryan put it: "The Japanese must be taught to walk, talk, think, and play all over again. Whether we like it or not, they are the wards of the United Nations. They can become an important factor in peace, or the breeding ground of a new and terrible atomic war."[36]

These journalists and others fell back on easily understood metaphors and relationships to explain to the American public SCAP's policy to reintegrate Japan into a U.S.-led liberal capitalist order. By casting the Occupation's objective as teaching problem students in "the world's largest reformatory school," they made it seem commonsensical that the United States needed to be patient and firm toward Japan, not merely punitive and vengeful. At the same time, regarding the Japanese once again as excellent servants rather than vicious foes helped Americans feel more kindly toward them. Time-Life journalist Noel Busch explained that Americans were able to get along with a hated foe so soon after the war because most of the daily contact between Americans and Japanese was "on a master-servant basis." An Army captain's wife, who had sworn she would never let "a Jap girl" hold one of her babies, found that living in a large, well-equipped house with four agreeable servants and having plenty of entertaining diversions made her life in Japan "a vacation."[37] Although the defeat of the Japanese meant that they were in an inferior, service position, their interactions with Americans were nonetheless cordial, and this fact was advertised back in the United States.[38]

Stateside media extended the vision of a gentler, more innocent Japan by highlighting Japanese females and children.[39] Although the American wartime press coverage tried to portray Japanese women as "fanatical" like Japanese men, women's faces were largely missing from popular and masculinized wartime images of the Japanese as apes, insects, or myopic, bucktoothed soldiers. After the war, magazine and news editors, and later filmmakers, while eager to survey all of Japanese society, tended to focus especially on Japanese women.[40] Of course they printed many photographs of Hirohito, Tōjō, and other Japanese leaders, but when it came to depicting everyday life in Occupied Japan, the editors showed a preference for one gender. It is true that American editors had fresh glimpses of Japanese women and children available to them for the first time since the war had begun, and that the population of Japanese men had been reduced by 1.3 million during the war. Yet this does not wholly account for the disproportionate lack of adult Japanese male images in the popular press.[41]

Decades later, former Time-Life correspondent Shelley Mydans helped explain this shift of focus. She lived in Tokyo during the Occupation while her photojournalist husband, Carl, headed Henry Luce's Time, Inc. operations in Japan. When asked about the striking ratio of adult female to male photographs in *Life* magazine, one of the era's most popular periodicals, she denied the disparity and mentioned a published collection of her husband's photographs of Occupied Japan that represented men and women equally. However, the *Life* editors at the time passed up many of the photographs he later chose for his 1995 volume, which would have indeed provided a more balanced portrayal.[42]

But Shelley Mydans insisted that the preference for some images over others simply resulted from the rules of photographic composition: "The aim of a good picture story (like an article in text) is to reveal in as interesting a way as possible what the photographer sees or understands." She gave a hypothetical situation of an editor having to choose from three photographs of the vista leading up to Yasukuni shrine: two men in western-style pants and soldiers' caps, two women in kimonos, and a woman with a child, both in native dress. She felt that having the women in front of the shrine's great *torii* "enhances the picture far better" than the men could. But the best shot would be the photograph of the woman and child: she thought while that the men and their outfits would reinforce the "starkly formal" mood at Yasukuni, the woman with the child would add color and contrast to it.[43]

Yasukuni's fame as the shrine for Japan's war dead may help to explain her thinking. Postwar journalists realized the need to counteract the wartime stereotype of Japanese as "little yellow beasts with buck teeth and glasses."[44] Putting colorfully dressed women and children in front of Yasukuni rather than a Japanese man in a soldier's cap certainly made sense for this objective. Soldiers' caps were a common sight on men in Japan after the war, but so were drab *mompei* or pantaloons on the women. The colorful kimonos in Mydans's hypothetical example were a luxury; many Tokyoites were forced to trade their prized kimonos to farmers in the countryside for food during and after the war. Beautiful kimonos were seldom seen especially in the first two years after the war, the period in question. American reporters, in attempting to "reveal" what they saw, chose exceptional images rather than more common ones, influenced by aesthetic considerations as well as partly unconscious presumptions about the innocence of women and children.

Mutually reinforcing notions of gender and maturity were

therefore integral to the perspective that had shaped Americans' understanding of Japan ever since Commodore Perry first sailed into Edo Bay. Despite the greatly changed circumstances of the twentieth century, westerners continued to view Japan in the framework established in the previous century. The Americans resumed the western custom—briefly interrupted by the war— of buying Japanese things, enjoying Japanese scenery, and being pampered by Japanese servants. In contrast to the prewar period, however, the U.S. government officially made itself Japan's caretaker to ensure that the Japanese did not threaten its neighbors or become seduced by the Soviet Union's antithetical "way of life." As a result, many Americans in Occupied Japan saw their *personal* relationships with the Japanese as having a larger international, or sometimes even geopolitical, significance. By learning to cope with the hated racial enemy—in the agreeable form of women and children—these Americans believed they were equipping themselves to be better world leaders.

"A G.I. 'Father' Greeted by His Happy 'Family'"

A *Honolulu Advertiser* correspondent predicted in mid-September 1945 that the GIs would have little difficulty upholding the nonfraternization rules after the war, since the "vast difference in language and customs" created "a natural barrier" between Americans and the Japanese.[45] But he underestimated the appeal of Japanese children to the Occupiers. "The children are attractive, and it's almost impossible not to be drawn to them," confessed an Army nurse who served during the early months of the Occupation. Moreover, it was difficult, Mark Gayn admitted, to see militarism in the faces of "little children in gay kimonos [who] looked like china dolls." Assertively friendly, they appeared to de-

light in the Americans. "The children wave at you and call after you wherever you go in Japan," reported Harold Noble for
the *Saturday Evening Post.* "'Hello,' they cry, or 'Good-by,' and
'Hubba-hubba,'" a popular GI exclamation.[46] Often the children
sought the treats tossed by the big Americans from passing Jeeps;
if an American stopped to distribute candy, he quickly found himself surrounded by twenty or so eagerly smiling children, all striving to get a piece.[47] Their pleas became so common during the
first weeks of the Occupation that the absence of kids crying out
for "chocoletto" or "cigaretto" was a sure sign that the Americans had not yet reached an area.

The children usually remained friendly and seemed to enjoy being near Americans, and the Americans, for their part, liked being admired.[48] Recognizing that the Japanese children could be
an ego boost to American soldiers, the American Red Cross began arranging popular "kiddy parties" for homesick GIs.[49] Thus
within a half-year of the Occupation, Americans GIs and Japanese children were "busily re-playing the pleasant age-old comedy of the soldier and the little kid," reported the *New York
Times.* "It is a natural fraternization no one could stop—not that
anyone wants to." Not many did, so the GIs felt free to give food
as well as joyrides in U.S. Army jeeps and lessons on how to play
baseball, even after SCAP established nonfraternization rules.[50]

Eventually SCAP promoted GI philanthropy toward Japanese
children to encourage caring and charity among its servicemen,
especially during the holiday season—a strategy that worked ex-
traordinarily well with Master Sergeant Hugh O'Reilly from the
Bronx. In December 1949, the 27th Regiment of the 25th Infantry Division got an order, as did all other Army units in Osaka, to
make a visit to an area orphanage to distribute some toys. A
member of the 27th "Wolfhounds," Sergeant O'Reilly was deeply

shocked at what he and the other Wolfhounds saw at the three huts that constituted the Holy Family Home for orphans. On a bitterly cold day, about forty children huddled around a single brazier in a dry corner of a leaking structure with a caved-in roof that had been patched with cardboard. Next door was a racetrack, and O'Reilly was outraged when he found out that the well-fed racehorses lived in heated stalls while the children at Holy Family were nearly freezing, living in unsanitary conditions, and unsure whether they would have enough food to eat from day to day. He thought something had to be done, and so O'Reilly convinced the Wolfhounds to "adopt" the Japanese orphanage.[51]

This was a surprising turnaround for O'Reilly, an Army veteran who had signed up with the Marines after Pearl Harbor rather than re-enlisting with the Army. He did not want to be stuck training troops and be denied an opportunity to "kill Japs." After the war he returned to the Army but, to his displeasure, he was assigned to Occupied Japan in July 1949. Before going to Japan, O'Reilly joked that he would "kick little Japanese kids in the head," but the desperate condition of the war-ravaged orphans, who ranged from six months to fourteen years, profoundly affected him. He talked the Wolfhounds into collecting money, appropriating food and medical supplies from their regiment, donating the contents of packages from stateside family and friends, and sending whatever help they could—including their regimental doctor for twice-weekly visits—to the children and the Sisters of Charity of St. Vincent de Paul at the Holy Family Home. Most other U.S. military units that sponsored orphanages did so at Christmastime with toys and a party, but as O'Reilly told a writer for *Catholic World,* he got the Wolfhounds to agree to the slogan "Christmas every payday." By getting them to donate on average

$3,000 to $4,000 every payday—about a dollar for every man in the regiment—O'Reilly had his Wolfhounds pay for the construction of solid, Spanish-style buildings within fourteen months of their first donation. The Wolfhounds continued their support even after they shipped off to fight in Korea in July 1950, and attracted additional donations from agencies such as CARE and other Americans in Japan who had heard about the Wolfhounds' efforts. With this support and the new facilities, the Holy Family Home expanded its care to approximately 160 orphans.[52]

It so happened that O'Reilly was his regiment's publicity man, and he regularly wrote articles in *The Stars and Stripes* about the Wolfhounds' exploits and about the orphanage. As word of the "Wolfhound Orphanage" spread, the Associated Press sent a photographer to capture shots of O'Reilly visiting the Holy Family Home on furlough from Korea and wired a story about the orphanage back to newspapers throughout the United States. The *New York Times* picked up the AP story and published it with the headline "A G.I. 'Father' Greeted by His Happy 'Family,'" along with an effective photograph of a very pleased O'Reilly surrounded by more than twenty chubby-cheeked, preschool orphans in clean white pinafores. The *Times* also commissioned an article about the Bronx native and the orphanage in its Sunday magazine; author James A. Michener wrote about O'Reilly in an article on Japan for *Holiday* magazine; and in 1953, E. J. Kahn wrote a long narrative for the *New Yorker* called "The Gentle Wolfhound." Half of Kahn's article focused on how O'Reilly courted and married Saitō Yuko, a young Japanese woman from a wealthy Osaka family. Two years later, the O'Reillys' interracial love story and the story about the "Wolfhound orphanage" became the basis of a Hollywood movie.[53]

Clearly, O'Reilly's paternal engagement with the orphans and

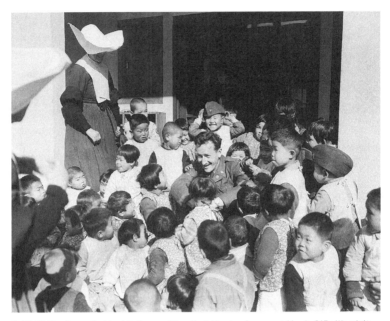

A GI "father" greeted by his happy "family." Master Sergeant Hugh O'Reilly visiting the Holy Family orphanage while on furlough from the Korean War, February 1951. AP/Wide World Photos.

his reaching out to unite with a Japanese woman was an appealing and heartwarming model for millions of Americans. O'Reilly was exceptional, yet he was presented as a symbol of American benevolence. Other units were ordered to visit Osaka orphanages in December 1949 but, as far as we know, only the lucky children at Holy Family got a new orphanage from their GI sponsors, while tens of thousands continued to live as homeless street children in ragged clothes. Not all GIs were thoughtful or kind; some threw candy from their Jeeps at Japanese children as amusement, the way one would throw food at birds.[54] The Wolfhound story, however, represented the GIs on their very best behavior and reinforced the prevailing metaphor of the United States as a father-figure provider to the Japanese "children"—an uplifting metaphor that helped American audiences forget the horrors of war, including the U.S. air raids that undoubtedly turned many of these children into orphans.

Images of happy children with conquering soldiers are important after any hostilities. Americans snapped and published so many photos of smiling GIs and Japanese children during the Occupation of Japan that the image became iconic.[55] As citizens of the conquering forces, Americans liked seeing the kindness and mercy of their soldiers. Highlighting their humanity after an armed conflict suggested that America's soldiers, and by extension their nation, were reluctant killers—kind rather than heartless and unforgiving. This response, of course, was not unique to Americans, but it helps explain why the *Saturday Evening Post* selected an official Navy photograph of three GIs treating the foot of a near-naked Okinawan toddler to grace the leading page of its May 1945 report on the deadly battle for Okinawa.[56] A few months later, images of smiling Japanese children posing with GIs were also reassuring because the children's friendliness and openness meant that they saw the "good" within American soldiers, and thus the "good" in America even after Americans had rained mass death upon Japan. "Do they hate us?" had been one of the most frequent questions that the Occupiers and stateside observers asked about the Japanese.[57] The children's reactions were particularly important because, as "innocents," they presumably expressed the truth—hence their great usefulness to propaganda. "You'll never convince these youngsters that there's anything wrong with America," said O'Reilly in 1951. When a GI walks into the Holy Family Home, he explained, the children run up to him because "they just know he's a good guy."[58]

Pointing out these propaganda benefits does not diminish the very real and truly appreciated efforts of O'Reilly, the city of Osaka's 1951 "Man of the Year," nor the generosity and kindness of many American soldiers to Japanese children—indeed, O'Reilly as a publicist understood this very well himself.[59] But there is no doubt that images of happy children after a violent confrontation were an important propaganda tool for governments and their supporters in the media.[60] Once a people were reassured about the "goodness" of what their soldiers were doing abroad, they were likely to continue to support the policies that kept them in other countries. Thus the construction of liberal paternalism entailed not only depicting the Japanese as children needing to be trained but also portraying Americans as their benevolent protectors and mentors. This helped to reshape how Americans viewed the Japanese, as well as how they saw their roles in Japan.

Baby-san: Madame Butterfly, circa 1945–1952

Americans of both genders reported liking Japanese women better than men because they found the women more cordial and friendlier. "I have seen a few samples of the Japanese male at work, both here and in the Philippines," wrote Lieutenant John Ashmead in the *Atlantic Monthly*, "and I trust very few of them. But certainly this feeling of mine does not apply to the women and children." He found that Japanese women "put little stock in [militaristic] concepts such as Bushido" and were generally easier to talk to about political subjects.[61] Another American writer asserted that Japanese women rarely displayed the "arrogance, fury when thwarted, and selfishness" supposedly characteristic of Japanese men.[62] To Lucy Crockett, the contrast between the two genders appeared so stark—one severe and brutal, the other pliant and pleasing—that Japanese men and women "might be two different races entirely."[63]

Although she liberally peppered her book with terms like "gooks" and "Japs" to refer to the former enemy, Crockett sang the praises of the charming, seemingly girlish manners of Japanese women. The Americans in the Occupation called the maids, clerical help, waitresses, or any other young Japanese women "Baby-san"—a name that combined an American pick-up line ("Hey, baby") with an everyday Japanese title of respect. "To us," Crockett explained, "Baby-san" was "like a bright-eyed, animated rag doll, quick to laugh, quick to shed tears, a giggling, singing, hard-working little creature, clinging like a vine that has found support to anyone who shows her the slightest kindness." Crockett's and other American women's use of the term indicated their sense of privilege vis-à-vis Japanese women and reflected the American perception of Japanese women as emotionally volatile and childlike. Perhaps the lack of fluency in English among most Japanese women, which made them appear inarticulate and somewhat simple-minded to Americans, contributed to this impression. To the Occupiers, the presumed naiveté of Japanese women—their curiosity and "childlike, pleasant and hospitable" personalities—was part of their charm. By lavishing "overwhelming affection" on whomever she served with "loyalty, sweetness, and untiring efforts to please," Baby-san helped "break down [the] indifference of the most bitter Jap-hater." Her "winning personality," asserted Crockett, "brought unexpected understanding and sympathy from Americans."[64]

Since the great majority of Americans serving in the Occupation were heterosexual men far from their spouses and girlfriends, their attraction to Baby-sans was hardly surprising. Naval reservist Bill Hume celebrated Baby-san in a tremendously popular, semi-pornographic, weekly cartoon series for the Far East edition of the *Navy Times*. Hume later published his cartoons in two volumes with added commentary by John Annarino: *Babysan: A Private Look at the Japanese Occupation* (1953)—a bestselling favorite with GIs in Korea—and *Babysan's World: The Hume'n Slant on Japan* (1956).[65] Hume and Annarino declared that Baby-san was a new postwar type of Japanese woman, not at all like the ones American servicemen expected— namely, the "'Madame Butterfly' type" with "an elaborate hairdo . . . and a fan coyly held before a face that wore a come-hither look."[66] Rather than wearing colorful kimonos and having their hair arranged stiffly, Hume's Baby-sans possessed narrow waists, long flowing hair, slim legs, and gravity-defying breasts.[67]

> Her face is oval. Her cheekbones are high. Her nose is pug. Her mouth is pouty. Her lips are a blazing scarlet, playing up what she judges from American movies to be the fashionable standard. Her hair is long and dark and slung into a peek-a-boo hair-do. Compared to American girls, she is short. But who cares? She has a heart that seems twice as big as many of her American sisters, and your every wish is her command. Since she is both a sensitive and a practical creature, let us suggest that our wishes be reasonable.

Hume's Baby-san was a beautiful sex kitten, the fantasy of a heterosexual Euroamerican man. Even though he was just some ordinary guy—often depicted as a tall oaf by Hume—she was "his Baby Doll . . . a tiny, but not fragile, doll." Unlike the decorative "Jap doll"—"the kind one would place upon the mantelpiece

Cartoonist Bill Hume, in collaboration with writer John Annarino, followed up the bestselling *Babysan: A Private Look at the Japanese Occupation* (1953) with *Babysan's World: The Hume'n Slant on Japan* (1956).

the HUME'N SLANT *on Japan*

NINGYO —IS A DOLL—
BUT NOT LIKE THIS
ONE !
THERE ARE CEREMONIAL
DOLLS — DOLLS FOR
CHILDREN — DOLLS TO
SELL TO AMERICAN
SOUVENIR COLLECTORS.
PERHAPS THE CUTEST
OF ALL ARE THE
KOKESHI

THEY ARE LITTLE WOODEN DOLLS
PAINTED IN BRILLIANT COLORS,
SOMETIMES CALLED "FRIENDSHIP"
DOLLS AND EXCHANGED AS
TOKENS OF AFFECTION.
THEY ARE MADE IN THE "SNOW
COUNTRY" (NORTHERN JAPAN).

back home," Hume and Annarino explained—she was a genuine plaything. And while they delighted in Baby-san's childlike nature, they also characterized her as petulantly blunt and coy: "Why you all time bring candy," pouts Baby-san to her lover in one cartoon, "why never *okane* [money]?" Despite her frequent demands for money, her creators insisted that Baby-san was no "gold-digger"; she shows her boyfriend photographs of her dependents—her widowed mother and younger siblings. Hume and Annarino agreed that the monetary exchange was fair, given her ability to bring "the sunshine into her boyfriend's life."[68]

As was typical of soldiers in conquering armies, American GIs who wanted to procure sexual services could count on the desperation of women, including young war widows, in the defeated nation. As an early Occupation report in *Life* noted, the "girls" were "plentiful."[69] Half of the $185 million spent by Occupation troops in Japan reportedly went for such services, although it is unclear whether this figure covers "onlys"—like Hume's Baby-sans who consorted with only one man at a time. Until mid-1949 when General Headquarters (GHQ) finally bowed to strong pressure from Japanese women's groups to eliminate the state-run brothel system, 70,000 women worked in them, and at least 59,000 other women engaged in sex work outside the state system.[70] Hume and Annarino saw Baby-san as Lieutenant Pinkerton saw Cho-Cho-san: someone to be left in Japan. Baby-san kept American servicemen "occupied while occupying." Dedicated to the servicemen who served in "the land of Fujisan," Hume's cartoons were meant to "bring many a chuckle in recalling the happiness some little Baby-san brought into their lives." This impermanence supposedly suited Baby-san just fine; she was a different sort of butterfly than Cho-Cho-san, who killed herself because of Pinkerton's desertion. Baby-san flitted from lover to lover, from one steady boyfriend to another as they rotated back to the States. Indeed, the verb "to butterfly" connoted the very opposite of Cho-Cho-san's devotion.[71]

Real Japanese women, of course, did not have gravity-defying breasts, and according to Kelley and Ryan, they failed "to match domestic [western] beauty standards," but soon the American servicemen grew to like the Japanese women's "winsome, bright, childlike personality." They "were swept off their feet by the deference and obedience of servile Japanese women."[72] Martin Bronfenbrenner, a language officer, depicted the GIs' exhilaration with such unaccustomed personal attention in his novella, *Fusako and the Army* (1946). It amazed and thrilled the protagonist, Bob Smith, to think about his girlfriend, Fusako, "waiting on *him* with such affectionate familiarity, doing little things for *him* to the point of embarrassment, calling him 'Babu-*San*,' appreciating every automatic common courtesy" such as opening a door for her. Bob was barely out of his teens, but Fusako made him feel important, like a man. And because of his relationship with Fusako, Bob tried to think of the "Japs" as "Japanese."[73] At the beginning of the Occupation, the Japanese government recruited lower-class women to be "shock absorbers" and, in the words of future Prime Minister Ikeda Hayato, to "protect the pure bloodline of the Yamato race" by satiating the conquerors' sexual appetites.[74] Without intending to, tens of thousands of other women like Fusako helped, with their ministrations and their bodies, to mediate, attenuate, and manage the hostility the U.S. servicemen felt toward Japan.

Relations with Japanese women, however, did not always mean a reduction in hostility. Some servicemen thought as little of their erstwhile Japanese sexual partners as naval officer Julien Viaud (a.k.a. Pierre Loti) did of his temporary bride while stationed in Nagasaki sixty years earlier. At a Kobe train station, Lucy Crockett witnessed two young GIs on their way back to the United States, callously saying their good-byes from their train seats to two tearful Japanese women on the platform. "When one sobbing girl asked, 'When you come back?' the young man answered with a laugh: 'Come back? Why, when you —— Japs bomb Pearl Harbor again, baby, I'll be back!'"[75] GIs weren't supposed to fall in love with these "gooks" of "such a strange and smelly country," as Mississippian Elliott Chaze described Japan. The future Associated Press writer and newspaperman claimed that most Occupation troops felt their mission was rather like being "suddenly handed a brimming bedpan and told to guard its contents carefully." Chaze's fictionalized memoir, *Stainless Steel Kimono* (1947), told tales of *schadenfreude* and GIs behaving badly in Occupied Japan while they waited to go back to the States where women had "good legs . . . long ones and very white."[76] Thus when Euroamerican servicemen did fall in love with their Japanese girlfriends, many tried to hide this apparently embarrassing fact.[77]

Trying to be antiracist in Occupied Japan was a challenge. SCAP enforced racial apartheid with Jim Crow–like regulations that ordered the Japanese to use different doors, ride on second-class rail cars, and keep out of certain areas—a system that did not exist in Occupied Germany.[78] Nonfraternization rules, although imposed at an earlier point in Germany, lasted nearly four years longer in Japan.[79] They were finally revoked on September 20, 1949, after U.S. policymakers, realizing Japan's growing importance as an ally in the Cold War and a model of capitalism in East Asia, instituted a "pro-fraternization" edict during the same month when the world discovered the Soviets possessed nuclear capability and a couple of weeks before the Communists triumphed in China.

The nonfraternization rules had always allowed GIs to have public dates with Japanese women, but they made it difficult for servicemen to marry their Japanese girlfriends. SCAP discouraged intermarriage in myriad ways: requiring servicemen to jump through a number of bureaucratic hoops; refusing, for a time, to allow U.S. chaplains to officiate at the marriages; and emphasizing the immigration law that made it illegal for the GIs to take their Japanese wives to the United States.[80] Commanding officers were known to transfer men out of an area to separate them from their fiancées, or to threaten to do so. In the real-life example of Kyo Wittrock, the officer who threatened to transfer her fiancé to Korea did not follow through, allowing them to marry. But the fictional *Fusako and the Army* ends unhappily, with Bob Smith suddenly forced to abandon the pregnant Fusako when his racist superior officer transfers him immediately out of the area to prevent Bob from marrying her.[81] Servicemen like Bob Smith could choose to recognize and support their children with Japanese women, but U.S. military law encouraged them to shirk responsibility. Because Japanese citizens were forbidden to take servicemen to court, Japanese women could not file a paternity suit against a U.S. serviceman. As a result, only 39 percent of the servicemen-fathers took responsibility for their Occupation babies, who numbered approximately 5,000.[82] Many so-called Baby-sans were devastated and socially ostracized when their GIs abandoned them and their children.

"The American Girls Could Take a Lesson"

Besides being a diversion in Japan, Baby-san was important to American men in providing a contrast to American women back home. Like the fictional Bob Smith, many American men serving in the Occupation were convinced that the typical Japanese woman had a heart that seemed, as Hume and Annarino put it, "twice as big as many of her American sisters," for their "every wish [was] her command." Soldiers polled by the *Stars and Stripes* corroborated these impressions and "praised the Japanese women for their kindly qualities, their submissiveness, and their eagerness to make the men comfortable." One serviceman declared, "The American girls could take a lesson in respect from these people over here."[83]

As the roles of American women were shifting during and after the war, Japanese women were held up as exemplars of femininity. American women saw a retraction of their wartime gains as employers laid them off or encouraged them to quit their relatively high-paying jobs in industry and the military to make room for the returning servicemen. Women in America also saw their public roles being attacked by men, as well as by other women.[84] "Women Don't Belong in Politics," argued a female author in *American Mercury,* a popular monthly, and the psychiatrists Marynia Farnham and Ferdinand Lundberg tried to convince women that their mental health depended on their staying at home in their influential *Modern Woman: The Lost Sex* (1947).[85] Although millions of American women, including most nonwhite women, lacked this choice and continued to work for wages, the postwar years saw a celebration of the hearth, family, and home-related consumerism and a contraction of women's career advancement opportunities outside the home.[86] Attending this development was a heightened misogyny in American public discourse, an assertion of the psychological dangers lurking in women, as expressed in Philip Wylie's *A Generation of Vipers* (1942, 1955), Edward Strecker's *Their Mothers' Sons: The Psychiatrist Examines an American Problem* (1946), and *Lady in the Dark* (1944), a Paramount film based on a Broadway musical hit.[87]

Stories from Occupied Japan frequently painted American women as difficult, prickly, and even smothering—the opposite of the winsome Baby-san. A general serving in the Occupation regaled a group of men with a tale about his wife asking him if he "thought men preferred women who were submissive, who didn't have strong ideas of their own and who were quiet, rather than women who would insist on taking part in conversations and insist on being an equal in the marriage." When he confirmed that men preferred submissive, quiet women, she left in a huff, slamming the door behind her. All the men laughed at this story, according to United Press reporter Earnest Hoberecht. They "agreed that any honest man would admit that he prefers to be waited on, that he prefers to have his own way, and that he really liked a woman who catered to him and granted him his every wish."[88] Similarly, in Carl Mydans's article on the Occupiers called "The White Man's Burden," the "burden" turned out to be one Texas captain's loud and obnoxious wife! This American woman embarrassed everyone on a special tour with a bilingual Japanese guide by complaining incessantly about Japan. Back home in Texas, she loudly stated, "You'd get . . . decent food and none of this fish, fish, fish, all the time. You'd eat with real silverware and you wouldn't be sitting on the floor." As the tour proceeded and the woman kept talking, her husband's shoulders sank lower and lower, Mydans noted with pity.[89]

Even Lucy Crockett and Margery Brown, a colonel's wife who lived in Kyoto, subscribed to this misogynistic view of American women. Explaining why Japanese men disliked American women, Brown wrote: "Seldom do we have the restraint, the elegant submissiveness or the subtle charm of their own women. We talk a great deal. We tower over Japanese men in the street and our noses are pointed heavenward."[90] Crockett agreed with the "verdict" that despite their "physical shortcoming[s]" and low status, "Baby-san and her humble sisters nevertheless are held up as having qualities which our own women would do well to emulate—qualities which make the proud American beauty in contrast seem harsh, petulant, talkative, restless, spoiled, and arrogant." Crockett cited the sergeant's wife who trained her Japanese maid to follow her everywhere with cigarettes and an ashtray, and the Public Health officer's wife who complained that the sliding shoji doors broke her fingernails. The many unmarried American women who went to Japan looking for romance, Crockett claimed, found single American men either too young or already attached to "a local incipient Madame Butterfly." An attractive, petite Japanese waitress told her, "American men like Japanese girls *very* much. Say Japanese girls no all time yappity-yappity-yap!"[91]

Although the Americans may have welcomed the Japanese women's silence and subservience to men as desirable traits, at the same time they condemned the social system that supposedly made Japanese women respond to their "every wish." "There is nothing so sad as to be born a woman in Japan," Kelley and Ryan stated, repeating a "Japanese proverb." "Shackled to an ancient feudal system which kept her inferior to the man," she had been until recently a mere "human incubator" for the Japanese empire.[92] Journalist John LaCerda professed amazement at the pay scale discrepancy between Japanese men and women, with Japanese men averaging two to five times as much income as women.[93] Lucy Crockett, who actually talked to Japanese women and men at some length about women's status in Japanese society, found women eager to improve their status while the men were perplexed, fearful, or hypocritical. One man talked extensively to her at his home about needing to bring equality for women while using the back of a maidservant as an arm rest. Another Japanese man, after hearing Crockett give a speech on emancipated womanhood, told her: "Well, I agreed with everything you said . . . but I still like to have my wife carry the bundles!" When she asked a group of Kyoto businessmen who were discussing *Gone with the Wind* how they would like it if all Japanese women were like Scarlett O'Hara, she noticed "the men visibly savoring the utter hideousness of the thought." Through an interpreter, one man told her: "We have accepted atomic bombing and defeat. But what you suggest is worse than either. It could not be endured."[94]

In tales ranging from melodramatic to humorous, Americans related the sorry state of women in Japan and depicted the Occupation as having a desperately needed salutary effect on Japanese women.[95] Many memoirs pointed out that Japanese women only gained the right to vote in 1946—without reflecting that American women had won suffrage by a margin of one congressional vote a mere twenty-six years earlier.[96] Ignoring America's own gender inequality, Americans interpreted their own men's polite or chivalrous behavior toward Japanese women as helping to liberate them: in small villages and towns, Kelley and Ryan wrote, the GIs "unwittingly" helped break "the feudalistic bonds which had held Japanese women for centuries." Making more modest claims, LaCerda asserted that American GIs had raised the standard of civility toward women in Japan. Japanese women quickly "succumbed to the charm of Americans," he wrote, overlooking the powerful material reasons why Japanese women dated American men.[97] American men rationalized their own liaisons with Japanese women by claiming to be better for them than the women's own countrymen.

On the other hand, criticizing the low status of women in Japan allowed American women in particular to be confidently optimistic about postwar gender relations in their own country and to see their role in the Occupation as helping to uplift Japanese women.[98] But when the Japanese Red Cross women of Osaka asked their American counterparts for advice about achieving gender equality at a forum on women's issues, the American women's response stressed their gender's "responsibility as a constructive force in the family." Likewise, in a lecture about American womanhood at Kyoto's Dōshisha University, Crockett disappointed an audience of several hundred highly educated women by telling them to be good housekeepers, to let husbands think they're the boss, and other such self-described "homely truisms."[99] This was nothing new for Japanese women; the "feudalistic" Japanese government had been emphasizing women's "constructive force" in the home since the 1880s with their slogan of "good wife, wise mother" (ryōsai kenbō).[100]

Crockett heard about her audience's disappointment with her speech, but the American Red Cross continued to emphasize middle-class American gender roles. Its programs to prepare Japanese brides for life in the United States did not show them how to become involved in local community affairs and politics, or how to become active members of a participatory democracy. Instead, American women showed them how to make beds, operate vacuum cleaners, bake a cake, bathe a baby, and prepare and serve dishes at a dinner party.[101] The Japanese women were being "uplifted" to do American-style housework—which was made easier by "modern conveniences" but was also harder because American housewives, unlike their Japanese counterparts, generally lacked the help of maids or extended family members. Assuming the superiority of the American system, a Red Cross volunteer told a group of Japanese brides, "I imagine all of you will be happy to have your husband provide the income. I know that I have found it very enjoyable."[102] Being self-supporting was overrated; after all, the housewife was her own boss and set her own hours. Reflecting and reacting to the social climate at home, the American women gave advice and lessons that emphasized women's power in the home.

War Brides and Racial Tolerance

Despite opposition and challenges, American men continued to marry Japanese women, and by the end of the Occupation, American public opinion had come around to viewing American military males' commitment to their nonwhite spouses as a demonstration of American racial tolerance. This was yet another lesson for Americans to learn about the fruits of war. It was developed more fully by Hollywood films on Japan in the decade following the Occupation, as well as in Occupation-era novels like Hoberecht's *Tokyo Romance* (1947).[103] A 1952 *Saturday Evening Post* article, "They're Bringing Home Japanese Wives," emphasized that the Japanese women were determined to work hard to make their marriages work in a potentially hostile environment, and it ended with a plea that Americans "try a fraction as hard to help them along." But the article also depicted the women as naive and inexperienced "youngsters" and included a prediction that only 10 percent of the marriages would survive the challenges the couples would face living in the United States. Several unsympathetic published reader responses seriously questioned the wisdom and viability of these interracial unions.[104] But another *Saturday Evening Post* article on war brides nearly three years later, entitled "Where are Those Japanese Brides?" was much more supportive of the marriages. By that time, the McCarran-Walter Act had revoked the racist 1924 immigration restriction and the number of GI-Japanese marriages had increased at least threefold. The author of this article found that despite hardships—and even some tragedies—the Japanese war brides had been assimilated into America. With *gaman* [perseverance], they had become American wives.[105]

By 1955, major arbiters of American popular culture were extolling GI-Japanese marriages as noble, successful efforts to fight racial intolerance. *Life* magazine commissioned an article on Japanese war brides from James Michener, by then the author of four works on American servicemen and Asians/Pacific Islanders: the Pulitzer Prize–winning *Tales of the South Pacific* (1948), *Return to Paradise* (1950), *The Bridges at Toko-ri* (1953), and *Sayonara* (1954), which first came out as a serial in *McCall's* in late 1953. In *Sayonara*, Michener had Air Force captain Lloyd Gruver part from his Japanese love, Hana-Ogi, and in the same vein, he recommended against interracial marriages to the many servicemen in Japan who asked for his advice. However, Michener's February 1955 article for *Life* about Sachiko and Frank Pfeiffer of Melrose Park, Illinois, was a story of victory over the "barriers of language and intolerance." He detailed their courtship in Japan, their trials and tribulations with Frank's mother and the racist neighbors in one Chicago neighborhood, and their triumphantly cozy life in a Chicago suburb, where their new neighbors—two World War II veterans who had fought the Japanese—and their wives immediately accepted the Pfeiffers as close friends. *Life* published seven responses to the article—all but one positive about the Pfeiffers' marriage. "I cried unashamedly, me a man of 45 years," a New Jersey man wrote, "because I have always contended that such interracial marriages can be successful." Michener must have finally agreed, for in October the *New York Times* announced that he too was marrying a woman of Japanese ancestry, Mari Yoriko Sabusawa, a Nisei.[106]

Hugh O'Reilly also wrote about his marriage to the former Saitō Yuko in article called "Our East-West Marriage Is Working" in the *American Mercury*'s December 1955 edition. Although the *Mercury* editors decorated O'Reilly's article with illustrations of kimonoed women whom Americans would recognize as "geishas," O'Reilly set out "to clear up some of the misconceptions" about Japanese women and why 20,000 American servicemen had married them. It was not because the women were "meek, submissive creatures," which they were not: "Don't let that politeness fool you," he asserted, "the girls we married have minds of their own just like the girls at home." He informed *Mercury* readers that the servicemen's Japanese wives were mostly modern urbanites and claimed that their being situated in Occupied Japan explained their marriages more than anything else. As for the viability of these marriages, O'Reilly predicted that GI-Japanese marriages had a "better chance than average" because neither spouse was permitted to go into their marriages "starry-eyed and certain that nothing could ever happen to mar their perfect bliss." Instead, he believed, all the paperwork and the talks with commanding officers and chaplains laying out the difficult road ahead served as truly useful pre-marriage counseling.[107] Happily for him, his prediction was correct. The O'Reillys have remained together for well over fifty years and raised six children together.[108] Michener's marriage to Sabusawa, his third wife, was also enduring; they were married for thirty-nine years until her death in 1994.

Thus, a decade after the war, the nonwhite war brides of a former enemy nation became "meaningful figures in the discourse on racial integration and cultural pluralism," to quote one scholar of the period.[109] One in four Americans who married a Japanese woman was either a Nisei or an African American, but images of those relationships were rare in the American mainstream press.[110] The American media may have regarded marriage between two people of the same ethnic ancestry as unworthy of comment and were probably at a loss to comment on an Asian-African union, since most Americans interpreted race only within a binary white/black or white/nonwhite construct.

The emphasis on the interracial aspect of the relationships between Euroamerican men and Japanese women served a couple of purposes. First, it allowed the relationships to stand metonymically for the relation of the predominantly white United States with Japan. Moreover, it allowed Americans to confront their racism in a modified way during the early years of the Civil Rights movement. For many Americans, relations with a racial "other" of medium skin hue were far less a social taboo than relations between American whites and blacks. And the fact that most of these interracial marriages occurred far away in Japan meant that most people could avoid visual and personal contact with them. Favorable portrayals of Euroamerican-Japanese romances in the mainstream media and popular culture provided an increasingly acceptable way to view the Japanese more sympathetically and to celebrate racial tolerance.

"If there were no other factors in fostering friendship between the two alien peoples," Lucy Crockett wrote, "the women and children would see that the proverbial twain shall meet."[111] Crockett was referring to actual Japanese women and children, and it seems to be true that Americans in the Occupation were drawn to them more than they were to adult men. But Americans were attracted not only by the purported innocence and charm of the women and children, but also by what they symbolized: a vulnerability, dependence, and naiveté that made them accessible and malleable. Ideologies about women and children were often conflated, but they were also distinct. Women represented a vision of excellent, attentive service and pampering, whereas the children represented the future—Japan as an enthusiastic young democracy ready to be educated and reoriented. Taken together, these experiences of women and children in Occupied Japan allowed Americans to transform their sense of Japanese inferiority from hostility into feelings of obligation and mercy toward Japan after a terrible war. Reframing their relationship with Japan in this liberal/paternalistic manner helped Americans begin to see a recently vilified enemy as a valued ally. The notion of Japan as childlike and feminine, of course, dated back to the nineteenth century when Americans and most Europeans began interacting with the Japanese. Even though the geopolitical priorities of the United States in the mid-twentieth century forced Americans to accommodate a more progressive vision of Japan's potential, the original nineteenth-century perception remained remarkably resilient in shaping the new picture.

In June 1955, *American Magazine* published Miriam Troop's "I've Got a Yen for Japan." An account of the author's spur-of-the-moment trip to Japan, this portrayal of Japan's visual and shopping delights varies little from prewar travelogues—except that it is completely sympathetic and glowing. The streets of Tokyo "glowed with thousands of lanterns, the kind we use over here to decorate garden parties," wrote Troop, but the ones she saw in Japan stretched two stories high. "Painted in bright yellows and reds, with dashes of black, they formed a kaleidoscope of color . . . and silhouetted the crowds of doll-like, kimono-clad men and women trotting along the streets." Things Japanese had once again become an enchanting spectacle for western visitors. If it were not for the mention of three GIs on liberty who accompanied the author on a day of sightseeing, one could forget that the war and Occupation had even occurred. Japanese motifs had become appropriate in consumer products again, and Japan itself was once more a desired tourist destination for Americans. Moreover, because of the Occupation, Japan's accommodations had been updated and refurbished with western conveniences, including luxuries such as American-trained chefs, more golf courses, and more English-speaking service personnel and shop attendants.[112] Returning servicemen and Occupiers gave free stateside promotion to the Japanese tourism industry with their photographs and stories about Japan. Although the number of prewar tourists had peaked in 1936 at 42,000 (of whom only 10,000 were American), roughly a half million Americans went to Japan within two years of the Occupation.[113]

Ten years after the war, major U.S. publishers like Simon and Schuster were no longer publishing thoroughly racist tracts like Chaze's *Stainless Steel Kimono*. Likewise, ten years later Lucy Crockett would have had to tone down her language and use "Japanese" rather than "gooks" or "Japs" in order to get her memoir published. A closer reading of Crockett and even Chaze, however, reveals that neither author had a completely negative view of the Japanese. Chaze prided himself on being hard-boiled, and his wise-guy stance shaped how and what he wrote about Japan. Crockett seems to have been trying to give a clear-eyed, neutral account of the Occupation, perhaps to avoid accusations of being womanlike and "soft" on the Japanese. Yet many of the tales she told were sympathetic to the Japanese, and she usually depicted the Occupiers as callous boors. The title of her book, *Popcorn on the Ginza*, refers to the "imperious" American women who, along with the GIs, emerged from the Ginza PX eating freshly popped popcorn or hot doughnuts, "sublimely indifferent" to the gaping stares of the hungry Japanese.[114] Unlike all the other memoirists, Crockett included an unflattering Japanese assessment of herself—by a Japanese man who sharply criticized her for the insipid speech she gave to college-educated Kyoto women. Others like Margery Brown and Honor Tracy showed some self-reflection in their writings, but only the blatantly patronizing Crockett allowed "the Other" to critique her personally.

The reimaging of the Japanese occurred with no master plan. Journalists and memoirists did not consult each other on how to depict the Japanese; they operated on half-conscious notions about the Japanese "character" that reveal more about American thought and worldviews than they do about the Japanese. O'Reilly did not set out to be the benefactor of a Japanese orphanage, or to fall in love with a Japanese woman. Yet the historical conditions and the pre-existing ideas about Japan made his actions, if not predictable, at least not surprising. And he was only one of many who went through a similar transition after the war—his story was just the best publicized. The former language officer Herbert Passin remembers a naval commander who also "did a one-hundred-and-eighty-degree turnabout" like O'Reilly. At the beginning of the Occupation, this officer refused to use a Nisei to monitor Japanese language communication because he "personally distrusted the Japanese," but he ended up marrying a Japanese woman and living in Japan after leaving the service.[115] Thus the real-life, individual stories and the publicly broadcast, constructed narratives dovetailed to create a shift in perception about the former enemy.

CHAPTER TWO

"Like a Boy of Twelve"

On May 3, 1951, General of the Army Douglas MacArthur testified before the Senate Committees on the Army and on Foreign Relations. The previous month, MacArthur had been relieved of his duty as the Supreme Commander of the Allied Powers by President Truman. The general had insisted on his plan of extending the Korean War into Chinese territory and using nuclear weapons against China, but the President, fearing a nuclear retaliation by the Soviets, refused to grant permission. When MacArthur would not desist, Truman fired him for insubordination. To investigate MacArthur's dismissal, the senators asked the general to assess the situation in East Asia. MacArthur was proud of his record there, especially in Occupied Japan, which had been under his direction. He pointed out, as he often did, the great progress made by the Japanese people in adopting democracy and asserted that democracy in Japan was likely to be permanent. History has shown, MacArthur emphasized, that no nation or race relinquishes freedom once having experienced it. A senator interjected, "Germany may be cited as an exception to that, however." The Germans, the senator continued, enjoyed a democratic government for a short period after World War I "and later followed Hitler . . . enthusiastically." But General MacArthur disagreed with this comparison between Germany and Japan, asserting that "the German problem is completely and entirely different from the Japan problem. The German people were a mature race."[1]

MacArthur then elaborated his meaning in a statement that became infamous to many Japanese for its condescension and racism:

> If the Anglo-Saxon was say 45 years of age in development in the sciences, the arts, divinity, culture, the Germans were quite mature. The Japanese, however, in spite of their antiquity measured by time, were in a very tuitionary condition. Measured by the standard of modern civilization, they would be like a boy of 12 as compared to our own development of 45 years.

Like children, MacArthur explained, the Japanese "were still close enough to [their] origin to be elastic and acceptable to new concepts," and thus the Americans could still "implant basic concepts" in Japan. The Germans, already an advanced or "mature" people, had to be handled differently since it was too late "to change the German nature." MacArthur posited that the German could be expected to "come back to the path that he believes is correct by the pressure of public opinion, by the pressure of world philosophies." The German, the general had no doubt, would "develop his own Germanic tribe along the lines that he himself believes which do not in many basic ways differ from our own." Similar to Euroamericans in race and culture, the Germans could be relied upon to shape their fate without American guidance, whereas the less advanced Japanese required more tutelage and control. MacArthur may well have compared the Japanese unfavorably to Germans to emphasize that his job in Japan had been more challenging than the one faced by General Mark Clark in Germany—after all, MacArthur was a defendant at a hearing when he uttered his words. In boosting himself, however, he nonetheless belittled the Japanese.

MacArthur's statement came as "a slap in the face" to the Japanese, who—until the general so candidly expressed his low opinion of them—had planned to erect a statue of their General "Makkāsā-san" and make him an honorary citizen of Japan. The Japanese eventually dropped these plans. MacArthur's depiction of the Japanese as 12-year-olds touched a raw nerve. Only recently, the Japanese themselves had been describing other Asians as immature in this same matter-of-fact way to justify the Greater East Asia Co-Prosperity Sphere. Once more on the receiving end of the insult, the Japanese were in an uproar about MacArthur's comment.[2]

In contrast, the general's words provoked almost no comment in the United States. This is not surprising, for Americans and Europeans had long believed that there was something immature and undeveloped about the "small" Japanese and their "toylike" nation. MacArthur had drawn upon widely held prewar American notions about manliness, civilization, and race—as well as about the underdevelopment or immaturity of nonwhite, "lesser" races.[3] When the general made his statement, most Americans, consciously or unconsciously, continued to have faith in a racial pecking order even though scientific racism had been generally discredited. Post–World War II liberals and internationalists increasingly relied on the more neutral-sounding language of development or cultural difference that nonetheless helped sustain old practices and beliefs. In this new framework, nonwhite peoples like the Japanese were no longer regarded as biologically inferior, but simply as delayed on a linear continuum of modernity that held democratic governance and a capitalist political economy as the primary indicators of a "mature society."

The Japanese might have been encouraged, however, by the fact that MacArthur at least compared them to "a *boy* of twelve." Women would always remain women, forever lacking the calm leadership skills, the vitality, the foresight, and the intellect to run a modern society, but "boys," in the general's conception, grew up into men. He fully expected the Japanese "boy" to mature into an adult man and take on the responsibilities and privileges of an advanced society, presumably by the time the Occupation ended. MacArthur's racialized paternalism at midcentury did not justify permanent subjugation of the Japanese, in marked contrast to the earlier racialized paternalism of slaveowners and imperialists toward their slaves or colonial subjects. The childishness of colonial subjects—or the superannuation of "old" European imperial masters—was depicted as gender-neutral, but a society that had reached or was moving toward the peak of its powers, the prime of its life, was usually gendered as male.[4] When Americans wanted to portray a nonwhite nation like Japan making progress toward becoming a capitalist democracy, they tended to depict that nation as a young male. Conversely, when they saw stasis, resistance, or barriers to "proper" development, they would describe the nonwhite nation as an inept, incorrigible child or a naive, foolish woman.

The American characterizations of the Japanese as an immature people helped to change a potentially bewildering postwar relationship into an easily comprehensible one that naturalized the unequal U.S.-Japan relationship and provided a basic template for appropriate action. The Americans told themselves and their servicemen that they were to be teachers and guardians to the impressionable, vulnerable Japanese "children." The ideology

As the original caption of this cartoon suggested, many Americans, including General MacArthur, believed that the Japanese—depicted here as a wind-up boy doll—were "not yet ready to walk alone" and needed to be manipulated by Americans to take steps toward democracy. From the *Jacksonville* (Florida) *Times,* February 1949.

of maturity more broadly gave Cold War liberals a conceptual framework and a working vocabulary with which to address the challenges they faced. The emphasis on the potential for non-white nations to grow into figurative adulthood fit the changing priorities of mid-century U.S. foreign policy, which was committed to containing communism and spreading American influence and dominance without establishing a formal overseas empire. The United States sought to encourage nonwhite nations to "develop" into modern, mature, democratic societies rather than to collectivize their economies or to redress social and economic inequities through violent revolution. The theoretical apparatus for this policy later became known as the modernization theory, but the basic ideas were refined in the postwar years and were heavily influenced by gendered notions of maturity.[5] Postwar liberals worried about whether Americans were sufficiently mature, knowledgeable, and open-minded regarding racial differences to hold the responsibility of leadership in a multiracial world. As MacArthur's statement suggested, self-assessment was intrinsic to using the concept of maturity.

Domestic conditions and intellectual trends made this ideology of maturity especially salient in the postwar era, helping to explain why Americans would see the Occupation of Japan as a "test of American civilization," and why they would cast their relationship with Japan as needing to teach a boy "how to walk, talk, think, and play all over again."

The "Feudal" Japanese Civilization

MacArthur's statement also provides clues as to why Americans so frequently described the Japanese as "feudal" after the war. They used this term so often that the British journalist Honor Tracy made fun of the way Americans in Occupied Japan labeled various Japanese practices as "fee-yoodle." She wrote, "No sooner was a custom or an institution pronounced fee-yoodle than they turned the full force of their noble rage against it."[6] As an outside British observer, Tracy thought that the Americans' pronunciation and usage of the word were both slightly ridiculous, but the Americans took the concept seriously. Calling the Japanese "feudal" justified why the United States, a much younger civilization, was in a position to be Japan's teacher. After all, to quote General MacArthur again, the Japanese "in spite of their antiquity measured by time, were in a very tuitionary condition." Although America was young, it was now, its people believed, the most advanced civilization, having superseded even Great Britain. Americans were therefore invested in seeing Japan as a less developed civilization, but one on the same evolutionary path that the Americans had taken. This view reaffirmed a belief in the linear progression of "civilizations," showed the United States to be the most sophisticated, and thus rationalized the U.S. role to lead Japan as only proper and fitting.

Some remnants of belief in scientific racism, however, may also help explain why postwar Americans frequently described the Japanese as "feudal" as well as childlike. The Americans were not necessarily mixing metaphors: both terms connoted underdevelopment, and the combination of feudalism and childishness would not have seemed contradictory to older Americans still informed by recapitulation theory to explain human history. Discredited decades earlier, it held that as humans grew, they relived all previous developmental stages, from the beginning of evolutionary life in utero through the experiences of their primitive ancestors during childhood, finally achieving the enlightenment of their parents. Nonwhite children supposedly stopped developing at a certain point because their ancestors had failed to attain great enough achievements or talents to pass down. Nonwhite adults were seen as similar to white children in intellectual ability, while younger white children were considered the "evolutionary equivalents" of dark-skinned "primitive savages." It is possible that MacArthur, schooled in the nineteenth century, meant that the Japanese were literally "like a boy of twelve," but he was probably using the term figuratively.[7]

More likely, MacArthur and others who described the Japanese as "feudal" were influenced by Freudian notions about psychological development and civilization. The cultural anthropologist Ruth Benedict drew upon Freud's ideas about psychic development in her famous study of Japan, *The Chrysanthemum and the Sword* (1946). The book was part of her national character studies for the Office of War Information (OWI) during the war. Benedict had never studied the Japanese prior to the war; she did not read Japanese; and she had never traveled to Japan. Nevertheless, her work had a tremendous influence on SCAP, Washington policymakers, and the postwar generation of Japanologists in the United States, and the book continues to be read and debated in both Japan and America.[8] While Benedict argued eloquently against racism in works such as *Race: Science and Politics* (1945), her "work in scientific anti-racism and the use of the culture paradigm ironically resulted in regendering Japan as the feminized racial Other," in the words of one American Studies scholar.[9] Behaviorist discussions of "cultural traits" allowed Euroamericans and European scholars to talk about what they formerly called "racial traits" with a more neutral-sounding language, one that unwittingly reinforced a racist ideology that was gendered. Although Benedict rejected the notion of the Japanese as biological inferiors and wanted to foster acceptance of cultural differences, her language depicted them as having a flawed culture that needed reforming in order to be more mature and masculine. Her suggestion, for example, that elements in the Japanese "national character" such as extreme "mood swings" had caused the Japanese to wage war in Asia neglected the economic and political reasons for their aggression.[10] Using notions of human development and cultural flaws to explain the "origins" of political conflicts remained popular in the coming decades.[11]

Studies by Americans that saw more points of similarity than contrasts with Japan were decidedly fewer and less popular. One such example was Helen Mears's *Mirror for Americans: Japan* (1948). As the title suggests, Mears did not orientalize the Japanese; she insisted that Japan was not the diametric opposite of the United States but in fact its mirror. Mears maintained that the "story of Japan's abrupt rise from peaceful isolationism to militaristic expansion in its brief modern period [was], in capsule form, the history of the Western World for the past four centuries." Thus Americans had much to learn from Japan's example—especially its overextension as a military power. Teaching a future generation that "Peace Pays," she pointed out, was "not likely to be accomplished by maintaining bases, huge armaments, keeping troops in foreign countries, backing warlords in China (or elsewhere), or acting, in brief, like old-style arrogant power politicians."[12] An early critic of U.S. militarization and Cold War policy, Mears warned about the folly, to paraphrase Senator Arthur Vandenburg, of "scaring the hell out" of friends, enemies, and the American people.[13]

Liberal Americans generally saw the United States in a positive light and tended to orientalize Japan. Regardless of whether they had little or no Japanese language ability, like Benedict, or were fluent in the language, like the famous Japanologist Edwin O. Reischauer, liberal Americans saw the Japanese and the Americans as very different people because of their different cultures and socialization. Americans who were more leftist—those with a more critical stance toward their country, like Mears—tended to see more commonalities between Japanese and American motivations and histories. Benedict, in the end, believed that the American democratic system worked, and that U.S. society was truly a melting pot. Mears, however, was less sanguine about Americans' ability to make a just and equitable society at home, much less abroad.[14]

Mears also possessed an ability to see past the strangeness of the Japanese. Like other western travelers to Japan, she had found the place odd and unfamiliar during her two prewar sojourns there, but she understood that her opinions mattered much more during her later trip in 1946 as part of an official advisory committee to GHQ's Labor Division. Whereas she had been an inconsequential "individual tourist and student" in her previous trips, Mears now held the power to affect millions of Japanese.[15] It disturbed her that the other ten members of her committee felt comfortable about going to Japan even though they knew next to nothing about the country or the situation in postwar Japan. They possessed, she thought, an unwarranted faith in universal economic principles and in the ability of Americans to make others embrace "The American Way." One committee member, she remembered, "carried with him slim volumes of Aristotle and Machiavelli, which—during the flight out [to Japan]—he had browsed from time to time getting a firm grasp on the principles."[16] Mears had little faith in the applicability of western principles to the current dilemmas facing either the United States or the world. She would have agreed with historian Bruce Cumings's observation that "[a] people that thinks its goals are self-evident and universal also has trouble grasping that it is bound by its own history and particularity."[17] As her book makes clear, she came to question the very basis on which her fellow Americans carried out the Occupation.

It should come as no surprise that while SCAP suggested both Benedict and Reischauer as recommended reading for its new personnel, it censored Mears's work in Japan. It is also not surprising that Mears's book was and remains in a "blackout" in the United States: "Without major popular success and without an academic post to speak from, Mears dropped almost completely off the map, figuring rarely on reading lists or in footnotes." Mears's publisher, Houghton Mifflin, recently reissued the sixtieth anniversary edition of Benedict's *The Chrysanthemum and the Sword* in 2005, whereas Mears's book remains out of print.[18]

Rather than looking at the political and economic factors that were operating in Japan, many liberal observers of the Occupation preferred to explain Japanese history as result of its unique culture, frequently depicting Japan as feminine and passive. Unencumbered with an appreciation of Japan's dynamic past, Lucy Crockett wrote that "until relatively recent years there [had] been few physical changes to mark the gradual passage of time."[19] In this frequently repeated interpretation, Japan had existed for most Americans in a timeless continuum until its contact with Perry's (big) black ships "forced *her* open," as if Japan had been an unwilling maiden. By ignoring Japan's pre-isolation contact with the Dutch, the Portuguese, and other Europeans, Americans remembered their nation as Japan's first suitor. In a December 1946 issue of *Life* magazine, Noel Busch suggested that an extension of America's "manifest" destiny led Americans to Asia to initiate contact with Japan:

> The Japanese are people who migrated eastward from Asia and were stopped by the Pacific Ocean. Trapped in a historical and geographical pocket, worshipping their own past in the form of ancestors, they made a virtue of retrogression and by means of it developed a fragile, nervous yet brilliant civilization which lay imprisoned in the 19th century like a butterfly in amber. For, while the Japanese had been receding toward a remote and upside-down perfection of their own, the European world had been racing in the opposite direction. When Americans reached the coast of California, it meant that two antithetical trends in human development were separated only by calm water; and that, in view of the nature of the Western trend, this water would be crossed.[20]

Busch's description of Japan as "a butterfly in amber" alluded to the femininity of Madame Butterfly and to her passivity, her inability to do little but wait for the American military man to cross the Pacific Ocean.[21] Rather than being progressive and forward-looking as Americans and westerners were, Japan was retrogressive; it was "receding," not proceeding, and "upside-down," not right side up. Most important, Japan was not simply passive, but "imprisoned in the 19th century." Other Americans also described the Japanese as being "trapped" in the past, weighed down with "feudalistic" traditions, or hampered by "medieval simplicity." This kind of language implied that while Japan was an ancient civilization, it lacked the vim and vigor of western civilization whose aggressive and confident genius allowed it to be hundreds of years ahead of the Japanese—or at least one hundred—in terms of development.[22]

The notion of Japan as a "butterfly in amber" waiting for American assistance attempted to erase the recent past. For Japan had not waited like a butterfly in amber for Americans to cross the expanse of the Pacific Ocean; instead, the formal hostilities had begun with the Japanese crossing the water in Mitsubishi Zeroes to surprise the sleeping Americans. This metaphor thus obscured Japan's aggressive, imperialist "penetration" of Asia and the Pacific islands. Moreover, portraying the United States as a gallant suitor or mentor not only humanized the Japanese but also helped rewrite history to take attention away from the moment when a vulnerable America was caught unawares and rendered helpless. Finally, the butterfly image ignored the U.S. immigration law—still valid for Japanese and Koreans until 1952—passed by Euroamericans to put a stop to Asians crossing the Pacific to establish themselves in the United States and U.S. territory. The metaphor therefore worked on multiple levels, all of which served to reconfirm a positive and flattering American self-image and to depict the U.S. military occupation of Japan as fated and benevolent.

In *Fallen Sun* (1948), an expansion of his *Life* essay on Japan, Busch argued that much of Japanese behavior could be explained by examining their childhood "conditioning." He claimed that the Japanese—despite their admirable civility toward one another—were extraordinary among all peoples and races in the way they projected "their infantile attitudes [onto] adult life."

Starting with the Freudian premise that humans "naturally cling to, or retrogress emotionally toward those periods of their lives which were most agreeable to them," Busch posited that the Japanese exhibited the immature behaviors associated with childhood, a stage when they were supposedly the happiest. Hence "a mere glance at the whole horizon of Japanese life, or the whole perspective of Japanese history, will show, as might be expected . . . this special yearning for the remotest past." Keeping in mind "this deep subconscious impulse," Busch asserted, would help Americans understand a laundry list of seemingly bizarre Japanese behaviors: their filial piety; the inclusion of the prenatal stage in calculating a person's age; their enthusiasm for Mount Fuji; their volatile mood swings; their physical agility; "their docility when confronted by authority and their lack of self-discipline when exempted from it"; and finally, their placid acceptance of the status quo. The Japanese, Busch stated, exhibited "the flexibility, the obedience, the unruliness and the stoicism of adults who possess and cling, in a way unimaginable to Occidentals, to the emotional status of childhood."[23]

Though Busch was clearly influenced by Benedict and her colleague Geoffrey Gorer, his view that the Japanese clung unreasonably to the past was evident in American discourse even prior to the publication of *The Chrysanthemum and the Sword*. A cartoon published originally by the *Detroit News* in September 1945 showed a little Japanese man in a kimono-like garment—an outfit that Americans would perceive as women's garb—proffering a flower to an American GI nearly twice his height who is preaching to him from a book titled the "Democratic Way of Life." Yet the Japanese man's mind seems to be clouded by the past. Behind him set in misty wisps are images of Mount Fuji, the Kamakura *Daibutsu*, the emperor, a *torii*, and other traditional symbols. "It

It Will Take a Long Time

Doubts about the Japanese ability to understand democracy, as illustrated in this cartoon, were prevalent among Americans during the occupation of Japan. From the *Detroit News*, September 17, 1945.

Will Take a Long Time," says the cartoon's caption; and indeed, the soldier's impatient stance and the Japanese man's vapid look suggest that none of the soldier's lesson on democracy is sinking in. Moreover, even though the Japanese man appears to be making a peace offering, a "present-o," he still carries a sword in its scabbard and appears capable of treachery.

To speak of the Japanese as "feudal," "medieval," or even "primitive" implied that the Japanese could be irrationally cruel because they lacked the combination of Enlightenment rationality and Judeo-Christian morality that Americans believed constituted advanced western "character." In this view, although the Japanese possessed the accoutrements of modernity, their fundamental character made them completely different from westerners. Although Japan "amaz[ed] the whole world with its swift and successful adoption of Western institutions and industrialization," Lucy Crockett wrote, "the Japanese were nevertheless a people of medieval minds under a thin veneer of civilization." Westerners should not be deceived by the evidence of "modern technology" in Japan, she commented, because the Japanese still possessed a "stone-age mentality." Crockett reported that an "Old Japan Hand" told her, "The Japanese only know the extreme. Always the middle is lacking. There is either complete self-control or complete lack of it. A woman is overly polite or very rude. She either smiles sweetly or she screams. There is no tact, no understanding, no real sympathy, only set rules that govern every thought and act." An Occupation officer stationed in Otsu declared: "The Japs are sneaky right down to their pagan souls. They are like animals. Ever since 1900 we had been saying and writing fine things about Japan. We told only about the beautiful scenery and the souvenirs. We overlooked the primitive aspect."[24] Although the man in the cartoon might be making a peaceful gesture, he could just as easily drop the flower and draw his sword on the American. The Japanese supposedly lacked the ability to make personal moral judgments. Influenced by Benedict, Americans increasingly explained this assessment of Japanese "character" by saying that the Japanese were a society governed by group shame, not by individual conscience.[25]

The notion that "every thought and act" of the Japanese was governed by "set rules" made Americans sometimes doubt whether the present generation of Japanese could ever understand democracy. Supposedly socialized and educated to lack individuality, the Japanese were thought to have poor analytical ability and little common sense. Part of Occupation lore—one of many such stories of Japanese incompetence—was a story of a Japanese "room boy" who was told to wake up a hotel guest at a given hour, but who was too considerate or timid to disturb the guest when the hour came. Instead, he allegedly tiptoed into the guest's room and noiselessly placed a note on the bureau: "Sir, it is 8 o'clock, please wake up."[26] Could such odd people comprehend and internalize the common sense that was essential to democratic living and thinking? Many Americans thought not. The journalists Frank Kelley and Cornelius Ryan complained that the Japanese wanted to reduce democracy to a number of rules to follow—they "wanted to know, almost pathetically, how they could become democrats and get on with life," they wrote.[27] The two failed to see how reasonable this Japanese response was, given the mixed messages about democracy sent by the military government and individual Americans. The Americans supposedly embodied democracy, yet many of SCAP's edicts, as well as individual Americans' demands for servility from the Japanese, were blatantly undemocratic.

Americans also noted that the Japanese conflated democracy

and affluent consumer culture. Advertisements in pictorial magazines like *Life,* Kelley and Ryan related, showed the Japanese that "bright cars, clothes, and cigarettes all meant one thing—democracy." Crockett concurred, observing that because of magazines and Hollywood films, the Japanese believed that democracy was "synonymous with all the dazzling features of Western life—sleek automobiles, cocktail lounges, fancy feminine shoes, electric gadgets, a helicopter on every roof." Drawing on an old stereotype, she asserted that the Japanese interpretation of democracy meant "zealous copying of many of those features of American life of which we have little to be proud, plus a naïve misinterpretation of liberty as license, individual rights as indulgence." A "pert housewife" asked Crockett, "If democracy means a Frigidaire, when do we start getting them?"[28] Crockett found this anecdote amusing because of the woman's apparent naiveté, not realizing that the Japanese housewife was actually interpreting the American message correctly. During the Occupation and throughout much of the world during the Cold War, the United States promoted democracy alongside the affluent "American way of life." It is possible that the Japanese housewife was trying ingenuously to point out the connection implicit in American thinking about democracy. At any rate, the point was lost on Crockett because the idea that the Japanese might have something to teach Americans lay outside the established framework.

Instead, stateside headlines such as "Teaching 'Demokratzi' to the Japanese" were typical and made sense to Americans because they implied that the Japanese, unable to lead themselves toward enlightenment, needed the Americans to show them the way.[29] Americans saw regenerative possibilities particularly in Japanese children and aimed to reorient the Japanese away from "feudalistic" and "militaristic" thinking by reforming the educational sys tem. Since Americans now rejected notions of immutable, biologically based racial differences, they believed that with the correct guidance, the Japanese could be reoriented within a generation or a lifetime rather than hundreds of years.[30] "Our greatest hope is in the children," the Stoddard mission declared after its tour of the Japanese educational system. Pundits like Harold Noble, the *Saturday Evening Post*'s Japan expert, agreed; he intoned to *Post* readers, "If there's anything which you and I must want more urgently from Japan, it is that this present crop of youngsters shall grow up decently and hopefully—that they will live in peace and understanding with their neighbors."[31] With this objective, SCAP implemented far-reaching educational reforms that were largely successful and appreciated by most Japanese. The reforms made education more accessible at both the secondary and college levels to women and to poorer, rural students; the schools were also made more egalitarian by replacing a multi-track system with an American-style single-track system consisting of six years of primary school, three years of middle school, and three years of high school.

But it was Japanese liberal educators and reform-minded bureaucrats who initiated the majority of the reforms, as Gordon Bowles later admitted. Bowles, a Japan specialist involved in the educational reforms, estimated that 60 percent of them originated with the Japanese. SCAP, to its credit, established a Committee of Japanese Educators that consulted with its American counterparts as equals. It was the chair of this group, Tokyo Imperial University president Nanbara Shigeru, who secretly persuaded George D. Stoddard to recommend the single-track 6-3-3 system and universal education for nine years—a recommendation that conservative Prime Minister Yoshida Shigeru protested would bankrupt the Japanese government.[32] Under the aegis of the American Occupation, liberal educators like Nanbara were finally able to achieve the education reforms that they had advocated for decades. Yet this Japanese input seems to have gone largely unnoticed by the American press, perhaps because it did not fit their conception of Japan as the bewildered pupil needing the firm guidance of the United States. Most reports on the Occupation gave the Japanese very little credit for taking positive, reasonable initiatives on their own, but preferred to depict them as over-eager students who, in their youthful, naive enthusiasm, could only imitate and misinterpret primary concepts. Thus the Americans—though not unique in this respect—saw and understood another people in the way they wanted to see and understand them.

Portraying the Japanese as less developed and imitative rather than advanced, wise, and innovative reassured Americans about themselves and their society. Amusing stories of everyday frustrations in Occupied Japan served to mitigate the hard fact of the Americans' conquest of Japan and its subjugation by "exposing their inner ambivalence concerning their prize."[33] Constant complaints about the Japanese inability to understand democracy implied that Americans were in full command of its principles. The journalists Kelley, Ryan, and Russell Brines even used the supposed innate resistance by the Japanese to democratic concepts to hint that the internment of Japanese Americans was justified. Because the Nisei were only a generation away from their Japanese origins, they supposedly had difficulty absorbing the principles of democracy: it "had not taken root in them," said the journalists, bizarrely ignoring the fact that Americans had denied democracy to their fellow citizens of Japanese ancestry.[34]

The most obvious use of the postwar American discourse about Japanese "feudalism" in justifying the U.S. occupation was to render the Japanese as helpless and naive as women and children supposedly were. Here again the discourses of femininity and maturity merged, but it is important to remember also how they remained separate. Drawing on old ideas about male activity and female passivity, Americans feminized stasis while portraying movement and advancement as masculine. They therefore described in feminine terms—"like a butterfly in amber"—what they perceived as the innate backwardness or inscrutability of the Japanese. When they spoke of the Japanese making strides and taking flight, they described them as young males—"like a boy of twelve."

How to Think about Western Civilization

Examining why Americans would cast themselves as wise teachers to the Japanese boy requires an analysis of how they looked at themselves at this historic juncture. On one hand, the construction of Americans as teachers was a continuation of previous and ongoing attempts to "civilize" nonwhites or those considered as marginally white others from southern or eastern Europe.[35] Whether expressed in the secular terms of modernization and development in the mid-twentieth century or explained as America's "manifest destiny" or "God-given" task in earlier periods, this outlook had served to justify public and private attempts by Americans to impose their values, culture, and institutions upon other peoples.[36] During the Progressive era, Americans finally succeeded in bringing what now constitutes the continental United States entirely under their control, and then engaged in a war with the Spanish that spread U.S. imperialism overseas. What the Native Americans, Native Hawaiians, Filipinos, Puerto Ricans, and Cubans characterized as immoral and unjust grabs for territory, the majority of Americans rationalized as destined and appropriate. Convinced that they needed to "uplift" the natives, religious and secular missionaries taught middle-class American culture to the children of the Yankton Sioux at White's Manual School in Indiana, the former black slaves at the Hampton Institute, the Sicilian immigrants at Hull House, the Hawaiians at the Kamehameha School, and the Filipinos in American-style "public schools." With a millennialist faith in America's national mission and its role as moral exemplar, as well as an adherence to Enlightenment creeds about universalism, science, and human perfectibility, nineteenth-century Progressives trusted that their attempts had the best interests of the "uncivilized" in mind.

After the Progressive era, however, the epistemological rationale for racism—and sexism—shifted from biological inferiority based on genes to societal inferiority based on psychoanalytical notions about "civilization" and social anthropological notions about "culture." Educated Americans were exposed to new theories by Freud, Franz Boas, and others that made them rethink how social hierarchies worked. Although Freud and Boas occupied vastly different intellectual and disciplinary universes, both perpetuated old beliefs about race. Freud's widely influential works, especially *Totem and the Taboo* (1913) and *Civilization and Its Discontents* (1930), continued a discussion about civilizations that not only presumed superior civilizations correlated to paleness of skin color, but also insisted that male endeavor created civilizations. "The work of civilization," he wrote, "has become increasingly the business of men, it confronts them with ever more difficult tasks and compels them to carry out instinctual sublimations of which women are little capable."[37] Women, like "primitives" and children, supposedly lacked the self-restraint to sublimate desires.

Similarly, the cultural anthropologist Franz Boas, whose scholarship helped debunk scientific racism, was only partially successful in separating variations in skin pigmentation or physiognomy
from cultural or social differences. Although he believed that African Americans deserved full citizenship because the average person of African descent was the equal of the average individual of
European descent in abilities and intellect, Boas held that neither Africans nor African Americans could produce the "men of
high genius" found among Europeans and Euroamericans.[38] By
overemphasizing culture in their studies, Boas and his students
conflated their ideas about a people's social traditions and behaviors with a people's political economy. Likewise, although Freud
was no champion of capitalism, he was more sharply critical of
communism as "a system based on an untenable illusion" that
there could be lasting harmony among humans.[39] The marginal-
ity of political-economic or class analysis in cultural anthropology and psychoanalysis thus resonated, decades later, with both
the vested class interests and the latent racism of most postwar
liberals.

Like their nineteenth-century predecessors, postwar liberals
felt supported in their beliefs by the latest social and behavioral
sciences. These liberals minimized class conflict and had faith that
free trade would create economic growth and could eventually
bring prosperity to all the world's peoples. As in the previous
era, most of them earnestly meant well—and felt philanthropic—
in their efforts to improve the lives of the "Other." But in the
postcolonial era, the notion that nonwhite nations could "grow
up" and "become like us with our help" was a sincere hope on
the part of American liberals, especially in Japan, in contrast to
the empty promises of western colonizers. And to be fair, the secular missionaries of SCAP did succeed to a significant degree in

bettering the lives of ordinary Japanese. But the postwar political climate created significant shifts in American liberals' attitudes toward the poorer, preindustrial nations of the world. First, they sought to use the state's power and wealth to address a wide range of domestic and international problems formerly left in private hands.[40] In addition, the emergence of the Soviet Union as a global competitor was a strong factor in making postwar liberals more concerned about "making them like us"—having the "Other" admire Americans enough to embrace liberal capitalism and "the American way of life."[41] Finally, since the United States possessed the most formidable ability in the world to project military and economic power after World War II, postwar liberals believed that the time had come when the U.S. could finally fulfill an anticipation that dated back to the founding of the their nation and be the leading light of the "civilized world."[42] War-devastated Great Britain had seemingly passed the responsibility of civilization on to the United States, who would thereafter preserve and spread it throughout the world.

Yet in the brave new world of superpower rivalry and atomic power, internationally-minded liberal Americans worried about their ability to be caretakers of western civilization. In a *Life* editorial, "How to Think About 'Civilization,'" Henry Luce pointed out that "the spread of concentration camps, the revival of torture, the official use of genocide, the splitting of the atom, and similar throwbacks and advances" from the recent war might indicate impending disaster. Noting that humans had thus far survived "the collapse of any particular civilization," Luce pronounced, "ours *might*, like Samson in the temple, so perish as to take the species with it." This editorial continued the message of Luce's famous February 1941 sermon, "The American Century": that Americans should "accept wholeheartedly our duty and our opportunity as the most powerful and vital nation in the world and in consequence to exert upon the world the full import of our influence, for such purposes as we see fit and by such means we see fit." At the beginning of the Cold War, Luce implored Americans to take on a role of world leadership commensurate with their military and economic power—but with the added urgency of preserving western civilization, if not world civilization itself. Loss of the former, of course, rendered the latter worthless in Luce's eyes. Therefore, the "U.S. must, in Britain's place, consciously become what it has been, in reluctant fact, since the beginning of World War II: the champion of the remnant of Christian civilization against the forces that threatened it." As another writer put it, the American could "no longer be a citizen of his own country; he must be a citizen of the world."[43]

This new responsibility highlighted the question of whether Americans were educated enough to be world leaders. "Are You Smart Enough to Be a Citizen?" asked the *Saturday Evening Post* in 1946. The answer was no, and that it was time Americans started to "study hard" and "the dry stuff," too, since recent events made "it easier to be a dope today than ever in history."[44] The Luce media empire, which included *Time, Life, Fortune,* and the newsreel series *The March of Time,* tried to inform its audience of 40 million people about international events and to give them a sense of personal obligation for peoples living under or threatened by Soviet rule. To encourage Americans to better appreciate their heritage, *Life* presented a lavish series on the history of western civilization, which ended with a look at America, "the heir and hope" of that history.[45]

That western civilization represented the acme of "man's greatest achievements" was clearly implied in Time, Inc.'s strong endorsement of British historian Arnold J. Toynbee's enormously popular *A Study of History.* Toynbee's multivolume opus came out in abridged form in the United States in 1947, with a lavish publicity campaign and glowing reviews.[46] Although Toynbee claimed to dismiss the existence of "superior races" in his ranking of twenty-one "civilizations," he placed western man—not woman, of course—in the top position. In its coverage of the book, *Life* provided a full-page, portfolio-sized illustration of Toynbee's metaphor of men climbing or resting on several mountains of various heights to denote the relative progress of human civilizations. The drawing presented the darkest-skinned people at the lowest level among the surviving civilizations, people of medium hue somewhere in the middle, and western man on top.[47] Perched above the "dead" civilizations were the "primitive societies," represented by a dark-skinned couple—a sitting man and a half-naked, supine woman. That the only woman in the illustration was a "primitive" and drawn lying down implied that climbing and striving to "make progress" was men's work. She and the "primitive" man seated next to her do not look up or forward; instead, they peer at the "dead civilizations" below them and back into the past. The "primitives" were those that "have never become civilized" but "being still alive, could develop fur-

An artist's rendition of historian Arnold Toynbee's metaphor of human civilizations, published in *Life* magazine in February 1948. The caption read: "The fate of civilizations is presented by Toynbee in an arresting metaphor. . . . Here the historian sees all mankind as on a mountainside. Lying on the ledge are the world's dead civilizations, which had climbed from depths where they were once subhumans and primitive men. Resting on another ledge are primitive societies which have never become civilized but, being still alive, could develop further. Stranded on minor peaks, unable to climb further, are five 'arrested' civilizations. Three of these, Eskimo, Nomadic, and Polynesian, are still alive. Five civilizations are still climbing. Healthiest is our Western civilization, the only one making any progress." Illustration courtesy of the Charles E. Martin trust.

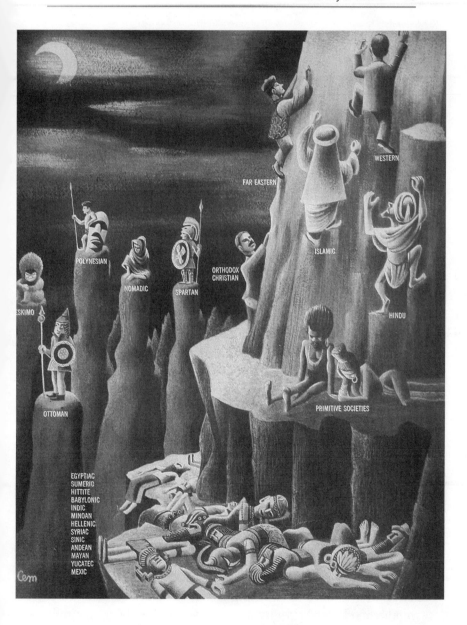

ther" (if they would only get up off the ground, the picture suggested).

This portrayal, incidentally, had Toynbee's full approval.[48] What it shows is that while Toynbee's work provided academic weight to the discredited Social Darwinist concepts about race and manliness, he modified the theory to indicate that other peoples were still engaged in the struggle to be "the fittest." Nonwhites or marginal whites were not necessarily left behind permanently; they were still developing and climbing toward the top. Toynbee's history became a bestseller. By 1956, Americans had purchased 7,000 sets of the ten-volume work and 300,000 copies of the abridged volume, which became a Book-of-the-Month-Club selection.[49]

At the beginning of the Cold War, Toynbee's study provided a convenient historical context for contemporary international politics. It sold extremely well in part because it was useful to Americans as they sought guidance in the new world order. "Western man" was now at the top, but the question was: "How much farther will Western man continue climbing before he comes to rest on a ledge or falls backward?"[50] Such questions revealed anxiety—not just on the part of liberal Americans but also by conservatives about the disorderly world abroad as well as the unruly or disturbing elements at home.

Some Americans worried that there were too many "mamma's boys" at home who had failed to mature properly. In his infamous *A Generation of Vipers* (1942), a book that continued to sell throughout the fifties, Philip Wylie charged that a generation of frivolous, petty, and domineering "moms" had smothered their sons into being sissies who lacked the physical and mental toughness to run the nation. Wylie's theory, which he dubbed "Momism," railed against the Victorian model of sentimental motherhood that held that mothers deserved undying gratitude from their children, as well as from the public, as nurturers of the home. "Moms," Wylie insisted, were simply unequipped to exert positive public influence: "'Mom's' suffrage was roughly concomitant with the start toward a new all-time low in political scurviness, hoodlumism, gangsterism, labor strife, monopolistic thuggery, moral degeneration, civic corruption, smuggling, bribery, theft, murder, homosexuality, drunkenness, financial depression, chaos, and war."

Not surprisingly, Wylie outraged many women and presumably some men as well. Yet "Momism" was legitimized by the psychiatrist Edward A. Strecker, a wartime government consultant who later became the chair of the Psychiatry Department at the University of Pennsylvania Medical School, a president of the American Psychiatric Association, and a charter appointee to the National Institute of Mental Health's advisory council. In *Their Mothers' Sons* (1946), Strecker—like Wylie—depicted "Moms" as a problem in national security, arguing that too many of them failed to raise mature, dependable, and patriotic sons who could serve their country. During the war, Strecker saw thousands of men deemed mentally unfit for service. He concluded that such men, along with draft dodgers and gay men, came from "Moms" who had kept their children "paddling about in a kind of psychological amniotic fluid rather than letting them swim away with the bold and decisive strokes of maturity from the emotional maternal womb."[51] By refusing to loosen the "emotional umbilical cord" and allow their sons to grow up, "Moms" created cowards and "sex perverts" who remained dependent, childishly self-centered, and devoted to "Mom" but averse to fulfilling adult, manly duties of citizenship, community, and fatherhood. As the scholar Jennifer Terry put it, "Mom's sons, gay or straight, therefore supposedly undermined the security of the nation."[52]

As Wylie's laundry list of complaints and Strecker's expansion of "Momism" revealed, Americans at mid-century feared that their nation was becoming effeminate, losing its previously forthright and sturdy character. With too much private and public power, women were seen to be emasculating men and thus presenting a danger to the nation's protection and health.[53] At the same time, women were held responsible for an "epidemic" in juvenile delinquency that many Americans mistakenly believed was caused by the American family's failure or "impotence" to enforce its values on a younger generation.[54] Adding urgency to this perceived crisis was not only global politics but also the knowledge that the numbers of idle, undirected, or disruptive youth would only increase in the immediate future, as the "war babies"—later known as the baby boomers—grew older.[55]

To ensure that the next generation of Americans would mature properly to maintain their society and be able lead the world, liberal educators and intellectuals called for more rigor in American education. Although they debated what a new curriculum should include or stress, most found the current U.S. system wanting.[56] Columnist Walter Lippmann complained that modern education was "destined to destroy Western civilization" for failing to pass down "the religious and classical culture of the Western world." Lippmann alleged that earlier reforms championed by John Dewey, which emphasized pragmatism and science, neglected the classical "study of moral wisdom" and threatened to turn Americans into amoral beings who would accept "abominable crimes" or immoral individuals who would play "with murder and robbery and the blackest brand of bad faith."[57] Lippmann and others believed that the antidote to this situation was a "liberal education" with a firm basis in the classics, a pedagogy most famously advocated by Mortimer J. Adler. In the 1930s, drawing on the emphasis on western classics that he learned at Columbia University, Adler created the "Great Books" curriculum at the University of Chicago.

Heavily criticized at the end of the Cold War as Eurocentric and sexist, the Great Books approach was also controversial from the outset and was hotly debated among educators. Columbia's Mark Van Doren—who co-taught one such class with Adler—endorsed the canonical approach, claiming that "the way to produce individual intellects is to teach all students the same things, and of course the best things."[58] Training all young American minds in the western tradition would presumably produce moral and intelligent citizens bound together, whatever their differences, in a community of ideas and ideals. Harry D. Gideonse, president of Brooklyn College, disagreed and pointed out, "Nothing is more clearly subversive of the true importance of the classics than the idealization of their definitive significance." He criticized Van Doren for repeating "the old complaint that American children cannot read, write, or speak their own language properly"—a lament also heard in other countries.[59]

Adler, however, never advocated an appreciation of western civilization for its own sake, but rather to encourage Americans to hone their critical thinking skills. Later, trying to answer charges of racism and sexism, he explained that he chose the "great books" based on their ability to provide suggestions for dealing with the "timeless" problems that beset humans. But at mid-century, criticisms about the canonical approach usually concerned methodology rather than its exclusive content, and the "great books" curriculum gained wide acceptance.[60] To spread this approach to a wider classroom beyond college campuses, Adler edited the highly successful *Great Books of the Western World* for Encyclopaedia Britannica and wrote extensively in journals and popular magazines, including *Harper's, Good House-*

keeping, Saturday Review, and even *Playboy.* He also published books geared to the wider public, such as his famous *How to Read a Book: The Art of Getting a Liberal Education* (1940) and *Aristotle for Everybody: Difficult Thought Made Easy* (1978).[61]

At the point when the United States finally reached a position of indisputable global preeminence, then, Americans looked out at the large, messy, and complex world, gazed inward at the problems in their own society, and wondered about the capacity of their fellow citizens and youth to live up to the profound challenge to bring about peace and order in the world. Emphasis on the canonical approach provided, its advocates hoped, a foundation in the western tradition, critical thinking skills, and a moral compass to guide America in this enormous task: the "finest books" of western civilization would help Americans make sense of and act upon a disorderly world. That this approach perpetuated the belief that individuals of "high genius" were invariably white and male mattered little to its advocates. What the situation called for was principles that were clear-eyed, rational, and unsentimental, and unlike Helen Mears, these thinkers believed that the western canon best provided this clarity.

The Mature Mind and Racial Tolerance

As liberals in the postwar period, Adler, Van Doren, and others all rejected blatant racism, and indeed they had an abiding faith that racism could be erased from American society through the efforts of rational beings of goodwill. To liberals, racism and bigotry were the result of outdated misconceptions and immaturity. Perhaps the individual who best articulated this position was Harry Allen Overstreet, a professor of philosophy at Brooklyn College. Committed like Adler to adult education, Overstreet preached what he called the "maturity concept" as another tool to help Americans navigate the postwar world. He explained his ideas in *The Mature Mind* (1949), another Book-of-the-Month-Club selection that sold half a million copies within three years and remained on the bestseller lists for seventy-two weeks, including nine weeks as the nation's top-selling nonfiction book.[62] Applying neo-Freudian insights to investigate what he regarded as the immaturity of Americans, he pointed out that since the average American left school at fourteen years—an age too young to grasp the significance of studies—most Americans were, "save in rare cases, a museum of immature fixations, snap judgments, picked-up prejudices, and unverified 'hand-me-downs.'" Too many individuals with "the mind of a child on the shoulders of an adult" caused the woes of modern American society, whether the problem was management/labor strife, religious intolerance, national chauvinism, or "white supremacism." All these problems, Overstreet advised, should be understood as a result of adults behaving as children—egoistic, selfish, rude, and sometimes cruel. Overstreet believed that maturity was a continual process of achieving, not a fixed final state, and described "properly maturing" adults as those who were open-minded, empathetic, patient, steady, generous, creative rather than destructive, and most of all, aware of the impact of their actions. With the Enlightenment's faith in reason and perfectibility, Overstreet held that mature individuals could, or at least should, tolerably work out conflicts of interest "with forbearance, courage, and fortitude."[63]

Particularly critical of continued racial discrimination in the United States, Overstreet—along with other postwar liberals—explained racism as Euroamerican immaturity. In 1945, he heartily endorsed an edited collection of essays published that year by the writer Bucklin Moon with a provocative title: *Primer for*

White Folks.[64] The collection upended a paternalistic discourse that infantilized African Americans by bluntly telling Euroamericans that in race relations, "white folks," not "black folk," were as illiterate as young children.[65] In his review of the book, Overstreet wrote: "'Primer for White Folks' is a book to teach us how to spell. White folk who think they already know how will not like this book; [they] probably will not deign to read it, since it seems to question their social and political literacy." To Overstreet, being an adult meant being sensitive to the African-American past and present and, most important, being aware of one's own racism. This history and self-knowledge were, as his book review title spelled out, "Some Things Adults Ought to Know."[66] Others agreed. Apparently believing that southern whites did not have this knowledge, John Gunther titled one chapter "The South: Problem Child of the Nation" in his bestselling *Inside U.S.A.* (1951). His chapter on southern blacks was called simply, "Negroes in the South."[67]

Echoing this theme of American immaturity to explain racism, Yale Law professor Eugene Rostow blamed the evacuation and imprisonment of over 110,000 Japanese Americans on the irresponsibility of the federal government in succumbing to racist and childish "mass hysteria." "In the perspective of our legal tradition," Rostow wrote in a September 1945 *Harper's* magazine piece condemning the internment, "the facts are almost incredible." "One hundred thousand persons were sent to concentration camps on a record which wouldn't support a conviction for stealing a dog," he disdainfully declared. It was a decision based on irrational "race prejudice" and on the preposterous notion that "race" or biology mattered more than "culture" in determining a person's "loyalty." This notion, as Rostow had explained more fully in his earlier *Yale Law Journal* article on the same subject, "was flatly contradicted by the evidence of the biological sciences, of cultural anthropology, sociology, and every other branch of systematic social study."[68] But by suggesting that the discriminatory Executive Order 9066 was egregiously inconsistent with a usually more responsible government, Rostow was ignoring the larger pattern of government-sponsored racial discrimination against Japanese Americans such as *Ozawa v. the United States* (1922), which reaffirmed denying the right of naturalization to Japanese immigrants, or the Japanese exclusion clause in the 1924 Immigration Act. Within this context, the internment, though unjust and unwarranted, was rational and consistent in the U.S. legal tradition—not a momentary lapse into childish hysteria.[69]

To point this out is not to castigate Rostow, an early and important critic of the internment. His law journal article helped influence Congress to give the Japanese Americans a small redress in 1948 and served as the basis for the successful effort to demand a larger redress four decades later. But there is a similarity between the presumption in Rostow's rhetoric, which called upon his fellow Americans to correct a grave, irresponsible, and shortsighted mishap, and the appeals about racial tolerance made by Overstreet. Rostow—and many other supporters of the Japanese Americans—labeled those who tried to use intimidation to prevent internees from returning to the West Coast as immature "hooligans." Against these punk-like or small-minded racists, the defenders of Japanese Americans held up the heroic, manly deeds of the Japanese American 442nd Regimental Combat Team. In so doing, they presented a choice to their American audience—many of whom might have been unsympathetic to the Japanese Americans—between siding with mature decency or with delinquent-like behavior and uneducated attitudes.[70]

This antiracist rhetoric helped the effort to refigure the Japanese enemy because it suggested that Japanese citizens could not be equated with the Japanese government. Rostow asserted incredulously that the internment was due to "the extraordinary proposition that all persons of Japanese ancestry are enemies, that the war is not directed at the Japanese state, but at the Japanese 'race.'"[71] As John Dower has forcefully shown, the Americans and the Japanese had indeed engaged in what they conceived as a race war. But at the end of the war, Rostow believed, mature and responsible people knew this idea was ridiculous. Well aware that many Americans believed they had fought the Japanese "race," he tried to convince them to be more open-minded and liberal about race, thereby being truer to their nation's highest ideals about equality.

The antiracism of Rostow, Overstreet, and other liberals fit into a larger worldview that supported capitalism as the economic system on which a "free," democratic society rested.[72] Rostow later wrote *Planning for Freedom: The Public Law of American Capitalism* (1959), while his younger brother, W. W. Rostow, published *The Stages of Economic Growth: A Non-Communist Manifesto* (1960), the classic of modernization theory that envisioned liberal capitalism bringing about a middle-class world of satisfied consumers. Overstreet, too, had an abiding liberal faith that capitalism could eventually create a middle-class or classless society with a strong, vibrant, democratic political system. Critical of unfettered capitalism that gave priority to profit margins over labor welfare, Overstreet advocated reform that would be more humane and more stable by allowing others, such as disenfranchised blacks, to have more of a stake in it. To Overstreet and other Cold War liberals, fighting communism and fighting racism were both vital for the health of a democratic society and world. "We realize," he stated at the end of *The Mature Mind,* "that the evils of our life come not from deep evil within us but from ungrown-up responses to life. Our obligation, then, is to grow up. This is what our time requires of us. This is what may yet be the saving of us."[73]

Overstreet's theory resonated at mid-century because it encouraged Americans to look both outward at their role in the wider world, and inward at the state of their own society, without fear. Like Toynbee and the neo-Freudians, Overstreet saw the potential of a people to "grow up" and develop properly rather than resorting to violent Marxist revolution. Thus it was not just antiracist rhetoric that helped recast the Japanese enemy, but the combination of antiracism and pro-capitalism in a framework of maturity. Having Japan properly "grow up," as U.S. policymakers desired, into a democratic, capitalist society would help invalidate Marxist critiques of racist, imperialist capitalism. Japan was a good choice, in the policymakers' view, because the chance of success was increased by the fact that Japan already had an industrial base and an educated workforce.

Policymakers saw the Cold War itself as a proving ground. In the *Foreign Affairs* article that laid out the policy of containment to the American public for the first time, George Kennan emphasized that the United States must "create among the peoples of the world generally the impression of a country which knows what it wants, which is coping successfully with the problems of its internal life and with the responsibilities of World Power, and which has a spiritual vitality capable of holding its own among the major ideological currents of the time." The struggle was thus "in essence a test of the over-all worth of the United States as a nation among nations"—a measure of Americans' maturity and ability to be world leaders as well as the "spiritual" health of their heritage.[74] The time had not yet come for Americans to relinquish the title of most advanced civilization to the Soviets or anybody else.

John Foster Dulles echoed Kennan in a 1950 *Life* magazine article: "There may come a time in the life of a people when their work of creation ends. That hour has not struck for us." He continued:

> We are still vital and capable of great endeavor. Our youth are spirited, not soft or fearful. Our religious heritage and our national tradition are not forgotten. If our efforts are still inadequate, it is because we have not seen clearly the challenge and the nature. As that is more clearly revealed, we shall surely respond. And as we act under the guidance of righteous faith, that faith will grow until it brings us into the worldwide fellowship of all men everywhere who are embarked on the great adventure of building peacefully a world of human liberty and justice.[75]

The future Secretary of State implied that America could prevail in this competition with the Soviets for the survival of the fittest. The United States would triumph because its citizenry was blessed with "righteous faith"—both religious and secular—and possessed the best intentions to make the world a better place where all could live in "fellowship" with "human liberty and justice." As with all testaments of faith, Dulles meant his words to persuade his audience of the truth of his witness. The correct path shall be "more clearly revealed," he asserted, and Americans "shall surely respond" to it. Drawing on long-standing ideas about masculine strength, vigor, and courage, Dulles cast the struggle as a test, an hour of reckoning—a moment to prove oneself a man. Proving manhood has been an important theme in American life, as it has been in the western imagination, at least since the Industrial Revolution. American boys became adult "men" in each other's eyes through a constant series of tests that gauged their worth by displaying skills and acquisitions.[76] As Dulles's words show, even elite policymakers adhered to a worldview in which men "proved" themselves worthy of admiration and power.

Cold War liberals therefore understood the rehabilitation of Japan and the success of U.S. foreign policy in Japan as a measure of their nation's manly skill, wisdom, and faith. In the liberal Catholic magazine *Commonweal,* senior diplomat William Franklin Sands asserted: "The right shaping of policy flows from mature conviction intelligently presented, and based upon sound historical knowledge, for the best good of all concerned." The stakes were high because it was not simply "the Japanese alone whose fate we have undertaken to settle . . . but the evolution of civilization." Or, as journalist John LaCerda put it, Japan's eventual adoption or rejection of "Anglo-Saxon democracy" would indicate "the direction and vitality of European civilization."[77]

Japan was particularly important because it had challenged the supremacy of western civilization during the war, and, as the Filipino leader Carlos Romulo reminded Americans, the Japanese had almost succeeded in their purpose. Until the war, Romulo told an American journalist, "the white man" of western Europe or the United States "was considered a god in the Orient and often an unjust and fearsome divinity. Japan broke that fetish and revealed him as a man who could suffer humiliation and defeat. That was an Asiatic victory that will not be forgotten by races who have suffered and resented imperialism."[78] Although Romulo had no love for the Japanese, he and other Asians gave Japan grudging respect for providing them with a model of "manly" resistance to western, even American, imperialism. Thus, even if Japan's new acceptance of "Anglo-Saxon democracy" could not re-elevate Americans to the position of "a god in the Orient," at least it could affirm American righteousness. Japan held regenerative possibilities for Americans, with the potential to reconfirm the universality of western civilization's principles and the wisdom of its political and social organization. The U.S. role as a mentor to Occupied Japan thus reassured Americans of their nation's righteousness and continued relevance—they could see themselves as a nation full of vigor rather than senescent has-beens.[79]

A Contrast with Germany

Since the Germans appeared to be the equal of Americans in both cultural achievement and physical height, they were, in General MacArthur's words, "a mature race." In contrast, the average height of the Japanese together with most Americans' lack of respect for Japanese society enhanced American impressions of Japanese immaturity. Although Americans also talked about the Germans in gendered terms after the war and lavished attention on German children, they seldom referred to adult Germans as childlike or childish. Americans talked instead about German pathology to explain the Germans' "deviation" from their common western heritage, as when they speculated about whether the Germans were "incurably" addicted to goose-stepping and militarism.[80]

Metaphors of maturity came easily to Americans in their analysis of Japanese "civilization." This is not to say that Americans never saw the Germans as immature, or that they never saw the Japanese as mentally disturbed. Japan could boast a much longer history than the United States, but Americans still regarded the Japanese as "feudalistic" and passively trapped in the past. Americans now saw themselves as the heirs to a great western civilization that could be traced back to ancient Greece and Rome. The metaphor of immaturity or arrested, feudal development could not be easily applied to Germans, who, most Americans believed, shared that civilization. Indeed, much of the "reorientation program" in Occupied Germany was intended to introduce American ways and culture to a large number of Germans who "were convinced that American culture did not exist."[81] Americans could not be as smug about their culture and tradition with the Germans, who after all had produced Goethe, Schiller, Beethoven, and other commonly recognized "great men" of western civilization.

Moreover, while the war in the Pacific had posed an external threat to western civilization, the war in Europe exposed, as Henry Luce phrased it, a fissure "within Christendom." The Nazis had international sympathizers in the United States and elsewhere, Luce pointed out, but "the cult of the Divine Emperor" attracted few, if any, non-Japanese.[82] Americans regarded the Japanese as distinctly unlike individuals of European ancestry because the Japanese did not share Western culture and a Judeo-Christian moral foundation. This difference, they believed, accounted for Japanese perfidies. Americans did not ignore Japanese brutality toward other Asians, but they were most enraged by the abusive treatment of Allied soldiers by the Japanese. Although the battle on Bataan and its subsequent "death march" resulted in thousands more Filipino than American deaths, the place name "Bataan" conjures up for Americans images of emaciated European and Euroamerican men with vacant stares.[83] Bataan, along with Pearl Harbor, came to signify a unique form of Japanese perversity: a manic intention to humiliate the west by brutal treatment and slaughter. But Americans found it harder to explain the German atrocities. The highly organized, systematic murders of millions by the Germans, utilizing the latest western technology, was profoundly disturbing to many Americans because it made them question the moral foundations of western Christian society.

This might explain why the bile toward the Germans was so much greater than the anger directed at the Japanese after the war in two of the era's leading liberal periodicals, *Life* and the *Saturday Review of Literature*.[84] The theme of German collective guilt and unrepentant Germans surfaced again and again in these two periodicals—not only in articles but also in readers' responses.[85] When *Life* published separate pictorials on displaced German and Japanese repatriates, the magazine showed sympathetic pictures of Japanese returning from China, but sent mixed messages about the Germans, suggesting that the Germans brought their suffering upon themselves: "These people allowed themselves to fall so low in the eyes of the world that the world, seeing their suffering, finds it hard to feel sorry for them."[86] The description of the Germans as "tragic" rather than criminal reveals the affinity the *Life* editors felt for Germans. It was for that very reason that they reminded their readers to maintain their emotional distance.[87] The reader responses published by *Life* agreed with the magazine's sentiments. Regarding the photographs, one reader unashamedly declared, "I gloated over them. May they continue to suffer long and hard for the monstrous crimes they inflicted on Europe."[88] In contrast, readers wrote no outraged letters about Japanese atrocities in reaction to these articles, at least none that *Life* published in later issues. While the Germans had "allowed themselves to fall so low in the eyes of the [western] world," the Japanese, it seemed, were already there. Or it may be that Americans were most infuriated by the killing of white people. The Germans killed Europeans, while the Japanese mostly killed other Asians.[89] Still, there was no purpose—no objective to be achieved—in reviling the Japanese further in public discourse. The very opposite was true: since the Japanese lacked the Germans' racial and cultural affinity to the vast majority of Americans, they required publicity to be seen as members of a friendly, if childlike and dependent, nation.

Thus the Euroamericans' greater affinity for Germans made Germany's wartime behavior seem less forgivable. Many Americans felt that the Germans, as a "mature race," should have acted more responsibly. "Whatever the German did in the dereliction of the standards of modern morality, the international standards, he did deliberately," MacArthur explained. "He didn't do it because of lack of knowledge about the world." In the general's opinion, the German wrongfully used military power as "a short cut to the power and economic domination he desired," but he felt that the German should "come back to the path" without too much difficulty. The Japanese, in contrast, "stumbled into" war "to some extent," the general pronounced.[90] Like children, they were not truly aware of what they were getting themselves into, unlike the Germans who should have known better than to start a war or commit genocide. This was why the Japanese needed the Americans to guide them back to "the path" and teach them all over again how to walk, talk, think, and play properly.

CHAPTER THREE

Sunday at Hirohito's

Six weeks after he announced news of the surrender, Emperor Hirohito presented himself to General Douglas A. MacArthur at the general's official residence. MacArthur had made it clear to the Japanese upon his arrival that he would call on no one, that even the emperor must pay his respects to Japan's new ruler.[1] The Supreme Commander for the Allied Powers appreciated symbolic gestures, small and grand. On his victorious return to the Philippines, MacArthur had the photographers in his company deposited on the beach first and then had his vessel pushed back away from the beach, so that the cameramen could capture frontal images of MacArthur walking boldly through the waves toward the shore. When he arrived in Japan, he disembarked from an unarmed plane that he had named *Bataan*. And at the formal Japanese surrender on the USS *Missouri*, MacArthur staged a climactic ending—an armada of three hundred B-29s "roared overhead in perfect counterpoint to Pearl Harbor" moments after the documents were signed.[2] Hirohito likewise appeared in a MacArthur production, arriving hat in hand to meet the general after hesitating for days. An American journalist noted that the meeting brought the "Son-of-Heaven . . . face to face with the man who was giving orders to the Son-of-Heaven."[3] Or, as *Life* magazine wryly commented, Hirohito "lost a good deal of his Shinto divinity" in humbling himself before the "big, ribbonless American soldier."[4]

Before retreating to a private office with the emperor, MacArthur allowed photographs to be taken of this historic occasion. One photograph instantly became the iconic image of the meeting between the conqueror and the vanquished. MacArthur, dressed in his everyday khakis with an open collar, stands next to Hirohito, who wears a formal morning suit, in front of a wide doorway. The general, with his hands on his hips and legs slightly apart, further affects a casual style, and his stance broadens the appearance of his upper body. In contrast, the much shorter emperor, with hands held stiffly at his sides and his chin slightly raised, unwittingly makes his shoulders look smaller and more rounded than perhaps they actually were. *Life*'s editors, who published the photograph in their magazine, pointed out approvingly that MacArthur "did not bother to put on a tie for the occasion."[5] The Japanese Imperial Household Ministry attempted to censor the photograph in Japan because it was deemed disrespectful to the emperor, but SCAP insisted on its wide circulation to impress upon the Japanese who would be the new leader. The general's refusal to dress up for the occasion signaled a confident, American "can-do" attitude, whereas the emperor's ceremonial dress—he came in striped trousers, a cutaway jacket, and a top hat—indicated, as everyone knew, his need to curry favor for himself and his nation. The photo also showed MacArthur's much greater height—five feet eleven inches as opposed to Hirohito's five feet three—a size differential that seemed to symbolize American might over Japanese weakness. Thus the photo

Iconic photograph of General Douglas MacArthur and Emperor
Hirohito, taken at their first meeting. Getty Images.

neatly summarized the new U.S.-Japan relationship: a powerful,
rugged America ready to work with a stiff, formal Japan, to make
changes to an overwhelmed nation.[6]

The photograph of MacArthur and Hirohito contrasted
sharply with the one of the emperor familiar to Americans during
the war. This earlier photo showed an elevated Hirohito on his

white horse, wearing a military uniform and reviewing his troops with a sword in hand. That image inspired Admiral William F. Halsey to brag at a press conference near the war's end that he looked forward to riding Shiroyuki, the emperor's horse. Demoting Hirohito from his godly status and getting him literally "off his high horse" was an American goal.[7] Although Halsey was never photographed riding the emperor's horse after the war, his colleague in the Army, Major General William C. Chase, had an opportunity to ride and be photographed on former premier Tōjō Hideki's "white horse."[8] Tōjō's horse was an appropriate substitute, since Americans increasingly came to interpret their victory over Japan as a victory over the general and the "militarists" rather than over the emperor.

During the war, Americans both inside and outside the government hotly debated the fate of the emperor after the expected Allied victory.[9] In the end, the Truman administration and State Department policymakers opted to retain the emperor, believing that this policy would make it easier to control the Japanese and help the United States avoid a prolonged occupation that would burden the American taxpayers. But Truman and his Secretary of State, James Byrnes, hesitated to approve this policy officially because they feared public repercussion—with good reason.[10] In 1943, former Ambassador Joseph Grew had come under heavy attack in the media after giving a speech in Chicago in which he advocated the postwar use of the emperor. Working with the emperor was unthinkable to influential radio personality Walter Winchell, who told his millions of listeners that the apparent U.S. policy not to bomb the imperial palace was "a brutal insult to the graves of our beheaded [Doolittle] fliers."

These reactions were consistent with polls taken from 1943 to 1945 which uniformly showed that a third of the American public believed Hirohito should be executed. Although the Office of War Information (OWI) began taking care, as early as November 1942, not to use the emperor to symbolize the Japanese enemy in its propaganda, a Gallup poll taken on May 29, 1945, revealed that 70 percent of Americans believed Hirohito should be executed, imprisoned, exiled, or put on trial. Only 3 percent agreed with what the Truman administration eventually decided to do: use him "as a puppet to rule Japan."[11] Some of the Japan "experts" outside of the government agreed with the idea of using Hirohito to help with the surrender, but most of them, along with those who advocated deposing the emperor immediately, insisted that Hirohito should ultimately bear responsibility for the war and step down from the throne.[12] So did the U.S. Congress. At the initiative of Senator Richard B. Russell (D-Georgia), Congress passed a joint resolution on September 18, 1945, demanding that Hirohito be put on trial as a war criminal.[13] The overwhelming sentiment against the emperor, save for a select few, explains why the "Initial Post-surrender Policy for Japan" (SWNCC 150/4/A), signed by Truman on September 6, 1945, left open the possibility of trying Hirohito as a war criminal. It was a compromise, an extemporizing strategy, to pursue a policy of least possible resistance.

Counteracting the enormous American public sentiment against the policy to retain Hirohito were narratives by American journalists and writers that began refiguring the emperor as a valuable U.S. ally. Gradually, these narratives of the "new" Hirohito became predominant in American public discourse. This process did not happen overnight, but developed unevenly over the first few years of the Occupation. Journalists for the mainstream press and writers who lived in Occupied Japan consciously engaged in this attempt to recast the emperor. More so than average Americans, they had privileged access to policy-makers or to SCAP and possessed better knowledge of policy rationales because of briefings and private conversations with policymakers or military leaders. Yet the new narratives did not result from a simple collusion between writers and policymakers. Like the policymakers and military leaders, the journalists and writers were socialized with the same cultural notions about race, gender, and maturity; imbued with the same beliefs about American greatness; and assured about the wisdom of the American political economy. This commonality meant that these journalists and writers easily came to identify with their government's policies toward Japan. This is not to say that the writers always moved along parallel tracks with the government, but that mainstream American writers chose their narratives about the emperor based on a combination of personal beliefs, particular epistemologies, cues from officials, and individual assessments of the situation.

The American journalists and writers gave the emperor a new image by casting Hirohito as a "good Japanese" who had been unwillingly taken to war by the "bad Japanese"—the "militarists." The erect, god-like emperor was transmogrified into a frumpy, absent-minded professor, complete with round glasses.[14] No longer did Americans see the emperor in a decorated military uniform atop his white horse, but rather in a plain suit and a fedora, walking among his people. This mild-mannered man, this amateur marine biologist, Americans were told after the war, had been forced to approve a war on the United States by the "militarists," especially General Tōjō Hideki. It was the militarists who were to blame for Japan's disastrous and terrible war, and they were the ones who deserved punishment to teach the Japanese the lesson that "aggression does not pay." Thus the "criminality" of the Japanese state became embodied in a smaller group of men, the "militarists," who were then tried in an international court of justice, convicted, and punished.

The term "militarists," however, obfuscates more than it clarifies, overemphasizing the difference between Japanese civilian imperialists and military imperialists. So-called "anti-militarist" Japanese leaders like postwar premier Yoshida Shigeru and the young Army officers who created an "incident" as a pretext to conquer Manchuria differed not in the goal of establishing a Japanese empire, but in how they thought Manchuria should be put under Japanese control.[15] Furthermore, before death, destruction, and starvation reached the home islands, the Pacific War was immensely popular among the Japanese public. Most Japanese thought it commonsensical that an advanced nation like theirs required—and indeed, deserved—more land to support their civilization and to develop resources that were underutilized by lesser peoples. The term "militarist" as applied to the Japanese is also arguably an Orientalist term—a word that masks U.S. militarism or militarization.[16] Yet Japanese militarism shared with U.S. militarization the same goal of ensuring security, as well as guaranteeing the control of resources and markets. Once Japan was forced to relinquish its autarkic dreams of controlling China, and after the U.S. and Japanese governments resolved the issue of the emperor, the goals of the two nations became quite compatible: to preserve and spread liberal capitalism in East Asia.[17]

The narratives that separated the "good" emperor from the "bad" militarists rested on notions of gender and maturity as they related to war activity and accountability. Americans sympathetic to the emperor tried to decriminalize him by constructing stories that depicted him as a principled opponent of the militarists, as well as an upstanding family man. On the other hand,

American observers who remained unsympathetic to the emperor cast him as a manipulated puppet who lacked the manly qualities of self-direction and personal control but who was nonetheless useful to the Americans in their control of Occupied Japan. In the case of Tōjō, Americans drew upon ideas about a kind of racialized, deviant masculinity to continue to criminalize him as an "Oriental" villain. Tōjō and Hirohito were the two most familiar Japanese figures to the American public; one was convicted for war crimes and executed, while the other's image was reformed to depict the Japanese as useful, reliable allies, worthy of American aid. Thus the "emperor's new clothes" were made intelligible by adapting pre-existing ideas about gender and maturity to Japanese actions and responsibility for war.

SCAP and Hirohito

MacArthur is usually credited—or criticized—for retaining the emperor and shielding Hirohito from prosecution as a war criminal. In the end, the Truman administration left it up to SCAP to make the final decision about whether the emperor was needed and sufficiently cooperative for U.S. purposes. MacArthur and Brigadier General Bonner Fellers, his military secretary and chief of his psychological warfare operations, were predisposed to protect Hirohito. Fellers had formed his opinions in the mid-1930s when he wrote a report on the "psychology" of Japanese soldiers. Having established himself as an authority on their mind-set, he reinforced MacArthur's belief that Hirohito was vital to the well-being of the Japanese people and the safety of U.S. forces. In a July 1944 report, Fellers avowed that the Japanese would react violently and "die like ants" if the Allied powers punished the emperor. "Hanging of the Emperor to them would be comparable to the crucifixion of Christ to us," he claimed.[18] SCAP therefore fended off demands from other Allied nations that the emperor be prosecuted and even rejected suggestions from some within the imperial household that Hirohito should step down. MacArthur had confidence in his convictions and did not need to be as attentive to public opinion as his less experienced civilian boss. In this matter, his opinion agreed with the wishes of Washington. Thus MacArthur was able to implement the policy that the Truman administration and Washington policymakers wanted but were unable to agree to put forth.[19]

After staging the initial publicity photo and setting the tone of the relationship between himself and the emperor, MacArthur lent SCAP's support to a publicity campaign to churn out images of a demilitarized, "democratic," more earth-bound and active Hirohito for both American and Japanese audiences. Despite presumptions of fanatical devotion to the emperor on the part of the Japanese, the propaganda officers at GHQ recognized that the emperor's image needed to be bolstered among Japan's war-weary, distressed populace. After all, fear of a social revolution had been one reason why the Japanese government put out peace feelers in early 1945. The Imperial Household Ministry, with SCAP's assistance, presented Hirohito as "the people's emperor," an emperor who was in touch with his people rather than closed off behind palace gates. To this end the ministry released photographs of the imperial family, presenting them as if they were just like other Japanese families. The first of these, published in Japanese newspapers the day after Hirohito renounced his divinity, included a photograph of the empress in a drab kimono kneeling to feed chickens with two of her children; the implication was that the imperial family had suffered like the rest of the country.[20]

For five years, starting in February 1946, the emperor undertook nationwide tours—with a U.S. military escort—to visit schools, hospitals, wounded veterans, families of deceased soldiers, factories, mines, and so on, traveling through most of Japan from large cities to isolated fishing villages. Three generations earlier, Hirohito's grandfather, the Meiji Emperor, had conducted similar travels throughout the land to legitimize his authority, and in both periods, the effort succeeded. Although a minority of the people angrily wondered why Hirohito did not end the war sooner if he had the power to do so, most Japanese accepted him as their savior from a terrible war.[21] They believed that he, the benevolent father-figure, not only stopped the American bombing, but also boldly told MacArthur that he was willing to be sacrificed if the Supreme Commander could guarantee the safety of the Japanese people.[22]

MacArthur reinforced and to a large extent fostered this image of a brave, honorable emperor who was manfully willing to shoulder the blame. He often repeated a story that he later published in his memoirs. "I come to see you, General MacArthur," he recalled the emperor saying at their first meeting, "to offer myself to the judgment of the powers you represent as the one to bear sole responsibility for every political and military decision made and action taken by my people in the conduct of war."[23] Because of an agreement to keep confidential what transpired in the eleven meetings between MacArthur and the emperor, MacArthur's version was not contested for decades. In the 1970s, however, detailed minutes written by the emperor's interpreter immediately after the famous meeting depicted a rather different conversation, with the emperor never offering to take responsibility.[24] But perhaps MacArthur truly believed that he heard the emperor take responsibility. The general was predisposed to work with the emperor: maybe MacArthur remembered hearing what he wanted to hear. Or perhaps he intentionally made up a quote to justify his decision. Or maybe the interpreter's notes cannot be trusted, and the emperor *did* take responsibility. Whichever scenario or combination of scenarios was true, the effect was the same. By the time the interpreter's account emerged, the endless repetition of MacArthur's story over the decades had made it an accepted truth in both Japan and the United States. The tale provided a coherent, simple narrative with heroic dimensions. And the fact that the emperor was not tried or punished as a war criminal appeared to be a just reward for courageously maintaining dignity and honor while confronting a greater and physically larger power.

Bonner Fellers also spun a tale that emphasized the emperor's courage and dignity. The Americans who were most sympathetic to Hirohito, like Fellers, portrayed him in a way similar to the Imperial Household Ministry: the emperor was a brave man who single-handedly faced down the "militarists" and stopped their madness. In an article published by the *Reader's Digest* in July 1947, Fellers put forth this narrative of "Hirohito's struggle to surrender" and stated that the emperor was committed to surrendering by the spring of 1945. Feller recounts that Hirohito told the imperial household "that he proposed to stop the war no matter what happened to him personally"—repeating again a theme put forth by the Imperial Household Ministry that recent scholarship has suggested was false.[25] Taking even greater creative license in his narration than his boss—at least MacArthur was witness to the tale he told—Fellers has Hirohito looking "menacingly" twice at those who opposed surrender at the crucial cabinet meeting of August 14th. The small ink drawing at the start of the article pictures Hirohito standing, back erect, at the cabinet meeting as his ministers sit, looking perplexed and weary. Interestingly, the artist depicted the emperor in a ceremonial morning suit (though it is unlikely he would have worn this in a working meeting), and standing in a pose similar to the famous photograph with MacArthur—but with noticeably squarer shoulders.[26] Fellers, who later became a charter member of the John Birch Society, related this supposed firm invocation of imperial authority in an entirely positive manner.

To put Fellers' and MacArthur's attitudes somewhat in perspective, however, we should remember that they would have been leading an invasion of Japan had the Japanese not surrendered in mid-August. Like the soldiers already engaged in or marked for combat in the Pacific, they understandably gave a sigh of relief at the war's end. Many soldiers believed that the destruction of Hiroshima and Nagasaki had spared their lives: "Thank God for the Atom Bomb," as the veteran and literature professor Paul Fussell has put it.[27] Likewise, those who served in the Occupation were relieved by the reception they received upon arrival in Japan, and they credited the emperor for the peace and order they found. The emperor, in this view, "stopped everything and turned night into day," as journalists Frank Kelley and Cornelius Ryan wrote in their Occupation memoir, *Star-Spangled Mikado*:

> The sense of discipline among the Japanese—however misguided during years of aggression—was superb. When the Emperor cried 'Halt!' they halted. Save for the few fanatics—who halted, too, when their miserable schemes faded in mid-August—seventy million Japanese were docile when we landed, even the three million or so who still bore arms in the mainland.[28]

Wielding this kind of supposed control over millions was something that military men like MacArthur and Fellers could admire in and of itself, as well as for the practical and humane reason of avoiding massive bloodshed. Of course, the Americans were overstating the emperor's authority and control; nearly all the Japanese were quite relieved to "halt" military action by this time and very grateful not to have to prepare to fight and die against a superior force. The two generals were, however, correct about the Japanese people's respect for their emperor's authority, and paradoxically, the Americans hoped to harness that authority to "democratize" the Japanese state.

The Emperor as a Puppet

The authors of *Star-Spangled Mikado,* however, were more ambivalent about the emperor than Generals Fellers and MacArthur, conservative supporters of the imperial system that emphasized Hirohito's character as forthright and steadfast. Those Americans who were less sympathetic to the institution and the man tended to present Hirohito as passive, weak, and spineless. While the defeated Japanese started revering their emperor as the brave man who ended the war, some of the conquering Americans preferred to ridicule him and the mythologically-based imperial institution. Some of the Occupation forces mocked the emperor's national tours as "ah-so" tours, so named for his usual response to the people he met: *"ah sō?"*—"Is that so?" "He is still pretty stiff" about meeting his people "and nervous, too," reported Kelley and Ryan. "His voice quavers; his phrases are still stilted. But he seems to be sweating it out manfully."[29] Less sympathetic, Red Cross volunteer Lucy Crockett scoffed at Hirohito as a "frightened brown face with . . . horn-rimmed glasses, receding chin, and absurd mustache" and derided his public appearances as a "democrat." She claimed that Americans of the Occupation regarded him as "the little man who [wasn't] there," and implied that he had always been an insignificant figure.[30]

Some Americans saw the emperor as a "puppet of the militarists" during the war—especially those who knew from Japanese history that powerful court families and military dynasties had exploited and manipulated the imperial institution throughout most of its existence. For Americans without particular knowledge of Japan, seeing Hirohito as a puppet without the ability to act autonomously also fit popular, preconceived notions about the Japanese being dolls—to be manipulated by others. Most Americans, if they knew anything about the Japanese imperial house prior to the war, got at least some of their impressions from William Gilbert and Arthur Sullivan's musical comedy *The Mikado,* which opened in 1885 and remained hugely popular for decades into the twentieth century. It was, incidentally, one of the first plays that Americans performed in Occupied Japan. It began:

> If you want to know who we are,
> We are gentlemen of Japan;
> On many a vase and jar—
> On many a screen and fan,
> We figure in lively paint;
> Our attitude's queer and quaint,
> You're wrong if you think it ain't, Oh!

> If you think we are worked by strings,
> Like a Japanese marionette,
> You don't understand these things:
> It is simply Court etiquette.[31]

The Mikado perpetuated Victorian notions of Japan as a childish "toyland"—a notion that Americans could not quite rid themselves of even after fighting the horribly real war. Although the second stanza says that the Japanese are not "worked by strings / like a Japanese marionette," the song and play's overall effect was the impression that the gentlemen of Japan could not determine their own destinies. The reason why Kelley and Ryan chose to call their book *Star-Spangled Mikado* becomes clearer with reference to Gilbert and Sullivan: the amusing, puppet-like Japanese characters were now being "worked by strings" that were controlled by the Americans.

Given the prevalent prewar notions of the Japanese as doll-like and easily manipulated, it made sense to many other American writers and journalists to depict the emperor as a puppet—either of the "militarists" or the Americans. For instance, *Senior Scholastic* in mid-September 1945 described the formal end of war by saying, "Today, Japan stands shorn of all her ill-gotten gains, and her God-Emperor has become General MacArthur's 'Charlie McCarthy.'"[32] The policy to retain the emperor, SWNCC 150, had been made public a little over a week earlier and made no reference, of course, to puppets or to ventriloquist Edgar Bergen's famous dummy. Yet the editors of this magazine for American high school teachers and students did not hesitate to use this metaphor because they felt it aptly described the situation, given their prior ideas about the emperor and the Japanese. Soon, "irreverent" members of the Occupation (who are unlikely to have read the *Senior Scholastic* description) were reportedly also referring to the emperor as "Charlie."[33] Hirohito was, journalist John LaCerda wrote, "a convenient dummy-on-the-knee for us" who mouthed the directives of SCAP. The emperor "serves as [a] cohesive force and it is expedient to allow him to remain as a safeguard against complete internal chaos," LaCerda explained.[34]

Such writers were not completely convinced by SCAP's efforts to present Hirohito as "a doll-like zombie secluded in the palace at Tokyo and as a prisoner of the naughty militarists," nor did they believe that "Charlie" was "a peace-loving recluse who was more concerned with birds and bees than autocracy and war." They complained that MacArthur looked upon the emperor as "a great liberal who was so much a prisoner of the militarists that he almost had to get their permission to go to the bathroom," and they suspected that Hirohito knew about, and approved in advance, the attack on Pearl Harbor as well as Japan's aggressive expansion in Asia.[35]

But these writers nonetheless approved the policy to make use of the emperor and defended it in their writing, emphasizing the practicality of using Hirohito to help rule Japan. A military government officer in a remote province told Crockett that Americans should be grateful that "the little men on Tokyo Boulevard" still stop and bow low toward the Imperial Palace. "Down here, fifty miles from the nearest tactical unit," he declared, "I personally am blessing an Occupation policy that uses psychology, not force."[36] Journalist Noel Busch agreed, noting that if the American authorities had eliminated the emperor, as "so widely recommended before the surrender," they would have "removed the basic motivation for Japanese cooperation with their conquerors." The United States would then have faced the nearly impossible task of policing and governing a hostile nation whose language was understood by very few Americans, "excepting the invaluable Nisei." Retaining Hirohito allowed Americans to utilize the "ready-made machine consisting of the two million or so Japanese citizens in government employ, from top-rank ambassadors to village postmen."[37]

This reasoning did not acknowledge the possibility of using the government bureaucracy without the emperor and underestimated, perhaps, the state of the war-weary Japanese, who were more concerned with surviving than with continuing to fight the Americans. To be sure, the emperor played an essential role in convincing some diehards to lay down their arms without a struggle, but those justifying U.S. policy may have exaggerated his continued usefulness to the Occupation. These rationalizations, of course, rested on an assumption that the Japanese supported the imperial system and would not be able to function without it. Arguing that the Japanese were "stagger[ing] beneath the impact of one sweeping democratic concept after another," Crockett asserted that they needed the imperial institution "for moral support until they could one day be wean[ed] from it."[38] Here, she echoed Fellers' statement about the centrality of the emperor to the Japanese belief system as Jesus Christ was to the American one, but she included the hope of cultural anthropologists Geoffrey Gorer and Ruth Benedict that the Japanese could "grow up" and move away from this invalid and childish belief system.

Memoirists and other American observers of the Occupation took it upon themselves, without any government directive or request, to justify U.S. policy to the "folks back home." It appears that they, too, after going to Japan, felt they had a stake in the success of the Occupation policies. These writers shared with most of the SCAP officers similar presumptions, prejudices, and blinders about the Japanese and "our job in Japan." And, as all good writers do, they pitched their narratives to their audience. Crockett, whose memoir is sympathetic to the Japanese overall, must have thought her potential American readers would be boorish and hard-bitten—an impression that was not unfounded, given the wartime bile her fellow Americans had released about the Japanese enemy. She thus summed up her discussion about retaining the emperor by stating: "General MacArthur brilliantly plays a gigantic poker game in which the Allies make full use of the joker in the Japanese's own deck."[39] Emphasizing the emperor's utility to MacArthur in ways that disparaged Hirohito was an attempt to appeal to fellow Americans' hatred of the emperor and to convince them of the wisdom of MacArthur's policy.

A Peace-Loving, "Model Family Man"

One strategy used to reach more liberal Americans was to depict Hirohito as an upstanding family man. America's most popular magazine closely reflected official U.S. thinking on the emperor's fate. As late as the spring of 1945, *Life* magazine was indecisive, like the Truman administration, about Hirohito's fate. But by August 1945 it commenced, as MacArthur and Fellers did, the task of shielding the emperor from war responsibility.[40] And by early February of 1946, about the same time the emperor embarked on his national tours, *Life* was presenting him as a thoroughly domesticated, ordinary, middle-class father in a pictorial report called "Sunday at Hirohito's." The photographs came from the Imperial Household Ministry, which had barred American photographers from taking pictures at the palace. The imperial photographs had been carefully shot over four consecutive Sundays (which suggested to *Life* the article's homey title). One "precedent-shattering" image showed the emperor smiling, while other photographs depicted him reading American comics, eating a meal with his family, listening to his daughter play the piano, and strolling outside with his children and grandchild. To highlight the imperial family's ordinariness, the photos not only showed these prosaic scenes of seemingly lazy Sunday afternoons but also omitted the servants, imperial household chamberlains, ladies-in-waiting, and royal tutors who were usually the constant companions of the imperial family members.

Acknowledging the photos as showpieces, *Life* stated that the photos revealed the

> not very subtle purpose of the Jap imperial household . . . to present Hirohito as a democrat, father, grandfather, citizen and botanist. It censored some photographs of him in uniform, happily revealed a

little shabbiness, such as of the baby carriage above, had him read a copy of the New York *Times* and got [a bust of] Abraham Lincoln into the picture. The emperor is in fact a qualified working biologist. He himself discovered the two pickled marine fauna shown below and named by him *Symposisphoea Imperialis Terao* (the shrimp) and *Lyrocteis Imperatoris Komai* (the jelly fish).

But even as it critiqued efforts to reshape the emperor's image, *Life* seemed to go along with this transformation, as an angry reader complained in a later issue. Ex-Air Force Captain Joseph D. Brasfield of Meridian, Mississippi, asserted: "To me your pictures of 'Sundays at Hirohito's' are playing right into the hands of propagandists who want us to believe the Japs were really nice folks, that Hirohito is a peace-loving family man who would never harm a thing, not even his well-preserved shrimp and jellyfish." The Pacific War veteran's complaint rings true. Although *Life* suggested in another paragraph that it was "obvious" that the Japanese were "build[ing] the emperor as a man understandable to Americans," the magazine also declared that the "facts" revealed him to be "a model family man," an admirer of Abraham Lincoln, a person well-versed in American literature and history, and a resolute opponent of the war. The text implied that had he not been a captive of unfortunate circumstances— namely a brutal, destructive war conducted in his name—Hirohito would have simply been a "decent," slightly "nervous" father, who loved his wife and read comic strips with his boys.[41]

In the succeeding years *Life* magazine, with Japanese cooperation, continued to focus on the imperial family as a way to humanize and popularize the institution. "Old married couple, the emperor and empress of Japan, posed for some vacation pictures Sept[ember] 2," reported *Life*'s gossipy "People" section in 1947. "Now experts at Americanizing themselves," the magazine ex-

plained, "Hirohito looked like a relaxed [and smiling] businessman, the empress like a housewife dutifully concerned with her
husband's mussed hair." The photo showed a matronly Empress
Nagako wearing a print dress with a hat, and the emperor in a
suit, carrying his hat.[42]

Because they interpreted democracy to mean freedom of
choice, Americans took special note that the emperor and his wife
had chosen each other as life partners. But the stories that they
had made a love-match were not accurate, for Prince Higashi-
kuni, the empress's father, had arranged the union while she was
still a girl. Yet the emperor seemed devoted to his wife; he had allegedly refused to take a second consort when she bore three
daughters before giving birth to a son—a story the Imperial
Household Ministry made much of. When one of those daughters
married a "commoner" in 1950, *Life* proclaimed the wedding as
"Democratic Nuptials" that overturned "a tradition 2,600 years
old." The nuptials, however, were only "democratic" in that the
bride could have rejected the bridegroom "handpicked by her
family": he was a distant cousin, an ex-prince who lost his title
after the war, and was only technically a commoner.[43] Nonetheless, the emphasis on the romantic coupling and domestic coziness in both generations was intended to make the imperial family seem less mysterious and backward and more ordinary to the
American public.

Life stuck to the new narrative of Hirohito's opposition to
war and published a version of it by Richard Lauterbach in the
issue immediately after the one carrying "Sunday at Hirohito's."
"On Dec. 8, hours after the attack began," Lauterbach related,
"Tojo called at the palace with a declaration of war. Squinting
through his glasses, Hirohito affixed his signature at exactly
11:30 a.m. He was not entirely happy." Lauterbach could hardly

have known that Hirohito was squinting or what his feelings were at the time, but he goes on to imply that Hirohito had no other choice in another imagined conversation, this time with MacArthur. Asked why he allowed Japan to go to war,

> The emperor looked at MacArthur with unbelieving eyes, as if the conqueror of Japan were a naive reporter. "If I had not," said Hirohito slowly, "they would have had a new emperor. It was the will of the Japanese people. No emperor could have turned against the popular desire at that point."[44]

It was "naive," then, to ask why the emperor had allowed the war to occur, and this put a stop to the question of why the emperor had the authority to end the war but did not prevent it from starting.[45] Also left unasked was the question of why the emperor did not abdicate if he was indeed so opposed to the war. If the allusion to the possibility of "a new emperor" meant that Hirohito feared assassination, it raises a moral question that was also left unexplored: should one be pardoned if one saved one's own life at the cost of millions of other lives? Lauterbach could just as easily have depicted Hirohito as a coward, but he did not. Lauterbach's fictional exchange was deceptive; even though it accurately attested to the popularity of the war among the Japanese people, his account falsely presented the prewar and wartime Japanese imperial system as a democracy, with the emperor accountable to the people rather than the other way around.

But like MacArthur and Fellers, Lauterbach—and by extension *Life* magazine—seemed to believe that creative license was justified to boost the image of the emperor. The embellishments and imagined conversations, in addition to the homey depiction of his "family life," made the emperor more real; he could be seen as an actual person with a voice and human emotions. It was appar-

ently also important to present not only a family man but also a
mature man with wisdom, agency, and bravery; this meant avoiding certain questions that could possibly cast Hirohito as a coward or as contemptible. Suspicion about the emperor's role did
not immediately or entirely disappear from the pages of *Life*, especially in articles authored by its journalists with war experience
in Asia, but those pieces repeated the story about the emperor as
an opponent of war. Although they often viewed the emperor's innocence with skepticism, these journalists nonetheless served to
spread the notion more widely.[46]

Life was not the only major publication that tried to remake
the emperor. The *New York Times* also humanized Hirohito and
rendered him more sympathetic to Americans. This was particularly evident in two separate *Sunday Magazine* articles by the
Times' Tokyo bureau chief, Lindesay Parrott. In the first, "At
Long Last Hirohito Begins to Enjoy Life," Parrott shows that defeat freed the emperor from the "militarists" and a stuffy court
regimen. Parrott describes Hirohito's daily routine to emphasize
his very human nature, and the article's accompanying photographs contrast "1944—the God-Emperor," a stiffly formal man
"forced" to be alienated from his people, with "1945—the Citi-
zen-Emperor": a smiling Hirohito enjoying breakfast with his
wife, a relaxed Hirohito consulting with a publicist, and a cheer-
ful-looking Hirohito doffing his hat while walking among a
throng of people who now stand with him rather than prostrating
themselves before him. The second article, published three years
later, repeats much of the same information and again emphasizes
the emperor's happiness at his new state. "There is sometimes a
twinkle in his eyes behind his heavy lenses," Parrott wrote. Perhaps Parrott, as the head of the most influential U.S. newspaper,
had a close audience with the emperor to see this twinkle. But

maybe not—this may have been another embellishment. Factual or fictionalized, such characterizations were intended to make the emperor a more likable figure.[47]

Windows for the Crown Prince

Efforts to humanize the Japanese imperial house also focused on Crown Prince Akihito. Fortunately for the imperial house, the heir to the Japanese throne was too young to have served in any official capacity in the war. His education prior to defeat had been semi-military—which made him similar to other Japanese boys of his age—but the Japanese and American media largely ignored this background. Instead, they emphasized his malleable youth, his presumable innocence, and the democratic, American education he received from his tutor, Elizabeth Gray Vining.

According to Vining, the emperor himself requested that an American Christian woman serve as the crown prince's English-language tutor. From a list of candidates, the Imperial Household Ministry then supposedly chose Vining, a young Quaker widow and author of numerous children's books. During her four years in Japan, from 1946 to 1950, she eventually taught English to all the unmarried royal children, Akihito's classmates at Gakushūin (the Peers School), the empress, and the emperor's brother. Published photographs of the crown prince during this time usually showed him with an indulgently smiling Vining.[48] With this maternal figure as an instructor—indeed, she was presented as if she were his only teacher even though he had other teachers for different subjects—Akihito seemed to American eyes to be under the right sort of influence. "Hirohito's son now studies under an American schoolmarm," the *Reader's Digest* stated approvingly. The Vining–Crown Prince relationship recalled the one between another western woman and crown prince: Anna Leonowens and Crown Prince Chulakongkorn of Siam in the nineteenth century, whose story had been recently popularized in Margaret Landon's *Anna and the King of Siam* (1944). The *New York Times* claimed that Leonowens had so successfully impressed upon her royal pupil "a burning faith in democracy and the dignity of the human being" that he later emancipated slaves and became one of Siam's "most enlightened rulers." Likewise, the *Times* editorialized, "If Mrs. Vining's tutelage inculcates in [Akihito] an appreciation of our way of life and of our thinking, the result will be favorable for peace in the Pacific."[49]

After returning to the United States, Vining penned a memoir about her experiences as Akihito's tutor in *Windows for the Crown Prince,* which won the Notable Book Award. It provided powerful, positive publicity for the imperial family. Not only was it a popular bestseller in America, but it also gave the impression of an imperial family willing to shake itself up. Vining did this through painstaking descriptions of innumerable "precedent-shattering" events, although these usually concerned relatively minor aspects of imperial protocol and her role in helping to break them. The Imperial Household Ministry undoubtedly emphasized their importance—given her frequent use of the phrase "precedent-shattering"—and she passed the importance of such groundbreaking events on to her American readers.[50] To cite one example, she noted that she was the first foreigner to be received by the crown prince with his parents.[51] As for the crown prince's progress, it deeply impressed her when the prince composed the sentence, "Democracy is the best organization of government." Since the word she had asked him to use was "organization," not "democracy," she believed the sentence revealed the development of his own thinking.[52] Whether or not he believed this sentence—

or even completely understood it, given that he remained committed to upholding the imperial dynasty—the prince's statement only echoed the tag line that SCAP was repeating ad nauseam. Any bright Japanese child would have known what to say to please a teacher, especially an American one.

The Imperial Household Ministry and SCAP could not have asked for a more favorable publicist than Elizabeth Vining.[53] The idea to have an American tutor in fact originated with SCAP, not the emperor, and choosing an author was a stroke of genius that might have been preplanned by the American authorities.[54] By emphasizing the emperor's role in selecting her, Vining added to the impression that Hirohito was not only a proper father personally overseeing his son's education, but was also liberal-minded, looking to have someone—a foreign woman, no less—open new vistas for the crown prince.[55] Vining found her main pupil a congenial preteen with an independent mind, and the members of "the world's most secret court" unfailingly gracious, considerate, and kind.[56] Indeed, she had held positive notions about the emperor even before her departure for Japan, having learned from people who had lived there that "the emperor was a man of simple tastes and habits, a scientist by avocation." Vining believed that Hirohito not only "disapproved what the war party did in his name," but also tried, at various points, "to avert war." She confirmed her opinion that Hirohito was an advocate of peace when she met him; she deemed him "a shy and sensitive man and a friendly one." Since Vining had a high opinion of Hirohito, she readily believed what "was generally said" about Kido Kōichi, the emperor's closest wartime adviser and a convicted war criminal, who allegedly "deceived the Emperor by withholding important information from him."[57] Apparently, it did not occur to Vining that Kido, a loyal imperial servant, might be taking the blame to protect his emperor, which in fact he was. Shielding the emperor from prosecution was his top priority after Japan's defeat. After Tōjō slipped in his testimony at the war crimes trial and stated that none of the emperor's high officials had dared to go against his will, Kido instructed the general to make a retraction, which he quickly did at the next possible opportunity.[58]

Vining, then, failed to follow her own parting homily to the prince and his classmates: "Don't believe everything you hear, no matter who says it. Don't believe all you read in the newspapers. Don't take other people's opinions without examining them. Try to find out the truth for yourselves." She admitted toward the end of her book that the Japanese she had come to know and admire were elites. It was Prime Minister Yoshida Shigeru, himself no champion of the people, who pointed this out to her, but she defended herself by referring to the many teachers and farmwomen she had met. Yet Vining seemed to have absorbed a Japanese upper-class distrust of the lower classes when she described Japan's agricultural class as the source for "ultranationalistic young officers" before and during the war and "a hotbed of communism" after the war.[59] She neglected to mention the poverty and misery in rural Japan since the Great Depression that were causes of unrest in the countryside. Instead, Vining maintained the urban Japanese elites' perspective and described them—especially the imperial family—as if the elites treated everyone else with the same courtesy and compassion that they had shown to her. Though a meticulous observer, she appears to have judged people at face value. Solicitous inquiries, numerous acts of kindness, and gifts from the imperial family and other Japanese to Vining were undoubtedly efforts (probably sincere) to put their best face forward. The fact that Vining was tactful, considerate, and respectful herself made their task easier. Vining's book promoted the imperial family so thoroughly that if her choice as the crown prince's tutor was truly fortuitous, this was certainly fortunate for the imperial household, SCAP, and U.S. policy.[60]

Tōjō and Deviant Masculinity

At the same time, it was fortunate and convenient for the postwar imperial publicity campaign that a personality such as General Tōjō Hideki existed. Throughout most of the war, Tōjō was the voice of the enemy. He was prime minister until late 1944, and it was Tōjō's statements, not the emperor's, that were reported in the American press. Americans read or heard about Tōjō accusing the United States and other powers of trying to "strangle" Japan; Tōjō justifying the war; Tōjō calling for a Greater East Asian Co-Prosperity Sphere; and Tōjō exhorting the Japanese to keep up the fight.[61] Americans saw Tōjō, according to journalist Clark Lee, as "sinister, threatening, brutal, a Hitler with the added danger of Oriental mysticism." Secretary of State Cordell Hull declared that Hitler and Tōjō combined "all the cruelty and fiendishness and inhumanity of Nero and Caligula and Attila as one."[62] Still, even though Japan was a repressive state with limited civil liberties, like Germany and Italy, Tōjō was never a military dictator and never wielded the authority of his supposed counterparts, Hitler and Mussolini. Imperial Japan, its expansionist policies, and even the ultranationalist junior officers who instigated war on China would have existed without Tōjō. But since Tōjō was the primary spokesman for imperial Japan, Americans found it easy to point to him as the primary instigator of the hostilities, which expedited the policymakers' goals of shielding the emperor from war responsibility.[63] Emperor Hirohito, Kelley and Ryan explained, was simply "a trumpet Tōjō blew."[64]

Blaming Tōjō as the main instigator of war, the Japanese counterpart to Hitler and Mussolini, provided a structural clarity to the story about the rise and fall of the Axis powers. A memorable figure with his bald head, mustache, round glasses, and fierce countenance, Tōjō personified the Japanese nation in many of the political cartoons and propaganda posters that depicted each of the enemy nations as a single character.[65] A couple of weeks after Pearl Harbor, *Life* used an image of Tōjō's face, not the emperor's, to illustrate the supposed differences in the physiognomies of Chinese and Japanese people in "How to Tell Japs from Chinese," a companion article to "How to Tell Your Friends from the Japs," published the same week in *Time* magazine.[66] At least one government agency, the Office of War Information (OWI), attempted to keep Hirohito out of propaganda, and Tōjō made a good substitute.[67]

Tōjō served as a good foil for the emperor because he happened to fit the part of an inscrutable, "Oriental" criminal mastermind, a latter-day Fu Manchu. Americans would have seen Tōjō, by his mere ethnicity, as "a Hitler with the added danger of Oriental mysticism," but his looks and actions reminded them of the stereotypical, evil Asian villain. Like Fu Manchu, Tōjō seemed to have delusions of grandeur, seeking to wreak nationalist and racial vengeance and to conquer the world. He was commonly singled out from all other Japanese wartime leaders. *Life*'s account of the Tokyo War Crimes Trial, for example, noted that Tōjō stubbornly continued to wear his military uniform without mentioning others who also did; that Tōjō was the most unapologetic; that Tōjō "sneered" while others "laughed" at an amusing incident; and that Tōjō listened "with great disdain" to the proceedings while Kido Kōichi assumed "an attitude of prayer."[68] Dr. Fu Manchu's creator, Sax Roehmer, described him as "the yellow peril incarnate in one man"; in the narratives about postwar Japan, Tōjō became that one man.[69]

Roehmer's bestselling series of novels about Fu Manchu made him a character recognized in most American households by the first decades of the twentieth century. Even Americans who never read the books, listened to the radio shows, watched the movies, or perused the comic strips about him knew what Fu Manchu represented. The original books revolve around plots that have Dr. Fu Manchu trying to best the western colonial Asian expert, Nayland Smith. Each seeks to defeat the other with superior knowledge and mastery of the other's civilization. Roehmer's stories tapped Progressive-era anxieties about modernity, race, nation, and masculinity and then resolved them by showing the triumph of the white man and his civilization as enlightened, superior, and morally upright. Unlike Smith, Fu Manchu is lascivious and seeks sadomasochistic control over whites—of either gender, since he is androgynous. But Fu Manchu is always defeated because his Anglo-Saxon nemesis is an outstanding specimen of white manhood and mature masculinity who can control his potentially unruly sensuous desires. In contrast, Fu Manchu is Asian, incapable of quelling his emotional, hysterical passion for world dominance, and his loss of manly control proves to be his downfall every time.[70]

Because Americans recognized Fu Manchu as the archetypal, nefarious oriental villain, they were primed to see in other Asian villains, fictional or real-life, the same hint of cruelty and an erotic/homoerotic desire to possess and control white women and men. This was evident in popular wartime images of the Japanese. Although the Japanese enemies in these images wear uniforms and do not sport long fingernails or wear the full-length, flowing silken robes of Hollywood's Fu Manchu or other Asian villains like General Yen of *The Bitter Tea of General Yen* (1933), they are depicted as threats to white womanhood and manhood. The "Jap militarists" are portrayed as rapists in wartime propaganda posters, leering and lustful, like the villainous Japanese general (Richard Loo) in his treatment of American prisoners in *Purple Heart* (1944), a film based on the story of the captured Doolittle fliers.[71] These Japanese film characters invariably wore a mustache—a pencil-thin or wispy, "Fu Manchu" one—and they were shown to deviate from the masculine ideals of candor, integrity, honor, and fortitude. They were treacherous and back-stabbing when evenly matched with their opponents; boastful and cruel when their opponents were in a weakened state; and hysterical and emotional in defeat.[72]

These notions of a racialized, deviant masculinity and the yellow peril intersected with Victorian descriptions of the Japanese as a "gay" people living in a childish "fairyland" that time had passed by. Although the Victorians did not necessarily associate words like "queer," "gay," and "fairy" with homosexuality, as twentieth-century Americans came to do, the Victorians did associate these terms with the precious, the affected, the irreverently carefree, and the immaturely irresponsible—the very opposite of what "true" adult men were supposed to be: duty-bound, "straight," and straightforward. Thus, circulating in American popular culture was the idea that Japanese men deviated from masculine norms—either charmingly or amusingly, as in *The Mikado*, or in a sinister way, like the type of Asian villain that Dr. Fu Manchu represented. The charming "queerness" of the Japanese and their culture and the sinister, suspect masculinity of Asian villainy appeared to be different sides of the same coin. As Kelley and Ryan noted: "We knew that the oh-so-artistic Oriental who had turned tea drinking and flower arrangement into somewhat mystic rituals was capable, too, of practicing cannibalism on captured American airmen. The supercivilized Jap also excelled in sticking bamboo stakes through the eyes of Allied prisoners."[73]

The Japanese, then, may have appeared modernized and even acculturated to the west, but in the eyes of many they remained savages or sadists with, as Lucy Crockett stated, "medieval minds underneath a veneer of civilization."[74] Writing for the Institute of Pacific Relations at the end of the war, William Johnstone echoed the same theme: "Fundamentally, we, and all peoples who have been the object of Japan's expanding conquests, failed to understand that behind Japan's thin veneer of modernism was a nation that had not discarded the ideas and structure of an autocratic militaristic feudalism."[75] In these descriptions, Japan is portrayed not only as underdeveloped and medieval, but as the embodiment of militarism itself, along with autocracy or despotism. To describe Japan as "feudal" allowed Americans to see the Occupation as ameliorative and beneficial to their former enemy. Describing Japanese militarism as "feudal" justified its excision from Japanese society and also served to differentiate American military might from that of imperial Japan.

The menace of the "yellow peril" was present in discourse about Japanese leaders who had attended elite American schools. The Japanese, like the fictional Dr. Fu Manchu, seemed to be seeking the expertise of the west in order to gain mastery, to "use western knowledge against westerners." The unctuous Japanese lawyer in *Purple Heart*, for instance, smoothly speaking English with a slightly European-sounding accent, introduces himself to the American prisoners as a graduate of an Ivy League school. One of the American prisoners, refusing to be impressed, snaps back and combatively asserts his state university credentials. In real life, when the *New York Times* referred to junior Japanese diplomat Kase Toshikazu's Ivy credentials, it depicted "Harvard man" Kase as wily and treacherous. Thus the *Times* raised the suggestion that Harvard University was a place where potentially dangerous learning occurred.[76] An alternative reading of the repeated mention of Ivy League degrees among Japanese leaders in the postwar press, however, is that journalists were suggesting that "reasonable" men with liberal training in the west existed in Japan and could become reliable U.S. partners. This was generally the attitude of the State Department and SCAP, but others continued to be skeptical. Clark Lee criticized the coziness between American officials and English-speaking Japanese elites; this led, he claimed, to the State Department's long-standing "tendency to favor monarchical and reactionary regimes."[77]

Emphasizing the deviant treachery and cruelty of Tōjō and the other "militarists" as archetypal "oriental" villains helped American writers and image-makers distinguish them from Hirohito, the "family man." Although Tōjō was also a family man—and one who had closer, more intimate contact with his wife, children, and grandchildren than his emperor did—and though he epitomized in many ways the proud, steadfast warrior and patriot, he was scorned by all and ridiculed by some Americans as a preening, slightly effeminate, former criminal mastermind. Similar to the stories of Jefferson Davis masquerading in petticoats to elude triumphant Union forces after the Civil War or the description of a beaten Hermann Göring "blush[ing] like a Rhine maiden," narratives questioning Tōjō's manliness spread. A telling example of such criticism of his manhood is the American accounts about his failed suicide attempt.[78]

On September 11, 1945, Tōjō tried to commit suicide when American authorities went to arrest him. But he failed to die, and Americans subsequently derided his attempt as "bungled." Occupation memoirs by journalists usually included an account of this, perhaps because many of them had witnessed it. Apparently news of Tōjō's impending arrest was leaked, and a horde of journalists and photographers had headed to Tōjō's house. The former premier refused to come out, and when the Americans outside heard a shot, they rushed into the house to find Tōjō bleeding profusely on a divan. He had aimed for his heart, but shot himself through the lung instead. As the Americans waited for Tōjō to die, the photographers manipulated his body as if he were a mannequin (another type of doll), crossing and uncrossing his legs to get the best image. As flashbulbs exploded in quick succession, the photographers instructed each other:

> "Move Tojo's head a little to the right. . . . Hold it . . . swell. . . . Do you mind taking your head out of the way . . . I want a shot of Tojo holding the revolver . . . do you mind pressing the gun into his hand? . . . Here comes the fly again. . . . I must get one of that [with the fly on Tōjō's forehead]."[79]

The writers, on the other hand, tried to capture what they believed would be the general's last words. Grimacing with pain, Tōjō declared: "The Greater East Asia war was a justified and righteous war. . . . I wait for the judgment of history."[80] The fact that he remained unrepentant to the end helped to secure his notoriety in the eyes of most Americans.

The Americans took full advantage of the spectacle of the general's suicide attempt. Small items were slipped into American pockets as souvenirs: writing brushes, items from his cupboard, automatic guns, and so on. Some even soaked their handkerchiefs with Tōjō's blood on the floor, and one had "clipped a neat triangle out of Tōjō's blood-sodden riding breeches."[81] Clark Lee recalled, "I saw a hand come through the window from outside,

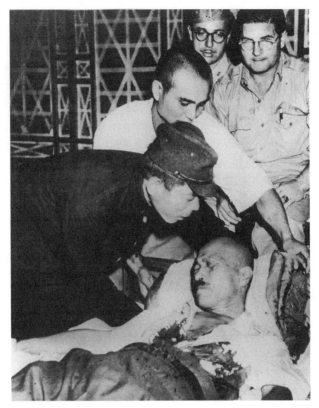

Former premier Tōjō Hideki's failed suicide attempt on September 11, 1945. Manipulation of his body—reportedly by two American journalists to speed his death—had the opposite effect of saving his life for trial and execution. Getty Images.

feel along the sill for the leather case, and then disappear with one of the samurai swords." This thief, a photographer, shoved the sword into the right leg of his pants and proceeded to limp toward his jeep, but a military police officer stopped him: "Nice going . . . but take it back."[82] After satisfying themselves with their reports, picture-taking, and new acquisitions, everyone waited for Tōjō to die. According to their own separate accounts and another one by Kelley and Ryan, Clark Lee and Harry Brundidge tried to hasten the former premier's death. While Lee was on the phone, someone mistakenly told him that Tōjō had died, and Lee ordered his colleague on the other end of the line to put out a "flash" about the death. By the time Lee learned that Tōjō was still alive, a long waiting line had formed for the phone, and he could not correct his error. Desperate, he called on Brundidge to help him expedite Tōjō's death by rolling him over a couple of times. They thought that this would make Tōjō bleed faster, but instead, their action caused two massive hemorrhages that had the reverse of the desired effect. Had they not moved him, Tōjō would have drowned by having his lungs fill with blood, but the two Americans, in their eagerness to speed his death, saved him for the hangman's noose.[83]

Disappointed that Tōjō had not died, Lee, Brundidge, and other Americans began to criticize him as a coward and a sissy. "The yellow bastard didn't have nerve enough to use a knife," said one reporter.[84] Another reporter insisted that the general's failed attempt "proves that Tōjō was partly effeminate," confirming his suspicions. He continued,

Did you ever hear of a male suicide shooting himself in the heart? Hell, no. They always point the gun at the mouth, the ear, or the temple. But there isn't a single case on record of a woman suicide shooting herself in the face. They always dress up in their best and put the pistol to their breast. Don't want to die with their faces mussed up. Tojo didn't either.

Tōjō had explained that he shot himself in the breast for identification purposes so that no Japanese would be in doubt about his death—as the Germans had wondered about Hitler's—and disbelieve it as an American trick. But this reporter failed to hear this, or remained unconvinced by it. He claimed that a "homosexual streak" existed "in these sadists," and argued that the "statistics showed a greater percentage of homosexuality in the Japanese Army and Navy than in any other armed forces in the world." The reporter further maintained that because the Japanese women "got damned little affection from their men," they fell in love with the cross-dressing actresses of Takarazuka Theater. The whole country, then, was a bit queer in this American's opinion.[85] Thus one of the ways in which Tōjō deviated from masculine norms, in the eyes of many Americans, was sexual deviance.

Americans had also frequently labeled Nazis as sexually deviant during the postwar period. One postwar psychoanalyst likened the Nazi's hatred of Jews to the homosexual's hatred of women and noted the "predilection of the Nazi hierarchy for homosexuality."[86] Labeling the Germans and Japanese as sexually deviant or effeminate after defeat was another way for Americans to distance themselves from their former enemies and to mark themselves as superior. To Americans, both Germany and Japan embodied a "sinister" evil, a cloaked, nefarious, and feminized danger that stood in contrast to their received image of the "normal" American adult male: healthy, straight, straightforward, calm, brave, and law-abiding. The enemies' evil, in other words, was explained as their deviance from the model of mature masculinity.

Because they saw their racial, cultural, social, and political differences with the Japanese in binary terms, most American policymakers, pundits, and politicians did not recognize or admit that their own nation had used similar methods to those of the Japanese. Demands that Japan become "a law-abiding, peaceful nation," as Secretary of State Cordell Hull argued in a 1943 deliberation about the postwar policy toward Japan, came with the advantage of having established in earlier centuries the political and economic security that the Japanese craved.[87]

To be sure, the overall objective of preventing Japan from waging another aggressive, murderous war was very worthy, but Americans talked about Japan with an unwarranted presumption that their own nation had always been and remained "law-abiding and peaceful," unlike the "gangster militarists." While Americans could see criminal deviance in the way the Japanese had tried to seize another people's territory, they failed to see how their own nation had gained territory in a similar manner, by violently seizing land and disavowing legal agreements. The refusal of the International Military Tribunal for the Far East (IMTFE) to consider the criminality of imperialism in a larger historical context or the "crimes against humanity" perpetrated by the victors thus vitiated the laudable goal of trying to outlaw preemptive war. Notably, the tribunal did not try to outlaw imperialism since Britain, France, Holland, and the United States all held or had recently held colonies. As Radhabinod Pal of India, the only jurist with expertise in international law, forcefully argued, laws must apply equally to all to be effective.[88]

American writers and media noted that the Japanese were also disdainful of Tōjō's unsuccessful suicide attempt. The Japanese saw him as a failure or a hypocrite for not carrying out what he had encouraged them, the Japanese nation, to do during the war: die rather than surrender. They wondered why he had not tried to commit suicide earlier than he did.[89] Americans learned that the Japanese despised Tōjō for getting them into the war in the first place, calling him *sono baka* ("that fool").[90] "How Beaten Japs Feel: It Was Tojo's Fault," reported *Newsweek;* "Japanese Lay Ills to Tojo Blunders," said the *New York Times* in mid-September 1945.[91] The phrase "Tojo no good" entered their limited English repertoire, along with "chocoretto," "cigaretto," and "jeepu."[92] Tōjō was so disliked, *Life* reported, that even the other Japanese wartime leaders in Omori prison ostracized him, refusing to take walks, play Go, eat meals, or talk with him, except for a curt "yes" or "no."[93] Later during the war crimes trial, another defendant—Ōkawa Shūmei, who was later dismissed for being mentally unstable—slapped Tōjō's bald head in the middle of the proceedings. So Crockett may have meant it literally when she called Tōjō "the nation's whipping boy."[94]

Separating the Militarists from Other Japanese Men

By driving a wedge between the emperor and his high-ranking, loyal servants, SCAP and its allies in the American media also separated the Japanese public, even Japanese men, from the "militarists." Allowing the emperor to be "the good Japanese," in other words, made it possible for other "good Japanese" to exist as well.[95] The process of creating a "good Japanese" developed in parallel to the notion of a good emperor, and both notions were mutually reinforcing. In the postwar narrative, the Japanese people, as well as the emperor, were seen as having been hoodwinked by the evil militarists into going to war—a plausible contention, but not unproblematic given the overwhelming public support for the war at its beginning.

Toward the war's end, the American media began showing ordinary Japanese soldiers more sympathetically as they pilloried Tōjō and other "militarists." Negative portrayals still appeared, but presentations of the Japanese rank-and-file tended to emphasize their humanity.[96] Americans discovered that Japanese soldiers seemed to want to survive the war and learned that Japanese soldiers were disinclined to surrender not because of fanaticism, but because the Japanese had been told that the Americans would kill those who surrendered.[97] By July 1945, even a favorable depiction of the "suicidal corps" appeared in American media. A year before gaining acclaim for his book *Hiroshima,* John Hersey authored an article on kamikaze pilots that portrayed them as generally crazed and desperate, but he also included a description of a more sensible kamikaze. Hersey wrote, "Quite a few have shown something less than the fanatical spirit which is expected of them," and he quoted a captured pilot:

> I come out to this Clark Field a couple of days ago and I have nothing to do so I go out to look at my plane. I find some dope of a mechanic has wired a bomb to my plane. I'm sore, I give this mechanic hell. He says, "Very sorry, orders." What are they trying to do to me? I go to headquarters and tell them what this dumb bastard has done. They say, "Oh, we all do that now." I say, "*You* do it, not me! I don't like this wiring business." So what do they do? They arrest me. All night I'm under guard . . . so in the morning I say, "Okay I'll take this ride for the Emperor." So they take the guard off me. Pretty soon I see my chance, I get my parachute in the plane. We got out on this mission, it looks lousy to me, so what do I do? I jump.[98]

Whether this translation matched the Japanese pilot's actual words can be questioned; given the usual strict observance of hierarchy in the Japanese army, it sounds somewhat dubious. But presenting any Japanese—especially a kamikaze pilot—as an ordinary human being with a normal desire to live marked a significant departure from the standard wartime images; this ex-kamikaze was depicted as a down-to-earth, "regular Joe." The passage also suggests that devotion to the emperor was more a forced party line than a cherished belief. Having to mouth an attitude that the "higher-ups" demanded was something that regular

Joes in the United States could understand well. After the war, many Americans learned that although kamikaze pilots "were willing to die for their country," like brave American soldiers, they much preferred to be alive. "The kamikazes are glad," a Japanese translator told Lee, "that they did not have to die crashing their planes into your invasion ships."[99]

Seeing their defeated combat foes up close helped to diminish harsh views, and American journalists in Japan reported their observations back home. Watching demobilized Japanese soldiers waiting—some for days—at a railroad station for transportation home, an American reporter described them as "very young, tired, forlorn and harmless."[100] *Life*'s Christmas 1945 edition invited feelings of goodwill toward the ex-enemy by detailing the return of a demobilized Japanese soldier to his family farm. With no references to Japanese barbarity or cruelty, the article portrayed the man as simply another veteran returning to his life's work after being pulled away from it by war and "humbly settling again into his immemorial place in the village, a place almost identical with that of half of Japan's population." A portfolio-sized photograph of farm fields with Mt. Fuji in the background suggested that this was the real Japan: the land of simple, "frugal" and "hard-working" folk—from the "able and conscientious" mayor to the farmer's wife who had worked in the fields and raised their young children by herself during her husband's absence. Japanese soldiers, the article suggested, came from people and communities like these, where entire families farmed small, miserable plots all their waking hours, lived on bland sustenance diets, and warmed themselves in the cold winter months by huddling around a charcoal heater. They were a people, the article implied, who needed uplift and modern conveniences, not condemnation from the world community.[101]

A demilitarized Japan meant a domesticated Japanese industry.

Americans described for stateside audiences the process of Japanese industry shifting itself from war production to consumer goods. In 1946, LaCerda reported that the former airplane prefabrication factories in Osaka were "making pie plates out of airplane gas tanks." Casings from depth bombs became stoves; "dehorned" sea mines became hog-feeding troughs; torpedo tubes turned into sewer pipes, rocket guns into hydraulic pumps, hulls of landing craft into fishing boats; and compasses became cosmetic cases.[102] LaCerda neglected to say where these goods would go, given that Japan could do no exporting and most Japanese people were using every bit of cash and bartering their valued possessions for food. But the notion of turning bombs into stoves and compasses into cosmetic cases—a modern-day version of swords into ploughshares—showed Americans the beginnings of a new Japan in compelling, gendered imagery. Postwar Japan would now abandon the masculine job of war-making abroad to focus on domestic and domesticated concerns.

During World War II, it was the Japanese who depicted American men as effeminate, soft, and corrupt. "The Japs," explained Clark Lee, "had been taught to think of us as an immoral, materialistic race, lacking courage, soaked in alcohol, neurotic, devoted to sissy sports and languorous past times."[103] Portraying themselves as the virile ones, they claimed that the effete, decadent, and cowardly Americans would be no match for the lean, muscular, disciplined, frugal, and spirited Japanese. In this propaganda, the Japanese directed their contempt mainly at American men, whom they saw as being too much under the control of American women. To be unable to handle one's woman was bad enough, deserving of ridicule and pity, but to lack manhood itself, in this view, was downright despicable. This view helped some Japanese justify their cruel treatment of the "effeminate" enemy.[104]

After the Japanese leaders accepted defeat as inevitable, the issue of the emperor's fate remained the outstanding point of contention. The Truman administration and SCAP gave assurance— or, in the case of MacArthur, bent over backwards—to honor and protect the imperial institution, and thus smoothed relations with Japan's elites. Ironically, although the United States repeatedly broke its pledge to uphold "self-determination" for many nations following World War II, it remained faithful to its promise to its ex-enemy, Japan. As Akira Iriye has noted, "the two governments included leaders with a shared past who had once worked together for similar goals and in accordance with alternative solutions to global and domestic problems."[105] Both nations shared a deep-seated aversion to communism, and Japan's leaders happily agreed to have their country be cast as a "bulwark" against communism in the Far East.

Given the coziness of the postwar bilateral relationship, Japan's subordinate role in it, and the worldview held by both Americans and Japanese that saw dominant partners as male and subordinate ones as female, it is understandable why the famous photograph of MacArthur and Hirohito has been described as a bridal portrait. In 1993 H. D. Harootunian, paraphrasing the Japanese literary critic Katō Norihiro, described the photograph as "a memento of a marriage with all of its attending associations of a sexual relationship and conjugal bliss between Japan and the United States at the beginning of the Occupation." Edwin O. Reischauer had also described the U.S.-Japan relationship as an ideal bourgeois marriage.[106] If we carried the analogy further, we could say that the emperor divorced his former partner, General Tōjō (though with some regret and pain, it is said), for another, stronger and more powerful general who was a better provider and protector. Yet the photo of MacArthur and Hirohito surely does not resemble a wedding photograph—the distance between the two men shows this to be no happy union—and it can be described as depicting "conjugal bliss" only in retrospect. The point here is how commonsensical this gendered framework appears. Easily understandable, it neatly encapsulates the more complicated relationships between peoples of two nations.

Despite the strong alliance that eventually developed, the issue of Japanese trustworthiness continued to circulate in American public discourse; old stereotypes about "Oriental" inscrutability persisted throughout the postwar era. SCAP and the Truman administration, however, did not require strong public support to work with Hirohito. They simply needed to avoid public outrage.

Interwoven with the practical reasons for the American public's acceptance of Japan as an ally were the pre-existing stories and themes that writers and journalists adjusted slightly to fit the new situation. These narratives, whether about upstanding family men, nefarious oriental villains, or manipulated Japanese dolls, derived their power from their very familiarity. What seemed familiar was also understood as true and valid at a gut level—more so, linguists say, than reasoned discourse that argues the opposite. Messages are best heard when they work within pre-established worldviews.[107] Depiction of the emperor in American postwar discourse used multiple strategies that ranged from respectful—as in the case of Vining and, for the most part, *Life* magazine—to disparaging and disdainful, as some Occupation memoirs demonstrated. Although it was not a coordinated effort, recasting the emperor as a peaceful family man and continuing to regard Tōjō as a vainglorious, even "perverted," oriental villain was largely successful: the Japanese fought in the emperor's name, but American memory thinks of the Pacific War as Tōjō's war. Americans, even historians like the late Stephen Ambrose, have tended to describe World War II as the one "when we beat Hitler and

Tojo."[108] Since 1945, Americans have come to consider Tōjō as the main Japanese miscreant of the war. Hirohito was not a dictator like Hitler, but it should not be forgotten that the Japanese equivalent to *Heil Hitler!* was *Tennō-heika banzai*—"Long live the emperor!"

CHAPTER FOUR

A Transpacific Treason Trial

In October 1946, a young war veteran and his wife went to the Sears, Roebuck department store in downtown Los Angeles. A survivor of the 1942 Bataan Death March, William L. Bruce had endured over three years as a prisoner of war and spent the last year of the war at a prison camp at Oeyama on Honshu, Japan's main island. Now resuming his life, Bruce was shopping for a lawn mower at Sears. He turned and accidentally brushed someone. Bruce started to say "Pardon me," but he was struck dumb upon seeing the other person—a familiar-looking bespectacled Asian man. The man seemed not to recognize him, and it took Bruce a few moments to put a name to the Asian face because, as he later explained, he had never seen the man "before in sports clothes." Then Bruce recognized the man: he was "Kaw-kida," one of the "strong-arm" men from the hated Japanese POW camp at Oeyama. The realization infuriated him. What was this Jap doing, walking around free in the United States?

Noticing the sudden change in his demeanor, Bruce's wife became worried. "My God, what's the matter with you?" she asked, trailing behind her husband, who began pursuing the Asian man.

"I've got a fellow I'm going to kill," he answered. Now truly alarmed, she cried, "You've gone crazy—get ahold of yourself!" Perhaps her words made him take heed. Being careful that "Kawkida" did not see him, Bruce followed him outside to a light green Mercury, wrote down the number of his car license plate, and reported him to the FBI. Eight months later, on June 5, 1947, the FBI arrested Tomoya Kawakita, a 26-year-old American of Japanese ancestry. A grand jury in Los Angeles indicted Kawakita on thirteen counts of treason, each count representing a separate act of abuse to POWs.[1]

Kawakita was one of two Japanese Americans who were tried for treason after World War II.[2] The other, Iva Toguri d'Aquino, was convicted—most now say unfairly—for broadcasting propaganda for Radio Tokyo. Though she never used the name during the war, this woman came to be known as "Tokyo Rose," a mythic character whose existence was never ascertained.[3] By coincidence, Kawakita and Toguri had attended the same Japanese American church, the Calexico Union Church, and took lessons at the church's Japanese-language school.[4] While Iva Toguri's family moved away to another part of California when she was still in elementary school, Tomoya Kawakita grew up and graduated from high school in Calexico, California. In 1939, after graduating from high school, Kawakita traveled to Japan with his father to visit his grandfather. His father, a successful grocer and merchant, returned to the United States, leaving his 18-year-old son in Japan to attend first a preparatory school for Nisei and then Meiji University in March 1941. Unlike Toguri, Kawakita entered his name into his family's *koseki* or family register to assure the rights of Japanese citizenship for himself and to secure employment.

In August 1943, Kawakita began work as an interpreter at the

Oeyama Nickel Industry Company, a mining and metal process-ing plant located a hundred kilometers from Kyoto near the Sea of Japan. During the war this company used Allied prisoners of war as laborers at the company's surface mines. Kawakita served as the interpreter between the Japanese military foreman in charge of the adjoining POW camp and the prisoners, who in-cluded British, Canadians, Chinese, and, after late 1944 and early 1945, about four hundred American POWs—most of whom had been captured on Bataan in 1942. Two other Nisei were there as interpreters: Kawakita's childhood friend, Meiji Fujizawa, who translated in the POW camps, and Noboyuki Inoue, who worked in the company's administrative office.

When the war ended, Kawakita served the Americans as an in-terpreter at Oeyama before making his way back to Tokyo. In December, he applied for a renewal of his American passport at the U.S. consulate, where he explained away his Japanese citizen-ship by asserting that he registered in his family's *koseki* only in 1943 and under severe pressure. Having heard similar tales from many other Nisei eager to leave war-torn Japan, the ex-amining officer did not find his story suspicious. When a check of the Eighth Army CIC records indicated nothing disturbing about him, the consulate issued Kawakita a new passport in June 1946, and he traveled home in early August. By October, he was en-rolled as a student at the University of Southern California when Bruce spotted him at Sears.

Kawakita's subsequent trial in 1947 must be seen within the context of the Cold War. His trial coincided with those of other alleged traitors of World War II. Most of these suspects had been investigated within months after the war's end, but they were re-leased or left free. Formal charges for most of them came only several years afterwards. Then, they were all duly tried and convicted for treason. In separate trials, Iva Toguri, John David Provoo, Martin James Monti, Herbert John Burgman, and Margaret Elizabeth Gillars, the so-called "Axis Sally," were convicted for broadcasting enemy propaganda during the war.[5] Like Kawakita, all had been investigated and released in 1945–1946 and then later formally charged by the Justice Department in 1947 and 1948, after the Cold War had truly begun.[6] The Cold-War-era treason trials, as well as the Red scare espionage trials of the period, allowed the federal government to pillory disloyal individuals. Kawakita's prosecution can therefore be seen as a part of the broader Cold War strategy of containment.

More specifically, Tomoya Kawakita embodied American anxieties about national disloyalty and the potentially sneaky Japanese as a Cold War ally. He symbolized the resentful minority male who seethed inside because the dominant society refused to treat him as a full-fledged adult man. News reports, prosecution testimony, and the court depicted Kawakita as having taken revenge for affronts he perceived to his manliness, but they also suggested that Kawakita truly was less than a man. Treachery and femininity or unmanliness have often been closely linked in American popular perception. People or nations commit treachery because they are too weak or poor in resources to stab, and so they backstab instead. In the United States, this gendered discourse divided the unmanly, devious, irrational cowards on one side and the manly, straightforward, brave Americans on the other. This oversimplified binary opposition helped Americans express their outrage about the attack on Pearl Harbor by establishing a narrative for retribution: justice was on the side of the United States, which should take whatever means necessary to punish the "cowards."[7] Some traitors were unmanly cowards who were unable to stick by their guns and remain loyal to their nation or people and instead caved in to the demands of the enemy. Kawakita represented the cowardly individual of "weak moral fibre" who was only brave when his fellow Americans were powerless and defenseless, who lashed out against Euroamericans only when they were unnaturally weakened as POWs. The U.S. government, however, did not punish Kawakita to justify the internment. His prosecution points to the very opposite: by showcasing Kawakita as a "bad" Japanese American— just as Tōjō was a "bad" Japanese—and as an exception among a majority of "good," loyal Japanese Americans, the state and the press urged the peaceful acceptance of Japanese Americans back into American society while still allowing an expression of racial hatred toward Kawakita, which they denied was racist. Ironically, the government's case against Kawakita reversed the infamous notion that "a Jap's a Jap." Forsaken and persecuted during the war, Japanese Americans now saw their government asserting in effect that "a Yank's a Yank" in order to punish one Japanese American.

The attempts to refigure the Japanese as postwar allies were linked to efforts to showcase the Japanese Americans as worthy citizens. But these endeavors operated within, and as a challenge to, a broader sentiment of continued hostility and distrust of the Japanese race. In this context, Kawakita's trial can be seen as an effort to individuate guilt and exorcise the former enemy. Clarifying and punishing what was bad about the Japanese in the Tokyo war crimes trials helped Americans understand at the same time what was good about the Japanese. Likewise, the focus on Kawakita's treasonous choices stood in stark contrast to the loyal and right choices made by most Japanese American men, especially the Nisei soldiers of the 442nd Regimental Combat Team. Kawakita's treason trial thus reaffirmed the fact that most Japanese American men had remained loyal to their nation. What distinguished Kawakita and Tōjō from other men of Japanese ancestry was their wrongheaded willfulness and their evil delusions of grandeur. That the potential for such "oriental" deviance and cunning still existed acknowledged an element of subversion or danger within the now seemingly safe, unequal power relationship between the United States and Japan. The treason of Tomoya Kawakita served as a site where Americans could work out the ambiguities of loyalty, allegiance, discrimination, and racial hatred that lingered from the previous war in order to conduct the Cold War more effectively. During the trial, both the American government and the press attempted to fine-tune the discordant notes in what was otherwise a performance of increasing bilateral harmony.

The Revenge of the Emasculated Minority Male

At his trial, Kawakita pleaded not guilty to the charges, and his defense rested on the status of his citizenship. His lawyer, Morris Lavine, contended that Kawakita regarded himself as a Japanese citizen with no allegiance to the United States at the time of his alleged crimes. At the very most, Lavine stressed, his client was guilty of "a series of isolated assaults and batteries—nothing more." Kicking a prisoner in the shins or forcing a prisoner to carry an extra bucket of paint "could not possibly rise to the dignity of . . . a treason case," he declared. He also pointed out that the alleged acts lacked the "element of secrecy and cunning" that characterizes treachery and asserted that Americans "have to be careful that our victory over Japan does not enable us for that reason to wreak vengeance against the defendant. We are all on trial here." The case, he stated, should not be "another chance to get a Jap."[8]

The government, of course, argued the opposite: that Kawakita understood that he still owed allegiance to the United States and thus had intentionally betrayed the country of his birth through his actions. Kawakita was on trial not because of his Japanese ancestry, the government's attorney emphasized, but because he had used his American citizenship so casually, casting off "citizenship in a country as great as the United States" or turning it off and on like a faucet. Head prosecutor James M. Carter pointed out that Kawakita had led the U.S. consulate officer to believe that he had remained loyal to the United States throughout the war, and the prosecution team disagreed with Lavine's minimization of Kawakita's actions and emphasized instead their seriousness. They claimed that Kawakita's exhortations helped the Japanese by forcing the prisoners to mine more ore and thus releasing more Japanese "man-hours" for other activities in their war effort.[9] Because this harassment of his fellow Americans furthered the enemy's cause, according to the prosecution, this made Kawakita guilty of treason—a charge strongly supported by many former Oeyama POWs.

In fact, former Oeyama POWs were so eager to testify against Kawakita that the prosecution team had to turn away at least a hundred and forty-nine of them, according to Walter Tucker, a former prisoner. A Texan captured on Bataan who spent the last thirteen months of the war at Camp Oeyama, Tucker had wanted to testify that Kawakita beat him "shortly before liberation," but by the time he came forward, the prosecution team told him they had more than enough witnesses.[10] When Kawakita was arraigned, Carter announced that the government planned to use the testimony of "close to 100" former POWs.[11] That so many veterans clamored to be prosecution witnesses just a couple of years after V-J Day should come as no surprise. How outrageous, it must have seemed to them, that a "Jap" partially responsible for their misery at a POW camp should go unpunished and worse, should be able to walk free in America. Many POWs had pledged to exact revenge against their tormentors as they endured the appalling conditions and cruelty of the Japanese POW–slave labor camps. One prosecution witness recalled that when he was a prisoner, he swore at the Japanese guards: "As sure as there's a Christ in heaven, you heathen bastards will pay for this!"[12] Kawakita's arrest therefore gave many former prisoners "a great deal of satisfaction," as it did to Charles J. Cushing, who had been beaten and starved from a prewar weight of 228 to a mere 107 pounds.[13] For Pacific War veterans like Cushing, personal knowledge of Japanese brutality convinced them of Kawakita's guilt.

Inflammatory headlines in the press prejudged Kawakita as guilty. At the time of his arrest and indictment, the *Los Angeles Times* inflated his importance at Oeyama: "L.A. Jap Arrested as Horror Camp Leader" and "Jap Camp Boss Indicted Here." The *San Francisco Chronicle* erroneously labeled him as "foreman in a prison camp at Oeyama," and the Portland *Oregonian*, playing up the image of a toothy, treacherous Jap, described Kawakita as "the Japanese American traitor who came smiling back to Los Angeles when the war was over, after having served Nippon as the brutal foreman of a Honshu prison camp." Even the *Pacific Citizen*, a Nisei newspaper, did not clarify the fact that he was an interpreter until nearly a year after his arrest.[14] As a civilian interpreter, Kawakita was neither a "camp leader" nor a "camp boss." Although he repeatedly asserted his innocence, the national press made no mention of his protests during its coverage of his ordeal and gave the impression that his case rested only on the status of his citizenship, not the truth of the charges. The *Pacific Citizen* only mentioned his claims of innocence when it reported Kawakita's testimony on the stand toward the end of his trial. Nor did the *Pacific Citizen* publish his or his family's side of the story when it broke. Instead, aghast at the damage Kawakita's case might do to their improved postwar image, the Nisei paper was quick to presume his guilt and try to distance Japanese Americans from him.[15]

Although public sentiment was convinced of Kawakita's guilt, his lawyer argued that the POW testimonies against Kawakita had fingered the wrong man. Lavine asserted that the more serious offenses Kawakita was charged with—like delaying medical attention to a prisoner who sustained a spinal injury, striking a mortally ill prisoner, or pushing a prisoner repeatedly into a cesspool as punishment for stealing Red Cross supplies—had actually been attributed to other camp guards in POW affidavits for the war crimes trials in Japan. The absence of Kawakita's name in a diary kept by the medical officer who recorded violations of the Geneva Convention at Oeyama also supported his innocence.[16] Quite tellingly, no prisoner retaliated against him after the war ended. Instead, the Allied officers chose him to be their main interpreter, and Kawakita was on friendly enough terms with some enlisted men, he claimed, to act as their tour guide for a trip to Amano-Hashidate after their liberation and to see them off at a train station with "friendly good-byes."[17] Nobody seized him when the war ended, when he went to the consulate, or when he went to the Eighth Army to secure transport back to the United States. Lavine emphasized that his client did not hide or change his name after arriving home; instead "he went to a university loaded with GIs"—an unlikely act for someone who had any cause to fear their retribution. Kawakita's lawyer also pointed out that it was strange that the prosecution called no officer to the witness stand during the trial—only enlisted men, who held an understandable grudge against the Japanese. Unlike the other two Nisei translators at Oeyama, Kawakita's role at the mine as translator of military orders meant that he handed down or barked orders to extract the most work from the mostly enlisted men under grueling circumstances. His job as a voice of the hated captors hardly made him a fond memory after the war for Camp Oeyama's former prisoners, Lavine asserted, and now Kawakita was being punished for merely being a messenger.

Yet the POWs insisted that Kawakita had added gratuitous, demeaning remarks as he interpreted and that he took unfair advantage of his association with their Japanese captors to act like "a big shot." They remembered him as an embittered minority man who declared that America "never gave [him] a damned thing" and who lashed out at white POWs because he was in the position to do so. Kawakita, reported one veteran, "seemed to take satisfaction in seeing Americans degraded in the presence of Japanese soldiers."[18] When exhausted Americans fell behind in meeting their required daily quota of mined ore, he showed no sympathy and berated them. "What the hell do you think this is?" he supposedly shouted at emaciated prisoners, "Hurry up and get to work."[19] The POWs also claimed that Kawakita delighted in pointing out the "inferiority" of American fighting men. "I knew that you Americans couldn't take it when the going got tough," he supposedly said, mocking their manliness. He also allegedly taunted them for surrendering: "It looks like MacArthur took a run-out powder on you boys."[20] One witness remembered that Kawakita was "strutting around like a cock" and boasting that Japan would win the war even if it took 100 years, an image the prosecuting attorney repeated in his closing arguments.[21] The press echoed this portrayal of overweening masculinity, describing him as "a swaggering sadist who brandished a wooden sword and abused the American survivors of Bataan."[22] The press also reported that Kawakita "appeared near tears" when informed during his arraignment that treason could be a capital offense, indicating that he was not as tough as he acted at Oeyama.[23] While the statements attributed to him may or may not be true, the overall depiction of Kawakita as a puffed-up male brandishing a phallic symbol indicated that the Euroamerican prosecutor, veterans, and the press—even the Nisei press—considered Kawakita a dishonorable minority who literally kicked other men when they were down.

Although the prosecution, the veterans, and the mainstream journalists conflated gender, race, and treachery during this trial, they did not automatically link treachery with Japanese ancestry, as they had commonly done during the war. They made a point of contrasting Kawakita's behavior with that of Meiji Fujizawa, his fellow Nisei interpreter at Oeyama, whom the POWs remembered as strictly adhering to his job of interpreting. Depicting Fujizawa as the "good" Nisei, they recalled that while Kawakita had tried to demoralize POWs, Fujizawa went around giving friendly slaps on the prisoners' backs and tried to instill hope by confidently telling them in the summer of 1945 that "we'll have Thanksgiving dinner in San Francisco." Walter Tucker, the Texan who claimed that Kawakita beat him, remembered Fujizawa a half-century later as an "excellent man" who secretly informed them in Spanish of the U.S. victories in Okinawa and Iwo Jima, in order to avoid the detection of English-speaking Japanese guards.[24] At the end of the war, a group of POW officers presented Fujizawa with an unsolicited document attesting to his good character. In part, it stated: "Although he is of Nipponese extraction, he has, under the most difficult circumstances, conducted himself in a manner worthy of merit and in accordance with the American idea of assistance and fair play. He has proven himself to be an American under conditions where many, if not most, would have failed and we feel that he has performed his duty here to more effect than if he had been an American soldier on the front lines."[25] In other words, Nisei men had the volition to be properly manful and loyal; an experience of racial discrimination was no excuse to act otherwise.

The prosecution and the press dismissed the racism that Kawakita had experienced while growing up in California as irrelevant and asserted, basically, that a Yank's a Yank. Carter argued that Kawakita was guilty of treason "not because he is of Japanese ancestry. He is being tried because he is an American citizen just the same as you and I."[26] But Kawakita was not "just the same as" Carter or the mostly Euroamerican members of the jury. He may have won a football letter during high school, but he grew up in a West Coast community that excluded Japanese Americans socially and discriminated against them racially. He and other Nisei were acutely aware that the larger society marginalized them economically, giving them only low-paying, dead-end jobs outside of their ethnic communities regardless of talent or education. As one of Kawakita's contemporaries, the future historian Kazuo Kawai, pointed out, "No matter what our qualifications may be, evidently the only place where we are wanted is in positions that no [white] Americans would care to fill—menial positions as houseservants, gardeners, vegetable peddlers, continually 'Yes, ma'aming.'"[27] Another Nisei, a fruit-stand worker and an essayist, sarcastically called himself "a professional carrot washer," referring to his restricted career aspirations.[28] "Before Pearl Harbor," observed *Pacific Citizen* columnist Larry Tajiri, "it wasn't just a bad joke to say that a Nisei needed a college degree to get a job as a clerk in a retail produce market on the Pacific Coast."[29] This restriction in career opportunities was the reason why Kawakita's parents had left him in Japan in the first place. Most Nisei lacked adequate Japanese-language skills, and the Kawakitas believed that if their son became fluent, he could work in a business importing Japanese goods, one of the few white-collar occupations available to prewar Nisei.[30]

Many Nisei men saw these limited opportunities and their overall treatment by American society—their "yes ma'am-ing"—as emasculation. They were quite aware of the larger society's depiction of Asian men as either effeminate, falsely full of bravado, or otherwise improperly manly. Some Nisei men harbored hopes to "get even" for this depiction of their race as unmanly and for the discrimination they suffered in the prewar years.[31] Nisei women also felt resentment about racial discrimination and their restricted opportunities, but unlike the Nisei men, they did not interpret their experience as an insult to their identities as females.[32] Men were different. Kazumaro Buddy Uno, another expatriate Nisei man who was known to abuse and harass American POWs, saw racial discrimination as emasculation. He claimed, "I was treated like a yellow skibby and not an American citizen. . . . So I decided, the hell with the United States. I'd go to Japan where my knowledge of the States would be appreciated." "Skibby" meant "Japanese prostitute" in western slang, and Uno was therefore comparing his racial experience to treatment as "a yellow whore by white men."[33] If the statements attributed to Kawakita truly captured his attitude and his words, it would appear that he felt similarly and wanted to "get even" by returning the insults to his manliness, telling the Euroamerican prisoners that they were cowardly and weak.

When Kawakita took the stand, however, he was not as forthcoming as Uno; he categorically denied any wrongdoing while at Oeyama, even verbal abuse.[34] The former POWs, he declared,

Tomoya Kawakita pausing during cross-examination at his treason trial in 1948. Los Angeles Times Photo.

made him into a scapegoat for all the mistreatment by Japanese civilian personnel and soldiers.[35] He claimed that he had never completely given his loyalties to the Japanese, and that he had refused a commission as a lieutenant in the Japanese army because he did not want to be in the position of fighting against his old high school friends. Stating that he had been distressed about having to deal with the Allied POWs and upset that his request for a transfer was denied, he nonetheless had to speak in a "stern, military manner" and avoid fraternizing with the prisoners because he was commanded to do so. He asserted, however, that he stuck to interpreting and even translated statements to sound less harsh than the original Japanese orders.[36] And the "wooden sword," he explained, was actually a cane to help him walk in the slippery mud; he claimed that he had never used it to strike a prisoner.[37]

Kawakita also testified that he helped prisoners, too—carrying one American prisoner on his back to the mine's hospital, escorting other prisoners to get medical or dental treatment several times, and asking for a workload reduction when he saw prisoners could not meet their daily quota.[38] He admitted to slapping one POW, but claimed he only did so because he overheard the man calling him a son-of-a-bitch in Spanish. During cross-examination, however, he conceded that he had also slapped British and Canadian prisoners, but implied in his answer that hitting prisoners of other nationalities was perfectly legitimate since he was on trial for treason against Americans—not necessarily the Allied cause.[39] His admission nonetheless raises suspicion about the veracity of his story. Perhaps he slapped Chinese prisoners as well; coverage of the trial and the trial itself completely ignored the treatment of Chinese POWs, as if only an Asian man's cruelty to white men mattered. To be fair, however, Kawakita, as an English-Japanese translator, may not have had much contact with the Chinese prisoners.

Punishing the "Bad" Minority Male

Today it is difficult to determine if Kawakita physically abused prisoners voluntarily or on the orders of his Japanese superiors. To give him the benefit of the doubt, however, some of his defense sounds plausible. It makes sense that he would not have risked returning to the United States if he were truly guilty of abusive behavior. During the trial, a prosecution witness testified that he had seen Kawakita slap three Americans who had stolen clothes from fellow prisoners, but admitted that as far as he knew, Kawakita "had never beaten anybody up."[40] Meiji Fujizawa testified that he, too, was commanded to whip a British POW for hoarding jam and did so because he feared the Japanese officer who had ordered him to do so. Fujizawa added that the Japanese even made the POWs punish each other. He saw one prisoner forced to shove another into a pond, and others who were "required to strike each other or hit each other."[41]

The POW camp, in other words, was a brutal place where violence was normalized and an everyday event. Years later, in a much different setting, Kawakita ineffectively tried to explain camp conditions by emphasizing a few times that he believed he might have been "severely punished or killed" for violating his duties. The prosecution demolished this explanation by demonstrating that Kawakita never came close to being killed, but rather was a very valuable interpreter whom his military superiors relied upon. Fujizawa told the court that he remembered hearing rumors about Kawakita's mistreatment of unnamed prisoners, but that he never received a complaint about Kawakita in his capacity as translator of POW requests and complaints to the camp commandant. As Fujizawa elaborated later, his childhood friend was "rough in speech" and "not diplomatic in talking," but he never saw him hit or kick anyone.[42]

Kawakita, then, was probably a bully and perhaps even voluntarily abusive at times in a place that encouraged violence. Many ex-POWs, when they discovered he was back in the States, wanted to punish him not only for his alleged harassment but perhaps also for the abuse they remembered suffering in Japanese POW camps. Kawakita tried to hide behind his temporary Japanese citizenship, and this led to a tortuous legal narrative during the trial about when Kawakita was or was not an American citizen. The presiding judge heavily influenced the verdict against the defendant. The jury approached Judge William C. Mathes several times for a dismissal during their eight days of deliberation, claiming they were impossibly deadlocked, but each time the judge insisted that they continue. At one point, the judge ignored the rule of double jeopardy and lectured jurors that failure to reach a decision in this "long and expensive" trial would mean that another "equally long and expensive" trial would likely ensue.[43] Finally, on September 2, 1948, the jury reached a verdict: Kawakita was guilty of eight of the thirteen "overt" acts of treason. According to the *San Francisco Chronicle*, he "showed no emotion when the verdict was read, beyond blinking his bespectacled eyes rapidly." Three days later, immediately before the sentencing, Lavine filed a motion for a new trial, charging that the jury had been unduly influenced. The bailiffs, he claimed, told the jurors, who had already endured a long trial in the sweltering summer heat, that the judge would keep them cooped up until they returned a guilty verdict. Lavine added that a juror told him that she had been pressured to agree to a conviction. Judge Mathes, however, had the authority to rule on this appeal, and he ruled that there had been no coercion. He then sentenced the 27-year-old Kawakita to die in a gas chamber.[44]

Mathes emphasized that Kawakita's Japanese ancestry had no effect on his sentencing. "My views would be the same no matter who he was," he claimed. Lest capital punishment be deemed too harsh, Judge Mathes went on to explain that Kawakita's crime of treason violated more than the well-being of a few American prisoners. Instead, the judge intoned, his "crime [was] against the whole people of this country where he was born and where he was fed and where he was educated." Not all traitors, Mathes asserted, are "given the chance to commit treason in a grand manner," and he speculated, without any evidence, that had Kawakita been given the opportunity, he would have "willingly blown up our Pacific Fleet and disclosed to the Japanese the secrets of our atomic bomb."[45] Mathes took special care to contrast Kawakita's behavior with that of the Japanese Americans who served with distinction in the 442nd Regimental Combat Team and the 100th Infantry Battalion:

> If the defendant were to go from this Court a free man, he would be condemned to live out his life in bitter scorn of himself. Haunted not only [because] of his base treason against the land of his birth, but also of Sadao Munemori, who won the Congressional Medal of Honor; of Private[s] First Class, Fumitaka Nagato and Saburo Tanamachi, who are buried with the American heroes of all time at Arlington National Cemetery; and the memory of almost seven hundred other boys of like American birthright, of like Japanese parentage, who stood the supreme test of loyalty to their native land, and gave up their lives that America and her institutions might continue to live.[46]

Mathes pointedly distinguished Kawakita—whom the press repeatedly identified as an "L.A. Jap" from the time of his arrest— from other Japanese Americans. The judge emphasized that the treasonous Kawakita who "[sold] knowledge of the English language which he had gained in the public schools of America" was the exception among Japanese Americans—that this one bad example stood against the hundreds who had died as American soldiers.[47] Mathes's remarks tried to reverse the collective wisdom of the war years that held every Japanese American—like the Japanese themselves—to be untrustworthy. But he unwittingly reinforced the notion that "the only good Jap is a dead Jap" by pointing to the Nisei soldiers who had been killed rather than to the thousands of Nisei soldiers who survived the war, many of whom continued to serve their nation.

The outcome of Kawakita's trial also reflected a national political climate that stressed national loyalty over personal concerns. About the time Kawakita was arrested, Truman had instituted the loyalty oath, and ongoing hearings by the House Un-American Activities Committee (HUAC) coincided with his trial. Along with headlines about Kawakita in the *Los Angeles Times* were larger ones such as "Thousands of Reds Holding Government Jobs, Witness Says" and "Four New Dealers Linked to Spy Ring by Ex-Red."[48] With national loyalty such an enormous concern, Mathes made it a point to note that Kawakita had also shirked the responsibility of Japanese citizenship by registering as a Japanese citizen in 1943, only after he had passed the age for military conscription in Japan. "The defendant was not," Mathes wrote, "the kind of traitor who gives his all to some real or fancied cause espoused by an enemy. His devotion first and last was to Tomoya Kawakita." Mathes thus concluded, "The only worth-while use for the life of a traitor, such as this defendant has proved himself to be, is to serve as an example to those of weak moral fibre who may hereafter be tempted to commit treason against the United States."[49] The appellate court, on June 22, 1951, and the Supreme Court, on June 2, 1952, affirmed both the conviction and the death sentence. A majority of the Supreme Court justices ruled that neither Kawakita nor any American should be able to "turn [U.S. citizenship] into a fair-weather citizenship, retaining it for possible contingent benefits but meanwhile playing the part of the traitor. An American citizen owes allegiance to the United States wherever he may reside."[50] The highest court of the land had spoken: unmanly cowardice and connivance deserved the sternest punishment.

Ironically, the *Los Angeles Times* seemed to think that Kawakita's trial and death sentence demonstrated that Californians were able to treat Nisei fairly and without prejudice. Ignoring the troubling issues about the jury's deliberation, the *Los Angeles Times* commended Mathes for presiding over a "meticulously fair trial" and declared that Kawakita's guilty verdict "completes the answer to the West Coast's Nisei problem." In this self-congratulatory editorial, the *Times* asserted that the decision demonstrated that the "American system" was color-blind. It could honor the Japanese American war hero with a Congressional Medal of Honor—awarded posthumously to Sadao Munemori—and punish the Japanese American who had betrayed the United States. Both men got what they deserved, claimed the *L.A. Times*, not for being a Nisei but for "being an American, possessor of a birthright not to be disdained."[51] Yet this writer's celebration of American fair play and justice for the west coast's Nisei featured one dead Japanese American and another who was soon to be sentenced to death. Ignoring this paradox, the *Times* used Kawakita's case to tout Californians' tolerance and progress in race relations. It published a photo of Fujizawa and a former POW embracing and smiling at each other with the caption "No Enmity" on the same page headlined by news about the trial, to send the message that "good" Nisei would be warmly accepted by the larger society whereas "bad" Nisei would be duly punished.[52]

The west coast's "Nisei problem" involved, most of all, the reintegration of the Japanese Americans into communities that were initially unwelcoming. By the time of Kawakita's trial, public discussion about the American sense of "fair play" and the blood sacrifice of the Nisei soldiers forced west coast residents to submerge public bigotry toward the Japanese Americans or be vulnerable to accusations of being "like Nazis" and un-American. Kawakita's case, however, seemed to endanger the progress made since the end of the war and threatened to dredge up the latent racism. Aware that headlines about a treacherous "L.A. Jap" could impede a peaceful reintegration of Japanese Americans into their communities, the press painted Kawakita as an egregious Nisei and continued to emphasize that the Nisei veterans were honorable and loyal Americans. This concern as well as a desire to appear balanced and tolerant explained why the *Los Angeles Times*' Sunday coverage of the city's V-J Day parade during Kawakita's trial focused on the sacrifice of the Nisei soldiers. Although the parade commemorated those who had served in the Pacific, the editors chose to portray the families of Japanese Americans who fought in Europe in two of the three photographs accompanying the article to show that Japanese Americans also celebrated the victory over Japan. A photo on the front page showed a brigadier general presenting a scroll to the mother of Congressional Medal of Honor winner Munemori, and another photo inside the paper depicted 3-year-old Sharon Anne Matsuzaki waving to her father, "a veteran of the famed 442 Combat Team in V-J Parade." "'There Goes Daddy!'" the caption read, and with this portrayal of a young, attractive family—in contrast to a depiction of Kawakita writing a letter to his mother as if he were still a dependent child explaining his actions to his "mom"—the *Los Angeles Times* showed readers that many Nisei soldiers were family men, with manly, adult responsibilities.[53]

Similarly, a newspaper near Kawakita's hometown urged after the trial: "Let's remember the patriot and forget the traitor." Worried that Kawakita's case had received "too much publicity" and was reviving or reinforcing prejudice in the valley, El Centro's *Imperial Valley Press* reminded its readers that Meiji Fujizawa also came from their area. "Kawakita was the exception to the rule," it asserted, citing the bravery of the 442nd Combat Team. The *San Diego Tribune-Sun* concurred, stressing that even though Kawakita had been convicted of treason, the principles of democracy had "succeeded marvelously" with thousands of other Japanese Americans. The Japanese American internment, the paper editorialized, would "not be one of the subjects toward which we will point with pride in future years," but "in spite of the privations, sacrifices and hardships which the nation imposed upon men of Mr. Kawakita's race, hundreds of them volunteered for military service and proved themselves to be among the most valiant of our troops."[54] The self-appointed opinion makers in the press thus attempted to control the perceived damage done to the image of Japanese Americans, but at the same time, these messages implied that while the internment was wrong, the "good" Nisei did not take revenge and were not resentful of their fellow Americans for their wartime mistakes or for other discrimination the Nisei might have suffered in the past. In other words, the mainstream media acknowledged the injustice inflicted on the Japanese Americans, but refused to legitimize their anger and resentment. Japanese Americans were still forced to fit inside a box—loyal or disloyal to the United States. What had changed since 1942 was that government officials and the press were presuming most of them to be in the "loyal" category.

The issue of Japanese American loyalty, however, was more complex and ambivalent than the way it was presented by the Justice Department, the U.S. courts, the American press, Kawakita's defense attorney, or even the defendant himself, who insisted that he saw himself as a Japanese citizen when he worked at Oeyama. During the trial, the government argued that citizenship should not be used so casually, and Carter, the government prosecutor, ridiculed the idea of fair-weather citizenship.[55] Carter ignored, as did everyone else, how the trial—and the war itself—forced an artificial binary opposition that oversimplified Japanese Americans' love or devotion to Japan or the United States. The decision by the great majority of Japanese Americans to embrace the U.S. cause was presented as easy and natural. Although this portrayal helped in the necessary task of condemning the internment, it masked the pain and regret involved in repudiating Japan—especially among the immigrant Issei, but also among their American-born children, the Nisei. Discriminated against in both the United States and Hawai'i, many Japanese Americans felt understandable, if unreflective, pride in Japanese nationalism. They rejoiced in Japan's rising power and its attempt to be a peer of western imperialists—rather than their colonial subject—and they did not seem particularly disturbed that the Japanese trounced other Asians in this effort. As a relatively new immigrant group, moreover, most Japanese Americans retained cultural, social, business, and familial connections to Japan. They believed their Japanese nationalism to be largely compatible with their attachment to the United States; they naively thought they could wear two coats, to use another one of Carter's images, and that they could love both countries. War disrupted this loose, unexamined worldview, forcing them either to reject the nation of their ethnic origin or to disavow the land of their current homes, businesses, and social networks.[56] The best scenario for nearly all Japanese Americans would have been if war between the United States and Japan had never occurred, as Kō Wakatsuki tried to explain to a young military officer who was interrogating him. Asked which side Wakatsuki hoped would win the war, the Issei immigrant answered, "When your mother and your father are having a fight, do you want them to kill each other? Or do you just want them to stop fighting?"[57]

But the war compelled Japanese Americans to make choices. Most of those in America, of course, supported the U.S. war effort; likewise, many of the Nisei in Japan threw in their lot with the Japanese, as they were encouraged—and expected—to do.

After the war most Nisei in Japan "switched" allegiances again, like Kawakita, or, perhaps more accurately, allowed their attachment to America, which they kept latent during the war, to reemerge. Understandably, they tried to use their birthright to leave the starving, war-devastated nation for reunion with family members and opportunities "back home." The dilemma of Nisei trying to return to the United States was a hot-button issue among Japanese Americans when Kawakita's case materialized in mid-1947 and continued to be throughout his trial and afterward. Thousands of Nisei stranded in Japan had lost their U.S. citizenship through ignorance or circumstances beyond their control. Some took on Japanese citizenship to gain employment, as Kawakita did; others automatically lost their U.S. citizenship by joining (or being drafted into) the Japanese military, by working for the Japanese government, or by voting. Hundreds of Nisei women lost their U.S. citizenship by rushing out to vote in 1946 when Japanese women were given suffrage. According to the *Pacific Citizen,* they "hadn't the foggiest idea they were canceling their American citizenship."[58] Kawakita initially was one of the lucky ones—easily able to return home—but had he remained in Japan, he probably never would have faced a treason charge and a death sentence. A month before Kawakita's trial, another Nisei was convicted of slapping Allied prisoners of war, but because Tsuda Taihei, another former USC student, had become a Japanese citizen, he was tried in Japan by the Eighth Army and got six months of hard labor.[59]

Rather than feeling sorry for Kawakita, many Japanese Americans were furious at him for making it more difficult for the Nisei stranded in Japan to return home. When Kawakita was arrested, Nisei columnist Bill Hosokawa conceded that he might be innocent of treason against the United States, but nonetheless charged that Kawakita was a traitor to other Nisei in Japan. Kawakita was, Hosokawa pointed out, "one who sought to save his own skin at the risk of [endangering] the position of thousands of his fellows."[60] Japanese Americans noted right away that Kawakita must have falsified or hidden his record in order to gain clearance to return back to the United States. "In so doing," the *Pacific Citizen* editorialized, "he has jeopardized the security and welfare of many thousands of Nisei who deserve the right to return to their families and homes."[61] As Kawakita's case was being tried, the *Pacific Citizen* reported that five thousand Nisei had lost their U.S. citizenship and were forever alienated from their homes and families except in "the unlikely event" that immigration laws changed to permit them to return to America.[62] Acutely aware of the federal government's injustice, the Japanese Americans nonetheless blamed a fellow Nisei for hurting their group's chances for fairness. A negative "by-product" of Kawakita's case was prison sentences for some Nisei who falsified passport applications in their desperate attempts to go back to the United States. Embarrassed that Kawakita had slipped back into the United States, the State Department enacted a "stricter policy" of checking passport applications, which delayed the return home for many Nisei.[63]

Many Japanese Americans were also upset with Kawakita for having "besmirched the name of Nisei," as a Nisei war veteran later put it.[64] At the time of his indictment, the *Pacific Citizen* criticized Kawakita for tarnishing the record of the Nisei, "one for which more than 600 Americans of Japanese ancestry gave their lives to achieve." This was a poignant observation, since flag-draped coffins carrying the bodies of Nisei GIs who had died in Europe were still coming back to the United States for burial as the Kawakita case went to trial a year later.[65] Kawakita's case, it seemed to the *Pacific Citizen,* attracted more attention than "the

33,000 Americans of Japanese ancestry who served in the armed forces of the United States during [the] war."[66] To their dismay, the Nisei learned shortly after the trial that RKO was making a film about the Kawakita case. Larry Tajiri observed, "Hollywood producers have replied on several recent occasions when a film on the 442nd Combat Team was suggested that there is no public interest in a film on the Nisei. However, a picture on a Nisei traitor, an isolated case in contrast to the 30,000 Nisei who served in the U.S. Army during the war, apparently is a matter of interest as far as RKO studio is concerned."[67]

Concerned and protective of their group image, the Nisei Veterans Association of Los Angeles even suggested requiring that Nisei seeking to return to the United States have their names and photographs published in American newspapers to "enable former prisoners and loyal Nisei to spot potential suspects."[68] Like Jewish Americans, Japanese Americans were aware of the larger society's hostility toward them, and these Nisei veterans—perhaps like the Jewish lawyers and judge who prosecuted the Rosenbergs and sentenced them to death—preferred to see racial guilt individualized rather than attributed to their entire group. As an even more marginalized group, whose internment was still a recent memory, Japanese Americans made preemptive moves to root out bad examples whom they believed might hurt the entire group. Thus the much-touted presence of a "Nisei girl" on the jury might have been disadvantageous to Kawakita rather than favorable to him, as it was presented. Many Japanese Americans had internalized Euroamericans' opinions of them, and most sought to be inconspicuous after the war. They were often quite critical of members of their group, especially those who did not seem "American" enough.[69] Rather than blaming the government for the internment, some Japanese Americans even castigated members of their own group for not assimilating enough or for acting in a manner that might reflect badly on the group in the eyes of the larger society. Moreover, the government's case in the Kawakita trial rested on its claim that Nisei were American citizens, whereas the defense argued that Nisei like Kawakita, as Japanese nationals born of Japanese parents outside Japan, had an allegiance to Japan—the very thing the Nisei in America had been denying since December 7, 1941.[70]

Japanese American fears that the Kawakita trial would undo the progress being made in the postwar years were nevertheless unfounded. Nobody publicly used the Kawakita trial to justify the internment. Instead, the media and the government continued to characterize the internment as an unwarranted mistake. The *Washington Post* editorialized in August 1948 that the "history of this country's treatment of its West Coast citizens of Japanese descent is a shameful one." The paper praised Federal District Judge Louis E. Goodman of California for restoring U.S. citizenship to internees who had renounced it in the camps. Rather than seeing those who had renounced their citizenship as "fair-weather citizens," the paper approvingly quoted Goodman when he said, "It is shocking to the conscience that an American citizen be confined without authority and then, while so under duress and restraint for the Government to accept from him a surrender of his constitutional heritage."[71] Californians also participated in this about-face, including Los Angeles mayor Fletcher Bowron, who had loudly advocated for the removal of the Japanese Americans in 1942, but praised them effusively in 1948. Speaking at a ceremony for the first reburial of Nisei soldiers in Los Angeles, Bowron pronounced, "The integrity of all those of Japanese blood born in this country, as well as the best majority (if not all) of Japanese nationals who had chosen this land as their place of permanent residence, has been definitely, completely established for all time."[72]

Progress on achieving racial equality for Japanese Americans thus continued despite the treason trial of Kawakita and that of Iva Toguri, the so-called "Tokyo Rose." In the same month when a federal grand jury indicted Toguri and Mathes sentenced Kawakita to die, the ACLU declared in its annual report, "These Uncertain Liberties," that the Japanese Americans had secured the "most encouraging results" in removing discriminatory laws against them. Although the Japanese Americans failed in their efforts to repeal the 1924 Oriental Exclusion act, they managed to win a number of victories: congressional approval to establish a claims commission for damages up to $2,500 for the losses incurred in the evacuation; the first step in repealing the Alien Land Law by allowing Issei to buy land in the names of their American-born offspring again; the U.S. Supreme Court declaration of the California anti-alien fishing amendment as unconstitutional; progress in bringing home Nisei "strandees" from Japan and taking home hundreds of Japanese Peruvians who were also interned in the United States; and the invalidation of Tule Lake internees' renunciation of U.S. citizenship by California federal courts. The ACLU report stated, "The tragic accompaniments of the wartime evacuation, hostility, and prejudices have not, as the record shows, been wholly overcome as yet, but they are on their way to such amends as can be made."[73]

The Japanese Americans even attracted prominent national leaders to their cause. Several months before he was appointed Secretary of State, Dean Acheson argued on behalf of the appellants of the Alien Land Law case, *Oyama v. California*, when it was presented before the Supreme Court.[74] A week after Kawakita was found guilty of treason, the Hood River American Legion, along with the Veterans of Foreign Wars, held services for a local Nisei who had died in Leyte. Also participating in the ceremony to honor Frank Hachiya were the state representative of the Daughters of the American Revolution, a former governor of Oregon, the president of Reed College, and Dillon S. Myer, wartime head of the War Relocation Authority (WRA).[75] Public leaders, even conservative ones, were now actively showing their support for a previously despised ethnic group.

Despite this progress, fighting for racial equality for Japanese Americans or any racial minority remained a tough battle in 1948 and beyond. Discrimination at public places remained an everyday reality. For example, ten members of the Los Angeles chapter of the Congress of Racial Equality (CORE), including Euroamericans, African Americans, and Japanese Americans, were water-hosed when they conducted nonviolent action in June 1948 to get the management of Blimini Hot Springs to admit blacks and Asians; it was their tenth failed attempt.[76] The Supreme Court ruled in 1948 that racial covenants restricting the sale of property to African Americans and Asian Americans were now unenforceable by the state, but still legal if individuals adhered to them on a voluntary basis.[77] A realtor in Glendale, California, received "upwards of forty protesting calls" when she announced that she planned to rent a house to a "fine Japanese family." A mysterious fire burned down the house the day before the family was to move into it.[78] The McCarran-Walter Act of 1952 finally allowed Issei to become naturalized U.S. citizens and allowed an annual quota of 185 Japanese to immigrate to the United States, but it did not represent a sea change in racial attitudes. It passed Congress only because its advocates promised that the legislation would improve relations with Japan without affecting the white majority of the United States. The Issei were a

group that was gradually becoming extinct, and the tiny quota—
less than 1/1500th of 1 percent of the total U.S. population—
meant that the immigration would not pose "any danger to the
United States, whether economically, culturally, socially, politically, or in any other respect."[79] Meanwhile, a disproportionate
number of Nisei and other racial minorities remained relegated to
low-paying, low-skill jobs in the immediate postwar period. The
California Employment Service reported in 1949 that 75 percent
of San Francisco Bay Area retail businesses stated that they did
not want "Orientals," while 90 percent said they did not want
"Negroes," and many unions remained hostile to the inclusion of
either group.[80] Despite the very positive 1948 ACLU report about
the advancements made in eliminating racial discrimination, the
task was hardly complete, as the ACLU itself recognized.

Japanese Americans nonetheless were correct in believing that
Kawakita's actions reflected badly on their group. To some of
their fellow Americans, Kawakita's death sentence probably
served as punishment for Japanese (and perceived Japanese American) sins. After Mathes sentenced Kawakita to die, Harold Keats,
the national commander of the American Veterans of World War
II (Amvets) telegraphed the judge commending him for his "courage" in exacting "justice."[81] When President Eisenhower was
considering clemency for Kawakita, Los Angeles resident Angela
Riggs wrote him to say:

> Don't get soft on these Japs Mr. President. I just read where they
> put up a monument to the Warlord Tojo, and you are forever mak-
> ing concessions to the Japs. They are not our friends, as you found
> out not so long ago, you should forever keep in mind our brave
> American heroes who were mutilated, bayonetted, eyes gouged out
> etc. Don't forget Bataan! . . . A Jap is a Jap always no matter where
> he is born.[82]

By the time Riggs wrote this letter, fifteen years had passed since the end of the Pacific War, but as her words show, old fears and hatreds persisted and were now expressed in a mixture of World War II and gendered Cold War lingo. The confusion between Japanese nationals and Americans of Japanese ancestry stubbornly remained. Mathes's pains to separate loyal Japanese Americans from disloyal ones had been lost on Americans like Riggs. But Mathes had undermined his own purpose by relying on the old stereotype that Japanese gained western knowledge only to use it against westerners. And the death sentence itself suggested that brutalities (notably not homicide) committed by a minority man against Euroamerican men deserved the ultimate punishment.

Aftermath

Unable to reverse the conviction, Kawakita and Lavine had tried to have the severity of Kawakita's sentence lessened. On October 29, 1953, President Eisenhower reduced Kawakita's sentence to life imprisonment, and the tireless Lavine continued to press for executive clemency. Eisenhower received many petitions—mostly from Japan—and continued to receive them after the commutation; they requested that Kawakita be released from prison and allowed to return to Japan. Kawakita's sisters referred in a letter to "a huge bundle of documents—appeals from Japan" at the Pardon Office, complaining that they had not been translated.[83] Kawakita had friends in high places. The governor of Mie, the Kawakita family's home prefecture, personally cabled Eisenhower expressing his appreciation when the President commuted Kawakita's death sentence, and at least one other Japanese politician—a member of the House of Councillors—wrote to Eisenhower on Kawakita's behalf.[84] Another politician, Miki Takeo, who became Prime Minister of Japan during the mid-1970s, was a family friend. The Kawakitas and Miki came from the same prefecture, Mie, and Kawakita senior, a wealthy grocer and merchant, had served as a mentor to Miki when he came to the United States for study. In fact, Miki was the one who found Kawakita the job at the Oeyama Nickel Company in the first place. By the time of the trial, Miki was a member of Japan's House of Representatives. Given his connection to his mentor's son's situation, Miki undoubtedly used his influence to make appeals to U.S. government officials as well.[85]

Racial discrimination against Japanese Americans had been a long-standing sore point in U.S.-Japanese relations dating to the beginning of the twentieth century, and the Japanese echoed the complaint by Kawakita's sisters that "injustice and prejudice" had prevailed in Kawakita's trial, conviction, and sentencing. They questioned the fairness of having Kawakita tried in California, given its history of racial animosity toward Japanese Americans—their evacuation and internment being a recent, glaring example. Japanese government officials generally cared more about the Japanese image abroad than they did about the welfare of actual Japanese Americans, but it seems that concern for Kawakita himself motivated members of the Japanese government, thanks to his connections. This reproach came at a time when the American government had become more sensitive to the effect of Euroamerican racism on potential and current nonwhite allies in the postwar world order. Indeed, an argument can be made that racism kept Kawakita in jail longer than others charged with World War II treason. For instance, the German émigré Hans Haupt also had received a death sentence for treason, which President Roosevelt commuted to life imprisonment, but he was able to return to Germany as a free man within five years.[86] The petitions for clemency for Kawakita continued into the Kennedy administration and emphasized racism. The president of Kawakita's alma mater, Meiji University, appealed to Kennedy on behalf of the university's faculty members and 33,000 students, and suggested that Kawakita had been denied a fair trial because of the "rather abnormal post-war situation."[87]

At first, the Kennedy administration stood by its predecessor's decision not to parole Kawakita. In 1961 the Reverend Haru Teriumi, a pastor to one of Kawakita's sisters, spearheaded a failed petition drive to coordinate the commutation of Kawakita's sentence with Attorney General Robert F. Kennedy's trip to Japan. Two years later, however, the Attorney General's office reversed its opinion and endorsed commutation to time served on the condition that Kawakita leave the United States forever.[88] A memorandum to the President signed by the Attorney General noted that various officials who had been involved in the trial held different opinions about granting clemency to Kawakita— Judge Mathes remained adamantly opposed—but emphasized that the chief prosecutor and the appellate judge who wrote the opinion affirming Kawakita's conviction now "unhesitatingly recommend[ed] clemency." Former U.S. attorney James M. Carter, by now a U.S. District Judge in the Southern District of California, the district that tried Kawakita, recommended that Kawakita be paroled on the condition that he never return to the United States.[89] The Attorney General passed on this recommendation to his brother, stating that although Kawakita had been found guilty of brutality toward fellow Americans, "justice would not be ill-served" if he were released since he had been incarcerated "a very substantial length of time," sixteen years, during which he had been a model prisoner. The cover memo by Robert Kennedy's executive assistant also mentions that the Japan desk at the State Department favored the action, as Kawa-kita's release "would be helpful" to U.S.-Japan relations.[90] President Kennedy paroled Kawakita on October 24, 1963. By mid-December of 1963, Kawakita was in Tokyo, where he lived until his death in the mid-1990s.[91]

In the end, Tomoya Kawakita survived his nightmare in the American legal system. Though he was probably guilty of some abuse, Kawakita's actions were not so heinous as to lead POWs to accuse him immediately upon the liberation of Camp Oeyama. Clearly something other than the purported crimes themselves warranted the expenditure of hundreds of thousands of dollars to prosecute this Japanese American.[92] That "something" included a complex mixture of personal goals, anxiety about national firmness in waging the Cold War, and domestic concerns, including resentment by minorities and the reintegration of the Japanese Americans.

Kawakita's treason trial revealed Americans' continued wariness about their new ally, Japan. During the war, Americans widely viewed treachery as characteristic of the Japanese, and before the war, they often regarded "orientals" in general as cunning. The smaller body size of the Japanese led Americans to assume they were physically weaker than westerners—as women were physically weaker than men—and thus they had to resort to sly, nefarious methods. Such perceptions, of course, had prepared Americans to see the preemptive attack on Pearl Harbor as an act of "yellow-bellied" backstabbing. In contrast, they portrayed Germany's invasion of Poland as rape by a stronger, masculine force that ultimately could not be "appeased." Americans have rarely viewed the attack on Pearl Harbor as a violation of a female body for the obvious reason that it was an assault on their country; this image would not fit their perception of America as a sturdy, virile power. Similarly, Kawakita's case, in the eyes of many Americans, proved that the Japanese (American) would not challenge Americans in a fair, manly contest and would only dare to attack when the American was already down. Although the postwar American media, working toward bilateral harmony, muted their anti-Japanese rhetoric, many Americans persisted in seeing the Japanese as mysterious and potentially lethal.

Public officials sought to condemn the self-seeking lack of patriotism that Kawakita represented among minority citizens. Some minority leaders, aware of this anxiety, testified in front of HUAC to vouch for the loyalty of their ethnic group.[93] Perhaps Kawakita embodied the ultimate "No-No Boy"—the name used to describe interned Japanese American men who refused on a questionnaire to pledge their allegiance to the United States and to serve in the Armed Forces, and who therefore were ostracized by other Japanese Americans after the war. The draft-dodger Kawakita, by managing to elude service in the Japanese armed forces, effectively said "no-no" to both countries and chose self-preservation over either nation.[94] Making an example of Kawakita served to remind racial minorities that they, too, were expected to be patriotic Americans. Claims of ill treatment or discrimination by the dominant society failed to excuse a member of a racial minority for being disloyal. In the same way that *Life* magazine used the example of Jackie Robinson to counterbalance the communism of Paul Robeson, Judge Mathes stressed the examples of "good" Japanese Americans—the 442nd Regimental Combat Team/100th Infantry Battalion and individuals like Meiji Fujizawa.[95]

Few today remember Tomoya Kawakita. Even at the time, the case of the other Japanese American tried for treason received much more extensive national coverage than Kawakita's trial.[96] The government prosecution of "Tokyo Rose," the enchantress who spoke freely over the airwaves, was what people remembered. Irreversibly implicated in a gendered myth about an enthralling, "oriental" siren, Iva Toguri was imprisoned for nearly a decade for a crime she did not commit. Kawakita and Toguri symbolized both a cultural and a racial menace—a "yellow peril"—to the national body, but more important, their trials reinforced wartime ideas about "cowardly" Japanese treachery. The rapid transition from "Jap enemy" to "Japanese friend," and from "sneaky Jap in our midst" to "our loyal citizens of Japanese ancestry," was not smooth. It included ambiguity and contradictions, although there were no significant setbacks. Like Kawakita, "Rose" in Toguri's physical embodiment was punished, but Toguri was officially vindicated; her tragedy is well known. Kawakita died in obscurity, in exile from the land of his birth.

CHAPTER FIVE

A Kamikaze Goes to College

Although the treacherous, myopic, bucktoothed "Jap" continued to make appearances in American popular culture after World War II, he competed with another character, less dehumanized and much better suited as a postwar ally. On December 26, 1956, ABC's prime-time series *Navy Log* presented its television viewers with a figure unimaginable during the war: a handsome, pro-American Japanese male worthy of American friendship and benevolence. Although the federal government's imprint was often invisible or missing from Cold War popular culture, it was emblazoned in *Navy Log*. The series announced its endorsements from the Departments of the Navy and Defense at the beginning and end of each episode. Produced for only three seasons in the mid-fifties, *Navy Log* tried to entertain, edify, and instill support for U.S. policies through its weekly dramatizations of stories from "official US Navy files."[1] That December night in 1956, *Navy Log* aired "A Guy Named Mickey," an episode that urged Americans to rethink lingering wartime images of the "Jap" enemy and to see the Japanese as students of democracy needing U.S. guidance and mentoring.

"A Guy Named Mickey" opens with a scene in wartime Japan. An American Navy pilot whose plane has crashed over enemy territory regains consciousness to find himself being nursed by a Japanese man in a clean but dilapidated hut, as an older Japanese woman looks on. The man introduces himself as Mikio Toyama and informs the pilot that he and his widowed mother will hide him from the Japanese authorities until the end of the war. Expressing amazement at their intention, the pilot stammers that they would be risking death for aiding an enemy. Mikio explains in impeccable English:

> True, but I don't consider you an enemy, lieutenant. There are a few of us here in Japan—many of us—who consider Pearl Harbor dishonorable—a violation of international law. It is true that there are those of my countrymen who would consider my having you here dishonorable, but this is a risk I take. My father was murdered for his beliefs. This is my chance in my own small way to repay you for this injustice [of Pearl Harbor]—Consider yourself a guest in my house.

Mikio, or "Mickey" as the pilot dubs him, explains that he learned his principles from his late father, a University of Michigan–educated judge who served on Japan's "supreme court." Recounting a prewar tale, shown as a flashback to the television audience, Mikio remembers his father giving him a sword, which he is surprised to find is welded into its scabbard. Judge Toyama intones that the sword, never to be drawn, should remind his son that "true law" lies not with brute force but with codes of justice inscribed in books. After hearing this story, the pilot nods his head in affirmation. As he sips the soup Mikio has given him, the American appears nourished not only by the food but also by the knowledge that kindred souls—sensible rather than fanatical people—could be found among the enemy.

In the next scene, which takes place a few years later, the American pilot is now the commander of a battleship. No longer the incredulous young man whom Mikio and his mother saved, the commander smokes a pipe as he paternalistically watches two enlisted men trying to choose a worthy cause for their ship's Christmas charity. Suddenly, the commander recalls "Mickey" and interrupts the men to suggest that the ship fund a college scholarship for his old Japanese friend. The two balk at the idea, explaining petulantly that they had hoped to give money to orphans near the U.S. naval base in Yokosuka until "another ship beat us to it." Seeing their reluctance, the commander urges the men to see a scholarship for Mickey as an "investment in our own future":

> If we educate Toyama in the United States then he can go back to Japan and tell his people how we think and how we feel. He can tell them that we don't wear horns. That we're not out to hurt anyone, only to help. He could become, well, what—a goodwill ambassador. If people could understand us—then maybe they wouldn't go out and start a war someday.

Helping Mickey, the commander asserts, would demonstrate America's goodwill, benefit U.S.-Japan relations, and prevent future Japanese aggression. Implicitly repudiating a stereotype of the Japanese as cunning and treacherous, the commander projects confidence that Mikio—like his American-educated father, who bravely criticized Japan's aggression during the war—would acquire a western education to promote, not undermine, peaceful relations with westerners. Convinced by the commander's wisdom, the men organize a fund-raiser and collect $5,000 to send Mikio to his father's alma mater. The final scene shows the commander and the same two enlisted men congratulating Mikio at his graduation. Mikio thanks them effusively and assures them that their generosity will bear fruit: in Japan, he says, there will be at least "one advocate of ideas of peace and, above all, understanding among men."

"A Guy Named Mickey" showed American viewers a "good" Japanese man, a character noticeably absent during the war. Although wartime discourse in America differentiated the "good" Germans from the evil Nazis, it did not redeem any Japanese until the war's end. Many postwar stories focused on relationships between Euroamerican men and young Japanese women, but since the only female in the television episode was Mikio's unattractive, unsmiling mother, all attention was focused on the positive presentation of Mikio. Mickey/Mikio is depicted as a humanitarian and a risk-taker, ashamed of and hoping to atone for Pearl Harbor. Rather than being embittered by his reduced state, he is properly grateful for the Americans' friendship and aid. Indeed, he understands the U.S. bombing raids on his homeland as justifiable retribution for the surprise attack, and he hopes his people have learned their lesson. He is even a fan of American football; Mikio seeks no information from the pilot other than that year's contenders for the Rose Bowl.

Unlike asexual or effeminate "oriental" characters like Charlie Chan or Fu Manchu, the "good" Japanese is good-looking and manly. The actor who plays Mikio in the television feature is a handsome Asian with erect posture, even features, and good vision; he speaks flawless American English as well as excellent Japanese.[2] He is the exact opposite of the stooping, bowlegged, myopic wartime caricature who barked guttural noises or bellowed "banzai!" Mikio's statement that many other Japanese found Pearl Harbor dishonorable suggested to American viewers that Japan had more men like him, and that teaching them "the

American way of life" would ensure an enduring peace between the two countries.

The moral of "A Guy Named Mickey" is one of Euroamerican magnanimity in racial tolerance: the Japanese can be our friends, if we let them. The sailors first recoil at the thought of helping a Japanese man, but later in the program they come to the aid of another Asian man. When they witness a boorish officer calling an Asian bartender by the wrong name, as if the man's identity did not matter, the two sailors angrily correct the officer to emphasize the man's individuality. Though left unsaid, the lesson, "Asians are not all alike," could hardly be missed. It is significant that *Navy Log*'s producers had working-class men—the regular Joes rather than the commander—come to the defense of an Asian and challenge a higher-up in the process, thus illustrating how the enlisted men had absorbed their wise commander's lecture on racial tolerance. Reminiscent of SCAP's orientation materials for GIs serving in Occupied Japan, this show urged the regular Joes in the television audience to contribute toward tolerance and world peace. The Asian bartender, although irritated and resentful of the officer, remains silent during the incident and relies on the Euroamericans to restore his dignity. He smiles gratefully at the sailors after they speak up for him. The lesson, then, was that Euroamericans should be correcting each other's rude, racist actions. Success in teaching the Mikios and other Asians that Americans were not "out to hurt anyone, only to help" depended on the social behavior of Euroamericans toward their new allies in Asia.

Sending the Junior Ally to American College Campuses

Scholarship recipient Mikio Toyama had real-life counterparts— the Japanese students who received American funding to study on

American campuses after the war. The scholarship programs for Japanese students reflected mid-century notions about race and civilization. American policymakers and their supporters continued to see their own culture and political economy as among the most highly developed societies in a racialized linear continuum of civilizations, but now believed that nonwhite, "primitive" or "feudal" societies could truly mature into "modern" ones. Cold War liberal policymakers espoused what later became known as modernization theory, a set of political and economic beliefs that not only compared societies to maturing, living species but also asserted that development or "modernization" could occur within a shorter period if a society was given the proper support and infrastructure. They claimed that economic growth—not societal overhaul—would bring increasing abundance, spread contentment, and diminish class conflict throughout the world. This view, embraced by former New Dealers as well as internationalist Republicans, characterized the Cold War liberal consensus. Although these liberals acted with self-interest in that they sought to guarantee foreign markets for American producers, they were also evangelists and true believers, convinced of the rightness of their nation's mission to extend its political institutions and free-enterprise system throughout the world.[3]

The Cold War liberal consensus and the program for Japanese students conveniently dovetailed with concerns that the occupation of Japan would divert energy and funds from America's primary international interest, the Cold War in Europe. U.S. policymakers decided to fast-track Japan's economic recovery so that it could, in John Foster Dulles's words, help "to resist and throw back communism in this part of the world."[4] With speedy economic recovery now the top priority, SCAP countermanded its former objectives during the Occupation's "reverse course" so that the purges, the land reforms, the *zaibatsu* trust-busting, the reparations—especially of industrial equipment to the victims of Japanese wartime aggression—and other grand goals to remake Japan and Asia into truly democratic societies were truncated and left unfulfilled. American policymakers judged Japan, the only Asian state with an extensive industrial base prior to 1945, as "the sole great potential military-industrial arsenal of the Far East." They chose to support Japan over other Asian nations, including America's recent wartime allies—such as the Philippines, which finally gained political independence from the United States in 1946.[5] Japan was selected to embody "the free way of life" and to be an exemplary student of democracy and capitalism that all other Asian countries could emulate.

Juveniles, Americans agreed, required proactive intervention and structured programs to keep them from becoming unruly; after all, children and youth presumably exercised less control over their behavior and tended to overestimate their abilities in hazardous ways. To prevent juvenile delinquency among youth, Americans promoted productive outlets for their time in community work, sports, civic clubs, and the like. To prevent the Japanese from becoming troublemakers—from thinking that they could "lick the whole cockeyed world"—the Occupation government started a scholarship program to foster the appropriate pro-American views in this "cornerstone" of America's Pacific security system. Called GARIOA scholarships because SCAP used public funds allocated by the 80th Congress for "Government and Relief in Occupied Areas" to finance it, this scholarship program brought a total of 1,066 Japanese students to American college and university campuses from 1949 through 1952 when the Occupation ended.[6] The stated goal for the GARIOA scholarships was similar to the ones funded by private individuals, like the scholarship given to the fictional "Mickey": that the students would return home and spread favorable opinions about America in "ever-widening circles" to their fellow citizens, and would instruct the Japanese that Americans, as the commander put it, "don't wear horns." By allowing Japanese "leader types" to live in America, the scholarships were meant to imbue them with an "enthusiasm to communicate" to their fellow citizens "accurate information and intelligent ideas" about American life and culture. Their experience in America, the sponsors hoped, would inspire the Japanese students to help their country develop "citizenship responsibility" and improve education along American lines.[7]

At the same time, the transformation from enemy to "junior ally" was closely tied to conscious efforts to make Americans more internationally minded and racially tolerant—as befitting their new role as global leaders. Cold War liberals were concerned about their fellow citizens' readiness for and willingness to embrace global leadership. Most Americans were preoccupied, pursuing consumerist dreams previously denied by economic depression and war. Others were prewar isolationists insistent, now that the war was over, on an "America first" outlook; still others were racists who continued to see the "Japs" as unredeemable enemies. The majority of Americans were probably either indifferent or hostile to the project of remaking Japan in America's image. Cold War liberals thus recognized that their fellow Americans—like the working-class sailors who had to be persuaded into sponsoring "Mickey"—needed to learn racial tolerance for the sake of national security and the international struggle against communism. Containing the Soviets meant not only supporting "the free peoples who [were] resisting attempted subjugation by armed minorities or by outside pressures," as the Truman Doctrine pledged, but also wooing newly decolonized nations and the former Asian enemy as client states.[8] Stark limits on the freedoms of America's minority citizens, however, made its claim to be the "leader of the free world" a hollow one—a contradiction that Soviet propaganda highlighted.[9] In Japan, American racism had been a source of anti-American sentiment since the turn of the century. To diminish racial friction, SCAP censored news of racial incidents and tacitly ignored racism as a problem. In contrast, the sponsors of the privately and publicly funded scholarships attempted to bring about positive change—they created the scholarships not only to educate Japanese students but also to teach Americans to confront their intolerance by dealing with Japanese students in their midst.

The presence of the recent enemy on American campuses full of World War II veterans thus provided a lesson in postwar reconciliation and racial tolerance. Although this lesson may not have been thoroughly learned, it nonetheless was one that American policymakers and internationally-minded fellow citizens promoted. The clean-cut, respectful Japanese students—like the Asian American "model minorities" of later decades—provided reassuring examples of proper social relations that allowed Americans to be self-congratulatory about their progress in race relations and to reaffirm the wisdom and decency of American society, its educational system, its free-enterprise economy, and its values. In short, the Japanese students served as another validation of the liberal consensus.

Ex-Kamikaze and Scholarship Student

Eight years before "A Guy Named Mickey" aired, the first Japanese national to attend an American college after World War II enrolled at Lafayette College in Easton, Pennsylvania.[10] His jour-

ney to America began because of a lanky, baby-faced Pennsylvania teenager, Robert S. Johnstone. A gifted student, Johnstone
skipped the last half of his senior year in high school to attend Lafayette at the beginning of 1944. He had already finished six
months of course work toward an engineering degree when he
was drafted into the Army in September. Bound by a sense of obligation, he refused to use his college status for a deferment and
sailed to the Philippines by Christmas, after three months' training at Fort Wheeler, Georgia. He faced combat at Leyte, enjoyed
a short furlough, and was then sent with his company to help secure Manila's water source—the Ipo Dam sector on Luzon. He
died there on May 14, 1945, while attempting to destroy a Japanese machine gun post. He was eighteen years old. The teenager had been armed with a Browning Automatic Rifle (BAR),
and BAR men, as they were called, often drew the heaviest fire
from the enemy because of their weapon's deadly potential. Johnstone's high school friend was on grave preparation duty and did
not know Robert was in the Philippines until he came across
Robert's body a week later, after the American forces were able to
retrieve their dead from Ipo Dam. Johnstone's family, who first
had learned that Robert was missing in action, received news of
his death.[11]

At a family conference shortly thereafter, Johnstone's father
convinced the rest of his family to use his $10,000 life insurance
policy to establish a tuition scholarship at Lafayette College in
his memory. Remarkably, Johnstone's father wanted the scholarship to go to a Japanese student, even though a Japanese soldier
had killed his beloved son. He invited the president of Lafayette,
Ralph Cooper Hutchinson, to his home to discuss the idea as
early as September 1945. Hutchinson greeted the plan with enthusiasm, and by the end of October, Lafayette's Board of Trus-

tees had approved the establishment of an international scholarship. Johnstone and his wife stipulated that the student given the
scholarship should visit their home "so we may exchange view-
points on international good will and establish a friendly and
homey contact during his stay at Lafayette." Hutchinson put it
more pedantically: the visits to the Johnstones were to impress
the scholarship recipient with "the spirit of hospitality and understanding in which this memorial is given and which makes it so
appropriate as a memorial to Bob."[12]

In January 1946, when the media reported the extraordinary
news of a dead soldier's family using his insurance money to fund
education for a Japanese student, Johnstone's father explained:

> I established this fund because I don't think we are going to have
> peace by settling the war with hate and hard terms. My wife and I
> are trying to do our small share by helping other people to keep the
> peace. Only by goodwill can we win out. I mentioned the Japanese
> in the scholarship terms because my son was killed by the Japanese.
> It would help, I think, if those people saw the light.[13]

The Johnstones believed that wars could be averted if all people,
including the Japanese, were enlightened by "the Christian spirit
of good will," and asserted that their dead son had felt the same
way.[14] Since early Occupation regulations prohibited Japanese
citizens from traveling overseas, the family conceded that the
scholarship could be given to "a Chinese, a Korean or Philippino
[sic] or other member of the yellow race" until the travel restriction on the Japanese could be lifted. Since the Johnstones meant
the scholarship to be an act of Christian humanitarianism, they
thought that giving it to "a member of the white race whose intention would be to serve as a missionary to the Orient would
also be desirable."[15] Although the Johnstone scholarship pre-

dated the GARIOA scholarships, they shared the overall goal of "re-educating" the Japanese in the ways of peace and democracy. Unlike the publicly funded scholarships, however, the Johnstones candidly relied on Christian ethics to justify their philanthropy. As committed Christians, the Johnstones held that the spread of a single set of values, which they believed to be heaven-sent, would ensure a better physical and spiritual world. They were part of a significant minority of Americans who actively sought postwar reconciliation with the Japanese and cited their Christian faith as their primary motive, taking literally Christ's message to "love one's enemies."[16] The Johnstones demonstrated exceptional goodwill to a people responsible for their son's death when emotions about the war were still so raw, and their contemporaries recognized their generous spirit. Positive press reaction to the announcement of the scholarship in early 1946 praised it as a shining example of "practical Christianity," a turning of "the other cheek," and an "expression" of "God's love."[17] This Christian outreach, however, did not mark a reconciliation of equals but rather paralleled the secular, liberal presumptions about American political, social, economic, and cultural superiority over the Japanese, who needed, according to the senior Johnstone, "to see the light." This Christian outreach, then, reinforced Cold War liberal ideology about spreading American economic and political institutions throughout the world, and it cast the effort to make Japan an American client state as a moral act of bestowing benevolence, enlightenment, and education.

As it turned out, the Occupation authorities would not permit any Japanese to travel overseas in 1946, so a Chinese student, Frederick Wong, was the first recipient of the Johnstone scholarship. A year later, Lafayette announced that with assistance from the American Presbyterian Board of Missions, it had selected the first Japanese scholarship recipient: Robert Yukimasa Nishiyama, 22 years old and a veteran of the Japanese Imperial Navy. He had been assigned to the kamikaze corps and had been prepared to "smash [him]self against some American ship" if the war's end had not saved him from certain death. Ironically, although Nishiyama had been prepared to kill Americans, he had considered Americans his friends since early childhood. As long as he could remember, his family and relatives had called him "Robert," a name suggested at his birth by his mother's American friend. Their family home bordered the compound for American embassy employees in the upper-middle-class Enokizaka neighborhood of Akasaka ward in Tokyo. Nishiyama remembered picking up some English from them and playing games like "cowboys and Indians, G-men and blind-man's bluff" with the embassy children. During his prep school years at Aoyama Gakuin, Nishiyama befriended more Americans—this time, Nisei who were studying in Japan—and he read many American books and magazines. Sympathetic to Nishiyama's curiosity about America, one Nisei friend provided him with uncensored, hence illegal, American magazines. For college, Nishiyama decided to improve his command of English and chose to attend the Tokyo Foreign Language University (Gaikokugo Gakkō or Gaigo). Given his personal history, it should not be surprising that Nishiyama later married an American. Although Helen Matsuoka Nishiyama was born in Japan—and thus was denied the right to become a naturalized U.S. citizen—she grew up in California, graduated from Stanford University, and was culturally, if not legally, an American.[18]

Nishiyama was in his third year at Gaigo when the Imperial Navy's draft broke off his studies. Like Robert Johnstone, he did not shirk from what he saw as his patriotic duty, even if it meant fighting against the countrymen of his childhood playmates, his prep school classmates, and his wife. He recalls that by the time he was in his mid-teens, he had accepted Japanese government propaganda about the Greater East Asian Co-Prosperity Sphere and its goals of liberating Asia from the yoke of western imperialism. Although he had read some uncensored American magazines and even discussed on several occasions the "evils of military actions" with an American teacher at Aoyama Gakuin, he later reflected that he "was much too young and did not have sufficient knowledge to analyze conflicting information to pass my own judgment." As he explained in his application essay for the Johnstone scholarship, he was ready to be a kamikaze, but the war ended and shattered any lingering belief he had in the Greater East Asian Co-Prosperity Sphere. By the time of his application Nishiyama, along with many Japanese, had "embraced defeat" and was working as a superintendent managing a construction job for the U.S. Air Force officers' club.

The Johnstone Scholarship selection committee chose Nishiyama over six other finalists on the basis of his letters of recommendation, academic record, application essay—which Lafayette President Hutchinson praised for its grammatical correctness— and his ability to support himself in the United States. Since the scholarship covered only tuition, the college asked applicants to demonstrate that they could pay for all other expenses, including room, board, books, and travel. Nishiyama showed that he could secure financial backing from his in-laws' former business partner, who had shared an agricultural enterprise in Berkeley with the Matsuokas. It was only a matter of time before the Occupation government gave Nishiyama permission to leave Japan. As he, the Johnstones, and Lafayette College waited, heated discussion about the scholarship ensued.

The announcement of the scholarship's establishment in early 1946 had elicited some media attention in America, mostly positive or neutral, although there was one angry letter to the college from a father whose son had died on the Bataan Death March.[19] But a year later in January and February 1947, news that an "ex-kamikaze" would be attending Lafayette brought renewed attention and more negative reaction to the scholarship and the college. A Marine veteran wrote President Hutchinson to "feverently [sic] protest the admission of Jap citizen Robert Y. Nishiyama to Lafayette College or any other similar institutions of higher learning." He claimed:

> I am voicing an opinion shared by hundreds of ex-servicemen like myself, and by the mothers of American Soldiers, Sailors and Marines who were brutally destroyed by the finatical [sic] "human bombs," naval and ground forces of Japan during the war. . . . I shall never graduate from the school that will always maintain that a Jap should be kept in his place (In a peep sight).[20]

According to this ex-Marine, the Japanese were still the enemy and should be kept at the end of a gun barrel. Another veteran with similar views wrote in response to an article about the scholarship in *Time* magazine. This former POW claimed he supported relief efforts and food kitchens for distressed Japanese children and adults, "but for God's sake, let's keep them out of our colleges and universities." He said that he felt "no bitterness" against the Japanese, but neither did he feel bitterness against a rattlesnake: "I see him for the venomous, treacherous reptile he is."[21]

The scholarship supporters could not let these criticisms go unanswered. The former Marine's contention that he spoke for "hundreds of ex-servicemen" may not have been an exaggeration. Cold War liberals understood that war hatreds could not be cast aside so easily and that, unlike the Johnstones, many Americans—veterans and families and friends of fallen soldiers—still believed that the Japanese were treacherous foes who deserved no mercy. In response, the scholarship supporters battled the continuing harsh sentiment against the Japanese by implying that the detractors were being "un-Christian." Hutchinson wrote back to the ex-Marine, defending the scholarship as "the dying wish of a fighting soldier" and reminding him that "Christ teaches us after standing and fighting for the right . . . to return good for evil, to love our enemies, and to reveal the love of God." "Who are we," he asked, "in the face of such commands, to say no?"[22] Below the letter comparing the Japanese to rattlesnakes, *Time*'s editors published a letter from another Pacific war veteran to counter it. "I ha[d] encountered so much intolerance and hatred since I came back," the second former prisoner wrote, "that I had begun to believe that the tenets of this fellow Jesus of Nazareth had been forgotten." Reading about the Johnstone Scholarship, however, made him consider that "just maybe" the three and a half years that he spent as prisoner had "not been in vain."[23]

The Johnstones believed that Robert would have approved the use of his insurance money as a means to educate his former enemy. It was not, however, his dying wish; as far as his family knew, he fully expected to come back from the war and resume his studies. After he died, the family felt "it was not quite right" to use the money to buy a new car or some new furniture for their house, and they agreed upon the idea of the scholarship. The Johnstones neglected, however, to correct the story about their son's dying wish for scholarship recipient Nishiyama, who continued to believe it until informed otherwise. Nishiyama admitted that he had been "treasur[ing]" the story "as a sort of romance" or idealized story. Perhaps the story that Robert had requested the scholarship himself had helped Nishiyama assuage some feelings of guilt for benefiting from the death of a promising youth who had been killed by his countrymen.[24]

In any event, arguments employing unapologetic Christian rhetoric presented a favorable view of the scholarship and helped to counteract public criticism by those resistant to accepting the Japanese as valuable Cold War allies. Public critics had to concede that the scholarship was a "noble act" that came from "the generosity of a fine Christian family," and they resorted to less forceful arguments against the scholarship—that it came too soon after the war, or that the Johnstones' charity came at the American taxpayer's expense since a government insurance policy would be funding it.[25]

The scholarship supporters were firm in their belief that Americans needed to learn the geopolitical significance of treating Japanese students well. The *Denver Post,* for instance, commented on Nishiyama's arrival by relating a story about another Japanese student who had studied at the University of Oregon decades earlier. Matsuoka Yōsuke (probably no relation to Helen, Nishiyama's wife) found campus life fairly pleasant, "but elsewhere he was despised and discriminated against as a 'Jap.'" As a result, a potential friend to America became an enemy. "It was the same Matsuoka," the editorial pointed out, "who led the Japanese delegation out of the League of Nations . . . thus starting the league's downfall. And it was Matsuoka who as foreign minister committed Japan to the Axis." The newspaper theorized that Matsuoka might have "struggled for friendship and cooperation between the nations with the same earnestness with which he plotted America's downfall" if only his experiences in America had been more positive.[26] This argument, of course, oversimplified the discord between the United States and Japan, reducing it to the personal, individual level while ignoring the fundamental conflict between Japan's ambition for security and wealth to be achieved by carving out an empire on the Asian continent, and America's commitment to keeping China "open" for America's own economic well-being. But despite the flaws in the editorial, this human-interest story worked well rhetorically: "Whether Nishiyama will 'pay back' the parents of the dead American who are giving him his chance, or leave the country with a warped outlook as Matsuoka did, will depend to a great extent on the reception given him by the American people."

As we have seen, Cold War liberals worried about the negative effect of racism on Americans' ability to be world leaders. The Luce publications, as well as other mainstream media, chastised those inattentive to this concern—whether they were racist Southern politicians like Eugene Talmadge, Theodore Bilbo, and Strom Thurmond, or ordinary citizens who wrote letters to the editor. Two individuals who wrote incensed letters to *Life* about an "ex-kamikaze" receiving a scholarship found themselves being publicly scolded in the magazine. Both *Time* and *Life* occasionally employed the responses of other readers to take issue with readers' letters that opposed the magazine's liberal editorial line—in the same issue or in a subsequent one. Paul Hunsberger of Reading, Pennsylvania, chided angry letter writers John W. McFayden and Robert C. Buchanan in the following issue of *Life*:

> I am sorry that these United States still harbor people like McFayden (a Yale student, no less) and Buchanan. Today, a fierce struggle is being waged to create a world in which all can live with one another. We won the war, fortunately, and because we won, we have the duty of re-educating our former enemies beyond the point of ever wishing to wage war again. . . . Let us hope that the ex-

Kamikaze pilot will travel the steep road ahead with the faith and sincerity of the GI who gave him his chance. Lafayette has enhanced itself by accepting the Japanese as a student. I hope that the Yale student and the ex-gob can see the fallacy in their way of thinking—soon![27]

Similarly, the editors at *Life* published a letter by Lafayette alumnus Harvey H. Hunerberg, who claimed that when he polled ten veterans, "nine of [the] ten showed a pleased reaction" to news of the scholarship.[28] Hunerberg's was hardly a scientific poll, but the editors could not resist publishing his letter because it essentially repeated *Life*'s editorial position urging Americans to take heed of the Soviet threat and bear more responsibility in world affairs. The impatient tone of both letters implied that Buchanan and especially McFayden should have known better about the global stakes involved in re-educating the Japanese. Racial intolerance hampered America's ability "to create a world in which all can live with one another."

Less troubled by the injustice of racism, the scholarship advocates tended to emphasize forgiveness, Christ's love, racial tolerance, and geopolitics. Tellingly, arguments supporting the Johnstone Scholarship never mentioned the need to redress wrongs committed against Japanese Americans. However, postwar discourse about the need for reconciliation with the Japanese certainly marked an improvement over wartime rhetoric, which had asserted that the Japanese Americans shared not only a common heritage with the enemy but also a predilection for treachery. The supposed disloyal nature of the Japanese Americans had been used to justify their internment—similar to the sophistry that the Japanese Americans could not be trusted because they had suffered discrimination. Not all Americans believed this—some students at Northwestern University, for instance, protested as antithetical to democracy the university's decision to ban Nisei admission in the spring of 1942—but they appeared to be in the minority of Americans.[29] After the war, focus on the former Japanese enemy, rather than on fellow Americans of Japanese ancestry, allowed Americans to feel charitable and less self-critical about the wholesale uprooting and imprisonment of an ethnic group. At least two recently interned Japanese American families—one at Topaz, the other at Gila River—inquired about the Johnstone scholarship on behalf of their sons, but both were politely rejected.[30] Just as their common ancestry with the Japanese nationals made them defenseless against abuse during the war, the Japanese Americans found their dual identity—American citizens and ethnic Japanese—a disadvantage again; the scholarship selection committee rejected them as attractive, viable candidates for the postwar scholarships.[31] There was thought to be no need for Japanese Americans to spread pro-American thought "back home." Indeed, their recent past served as a reminder about the uneven distribution of American democracy and civil liberties. The available records do not show any Japanese Americans attending Lafayette during the Nishiyama years.

The spotlight on the Japanese in the postwar period resulted in the neglect of not only Japanese Americans but also other Asians—especially the Filipinos, whose country George Kennan had marked as the other "cornerstone" of America's security in the Pacific. The *Manila Times* reported news of the Johnstone Scholarship in January 1946, repeating the Johnstones' wish that the scholarship go to a Chinese, Korean, Filipino, or other Asian should it be impossible for a Japanese student to take it. This prompted at least nineteen Filipinos and one Chinese student living in the Philippines to present themselves as candidates for the scholarship, including two veterans—one with a debilitating hand injury and another who had survived a Japanese POW camp. The letter writers from the Philippines described the destruction of colleges and universities and the lack of resources in their country, their poverty and personal hardships, their "ardent desire" to begin higher education or to continue studies that had been interrupted by war.[32] Cyrus Martinez, Rosario Bobila, Leonardo G. Alfuente, and other Filipinos did not need Japan to be a shining example to them—they simply asked for and thought they deserved, after years of service to the United States, the opportunity to further their education and improve their station.[33]

But this was not to be. The Johnstones unwittingly followed official U.S. policy that by 1948 favored giving aid to Japanese over Filipinos. By withholding opportunities given to the Japanese, the United States kept the Philippines and other Asian nations underdeveloped in their role as suppliers of raw goods for Japanese industries and as consumer markets for Japanese products. This decision understandably infuriated the Filipinos: the *Manila Times* demanded, "Why should the Philippine republic agree to a deal under which the Japanese will profit and prosper and the Philippines will remain on the old colonial basis of providing basic raw materials to a former enemy in exchange for the modern equivalent of glass beads, brass rings and mirrors? Especially when the Philippines can make its own."[34] Despite their rhetoric of holding up Japan as an example to the rest of Asia, U.S. policymakers did not encourage the efforts of other Asian nations to achieve a level of industrial strength similar to Japan's.

The neglect of the Japanese Americans and other Asians like the Filipinos showed the limits of Cold War liberal concern for civil rights at home and anti-colonialism abroad. The scholarship program may have addressed racism, but by promoting magnanimity toward a single former enemy, the Japanese, it masked larger, more intractable domestic problems in America. While the press applauded the kindness shown to one Japanese student on a college campus, African Americans, Native Americans, Latinos, and other minorities throughout the country were struggling to obtain a decent basic education and access to higher education. Similarly, the success of America's experiment of bringing democracy and free-market capitalism to Japan ignored the continued exploitation of Asians, who found that the United States had another version of the hated Greater East Asian Co-Prosperity Sphere. By focusing on the Japanese students as examples of the wisdom of American policy, Cold War liberals managed to reduce race relations and international relations to personal, human-interest stories with easily comprehensible morals that omitted complex realities. The story of the Japanese scholarship students was a simple one of American generosity and triumph over racial intolerance. As the first Japanese postwar student, Nishiyama and his reception at Lafayette College set the course for this narrative.

Despite some outcry against Nishiyama's admission to Lafayette, most of the press coverage continued to be positive or neutral in 1947, as in the previous year.[35] The *Pittsburgh Press* headlined an article with "Storm Brewing over Jap Getting College Scholarship," but the text of the story was sympathetic toward the scholarship and the Johnstones' purpose to educate the former enemy. The "storm" turned out to be a formal protest signed by 51 Philadelphia-area veterans who had been denied admission to colleges, and a couple of sarcastic remarks reported in *The Lafayette*, the school newspaper. A sophomore, for instance, was overheard suggesting that the "ex-kamikaze" should make a splash at Lafayette by doing a "spectacular" suicidal dive into a campus building. *The Lafayette* printed these comments with a disclaimer that they did not reflect the opinions of the editorial staff and juxtaposed them with an editorial that called the Johnstone Scholarship "the most important thing that has happened to an American college in the last twenty years."[36] The editorial also chastised President Hutchinson for appearing to be "apologetic" in his message to the students about the scholarship. The school paper was correct in its assessment of Hutchinson, who feared a large, sustained public outcry over the admission of a recent enemy to Lafayette; but contrary to his expectations, not much more public opposition occurred.[37] Critics of the scholarship found their views immediately challenged and suppressed by a public that supported the Cold War liberal worldview.

When Occupation authorities finally permitted Nishiyama to travel to the United States in the fall of 1948—not coincidentally, after the Occupation's "reverse course" had taken effect—the college cooperated with *Life* magazine's feature on the "former suicide pilot." *Life*'s October 1948 story, "A Kamikaze Goes to College," portrayed Nishiyama as a bright, conscientious, and grateful scholarship recipient. Like other articles on Nishiyama that autumn, the *Life* article portrayed him in reassuring ways: he was Christian, not embittered about Japan's defeat, eager to learn about democracy, and, like the fictional Mikio Toyama, even handsome and a fan of American football. The article was sympathetic in describing Nishiyama's apprehensions about being at an American college. "Nishiyama was prepared for almost anything," *Life* reported, "but the casual reception he got from his Lafayette classmates." Instead of hostility and blame for the war, the magazine asserted, he found that his classmates "were friendly and paid little attention to him." Soon after his arrival, Nishiyama "was just one of 500 confused freshmen going through an indoctrination program" at Lafayette.[38]

The vast majority of the other bewildered freshmen were, like Nishiyama, World War II veterans. Mostly returnees on the GI Bill, the veterans constituted as much as 85 percent of some post-war classes at Lafayette. Enrollment at the small-town college ballooned suddenly from 142 students in June 1945 to 1,250 by the following year. When Nishiyama matriculated three years later, Lafayette counted a little over 2,000 men in its student body. Because the veteran students brought their wives and families to school with them, Lafayette—like many campuses after the war—had to build temporary housing, nicknamed "passion flats" or "stork villages" by Lafayette students. Most of the students came from Pennsylvania, New York, and New Jersey; some came from other eastern states; and a very small number were from areas outside the East Coast.[39]

Though *Life* probably overplayed the Lafayette student body's acceptance of an ex-kamikaze pilot in their midst, the veteran students appeared to be fairly progressive in their attitudes. During the second half of Nishiyama's freshman year, for example, the Lafayette student body demonstrated against racism—years before such student protests became a familiar event on American campuses. The Lafayette students forced the college to be more forthright about tackling racism in a case of racial discrimination against David Showell, an African American on Lafayette's winning football team. The Lafayette faculty had voted to turn down an invitation to the Sun Bowl in El Paso, Texas, because they anticipated that the Texans would not permit Showell to play. This decision outraged the students, including Nishiyama, who remembered decades later how he and a "mass" of other students "paraded down to a local radio station [and] gathered in front of the President's house" to insist that he tell the Sun Bowl organizers that Lafayette still wanted to participate *with* Showell. Hutchinson acquiesced to the students' demand, but the Texans told Lafayette that Showell was not welcome, at which point the Lafayette students telegraphed President Truman to denounce the Sun Bowl organizers. The school stood on principle, and its team stayed home.[40]

Despite this early activism for civil rights, the Lafayette student body remained overwhelmingly Euroamerican, with only a handful of minority students like Showell. When Nishiyama attended Lafayette, eight minority men among a couple of thousand were enrolled at Lafayette: Showell, another African American, two Chinese, two Okinawans, one Chinese American, and Nishiyama. Both Okinawans, Aso Kawahira and Kankichi Taira, entered Lafayette in 1950 as GARIOA scholars. Kawahira graduated with Nishiyama in 1952; Taira graduated a year later. In contrast to Nishiyama, the college files of the Okinawans did not include publicity or even student newspaper articles mentioning their arrival and adjustment to Lafayette. Their status as Okinawans complicated the simple narrative of former enemy transformed into ally. Subjected to Japanese colonization and abuse before and during the war, Okinawans after the war saw their small homeland of 454 square miles settled by tens of thousands of U.S. military personnel and controlled by U.S. military officers. Kawahira and Taira were essentially American colonials when they attended Lafayette. But technically they were Japanese nationals, and were undoubtedly perceived as former enemy Japanese by the largely Euroamerican student body and faculty.[41]

Showing Americans at Their Best

Lafayette's lack of racial diversity did not adversely affect Nishiyama, according to both his statements at the time and his recollections. He asserted that his reception by the nearly all-white La-fayette campus was solicitous and even warm. An article he wrote for *American Magazine* in 1949 extolled the generosity, open-ness, and goodwill of the Americans he had encountered. When leaving Japan, he wrote, "I was lonely and more than a little frightened. How would Americans treat me? Would I still be an enemy?" Nishiyama felt nervous about meeting his benefactors who had lost their son to his countrymen, but the Johnstones, he emphasized, went out of their way to make him feel welcome and invited him to stay for a week at their Downingtown home before school started. "Throughout the first weeks," Nishiyama wrote, "I was extremely shy, afraid I might run into embarrassment. But always my fears were dissolved by American friendliness." He found many of Easton's residents to be as welcoming and recep-tive as the Johnstones—inviting him into their homes for dinners, parties, or conversation—and he reported experiencing no ani-mosity on campus. In addition to American generosity and open-ness, Nishiyama cited his admiration for Americans' civic action and participation in the political process at the community level. Toward the end of the article, he asserted: "I hope to make a ca-reer as a teacher of history. I would like to contribute my one small voice to creating better understanding between America and my country."[42]

Lafayette and the Johnstones appeared to have selected their candidate well. The photograph accompanying the article re-vealed Nishiyama to have an agreeable, reassuring appearance that refuted the wartime stereotype of the Japanese as monkeys with bad eyes or the prewar images of Fu Manchu or Char-lie Chan. Handsome, clean-cut, with excellent vision and good posture, Nishiyama looked like a typical male college student. Wearing slacks and a sweater and carrying his books on his hip in

"Just another college student": Robert Nishiyama with fellow Lafayette College students. Photograph by Donald Riley, courtesy of Robert Nishiyama.

this photo, he walks with a casual but purposeful stride. Here was "the junior ally," a young Japanese male who "embraced defeat" and was figuratively moving toward the American way; his portrayal in the American media reflected this transformation from enmity to admiration. Unlike Tomoya Kawakita, Nishiyama seemed to be a worthy, manly, and honorable man, who did not try to evade military service to his nation and who had quickly learned to appreciate American society and values.

Nishiyama went along with this portrayal of his transformation because it allowed him to educate the Americans about the

Japanese. Decades later, Nishiyama recalled, "I felt I had to do my best to prove that I, a Japanese, was not too different from them as a human being. I think . . . I endeavored to participate in [a wide variety of] activities including intramural touch football."[43] This goal explained his patience with the numerous requests for interviews from the press and speeches at churches, schools, and civic organizations. Traveling all over Pennsylvania, New Jersey, New York, and even as far as Louisiana, Nishiyama talked to schools and civic associations like the Shriners, the Lions Club, and the Kiwanis Club. His freshman-year roommate, Lewis Bender, remembered Nishiyama often being away from campus to meet those requests. "He was caught up in all the interviews," Bender stated. "I wished they would have let him alone, but it made a tremendous human interest story back then. He used to get so many phone calls, and some of the calls were just not good. For me, I would have had trouble with it. I would have told them to go fly a kite."[44] Nishiyama, on the other hand, seemed happy to oblige and played down or suppressed incidents like phone calls from hostile Americans. Nishiyama was able to reflect back to Americans what they wanted to believe about themselves, while showing that the ex-enemy appreciated them and had been wrongheaded to go to war with them. In contrast to Kawakita, who unleashed upon Euroamerican POWs his resentment about the racism he had experienced in his native California, Nishiyama was a grateful pupil of American altruism and wisdom.[45]

In general, Nishiyama remembered his years at Lafayette as an enriching experience, especially in comparison to his wartime education at Gaikokugo Gakkō. Rather than striding in military formation, as he was forced to do at Gaigo, he marched to protest discrimination against the football player David Showell. Rather than listening to patriotic speeches and participating in military drills, he heard and participated in discussions on a variety of political issues, including debates on the meaning of democracy. Nishiyama recalls that some of his classmates were critical of America, pointing to the "WASP supremacy and minority problems," while others "more or less believed in the American system." He explained his appreciation of these exchanges by saying, "Coming from a country where such open debate was taboo, and having had the experience of forced obedience to authority like in the Navy, [this exposure] to such open debates [was] . . . new and fresh."[46] Nishiyama sincerely believed the glowing message he gave to Americans about themselves, but he nonetheless remained sufficiently aware of racism to have worried about his reception by Euroamericans until he was reassured by the welcome and warmth he received from many members of the Lafayette community.

Some postwar Japanese scholarship students, however, chose to ignore racism. Mitsuya Gotō, who attended Wabash College in Crawfordsville, Indiana, as well as Princeton, maintains that a Japanese student could avert negative treatment with his attitude and behavior. "I felt it all depended on how I approached others, especially Americans," he later insisted. Gotō's approach was one of tact, flattery, and humorous self-deprecation. In his commencement address as the valedictorian of Wabash's class of 1955, Gotō emphasized how his perspective had been broadened by his American education. He credited a world history course at Wabash for being "the first objective view of . . . world history I'd attained. I began to see the faults and flaws of Japan." The Wabash campus, Gotō declared, happily contradicted the familiar Rudyard Kipling refrain: "East is East, / and West is West, / and never the twain shall meet." His four years at the Crawfordsville campus, he explained, were a struggle to fuse my Oriental mind, though it may be crooked, with your minds, the American minds. At first I found a great gap between your minds and mine. . . . Then I started to build what I call "the bridge of understanding" in order to help bridge this gap. The bridge is still unfinished, but at least the traffic has begun to flow. I hope that in the future an ever-increasing traffic, not just a one-way traffic but a two-way traffic, will continue to flow over the bridge spanning your minds and ours.[47]

More explicitly than Nishiyama, at least according to the available sources, Gotō addressed cross-cultural communication—the bridge of understanding—in geopolitical terms. As a member of the Wabash speech team in the early 1950s, Gotō made over 200 speeches to various civic organizations and audiences all over Indiana, in other midwestern states, and as far away as Georgia. The *Indianapolis Star Magazine* quoted Gotō as telling American audiences that he was "convinced that Japan has found her most reliable ally in the United States" and that "with continued American economic aid, Japan can stand with the Western allies as a bulwark against the tide of Communism in the Far East."[48] By the time Gotō began his American college career, phrases like "bulwark against Communism" had entered common parlance.

Both Gotō and Nishiyama knew how to appeal to their American audiences. They were polite, earnest, grateful, and complimentary. They challenged their readers or listeners to rethink their preconceptions about the Japanese, but did so modestly and judiciously. Gotō explained in his commencement address that the Japanese could be re-educated to think more like Americans, but he also emphasized that "the bridge of understanding" should carry "two-way traffic," not simply function "one-way." Phrasing his plea diplomatically and with self-effacement, he urged Americans to learn from the Japanese as the Japanese had started to learn from them. Expediting the two-way flow of traffic on the bridge meant avoiding potential points of conflict, and for Gotō, this meant ignoring racism. Nishiyama, on the other hand, may have minimized racial discrimination directed at himself, but he was not blind to racism. Still, like Gotō, he tended to accentuate the positive. Recalling his Lafayette years, Nishiyama stated, "It deeply impressed me that, while the ugly sign of racism was evident in many areas in the US, there were good common people who believed that racism should not be tolerated."[49]

Gotō and Nishiyama were and still are genuinely grateful for the opportunities afforded them in the United States. The postwar scholarship students felt what the Japanese call *on*, or moral indebtedness, to their *on-jin*, their American benefactors, and they would consider it unmannerly to voice criticism or focus on their host country's problems.[50] Even Koya Azumi, another postwar Japanese student, chose to minimize racism even though he found it difficult to be positive in the early 1950s about race relations in the United States. After facing blatant hostility in California, Azumi chose to continue his education at Haverford College in Pennsylvania—thousands of miles away from the west coast and its long history of anti-Asian sentiment.[51]

Nishiyama and Gotō seem to have embraced their roles as "goodwill ambassadors," but some Japanese students resisted this role. As one might expect, many scholarship recipients thought of their careers first and bilateral amity second. The program directors, in contrast, put friendship first and emphasized that "the objective of the student program is by no means entirely scholastic." As the chief of SCAP's CIE Section explained, "We wanted as many Japanese as possible to live among us, not only to see what sort of people we are but also to help our people know through them more about Japan." The GARIOA program therefore placed Japanese students on a variety of campuses throughout the United States for the dual purpose of giving the Japanese a wider look at America and exposing more Americans to the Japanese. This decision did not please some of the GARIOA scholars. Enough of them expressed disappointment about not being placed at big-name East Coast schools that the program directors felt compelled to point out that "the Pacific Coast and Middle West are not intellectual deserts."[52] The program also ejected and deported one Japanese student for failing "to accept the limitations and the purposes of [the] program." This student, Torao Miyamori, met a Spanish national who became his girlfriend during an orientation for international students, but his placement at Iowa State divided them. Upset about the separation, he left the Ames campus without permission to be with her in western Massachusetts. Subsequently apprehended, Miyamori was handcuffed and sent to a detention camp for illegal immigrants on Ellis Island, where he wrote a letter complaining that the program had "forced [him] to be put in a narrow framework." Soon back in Japan, he expressed his intention to go back to the United States to be with his lover. Rather than spreading pro-American propaganda in Japan, Miyamori wanted to escape his country, a desperate, poverty-stricken place that he loathed.[53]

Open defiance against the scholarship program, however, seems to have been the exception. During Miyamori's ordeal, the Japanese involved in the program were embarrassed and apologized profusely for his behavior. "We are very sorry for America who has shown so much kindness," wrote a Japanese official whose office helped coordinate the selection of the students. A fellow Japanese scholarship recipient at Iowa State asserted, "I am very grateful for the people of this college who have attributed this trouble to his personal character and have never shown any misunderstanding to the Japanese nationality."[54] Vulnerable and dependent on American charity, the Japanese students and program administrators wanted to prove themselves worthy of American magnanimity. At the same time, they did share the American vision of a secure and prosperous global order. The American goals were not simply forced on an unwilling people.[55] Indeed, many Japanese experienced a profound disillusionment with the Japanese authorities, and at the end of the war more Japanese than at any time before or since sincerely believed that Americans knew the path to prosperity and happiness. This belief resulted in widespread support among the Japanese for Cold War liberal goals, particularly among the postwar students whose career goals—mostly in education, business, law, or government—benefited from the U.S. agenda.

It should be noted that the Japanese students represented a minuscule portion of Japanese society—only the relatively wealthy (or once-wealthy) were represented. The selection process for both publicly and privately funded scholarships tended to yield overwhelmingly male candidates from well-connected, well-educated, cosmopolitan families. Nishiyama's father, for example, was an architect with training in France, and both parents socialized with Americans; Gotō's Sorbonne-educated uncle taught French to Crown Prince Akihito; Koya Azumi's father was once governor of Tochigi prefecture; and another student, Steve Yukeyasu Yamamoto, was the son of an admiral and a great-grandson of the first chairman of Mitsubishi Heavy Industries and Mitsubishi Electric.[56] Two of these men, moreover, had been baptized with western names—which was fairly unusual in pre-war Japan—and a third, Gotō, converted to Christianity while in college.

Women among the postwar exchange students were far fewer; the ratio was perhaps as low as 10 to 1, according to one alumna.[57] Wealthy Japanese families saw American degrees as investments for making connections and enhancing family prestige. They therefore reserved this expensive experience for their *chōnan*, their eldest sons, or for other sons preparing to take over the family business. In contrast, female Japanese students at U.S. colleges in this period usually had no family funding but relied on merit-based scholarships or funding from other sources. The women, however, also tended to come from well-connected, upper- or upper-middle-class backgrounds, including the youngest daughter of General Tōjō Hideki, who received a scholarship arranged by an American patron to attend graduate school at the University of Michigan at Ann Arbor in 1959.[58] The screening process thus tended to select candidates whose class interests were likely to make them receptive to building Japan as America's most important junior partner and the leading capitalist nation in Asia.

As the first Japanese student to study in the United States after the war, Nishiyama probably received more attention from the American media than any other Japanese student. He arrived in the United States only three years after the end of hostilities, and the unusual origins of his scholarship as well as his own status as an "ex-kamikaze" made intriguing copy about the reversals of war. Discussion about the Johnstones' scholarship gave Americans new ideas about how they should view the former enemy. Because many Euroamericans understood racial tolerance as a necessary part of their postwar education, they knew that by hosting Japanese students, lessons would be learned on both sides. Most readers of the *Lancaster New Era* were probably heartened when they read what Nishiyama said he intended to do with his American education. "When I graduate," the paper quoted him as saying, "I will return to Japan and will teach Japanese children the true meaning of democracy."[59] Some may have been cynical or skeptical about his declaration, but the media remained predominately positive about this story that proved Americans capable of being wise and altruistic patrons despite troubling domestic strife.

Upon graduation, Nishiyama returned to Japan, but he did not become a diplomat or a teacher to educate children about the meaning of democracy. He used his "small voice" to further the bilateral relationship in a less vocal but perhaps more significant fashion. Rather than becoming a "goodwill ambassador" to convince fellow Japanese to become willing participants in an American-led global capitalist economy, he participated directly in the U.S.-Japan economic relationship. Most of his subsequent career was in business; as a representative of American corporations in Japan, he helped to cement capitalist ties between the two nations. From 1962 to 1985, Nishiyama worked for a Pennsylvania-based manufacturer of electrical and electronic components. He helped establish this company's Japanese subsidiary, and served as its president and general manager for twenty-three years. He then worked for another American electronics company as its vice-president of marketing for the Pacific Basin before retiring in 1991 to set up his own consulting and electronics import company, which he was still running into his eighties. Today he is still active as a Lafayette alumnus and interviews prospective students for the college in Tokyo—usually high school seniors from one of the city's international schools for foreign expatriates and Japanese returnees. In 2002 he attended his fiftieth class reunion at Lafayette.[60] Although he became neither a diplomat nor a teacher, Nishiyama has worked with Americans throughout his career and has achieved financial security and affluence.

Although scholarships for Japanese students were created to spread pro-American attitudes in Japan, a small but significant number of these students did not return to Japan, making their careers in the United States instead. Koya Azumi and Steve Yamamoto became educators, teaching and researching at American universities for the majority of their respective careers in sociology and physics. Two other Japanese students who attended Haverford College with Azumi did likewise: Akira Iriye taught history at Harvard, and Robert Togasaki was professor of biology at Indiana University. Iriye has devoted his illustrious career to examining the bilateral relationship. He is equally at home among American and Japanese academics, but he has spent the bulk of his professional life with American colleagues and students. Gotō, on the other hand, spent a large portion of his career in Europe, as well as in the United States, representing Japanese business interests. Throughout his career he gave talks on the U.S.-Japanese relationship, but to mostly non-Japanese audiences. In the nearly fifty years since he graduated from Wabash and Princeton, where he received a master's degree, he has spent far less time explaining Americans to the Japanese.

U.S. international aid programs often fail to meet their lofty goals, but they nevertheless tell us much about the American self-image and American needs.[61] Such was the case with American scholarships for Japanese students. A good fit between domestic concerns and the needs of an alliance made the notion of the Japanese as students of democracy compelling. American depictions of Japanese males studying in the United States, like American portrayals of Japanese women, reflected specific attitudes toward youth, education, race, western civilization, and American destiny. Although these images were less racist than those of the bucktoothed "Japs" during the war, they were nonetheless still mired in a colonial and racialist discourse that linked lighter skin color with a more mature civilization. Given this context, an effort to present reformed images of Japanese men could work only if the depictions resonated with, rather than disrupted, the prevailing racialist worldview. Making the United States a mentor and teacher to Japan, the pupil, reinforced notions about American superiority while humanizing geopolitical power relations between the two nations. No longer an enemy, the Japanese were to be "star pupils" or international model minorities—the only nonwhite nationals chosen to serve as an "example" of free-enterprise capitalism to the rest of the "developing" world.

The decision to privilege Japan not only resurrected the prewar notion of Japan as the model or leading nation in Asia, but it also provided a rationale for overlooking other powerless peoples—just as the "model minority" concept in later decades rationalized neglect of the less powerful members of American society. At the same time, the trope of maturity helped Americans cope with cultural and social fears of delinquency at home and deviance abroad by projecting the United States as the able and qualified teacher of grateful wards. The scholarships no doubt benefited individual Japanese, but instead of fulfilling their stated mission to promote pro-American sentiments in Japan, these programs were more effective in allowing some earnest Japanese individuals to show their people in a better light. Rather than spreading good news about America in Japan, the students helped Americans accept the Japanese as their "junior allies" in the Far East.

CHAPTER SIX

Channeling Atomic Guilt

A little over a year after the Americans dropped atomic bombs over two Japanese cities, Reverend Marvin W. Green, a transplanted Kentuckian living in New Jersey, picked up a special edition of the *New Yorker*. In an unprecedented act, the magazine had devoted the entire issue of August 31, 1946, to John Hersey's narrative of six residents of Hiroshima who survived the bomb. Reading Hersey's account, Reverend Green soon discovered that one of the six survivors had been his classmate at Emory University's Candler School of Theology in Georgia. Relieved and delighted to learn that Reverend Kiyoshi Tanimoto was still alive, Green immediately wrote to him. Green feared that the Occupation authorities might not allow his letter to reach his old classmate, but to his surprise, he received a response and began a correspondence with Tanimoto. Green reported the re-establishment of communication with Tanimoto to other members of the class of 1939 and spread the good news of his survival to those who had missed Hersey's article. Moved by Tanimoto's plight of ministering to atomic bomb victims, his former classmates began sending money and supplies to Tanimoto. They also petitioned the Overseas Methodist Mission Board to invite Reverend Tanimoto to the United States for a speaking tour when Occupation authorities would permit Japanese to travel abroad. On October 5, 1948, Tanimoto arrived in San Francisco to begin a year and a half of "evangelical barnstorming" across America, speaking to 472 audiences with a total of 160,026 people. He raised $10,000—more than enough to rebuild his church in Hiroshima. The Methodists' contact with Tanimoto marked an early episode of stateside American humanitarian aid to the victims of the atomic bomb.[1]

The U.S. government, in contrast, never officially provided aid to the victims of the atomic bomb. Although it established the Atomic Bomb Casualty Commission (ABCC) to study the effects of bomb-induced injuries and radiation on humans in Japan, the U.S. government forbade ABCC doctors from giving medical treatment to their subjects. Treatment, the government maintained, would be tantamount to apologizing for the bombing—something the United States stoutly refused to do. With plans for subsequent, more powerful nuclear bombs already under way, the Truman administration feared that widespread domestic and international censure of the bombing of Hiroshima and Nagasaki would thwart a future U.S. defense policy based on nuclear weapons. This American sensitivity about the bombs meant that the *hibakusha* (atomic bomb victims) of Hiroshima and Nagasaki received no special medical aid from the Occupation authorities. Moreover, the victims received hardly any relief from their own government, already besieged with other problems that it found more pressing—since all Japanese cities, not just Hiroshima and Nagasaki, lay in ruins by mid-August 1945. Reverend Tanimoto's tour, the first of his visits to the United States, thus marked a positive step to help the atomic bomb victims, and its success revealed a way in which Americans—in opposition to the official policy—could assuage their feelings of remorse for being the first people to use the terrifying new weapon.

In the decade after U.S. bombardiers destroyed Hiroshima and Nagasaki, Americans continued to express ambivalence about atomic weapons. While many believed that use of "the bomb" in Japan was more than justified, other Americans continued to be troubled by their nation's use of atomic bombs—whether or not they believed former secretary of state Henry Stimson's 1947 assertion that the swift devastation of two Japanese urban centers truly prevented "over a million" American casualties. Many Americans had turned away from the disturbing pictures of mass death and suffering humanity even before their government officially censored such images. Americans preferred instead to "imagine the unimaginable horror" of a possible future atomic attack on an American city rather than confronting the reality of Hiroshima and Nagasaki's past and present. Imagining such a cataclysm, of course, would have been inconceivable if the United States had not dropped atomic bombs on Hiroshima and Nagasaki. Americans therefore back-handedly admitted to wrongdoing by simultaneously acknowledging and denying their guilt about the atomic bombs.[2] Although a minority of Americans were more forthright about what the *Christian Century* called "America's Atomic Atrocity," they, too, focused less on Japanese suffering and more on the U.S. image abroad or on their guilty conscience as practicing Christians.[3]

The rapprochement between Americans and victims of the atomic bomb, as exemplified in two humanitarian programs, attempted to redirect American guilt about the atomic bombs into emotional, ethical, and political reconciliation between the United States and Japan. The two programs, both spearheaded by

Saturday Review of Literature editor Norman Cousins, predictably chose Japanese women and children as the beneficiaries of their aid. The "Hiroshima Maidens" project (1955–1956) arranged plastic surgery in New York City for twenty-five women disfigured by "Little Boy," and the "moral adoptions" program (1949 to the mid-1960s) assisted roughly 300 children orphaned by the bombing. Although the "moral adoptions" project predated and outlasted the Hiroshima Maidens program, it has attracted only passing attention over the years; in contrast, books, articles, and even a fictionalized children's film have been devoted to the Hiroshima Maidens' story.[4] But both programs neglected the adult male victims of the atomic bomb, providing yet another example of the postwar interpretive framework that cast the Japanese as the dependents of a big-hearted and wise U.S. breadwinner, protector, and parental figure.

Since U.S. policy forbade official American aid to the *hibakusha,* private efforts became essential in reconciling Americans and victims of the atomic bombs. It was thus up to individuals like Reverend Green and Norman Cousins to help Americans "make peace" with the Japanese *hibakusha* through private charity initiatives.[5] The private efforts employed metaphors of familial obligation that cast Americans as parental saviors to the victims, and this helped to mitigate, at least in American minds, the "unimaginable horror" visited upon Hiroshimans. The depiction of the Hiroshima Maidens as "daughters" and the Hiroshima orphans as "children" to their American "parents" naturalized American beneficence as well as their authority over the Japanese. By emphasizing bonds of love and connection, the use of familial metaphors helped to mask intractable social, political, and material inequities.[6] The Hiroshima Maidens and "moral adoptions" projects privatized reconciliation and provided liberal

Americans with a rationale for the unequal U.S.-Japan relationship. Both projects offered individuated, sentimental solutions to
the national problem of making peace with the *hibakusha,* and
allowed Americans to channel their guilt about the bombs in a
positive way—an attitude, moreover, that supported U.S. nuclear
policy.

Norman Cousins and the Moral Adoptions

The most significant contact that Reverend Tanimoto made during his first postwar tour of the United States was Norman
Cousins. Cousins, the young editor of the *Saturday Review of
Literature,* had been deeply disturbed by the atomic bombing and
had written in its aftermath an impassioned editorial denouncing
the bombing as "a stain" on the nation's history. He deplored
the fact that modern man had been "willing to mobilize all his
scientific and intellectual energies for the purposes of death [but]
. . . unwilling to undertake any comparable mobilization for the
purposes of life."[7] Three and a half years later, when he came
across Tanimoto's proposal to establish an international, nonsec-
tarian "World Peace Center" in Hiroshima, Cousins thought he
had found what he sought: a positive step toward affirming and
protecting life. By this time, Hiroshimans were already commem-
orating August 6th every year, but Tanimoto envisioned a bolder
plan. He wanted to establish a charitable and educational institution in Hiroshima with a twofold mission: to minister both physically and spiritually to the *hibakusha,* and to publicize the first
atom-bombed city as an omen of what could happen elsewhere if
all people did not work toward global peace.

Cousins published Reverend Tanimoto's proposal in the March
5, 1949, issue of the *Saturday Review,* strongly endorsing the Jap-

anese pastor's appeal for American help to establish an institute to research, plan, and spread "peace education throughout the world." Soliciting American support pointedly but tactfully, Tanimoto asserted: "We believe a world which used us as its laboratory test in time of war will want to make it possible for us to explore the ways of peace."[8] By blaming the "world" for the destruction of his city, he pricked the conscience of Americans without accusing them directly, and he suggested that even those who believed the atomic bombs were necessary to end the war could now work constructively toward peace.

In August 1949, five months after Tanimoto's guest editorial, Norman Cousins traveled to Hiroshima. With letters of introduction from Tanimoto to Hiroshima's civic leaders, Cousins arrived in the city just in time to participate in the ground-breaking ceremony for the Peace Memorial Park on the fourth anniversary of the atomic bombing.[9] Although Cousins went to Japan at General MacArthur's invitation to examine human-rights conditions in the country—as General Mark Clark had asked him to do in Germany the previous year—he ignored most of Japan and wrote articles about Hiroshima almost exclusively. In an essay that he wired back to New York, Cousins reported to *Saturday Review* readers that what he saw in Hiroshima both encouraged and shocked him. To his admiration, the Hiroshimans had almost rebuilt their city and were "not defeatist," but to his horror, they lacked basic medical facilities. An operating room in a hospital that he toured "seemed little better than a crude abattoir," and "nothing [he] had seen [in displaced persons camps] in Germany or anywhere else put human pride to such a strain." During this hospital tour, Cousins related, a sobbing woman threw herself at his feet and begged the American to procure medication for her tubercular daughter. Profoundly moved, Cousins engaged in "a little black marketeering" and succeeded in obtaining the badly needed streptomycin from Tokyo. The Church World Service then sent more streptomycin by air to supplement the batch from Tokyo, and the girl began to respond to the medication.[10] What ultimately happened to the girl remains unknown, but Cousins believed that he may have saved her life, providing a lesson to his readers about the power of American altruism.

Hiroshiman children continued to hold Cousins' attention during his visit. While touring the city, he noticed many small children "on the loose" and asked Mayor Hamai Shinzō about them. The mayor explained that many children orphaned by the atomic bomb lacked proper care because all the orphanages were at full capacity.[11] Cousins was then led to a makeshift orphanage started by a couple named Yamashita, who had been gathering in homeless children without families from the streets. Cousins promised to write about their plight and devoted a portion of his longest essay from Japan to Mrs. Yamashita, who despite her own injuries from the blast was caring for as many needy children as she could. Cousins said almost nothing about Mr. Yamashita, without whose purchasing power and vision the orphanage could not have existed. One Yamashita orphan recalled that he and the other children "grew up in the warm hands of Mr. Yamashita," but the American editor focused on the universality of maternal love by describing how "dozens" of the younger orphans clung to Mrs. Yamashita "like kids hanging on an American mother's skirts in a department store." Cousins wrote that the orphans' living quarters were "better and brighter" than elsewhere in the city, and that the children received good food, a decent education, adequate playing space, and most important, enough affection. Although the Yamashitas appeared to be doing an excellent job, Cousins wrote, "there was one thing wrong with the Yamashita orphanage. There was not enough of it. It should be five times as large, and would be, if outside help were forthcoming."[12]

Cousins wondered out loud in his essay what Americans could do for these children. He pointed out that U.S. immigration laws, which forbade the immigration of Japanese and Koreans, made it impossible for Americans to formally adopt the Hiroshima orphans. Cousins then urged his readers to do what he called "the next best thing" and make "moral adoptions" of Hiroshima orphans. The Yamashitas needed only $2.25 a month to feed, clothe, and educate a Hiroshima orphan. This seemed a ridiculously low sum for such a gain—surely the *Saturday Review*'s readership could be called upon to help out. Cousins proposed that American families "adopting" Hiroshima orphans be financially responsible for the orphans' upbringing and care. When and if Congress revised its immigration laws, then the children could join their adoptive families in the States. To simulate real family bonds—and to prepare for a possible legal adoption in the future—Cousins even suggested that the children take on the surnames of their adoptive families.

Cousins' proposal for moral adoptions received a prompt and gratifying response. Within three weeks, the *Saturday Review* published excerpts from twenty-three letters and the names of another twenty people who were taking up Cousins' offer to facilitate their donations to the Hiroshima orphans. The letter writers included heads of families, college women (from Swarthmore and Radcliffe), and single women who cited as their motivation their inability to adopt a child legally in the United States because they were "spinsters." The program thus allowed these women to participate, even if in a limited way, in the postwar "baby boom." "You have no idea how proud I will be to have a child somewhere I can call 'my own,' morally at least and provide the little things a mother likes to provide the year 'round," wrote Dorothy M. Boyington of Northfield, Illinois. "I have tried to adopt children here, but there are state laws which prevent a single person from adopting a child, the theory being that a child must have *two* parents."[13] While most of the donors implied or confessed that they would be unable to actually adopt a child even when the immigration laws changed, a few seemed committed to it. "We have discussed the obligations involved," wrote R. E. Downing of Chicago, "and we are ready to offer our home, when possible, and our aid to bring some measure of family life and love to one of these youngsters. We are of moderate means and have two children of our own, but feel we can afford the sum of $2.25 each month to help some child." Other individuals wrote that they could not make a financial pledge but included a one-time offering (usually around ten dollars), or tentatively made a payment which they would continue only if they could afford to do so.

By November 5, 1949—a mere seven weeks after Cousins' initial suggestion—149 individuals and families had made an indefinite financial promise. "Moral parents" eventually represented all regions of the nation, rural and urban. They even included the fourth grade class of the Roger Wolcott School in Wilson, Connecticut, two expatriates (one each in Guam and Venezuela), and later, a celebrity: Helen Keller.[14] Two Japanese Americans (identified by their surnames) also became moral parents: Edith Saito of Philadelphia and James A. Yamamoto of Chicago. The rest of the donors had Anglo or German surnames, indicating that most came from Yankee stock in the New England and New York areas. Women constituted the majority of moral parents: at least 62 percent of those listed were single women or married (or possibly widowed) women who identified themselves by their husband's name but did not include their spouses as co-donors. Single men were the next largest contingent, accounting for about 25 percent. Although Cousins had two-parent families in mind for the adoptions (moral and eventually legal) of Hiroshima orphans, only 10 percent of those on the preliminary list were married couples.[15] A later update listing some of the occupations represented by the moral parents showed that they tended to be professionals rather than working-class, reflecting the readership of the *Saturday Review*.[16]

The limited information available about the moral parents prevents a complete analysis of this group, but their personal letters to the *Saturday Review*'s offices indicate that guilt about the atomic bombs motivated many of them. Upset that her country had "cast aside all decent scruples and committ[ed] mass murder in the name of military necessity," Genevieve Tiller Garland of Beaver Dams, New York, pledged to support a Hiroshima orphan. "I have a vague hope," she wrote, that sending money to "a child who was hurt on that awful day will give me some rest from the feeling I've had ever since."[17] A former pilot who flew twenty-six B-29 missions over Japan confessed to being haunted since the war because of "the indiscriminate fashion with which [he and others] used to burn out slum areas with fire bombs" as well as the "unwarranted and needless use" of the atomic bombs. To him, Cousins' proposal "presented an easy way to soothe an elusive feeling of collective guilt." "I know I can't buy back my teenage ideals for a small sum," he acknowledged, "but everything is worth trying today."[18]

Some readers, however, were not pleased by Cousins' proposal to help Hiroshimans. "In the face of such nobility by fine people towards the orphans of Hiroshima," wrote Belinda Jelliffe of New York City, "I feel that maybe I'm a heel, some inferior type, in saying that before I get into a lather about the orphans of Hiroshima, I would like to know what happened to those made by the attack on Pearl Harbor. Where could this information be obtained?" Another New Yorker wondered, "Can it be possible that all your readers are willing to forgive those who tried to perpetrate by force, the fraud that they were the supermen of at least their half of the world? Can it be possible that all your readers have forgotten so soon how the little men of Japan treated those whom they conquered?"[19]

Cousins' detractors included a personal friend who accused him of becoming a "softy" toward the Japanese.[20] Responding publicly to his friend and all other detractors, Cousins empathized that "it must seem strange indeed that Americans today should be going out of their way to help those who only four years ago were a monstrous threat to our freedom and our physical safety." But, Cousins explained, his attitude changed as he began to see the Japanese as individuals rather than as part of an enemy nation. Earnest Japanese who queued outside his hotel room every day to talk to him about political philosophy or ask him small favors to continue their political education impressed Cousins with their idealism. "Was it 'soft' to work with people such as these, to encourage them, to get them to deepen their commitments to free institutions?" Cousins asked. He also hinted that Americans had a special obligation to these particular orphans who lost their parents in the first atomic bomb explosion; the youngest, Cousins added, was born just hours before the explosion.[21] In 1949, it would have been a stretch for Americans to see Japan as the equal of the United States; more liberal Americans like Cousins thus imagined a relationship that encouraged his fellow citizens to feel responsible toward the Japanese.

Cousins had called for moral adoptions of children in the Yamashita orphanage only, and less than a month after he printed his proposal, all the children at Yamashita's had been covered.[22] He wrote to Mayor Hamai that he hoped the response to the project would grow so that Americans would provide "for all the atomic-bomb orphans of Hiroshima, and not merely those at the Yamashita orphanage."[23] The moral adoptions program eventually covered seven orphanages, and a total of $70,000 was sent to provide for more than 600 children over a period of approximately a dozen years.[24]

The American "parents" seemed happy with their new wards; some were even gushing. "We are delighted with our little butterball!" wrote the "moral mother" of Keiko Kihara Snoddy, while the "moral father" of Mitsuko Yoshikawa Fuson said that adopting her was "the biggest and most exciting dividend of pride and happiness that we can imagine getting for $2.25 per month invested." Photographs of some morally adopted children in the *Saturday Review* in June 1950 showed one of a smiling Mitsuko next to a photo of her "family" with their dog.[25] Moral parents also received newsletters filled with glowing reports, and occasionally letters from the children themselves. One 9-year-old wrote, "Spring is coming round to the world but it has already come to me. I feel as if I were dreaming a happy dream. I will try to study very hard and be a good daughter to you." In addition to money, moral parents sent clothing, toys, primary English readers, baseball bats, and even pianos to Hiroshima during the first year of the program.[26]

To the deprived Hiroshima orphans, the gifts were a miracle, but the donors' words suggest that they, like the former B-29 pilot, were trying to "buy back" their innocence at a distance from the victims of American air power. The number of words signifying currency—profit, dividend, investment, even tax—are striking in the moral parents' language. The "adoptees" almost seem like purchases—perhaps an unavoidable situation, given the simple exchange of money.[27] The sense of parental duty in these Americans was intrinsically limited not only because the children lived thousands of miles away, but also because private families could not accommodate the situation's great financial need. A smaller group of Americans, however, went further than the "moral parents" and served as quasi-foster parents for a group of twenty-five women who became known as the "Hiroshima Maidens." The project originated with a support group at Reverend Tanimoto's church for women scarred and injured by the atomic blast.

The Hiroshima Maidens

As Cousins dealt with the logistics of the moral adoption program, Reverend Tanimoto continued his mission to establish the organization he had described in the *Saturday Review*. He returned to Japan in the spring of 1950, and he and some Hiroshima dignitaries formally founded the Hiroshima Peace Center (HPC) on August 8, 1950. Reflecting the name change from "World Peace Center" to "Hiroshima Peace Center," the new organization's core activities centered on their city—a difference in focus that eventually led to a rift between Tanimoto and Cousins.[28] These troubles, however, lay in the future when the pastor embarked on his second fund-raising tour of the United States in the autumn of 1950. Tanimoto spoke before far fewer audiences during this shorter visit than during his previous 1948–1950 tour, but he probably reached more Americans by appearing on three television shows and fifteen radio programs. The nation's capital treated him as a "distinguished statesman": he met members of Congress, was given a luncheon by the House

Foreign Affairs Committee, delivered the opening prayer at the U.S. Senate, and made a broadcast for the State Department's "Voice of America."[29] In May 1951, Tanimoto—with Cousins and Marvin Green—established an American organization, the Hiroshima Peace Center Associates (HPCA), to help support the activities of the HPC. Pearl Buck, John Hersey, Dr. Harry Emerson Fosdick, pastor emeritus of Riverside Church in New York City, Dr. Garland Evan Hopkins, associate editor of the *Christian Century,* Dr. H. B. Trimble, dean of the Candler School of Theology, and G. Bromley Oxnam, Methodist bishop for New York City, all agreed to serve on the HPCA's advisory board.[30] Norman Cousins, the new organization's chair, provided space in his office in New York City for board meetings and administrative work. The *Saturday Review* office—and later, Reverend Green's church office—served as the HPCA's clearinghouse for donations, requests for interviews, and correspondence for the HPC as well as for the moral adoption program.

After seeing to the founding of the HPCA, Reverend Tanimoto returned to Hiroshima with a full money belt and embarked on a variety of activities. With other directors of the HPC, he founded homes for war widows, juvenile delinquents, and deaf victims of the bomb; started classes that would teach practical earning skills, such as sewing classes for women; and worked out an expansion of the moral adoption program. Angry at the Japanese government's neglect of the *hibakusha,* Tanimoto also helped organize the Atomic Bomb Victims Association, which initiated a campaign for a national medical treatment bill.[31]

During his rounds of the city, Tanimoto noticed young women with extensive keloid scars hiding in the shadows. He began a support group for these women, who were shunned by others, so that they could talk and discuss treatment. Members of the group spread the word, and it eventually grew to include eighty-eight women (a few badly scarred men attended the meetings once or twice but never returned). Every Monday evening, about twenty women regularly gathered in the basement of Tanimoto's Nagaregawa Church, and Tanimoto called their group *Shion-kai* or the Aster Association.[32]

Tanimoto first approached Hiroshima city officials and the medical establishment about getting medical treatment for his "keloid girls," but they stonewalled him with excuses. Some months later, Tanimoto appealed to Masugi Shizue at the Japan PEN conference, which met in Hiroshima that year. Masugi, a famous woman novelist and columnist for Tokyo's *Yomiuri Shimbun,* agreed to help and spearheaded efforts to get treatment for nine *Shion-kai* women at Tokyo University. When the women arrived in Tokyo on June 6, 1952, for preliminary examinations, they received tremendous media coverage. The press started calling them *genbaku otome* or "atomic bomb maidens," focusing on the women's tainted beauty; their chances for marriage had been ruined by looking up at the sky at the wrong moment on that sunny morning in August 1945, incurring hideous scars on their faces, necks, or hands.[33] Masugi organized a Tokyo branch of the HPC, supported by wealthy matrons, to fund a series of operations for the scarred women in the autumn. A similar effort took place in Osaka, Japan's second largest city, where wealthy women established another HPC affiliate. The Osaka affiliate arranged for another group of Hiroshima women to receive surgery in their city at the end of 1952. Sadly, the operations in Japan were a failure: the keloid scars quickly grew back after being surgically removed by scalpels. Since knowledge of plastic surgery techniques in Japan at that time was very limited, the Japanese doctors could do little more.[34]

Reverend Tanimoto began thinking that surgery in the United States might be the only hope for these women; but Cousins expressed no interest in the "keloid girls." Cousins was reluctant to take on another major commitment, and by this time he had heard about, and wanted to stay clear of, the political in-fighting between Tanimoto and the HPC's other directors. Tanimoto then entreated every visiting American to help the women. Matsubara Miyoko, who had been a member of *Shion-kai,* remembered that Tanimoto took every opportunity to introduce American missionaries and others to their group, to show how "horrible" their scars were.[35] Tanimoto even appealed to Eleanor Roosevelt when she visited Japan in 1953. But the former First Lady offered only sympathy and refused to become involved.

Meanwhile Masugi wrote to a fellow female novelist, Pearl Buck. Masugi highlighted the "fortitude" and "warm-hearted" nature of "these children of the atom bomb," and noted that politicians in Hiroshima and Nagasaki were planning a protest against the ABCC's refusal to treat the *hibakusha* or share its findings with Japanese doctors. Accusing the Americans of using Japanese bomb victims as "guinea pigs for scientific investigation," Masugi claimed, would "only serve to create ill-feelings on both sides, particularly over here, where the Japanese people are at a very critical juncture psychologically"—probably a reference to the end of the Occupation and the return of Japan's sovereignty earlier that year. Masugi's pleas led Pearl Buck to make repeated efforts to interest Cousins in the "keloid girls," but to no avail.[36]

The next year, however, Cousins and his wife stopped in Hiroshima on their way to the Bandung Conference, and Tanimoto made sure that they met some *Shion-kai* women. In the church basement, face to face with women missing an ear, with a caved-in face, or with "a nose shoved into a snout," Cousins could no longer ignore them. When Tanimoto asked several women to push up their sleeves and reveal their arms, Cousins saw "elbows and wrists . . . yanked out of position as if from some muscular frenzy and locked into place by gristly straps of scar tissue." One woman held up both hands, "revealing fingers that were curled and webbed like talons clutching at prey." Now that he had Cousins' complete attention, Tanimoto simply stated, "I can give them things to do, and I can help restore some of their self-respect, but the important thing now is medical treatment." He repeated his belief that the women needed to receive this treatment in the United States. Before Cousins had a chance to reply, Ellen Cousins looked at him and said, "It may not be as difficult as you think."[37]

Still, it took almost two years before a group of Hiroshiman women came to America for surgery. Unlike the moral adoption program, which was a relatively simple matter of sending money and goods abroad, the "Hiroshima Maidens" project, as it soon came to be called, took more detailed planning. Transportation, doctors, hospital beds, food, and lodging would all be required. Knowing that the project would costs hundreds of thousands of dollars, Cousins tried for six months to get support from a major foundation. All the ones he approached, however, turned him down because each foundation thought the project carried a high risk for negative publicity. Undaunted, Cousins changed his tack and started soliciting services rather than funds. He signed on physicians who would perform the surgery; got hospital beds provided at Mount Sinai Hospital; convinced Quakers in the New York area to be host families for the women; and finally, through an intermediary, secured transportation through U.S. military personnel stationed in Japan.

The pieces of this improvised plan fell into place, one by one. One of the last essential pieces came when Cousins was already in Hiroshima to escort the women to America: a Nisei employee of the ABCC offered herself as a translator and "liaison assistant" for the project. Hatsuko "Helen" Yokoyama was an alumna of the University of California at Berkeley who had spent the war years in Japan. By pure luck, she had her passport papers prepared to return to the United States and was ready to leave Hiroshima when they were.[38] Yokoyama became indispensable to the women, serving as their confidant, adviser, and go-between not only during the project but also for years afterward.

Getting the Quakers to agree to host the women, however, did take some effort. Although Cousins thought the Quakers' antiwar beliefs made them logical hosts to help the victims of war, the New York-area Friends did not jump at the opportunity to be part of the project when approached by the HPCA. The Quakers hesitated for a variety of reasons. How would they communicate with the foreign women? Would the women require special Japanese foods? Did the women, as victims of the bomb, require special care? What should they do in case of an emergency? Moreover, they were not sure they wanted to host foreigners who were nonwhite ex-enemies.

Rodney Barker was nine years old when his family served as hosts to Suzue Oshima Hiyama and Misako Kannabe, but the Barkers nearly didn't participate in the project because Rodney's veteran father had serious reservations. Although he agreed when his wife opened their home to youth and students less privileged than their own three sons through summer programs like the Fresh Air Fund, the senior Barker felt uneasy about inviting Japanese individuals to stay with them. As an Army officer-clerk at the end of World War II, he had interviewed newly released American

POWs from Japanese camps in order to identify possible Japanese war criminals. Day after day, he heard gruesome stories of Japanese barbarity, and this experience left him with "a strong anti-Japanese residue" that lingered for at least a decade after the war. But as a man committed to social activism, he decided that the Hiroshima Maidens project would be "a way to test his prejudice." Many of the other Quakers who became hosts had also been "personally touched" by the war, and wartime animosity against the Japanese still remained relatively high at the time. Sending monthly allotments to an alien child halfway across the world was one thing; having the ex-enemy right in one's home for an extended period of time was another.[39]

Some Quakers were also suspicious about the political purpose of the project. Was it, they wondered, simply a ploy to counteract bad publicity about the irradiated Japanese fishermen on the *Lucky Dragon?* In March 1954, a Japanese fishing boat called the *Lucky Dragon* unknowingly sailed close to the testing site of an American atomic bomb explosion in the Marshall Islands, and within three days the crew members manifested symptoms of radiation sickness. The episode caused a panic in Japan, where people feared they had been eating radioactive fish, and spurred anti-American demonstrations, which increased when one crew member subsequently died.[40] Even though the plans for the Hiroshima Maidens project predated that nuclear accident, the Quakers were unaware of this fact, and they speculated that the program had hidden, leftist political motives rather than being "simply" a people-to-people humanitarian project as Cousins said it was.

Addressing such fears, the New York Friends Center Association sent a letter of appeal to New York-area Quakers that described the "dangers" of Japanese Communists using these vulnerable "girls"—"mostly orphans"—in "an anti-American propaganda campaign." The letter claimed, "Several of the girls were offered free medical treatment in Russia, with the apparent intent of exhibiting their unfortunate disfigurement to the world as a sort of chamber of horrors of 'imperialist atomic aggression.' Only the fact that Mr. Tanimoto through his program of social service provided a haven of true friendship and comfort saved them from becoming innocent victims and tools of a Communist propaganda scheme."[41] The letter therefore emphasized that the "girls" were never enemy combatants but rather the innocent victims of war, and that it was up to the New York Friends to extend a hand of genuine friendship and provide parental protection from the scheming Communists. Unlike the Communists, the letter implied, the Quakers would be free of any underlying motive other than a desire to help and reconcile with former enemies. Thus put at ease, one group of Friends finally decided to be hosts for the women; then other groups of Friends joined the bandwagon and volunteered their own services. "It developed like wild-fire," Marvin Green recalled. "The moment you get the Philadelphia group, the Montclair group opens up, and so forth on up in Connecticut. And suddenly we got everyone saying 'Send us some girls.'"[42]

Like the Quakers, the State Department also feared that Cousins might have a hidden, leftist agenda. But an FBI background check on Cousins, along with the other members of HPCA, found that Cousins was no political radical, associated with only "several left of center organizations" like the American Civil Liberties Union and the World Federalists.[43] A mere review of Cousins' body of work would have shown that his *Saturday Review of Literature* had more in common with DeWitt Wallace's *Reader's Digest* than with the *Daily Worker*. Like the *Reader's*

Digest, the *Saturday Review of Literature* embraced universalism and refused to see America as an empire.[44] Although Cousins did not explicitly hold up the United States as a model for the entire "free" world, he believed that U.S. citizens should be engaged and reach out to the wider world. He presumed that greater understanding meant greater concord, and he steered the Hiroshima Maidens project away from any impression that it was associated with communists. Declining an opportunity to receive the box office profits from the New York City showing of *Hiroshima,* a documentary film made by the "leftist" Japanese Teachers Union, he chose instead a popular television show to help sponsor the project. *This Is Your Life,* a nationwide program that chiefly celebrated American success stories, also happened to be the more lucrative choice, and it cast the Maidens project as a narrative about the benevolence of "the American way."

During the mid-1950s, *This Is Your Life* consistently ranked among the top ten TV shows and reached a weekly audience of approximately 40 million viewers. Every Wednesday night, host Ralph Edwards surprised a celebrity or some other worthy personality with a presentation of that person's life story, complete with appearances by family, friends, and figures from the person's past like a teacher or an old classmate. In Cousins' retelling of the story, he serendipitously bumped into Edwards at an airport and told him about the Hiroshima women and Reverend Tanimoto, and they decided that Tanimoto would make an ideal candidate for Edwards' show.[45] On May 11, 1955, a few days after the women and Tanimoto arrived in New York, Tanimoto went on the show. Edwards surprised him with the appearance of his wife and four children (whom he had thought to be at home in Japan) as well as Robert Lewis, who had co-piloted the Enola Gay. At the end of the program, Edwards explained the situation and

made an appeal for the plastic surgery project. He told television
viewers to send contributions to "Maidens, Box 200, New York
1, New York." The first to make a contribution, Lewis handed
Edwards a check for $50, saying that the money came from him
and his fellow crew members.[46] Some viewers wrote to object
about the shameful exhibition of an Enola Gay co-pilot almost
crying in front of television audiences; others declared that the
Japanese still had much to atone for in regard to Pearl Harbor before receiving any American charity.[47] But the overwhelming majority of letters about the TV show were positive: HPCA got only
fourteen critical letters while receiving 23,000 that praised the
project.[48] The show brought in $52,422 and solved the project's
cash flow. "It was manna from heaven," Cousins later recalled.[49]

Tanimoto's appearance on the television show also alarmed
those with a vested interest in U.S. nuclear policy. A former ABCC
director complained to Assistant Secretary of State for Far Eastern Affairs Walter Robertson that the "maudlin" episode could
be used by communists "to reinforce leftist propaganda of American guilt" and lead to "further anti-American demonstrations."[50]
The State Department forwarded this letter to Cousins, who
agreed that Japanese communists were "denounc[ing] the project
as a manifestation of American guilt" or as a way for the U.S.
government to "offset the bad impression" created by the irradia-
tion of Japanese fishermen on the *Lucky Dragon.* "But the Communists," Cousins argued, "were shamed into silence by the tremendous enthusiasm among Japanese in all walks of life for what
is being attempted. An overwhelmingly large proportion of Japanese have seen this project for what it really is—a genuine attempt by a few Americans to do that which is in their power in
behalf of human beings who might not be helped otherwise."[51]
Cousins firmly believed in the power of American benevolence.[52]

Though critical of the extremes of the Red Scare and the State Department, Cousins operated within, not against, the dominant political paradigm, on the left flank of the Cold War consensus.

The U.S. State Department, however, remained wary of the Maidens project because of its potential to undermine U.S. nuclear policy as well as the U.S.-Japan security pact. After he became president in 1953, Eisenhower reduced Truman's defense budget and attempted to secure containment cheaply by drastically increasing the number of nuclear warheads. Experienced with the devastating effects of nuclear weapons, the Japanese were deeply disturbed by Eisenhower's policy and anxious about being in the firing line between the two superpowers in East Asia. Two years earlier, many Japanese had vigorously opposed the U.S.-Japan security pact because they were terrified that their nation's ties to an unpredictable United States waging a cold war against an equally dangerous Soviet Union might bring another, even greater nuclear attack upon Japan.[53] Aware of this fear, the State Department speculated that the Hiroshima Maidens project's focus on victims of U.S. nuclear policy might reawaken anti-American sentiment overseas. The Department also worried about anti-nuclear protest in the United States. Unlike the moral adoptees, who would stay in Japan, the Hiroshima women would be more visible and had the potential, as the New York Friends Association warned, of being showcased as a "chamber of horrors." The State Department therefore tried to stop the project from literally getting off the ground by telegramming an order to stop the women's flight from Japan. But General John W. Hull, who had authorized the military plane for the project, ignored the order until the plane departed. He then reported the flight as a fait accompli and stated that reversing the plane in mid-flight might cause international embarrassment.[54] Conceding defeat,

State Department officials vigilantly and successfully guarded against "a rush of 'Hiroshima girl' projects in major American cities."[55]

The State Department was alarmed because it had heard about interest in replicating the project in San Francisco, Philadelphia, and elsewhere. But the most serious proposal for another "Hiroshima girl" project came from Mobile, Alabama, which the Department managed to nip in the bud. Dr. A. Carl Adkins, a Methodist minister and spokesperson for the plan, explained that the proposal had the "unanimous enthusiasm" of Mobile community leaders and that they were partly motivated by a desire to mitigate an image of Southern racism. "Mobile is in the center of a section of our nation which no doubt in the minds of the Japanese is synonymous with race prejudice, and to bring these girls into the homes of the citizens of this community would be a tremendous gesture of good will," Adkins claimed.[56] State Department officials appeared unimpressed by the project's potential value in assisting their government to woo Third World nations. In the view of these officials, nuclear weapons alone "stopped communist aggression" and "protect[ed] the free world."[57] Max Bishop of the Under Secretary of State's office added that "the sooner the 'Hiroshima Anniversary' is forgotten or at least ignored, the sooner we can bring about a solid foundation for good relations between the United States and Japan."[58] The Department tried to convince Adkins that the *hibakusha* had access to good plastic surgery services in Japan, even though Cousins had reported that such facilities in Nagasaki were "only fair" and in Hiroshima, "definitely third-rate." Adkins, who had been talking with Cousins, was not fooled, but he was powerless to make his project work unless he had State Department cooperation for basic necessities such as visas.[59]

Cousins later claimed that he "didn't give a damn about what the State Department thought," but he never sent the women on a publicity tour throughout the country to show the effects of the atomic bomb. The official government line was that the atomic bombs not only shortened the war and saved lives, but also caused deaths and injuries no different than those from conventional weapons. The State Department maintained this position even after the *Lucky Dragon* incident and thus feared that the women chosen for the project would be "disfigured in a ghastly manner."[60] But the project did not include women with terribly deformed facial features—the one with "a nose shoved into a snout," for instance—because the plastic surgeons understandably chose women with high probability for successful outcomes. Always trying to be considerate of the Hiroshima women's sensitivities, Cousins believed that "parading the girls around" and making a spectacle of their injuries—injuries that the women had gone to great lengths to try to hide—would be "exploitative." He did not believe such a publicity tour would be effective in molding public opinion. Although he personally thought nuclear weapons should be outlawed, Cousins did not want to cast the project as a plea against nuclear weapons. First and foremost, he wanted to help the selected twenty-five "girls," victims of what he believed was an immoral use of the bomb by his country. He also "wanted to shame the bastards" responsible for the ABCC policy; and finally, if the project raised awareness about the horrors of nuclear weapons, so much the better.[61]

But Cousins' attentiveness to the women and his modest goals for the project ended up serving State Department interests. The women, after all, *were* acutely self-conscious about their injuries. As one Hiroshima woman recalled, "Having a maimed face can really depress you and deprive you of all incentive to do anything. Whatever people say, the face is what counts if you're a woman." Two other women later admitted separately that their shame about their appearance meant more to them than helping to bring about global peace.[62] Individual, gendered attitudes about beauty and self-worth therefore also worked in the State Department's favor. The project's focus on rehabilitation—on the women's future rather than their unfortunate past—helped it conform to State Department concerns, as well as to a forward-looking, nationalist ethos that celebrated a spirit of "can-do-ism." This was reflected in the English translation of *genbaku otome* as "Hiroshima Maidens," in which "atomic bomb" was replaced with "Hiroshima." By making Hiroshima a metonym for atomic destruction, the name not only omitted Nagasaki, but also allowed English speakers to imagine that atomic destruction was unique to Hiroshima and would not happen elsewhere.

If Hiroshima was a metonym for atomic destruction, the Hiroshima *hibakusha* who were appealing for American help had to show acceptance of the reason for dropping an atomic bomb on their city. In his tours around the United States, Reverend Tanimoto stressed that the Japanese were not bitter about the atomic blasts. He told an audience in Dallas, Texas, that the Japanese "believe that the Hiroshima disaster was a sacrifice for their own mistakes. They firmly believe that Japan started the war and feel that what happened in Hiroshima and in Nagasaki was a price they had to pay."[63] En route to New York, the Hiroshima Maidens stopped in Hawai'i and paid a visit to Pearl Harbor to show that they recognized that Japan started the war.[64] Once on the U.S. mainland, a few of the women spoke to the press in prearranged interviews to stress, as the *New York Herald Tribune* reported, "that they bore no hatred for their injuries." The *Herald Tribune* noted that Michiko Sako, one of the Maidens, mentioned their visit to Pearl Harbor and stated, "The Japanese Navy took the first step in the last war. We survivors of Hiroshima got a terrible destruction upon us, but we should have repentance rather than hatred, and we began to hate war in general."[65] Relying on the subjunctive "should have," Sako's perspective slightly varied from Tanimoto's claim that Hiroshimans accepted the bomb as punishment for their own wrongdoing, but got across the message that some Japanese understood their sins and were willing to atone for them. Similarly, in a later interview, Suzue Oshima told an Associated Press reporter, "When I think about how kind everyone is, I'm glad I've never been bitter about the bomb. Just please—no more Hiroshima[s]."[66]

The Japanese understandably tried to appeal to American feelings in order to achieve a desired outcome. This call to make Hiroshima a symbol of peace was what had attracted Cousins to Tanimoto's plans in the first place. Tanimoto tried, but failed, to have the women meet either former president Truman or President Eisenhower because he took seriously the concept of atonement and reconciliation—and probably because it would have generated more publicity.[67] Tanimoto continued to praise American audiences for their nation's generosity to Japan after the war and for preventing "famine and suffering which would have been even greater than the losses of war itself." He informed Americans that the Japanese were "filled with gratitude" toward their country and "eager to show [their] appreciation."[68] Appealing to Americans to reach for their pocketbooks, Tanimoto and the women understandably emphasized what they wanted to hear.

Many Hiroshimans, of course, felt hostility toward the United States for dropping the bomb.[69] Tellingly, the journalist Clark Lee titled the chapter on Hiroshima in his Occupation memoir "Hiroshima Doesn't Hate Us," obliquely acknowledging that there was a reason for Hiroshima to hate Americans.[70] Postwar writings, however, usually failed to state the reason directly: that Americans were responsible for a wholesale massacre of civilians. Indirect admission through speculation and rhetorical questions were more common in public discourse. Lee mused, "Imagine what would have happened in a war-crimes court—if we had lost—to the Americans who invented the atom bomb and the Americans who dropped it!"[71]

Reverend Marvin Green, Tanimoto's old classmate and the HPCA treasurer, could not adhere to such wishful thinking. Years later, he reflected, "I had always felt that we [Americans] were the most hated group in the world. . . . And very seldom did we ever have any love or affection [from the Japanese]." At best, the Japanese regarded Americans with "apathy," in his opinion: "Those Japanese students had nothing but antagonism for [American] Christians. It came out in some of the discussions and lectures that we had, the questions that were thrown out at us. . . . And it could hardly be otherwise."[72] Green thought that Tanimoto "was speaking politically" when he told Americans that Hiroshimans did not dwell on the past and simply wanted to move on with their lives or dedicate themselves to world peace. "It wasn't that [Tanimoto] was insincere," Green explained. "It was just he felt this was the best approach to Americans." Green himself took this approach; when he coordinated a campaign to give a scholarship to Tanimoto's daughter, Koko, he talked not about Hiroshimans' resentment but about the Christian love between the two peoples.[73] Reverend Green did not believe that Hiroshimans were exploiting Americans' guilt or generosity: "I think it was desperation, borne of starvation and suffering and death. It was just the pure horrors of the war crying out in the aftermath."[74]

Green wanted to respond to the cries of those who had suffered so greatly in the war. He and others like him understood how fortunate stateside Americans had been, buffered from the fighting and the misery by two oceans. For these Americans, Hiroshima and the Holocaust epitomized "man's inhumanity to man" in their respective "theaters" of war, and as such, the two acts of mass murder preoccupied the humanitarian members of the HPCA.[75] Cousins, for instance, went to Germany the year before he first went to Japan, and wrote a long article with a title professing guilt for having suffered so little: "An Apology for Living." The article, about the displaced persons (then known as "DPs"), concentrated on the Nazis' youngest victims and featured a photograph of some Jewish children who had escaped the Holocaust.[76] John Hersey, having examined the war from the soldier's perspective in two novels, wrote not only *Hiroshima* but also a novel about a Jewish community in Warsaw under Nazi occupation.[77]

Although the *New York Daily News* wryly repeated "the acid crack . . . 'the way to win a war is to lose it to the United States,'" the predominantly positive reactions of the print media to the Hiroshima Maidens suggest that the strategy of emphasizing the Hiroshimans' lack of resentment was largely effective.[78] Most printed commentary referred to the ongoing Cold War, citing the Maidens project as evidence of the goodness and moral rectitude of the American nation in contrast to the Soviet enemy. Calling the project "a gesture in keeping with the finest American humanitarian tradition," the *Savannah News* claimed: "This act of generosity demonstrates to the world that the United States wishes to serve peaceful purposes in the interest of civilization as opposed to war-like objectives which our enemies persist in supporting."[79] Trying to depoliticize the project, the *Dayton News* clearly rejected the notion of American culpability or error for using the bombs and asserted that the project "is not subject to interpretation as an act of national penitence for dropping the bomb in [the] interest of shortening a murderous war. Nor is it suspect as a gimmick of official propaganda. . . . It is individuals in one country saying to individuals in another: 'We're sorry it had to be you—and we want to help you!' Of such stuff and no other are made man's finest adventures in brotherhood."[80] While sounding regretful, this article, like most opinions composed for publication, makes no actual apologies, thus adhering to the U.S. government's rationale for the atomic bombing and the view that the *hibakusha* should be helped through private acts of charity.

As victims who survived another sort of holocaust, the Hiroshima women evoked sympathy among American Jews. The wealthy Jewish lawyer who paid for the women's hospital stays was also heavily involved in Jewish charities that, after the war, concentrated their efforts on alleviating the suffering of Holocaust survivors.[81] The *Kansas City Jewish Chronicle* praised the Hiroshima Maidens project for "repair[ing] some of the damage of the last world war . . . damage that can still be repaired"—reminding its readers, once again, of the lives lost in the Holocaust. The *Chronicle* also proudly pointed out that "Jewish generosity and kindness" made the project possible. Like the mainstream press, Cousins had downplayed his Jewish ethnicity and the crucial role of Jewish charity in the Maidens project, preferring to present the program as an "American" benevolence. This article, however, proudly noted that "a great New York Jewish institution," Mount Sinai Hospital, was donating the plastic surgery services, and that the "Hiroshima Peace Society of New York," led by the Jewish Cousins, would cover all other costs, including pocket money. "As the holiday of Shavuoth, which celebrates the giving of the Law on Mount Sinai, approaches, we are happy to note that a Jewish hospital which carries the name of that hallowed mountain in the Egyptian desert is giving concrete expression to the principles once proclaimed on that mountain, to those ideals of justice and kindliness which Judaism first gave the world."

The *Chronicle* article also stated that Japan had helped Jewish refugees fleeing from Nazism, which was half-true. Against the orders of the Japanese Foreign Minister, Sugihara Chiune, the consulate at Kovno, Lithuania, saved at least 1,600 Polish Jews by granting them visas to Japan in 1940—an act for which the Japanese Foreign Ministry punished Sugihara.[82] Unaware of this, the newspaper quoted a New York Yiddish paper and argued, "In an indirect way the Jews have expressed their gratitude to Japan through Norman Cousins and through Mount Sinai Hospital for the humanitarianism which Japan had displayed toward Jews."[83]

In contrast to the *Kansas City Jewish Chronicle*, the liberal nondenominational Protestant magazine *Christian Century* published a rare editorial criticizing not the project itself but the effusive publicity about it. The magazine conceded that "everyone connected with this mission of friendship and mercy has a right to feel deep satisfaction," but it remained consistent with its 1945 position that the bombing was "America's atomic atrocity." Ten years later, the magazine asserted, "It is, we repeat, a lovely story in all its parts—except that it should have never been." The *Christian Century* argued that "an American sense of guilt at the way in which we ended the war" motivated Americans to conduct a project to "wipe out the scars" of U.S. aggression. But it suggested that the effort was futile because "there are some scars that no plastic surgeon can erase, and Hiroshima is one cut deep into the American conscience."[84]

Such a straightforward admission of guilt was rare in published commentary, but individual letters to the editor or private correspondence sent to the HPCA tended to support the *Christian Century*'s assertion about American guilt. Although private letter writers sometimes repeated themes stated in the media about working toward peace rather than universal destruction, more often than not their letters expressed feelings of contrition and sorrow that were missing in most newspapers and magazines.[85] These Americans frequently used the word "atone" in their statements. In her contribution Lois P. Munroe wrote: "As an American who has felt guilty ever since the atomic bombs fell on Hiroshima and Nagasaki, it gives me great please [*sic*] to be able to do some small thing to help atone for this blot on our national honor."[86] Still, these writers often referred to the bombing indirectly, in the passive voice, or in a prepositional phrase. But an octogenarian thanking Cousins for the Hiroshima Maidens project nearly thirty years later addressed the subject forthrightly. "When we dropped the bomb on Hiroshima," Jessie Borchers explained, "my husband was shocked when I said: '*I* did it—it was done in the world in which I live'—and you gave me the blessed privilege of being a part of the program designed to show how much we cared for the victims."[87] Distance from the event, perhaps, made admission easier. Nevertheless, all these letter writers expressed gratitude for the chance to help "heal," an opportunity available only through private channels.

The exception to such reactions among those who sought to help the Hiroshiman women were the New York-area Japanese Americans who invited the Hiroshiman women on outings and for Japanese meals in their homes. Many, like Yuri Kochiyama, were former internees. After the war, Kochiyama and her 442nd veteran husband, Bill, had settled in Harlem to raise their family.

Recalling her involvement with the project, Kochiyama explained that Japanese Americans were not called upon to be host parents because they were not as financially well off as the Quaker host families living in the suburbs. Ten years after the internment, most Nisei were raising young families on a tight budget—the median age of the Nisei at the time of the internment was nineteen—and most of the older Issei generation of internees had not been able to recoup their losses. Kochiyama's involvement, which she insisted was not much compared to that of other Nisei, reflected her political sympathies; she later became and remains a political and community activist and was an associate of Malcolm X. Haruko Akamatsu, widow of the pastor of the Japanese American United Church in New York, related that she and her husband were motivated to help welcome the Hiroshima women because they too believed that the atomic bombings were wrong. She recalled going to a peace rally at Central Park in 1950 where she heard a speech saying that the United States did not need to drop atomic bombs on Japan and that its "fear of Russia" prompted the U.S. to use the people of Nagasaki and Hiroshima as "guinea pigs" to test uranium. Both Akamatsu and her late husband had relatives in Hiroshima prefecture, but it was not the connection to Hiroshima that compelled her to reach out to the Hiroshima women. As a Japanese American who had recently been treated unjustly by the U.S. government—she had been interned at Topaz—Akamatsu felt that the bombing of the two Japanese cities was also "unfair."[88]

Decades after the project, some have wondered why this program treated Hiroshima women only, no men and no Nagasaki women, and why the American coordinators referred to the women by the archaic term "maidens."[89] The fact is that the Americans picked up a program that the Japanese had already put in motion. Reverend Tanimoto assembled the women, Masugi and Japanese matrons took up their cause, and the Japanese press dubbed them *otome,* a word that also translates as "virgins." The name "Hiroshima Maidens" implied that the young women, who were in their late teens or early and mid-twenties, would remain virgins—that is, unmarried—unless they received treatment to make themselves "presentable" candidates for marriage. Tanimoto had stressed the women's unmarriageable state when he first tried to interest Cousins in the project, taking for granted that the American would understand his meaning[90]—an assumption that was not unwarranted, for Japanese and Americans held similar ideas about women's dependency on men. Many people in both cultures believed that women's financial security came through an attachment to a male provider, since men had greater access to good jobs and earned more for most work after the war, and that women's primary fulfillment came through bearing and raising children. Without treatment, the Hiroshima women "were to be forever removed from the fulfillment all women look to: marriage, the home, the family, the dignity of one's own life," observed a sympathetic contemporary. "Who, as they grew older, would cast a second look at such caricatures of womanhood?"[91] Men, on the other hand, were expected to find "dignity" in their profession, craft, or job—in roles usually not carrying a requirement of physical attractiveness—and thus male victims of the bomb were assumed to be in little danger of becoming "caricatures" of manhood.[92] The HPCA kept records of how many children the Hiroshima women bore after their surgeries in the United States, as if that were a measure of the project's success. Someone penciled in "19 children" on a 1969 update on the women that listed their ages, occupations, marriage status, and number of children.[93]

The Americans thus took up a theme stressed by the Japanese

that these young female victims of the bombs were "good girls," very worthy of help and kindness. Presented as cheerful individuals, the women supposedly were not resentful despite their injuries. Even those who missed the chance to receive treatment in the United States, Americans assured themselves, were not angry or jealous—a convenient palliative for any guilty feelings that might arise for giving aid to only a small group. According to the *Ann Arbor News,* the women "were incredibly selfless about the selections," remaining "gentle" and acting "happily" throughout the long selection process.[94] The press failed to mention the deep disappointment of the women denied the trip, especially since promises of subsequent trips for other groups never materialized.[95] Instead, Americans glowingly described how the deserving young women from Japan enjoyed American consumer products that were largely unavailable in Japan: hamburgers, electric vacuum cleaners, television, and U.S. fashions. The women reportedly also helped with chores at the host families' homes, voluntarily offered to baby-sit, and even demonstrated the Japanese tea ceremony at local churches.[96] Hatsuko "Helen" Yokoyama later said she had encouraged the women "to behave just as they would to their own parents back in Japan . . . [and] to help with the dishes after each meal; to give massages to their 'American parents' when they seemed tired; never to forget to say 'thank you' when a favor had been done; and not to say 'yes' when they didn't really mean it."[97] The twenty-five women came from a range of social backgrounds and class positions, but Americans ignored the differences. As dutiful daughters on their very best behavior, the "maidens" as a group represented the best of Japanese culture, and their example helped Americans adjust notions of their old enemy by appealing to deeply ingrained beliefs about mutual obligations between young women and their parents.

A few of the hosts had less than altruistic motives for opening

The original AP caption for this photograph read: "Mingled emotions bring tears to the eyes of Motoko Yamashita, one of Japan's Hiroshima Maidens who are victims of the world's first atomic bombing, as American girlfriends bid her farewell at New York's Idlewild Airport on June 12, 1956. Miss Yamashita, whose facial scars are scarcely visible after the series of plastic surgery operations performed on her and her countrywomen, is one of the group returning to Japan." AP/Wide World Photos.

their homes to the Japanese women, who were always paired when they stayed in Quaker homes to prevent loneliness. One host, a writer, saw them as subjects for a series of articles he wanted to sell. Another hostess, apparently still embittered by the loss of a relative in the Pacific during the war, saw the project as an opportunity to make household servants out of two former enemies. The women staying with her quietly informed Yokoyama of the situation, and she verified their plight by spending a full day with them. An emergency hospital stay was arranged for the women to get them out of the hostess's house without insulting her, and soon the women were transferred into the home of a more gracious host. Fortunately, the insensitive hosts proved to be in the minority; most lived up to their liberal values.[98]

The Quaker hosts and their Hiroshima guests, of course, could not replicate an actual parent-child relationship. Everyone recognized that Yokoyama served as the women's surrogate parent for the duration of the program. It was Yokoyama, not the host "parents," who held the hand of each woman as she went into surgery and helped her count numbers aloud as she received anesthesia.[99] But as the warm correspondence between the women and their host parents attests, many kept in contact for decades after the project, some of them continuing to call the host parents "Mother" and "Dad." And this contact is still maintained to some degree among the surviving Hiroshima women and their hosts.[100]

Predictably, American interest in supporting charity initiatives for the people of Hiroshima waned. What Tanimoto saw as the beginning of a host of projects became the end of Cousins' activism for Hiroshima. The American organization that Cousins helped found stayed with the theme of violence to women during war but took their funding, which Tanimoto had helped to raise, to another part of the world. After the Hiroshima Maidens project the HPCA, at Cousins' bidding, sponsored a similar project for a group of Polish women who had been scarred mentally or physically by Nazi biological experiments. These women, mostly highly educated professionals ranging in age from thirty to sixty, became known as the "Ravensbrueck Lapins" ("lapins" indicated their status as "human guinea pigs"). Reverend Green remembered them as the "Polish Maidens" despite their age and status, expressing a link he saw in not only the atrocities both groups had suffered but also their rehabilitation goals.[101]

After the "Maidens" project, the HPCA made an attempt to establish a partnership between American and Japanese doctors for treatment of *hibakusha* in Japan. But the Japanese medical establishment, upset because they felt the project implied an insult to their skills, were resistant to further programs with the HPCA. The Americans had, in Barker's words, "outstayed their welcome." When proposals to establish this venture also failed, plans came to a complete standstill.[102]

The HPCA board members and workers also lost momentum. The organization's printed stationery showed names crossed out from its list of board members as time went on.[103] "Americans," Reverend Green recalled, "wanted to do something for the kids, the orphans, and the girls. But they weren't interested . . . in buildings, structures, institutions."[104] By July 1956, during the midst of the "Maidens" project, the earlier moral adoptions program retained less than half of its active support. Green sent a newsletter urging lapsed "parents" to assist the orphanages in continuing their "wonderful work" by giving to a general fund. "Such financial support," Green argued, "will be no less effective in terms of world friendship and helping to bring understanding and peace between our two nations."[105] But the appeal fell on deaf ears. By the mid-1960s, the program "petered out" completely.[106] On the Japanese side, the Yamashitas had been forced to give up running their orphanage much earlier; by 1954 they had been replaced with trained social workers.[107]

Despite its stated goal of providing aid to atomic bomb orphans, the moral adoptions program ignored Nagasaki orphans and covered only a fraction of the six thousand children of Hiroshima who lost their parents on August 6, 1945, and in the days that followed.[108] Moreover, the program made no formal provisions for children when they reached the age that required them to leave the orphanages. Norman Cousins initially saw the moral adoptions as "lifetime commitments," but as it worked out, most "parents" stopped payments after their "children" had to leave the orphanages at age sixteen, according to Japanese law.[109] Even though some "moral parents" had expressed interest, no legal adoptions seem to have occurred after Congress made Japanese immigration legal again three years after the program started.[110] Cousins had strongly suggested that moral parents do as he tried to do and bring their wards to the United States for education, or else support their continuing education in Japan.[111] Some moral parents may have done this, but the available records suggest that they did not. Instead, the records indicate that a problem of juvenile delinquency occurred among some of those teenagers once they were cut loose on the streets of Hiroshima.[112]

Not surprisingly, the ties between the orphans and their "moral parents"—tenuous from the beginning—broke off. But at least the donors tried to make amends, in however limited a way, for the horrors inflicted by their nation upon Hiroshima—a gesture attempted by very few Americans. As a result of the efforts of those who did participate, the program brought material benefits to 600 children and youth. Most of the orphans and their "moral parents" had never met face to face and lacked fluency in each other's language, making overseas communication difficult in a time before the Internet or even cheap international phone calls. Sustaining ties in the face of such challenges would have been extraordinary without ongoing institutional support. In contrast, the U.S. Army 27th Infantry "Wolfhounds" who "adopted" an orphanage in Osaka in 1949—the same year when Cousins began the moral adoptions program—continue, more than fifty years later, to arrange short home stays each summer for two to three orphans from the Holy Family Orphanage with a Wolfhound family in Hawai'i, where the 27th is based.[113] In the end, however laudable these private American efforts may have been, they could not match their government's ability to compensate the victims—if the U.S. government had been willing to pay reparations to the *hibakusha,* which, of course, it was not.

Some of the relationships and friendships forged through the "Maidens" project, however, lasted a lifetime. One of the women, who became particularly close to the Cousinses, even named her son "Norman Cousins." The other women remained loyal to their American benefactors, and whatever complaints they might have had about their experience in America, they kept to themselves. Practically everyone involved heralded the project as a success and continue to do so. Even the skeptical State Department breathed a sigh of relief: "Despite the unfortunate publicity which accompanied the arrival of the Hiroshima maidens last spring, the Hiroshima maidens project has earned the United States considerable good will in Japan to date," reported an official. "It has not been exploited as a publicity stunt nor has it been regarded as an official apology for our wartime use of the atomic bomb."[114] The State Department could tout the project as an act of American benevolence, an act demonstrating, to quote Assistant Secretary Walter Robertson, "the American spirit of humanitarianism of which we are justifiably proud."[115]

Under the rubric of morality and parentage, both projects implicitly challenged the rightness of dropping the atomic bombs and asserted American accountability for the bomb's "most innocent" victims. Neither program, however, sought to end or overtly criticize U.S. policy on nuclear weapons. The projects represented reconciliation with a hated former enemy in the agreeable shape of children and young women and, to some, atonement and partial compensation for dropping the atomic bombs. These "people-to-people" programs were avowedly antiracist—encouraging liberal-minded, politically engaged Americans to forge relationships across national, racial, and class boundaries and to see their interdependence with the wider world.[116] During the Cold War, the overall political objective was to clean out the "breeding ground for communism," and providing a "wholesome" environment for Hiroshima women and youth dovetailed with Americans' deeply held beliefs about responsibility, sympathy, and humanity. But it also tied in with a postwar American "global nationalism" that combined convictions about "American chosenness, mission, and destiny" with the notion that the United States had an obligation to spread "universal" values such as liberty, democracy, and freedom throughout the world.[117] The family trope both naturalized the hierarchy between Americans and their former enemies and privatized the responsibility for the Hiroshimans' care.

The fact that the moral adoptions program and the Hiroshima Maidens project were more symbolic than substantial did not seem to matter a great deal to Americans, then or since. At the start of the "Maidens" project in 1955, the *Ann Arbor News* had enthusiastically claimed: "The excited girls are starting out on a journey that will lead to a new life. The persistence of a few compassionate people in this country and in Japan made it possible. While the project is not a large one in scope, it is tremendous in implication. And it is surely one of the most touchingly worthwhile undertakings that has come to our attention in a long time."[118] Cousins, thirty-five years afterward, declared satisfaction with the Hiroshima Maidens project despite its small reach and lack of lasting impact. "The world can be improved only one person at a time," he stated, deflecting his interviewer's attempt to find a larger meaning for the project.[119] The two projects improved the lives of twenty-five women and, for a time, assisted in meeting the needs of six hundred children when no help appeared to be forthcoming from any other quarter.

CHAPTER SEVEN

Hollywood's Japan

On December 5, 1957, at its studio headquarters, Warner Brothers put on a lavish spectacle for the premiere of what it touted as "one of the most eagerly awaited films of the year": *Sayonara*, starring Marlon Brando and Miiko Taka. As invited guests and an international press corps entered Warner Brother's North Gate, they encountered a "gigantic display" of "tropical plants, tapestries, oriental prints and other items of Japanese culture . . . spotlighted by a bank of multicolored lamps" on the 213-foot wall adjoining the gate. Once inside, they were welcomed by "sixteen of the most beautiful Southern California girls of Japanese ancestry" wearing "the traditional costumes of Japan," including Mitzi Miya, Miss Nisei Queen of 1957–58. The kimonoed Nisei women escorted guests to their seats in one of ten studio theaters used for the gala event, hosted by Jack Linkletter, along with Andy Griffith and Ed Wynn. To give "spectator fans a full unobstructed view of the glittering affair," Warner Brothers erected sixteen sections of bleachers in the studio parking lot and illuminated the Thursday night sky with 10,000 one-hundred-watt bulbs.

Although *Sayonara* premiered with tinsel-town fanfare and expectations for huge profits, the film's makers also held the loftier goal of promoting international friendship between Americans and Japanese. Explaining the film's higher purpose, *Sayonara*'s director, Joshua Logan, explained: "We want to bring the issue of intermarriage between America's GIs and Japanese women into full focus—to say that modern communication has discarded forever that old saw that 'East is East, and West is West, and never the twain shall meet.'"[1] The film *Sayonara,* based on James A. Michener's bestselling novel of the same name, told the story of how U.S. Air Force Major Lloyd Gruver (Brando) learns to overcome his racial prejudice against the Japanese when he falls in love with Hana-Ogi (Taka), the star of an all-female musical company. Warner Brothers' film became the third highest grossing movie of the year, earning the studio $10.5 million.[2] It was nominated for ten Oscars, including Best Picture and Best Director, and won four, though not in the major categories.

A high-budget spectacle with Academy Award nominations and an A-list cast, *Sayonara* probably remains the best-remembered film of this genre. For indeed it was a genre. From 1949 to 1967, Hollywood produced over a dozen films set in Japan—some of them forgettable and forgotten B-films such as *Tokyo After Dark* (1959) and *Cry For Happy* (1961). But some were films with prominent A-list talent like *The Barbarian and the Geisha* (1958), which starred John Wayne, and, of course, that other Marlon Brando hit, *The Teahouse of the August Moon* (1956).[3] These were a subset of dozens of Asia-related, Cold War Orientalist films screened in American theaters—films featuring or concerning Japanese Americans such as *Go For Broke!* (1951) and *Bad Day at Black Rock* (1955); silver-screen East-West love stories such as *Love Is a Many-Splendored Thing* (1955) and *The*

World of Suzie Wong (1960); and nearly two dozen war movies set in Asia, including *The Bridge on the River Kwai* (1957). The emergence of this genre can be traced to several factors. The U.S. wars in Asia made American filmmakers and audiences pay more attention to Asia, Asians, and even Asian Americans. The weekly bestselling lists in the *New York Times Book Review* and *Publisher's Weekly* from 1931 to 1980 showed that fiction and nonfiction works about wars set in China, Japan, Korea, Burma, the Pacific, and Southeast Asia dominated bestsellers on Asia.[4] It was easier for American writers to follow the familiar and accepted plot line about American heroism in stories about Americans in Japan. At the same time, Hollywood studios began breaking the taboo against films that confronted racial prejudice. Before World War II, the studios—largely owned by Jews who were well aware of society's prejudices—calculated that the majority of their customers would be unsympathetic to films that championed racial and ethnic minorities. But after the war, the studios tuned into the changing opinions about race—more Americans recognized that racism lacked a scientific basis and believed that such "immature" beliefs and practices hampered their nation's ability to provide equally for all citizens at home and to maintain nonwhite allies in the Cold War.[5] In contrast to the tragic endings of interracial romances in prewar films, postwar films allowed interracial couples—if the couple consisted of an Asian woman and a white man—to have a happy ending. The Production Code Office had initially judged the Michener story in 1953 as "an unacceptable treatment of illicit sex" and encouraged a script change that showed the couple attempting to marry.[6] It was fornication, not miscegenation, that concerned the code office of Joseph I. Breen, a Roman Catholic.[7] Revising the end of Michener's novel to have the protagonists become a married, procreative couple satisfied the censors and allowed the Warner Brothers publicity mill to crow: "Inter-racial love and marriage have come a long way since 'Madame Butterfly.'"[8]

Michener's novel was immediately recognized as a potential hit movie by a film industry eager to offset a decline in movie attendance after the war.[9] The author received bids for the movie rights to *Sayonara* from individual filmmakers and studios even before its publication as a book in 1954. Filmmakers like Joshua Logan had both monetary and artistic reasons for making films about Japan at this time. Logan, for instance, nursed an ambition to introduce Japanese theatrical arts to a wider American audience and used *Sayonara* to highlight kabuki and *bunraku*. He took advantage of new technologies to offer sumptuous spectacles of Japanese gardens, landscapes, architecture, and costumes in Technicolor—as did almost all Hollywood films about Japan.

These postwar films indicated the degree to which American perceptions of the Japanese had changed since the end of World War II. Wartime films like *The Purple Heart* (1944) had emphasized the depravity of the Japanese; now Hollywood promoted visions of a kinder, gentler Japan.[10] Even postwar films about the Pacific War itself often carry this message of humanizing the Japanese enemy. *The Bridge on the River Kwai,* for example—the top grosser the year *Sayonara* came out—had a story line driven by conflict among the Allied POWs; the struggle against the Japanese was secondary.[11] The film shows sympathy for the Japanese soldiers: they seem to fear the imperious commandant, Colonel Saito (Sessue Hayakawa), who represents "militaristic Japan." The film thus reflects the distinction made in postwar American media and memoirs between "ordinary" Japanese men and evil, high-strung "militarists" like Tōjō.[12]

By the mid-1950s and early 1960s, these films set in Japan represented a culmination of an earlier postwar process that helped make the former enemy into an ally. Americans, to be sure, never completely forgot that the Japanese had been wartime enemies responsible for heinous brutalities. But vision after vision of cherry-blossom Japan, receptive Japanese women, and grateful, smiling Japanese children in postwar Hollywood films helped Americans accommodate a more tolerant view of the Japanese. Although these gentler visions of Japan were not new to American audiences, the wider circulation of such images after the war and the repetition of the tropes in films helped fix a transformed version of the prewar image in American popular culture.

During the war years, the Office of War Information (OWI) had enlisted the studios to mobilize public support for the war, but the OWI was disbanded after 1945.[13] After the war, Hollywood nonetheless continued to produce films that reflected American attitudes and generally supported U.S. foreign policy objectives without direction from Washington or conscious collaboration among themselves. The filmmakers who created films on Japan attempted to depict a friendlier, more humanized relationship with the Japanese while at the same time trying to make a hefty profit. In the hands of Hollywood filmmakers, the effort to depict the Japanese as friends became thoroughly commercialized—which was, of course, completely consistent with the policymakers' goal of propping up Japan as a democratic "bulwark" against communism in the Far East.[14] With a trained and educated workforce, a corporate infrastructure, and a centralized government bureaucracy, Japan had not only an existing industrial base but also a location in northeast Asia—near China and the Soviet Union—that made it important to U.S. Cold War geostrategy. Continuing the Truman administration's policy of striving to "keep the Japanese on our side" by strengthening the "workshop" of Asia, the Eisenhower administration pushed to soften domestic and international opposition to opening markets for Japanese products.[15]

Hollywood spectacles about any subject dazzled viewers, inducing forgetfulness and momentarily overwhelming their sense of time and space.[16] The Hollywood films about Japan urged viewers to forget, to put aside any remaining wartime enmity and buy visions of an exotically attractive Japan and happily ending romantic tales. The studios' promotional "commercial tie-ins" encouraged filmgoers to purchase Japanese products and tours. Hollywood thus packaged and marketed the effort to remake America's former World War II enemy into a postwar ally. The filmmakers, however, could not avoid reinscribing the same Orientalist notions they thought they were challenging. As the Warner Brothers premiere for *Sayonara* illustrates, Hollywood promoted racial tolerance by selling Japan as an exotic spectacle to be enjoyed by western viewers and by resorting to an imagined, mysterious, and feminized "East." Thus the Japanese—even the American-born Nisei hostesses at the *Sayonara* premiere—remained culturally distant figures in Hollywood's view.

Hollywood's films on Japan that involved interracial love were romantic tales that aimed to deliver the uplifting message that love could overcome seemingly insurmountable barriers, healing racial divisions and enmity between the Japan and the United States. Like the charity initiatives and American programs that bettered the lives of the Hiroshima Maidens, a number of Hiroshima orphans, and postwar scholarship students like Robert Yukimasa Nishiyama, these romantic adventures in postwar films reduced the bilateral relationship between nations to an individual, personal level that both simplified the contemporary U.S. policy in Asia and commended it as humane and wise. The films glossed over the social and economic ambiguities of the larger, conflicted relationship between the two nations and portrayed the bonds of "love" as holding together the international, interracial "family." The postwar movie spectacles of Japan affirmed not only the American policy to reintegrate Japan into the U.S.-led liberal capitalist framework, but also beliefs that Americans were legitimately equipped to lead it.

Interracial Love

The romantic liaisons between so many American GIs and Japanese women mystified and disturbed some stateside Americans. The "folks back home" could accept the soldiers' giving out chewing gum and chocolate to Japanese children: the contact was minimal, and the action fit Americans' image of themselves as kind and generous. Even temporary sexual liaisons made sense to those who made allowances for young men's libidos, but most Americans—including many who served in the Occupation—wondered why a GI would want to marry and spend the rest of his life with a "Jap." In the immediate postwar years, memoirs and popular press articles of the Occupation tried to answer this question in print, and in the 1950s Hollywood began addressing this phenomenon on the big screen, using an old formula—love conquers all—to help explain cross-national, cross-racial relationships during the Cold War. More specifically, the films treated these romances in a traditional literary sense, where the man struggles, learns, and emerges from a relationship—usually with a woman—as an enlightened and empowered individual. These interracial love stories are tales of transformation and maturation that show Euroamerican men learning to become more open-minded, understanding, and wise—in short, mature men—

through their relations with the Japanese. Three films that premiered in consecutive years—*Three Stripes in the Sun* (1955), *The Teahouse of the August Moon* (1956), and *Sayonara* (1957)—have plots featuring a white American male protagonist who learns to become more competent in his patriarchal responsibilities.

Although *The Teahouse of the August Moon,* set in Okinawa, satirized the Occupation and presented a more ambiguous view about who should be in charge and who should be teaching whom, it depicts the Okinawans as childlike, hard-working people who squabble about trifling matters, trivialize the meaning of democracy, and care most about creating a teahouse for their amusement.[17] The local interpreter, Sakini (Marlon Brando), may be wise, but his bailiwick is clearly limited to a group of small islands off the southern tip of Japan.[18] But Captain Jeff Fisby (Glenn Ford), an earnest but incompetent Occupation officer, has learned not only to appreciate Okinawan traditions but also to communicate and operate successfully in an alien culture. He takes from Okinawa a skill that he can apply elsewhere, presumably in his capacity as a U.S. Army officer. While the characterizations reinforce the hierarchy between the U.S. military and the Okinawan or Japanese natives, the film's ending seems to justify the Occupation itself. The Okinawans invite the blundering and high-handed Americans into their teahouse for a celebration—no hard feelings about the Okinawans' subordinate status in their own homeland. The closing scene of American military personnel among happy, dancing Okinawans is at best a rose-colored and enabling vision of the U.S. occupation of Okinawa that persists to this day. As a satire and comedy, *The Teahouse of the August Moon,* like many memoirs and articles written by Occupationers, served to soften and minimize the cold, hard fact of Occupation.[19]

Three Stripes in the Sun is a movie based on the real-life story of Army Master Sergeant Hugh O'Reilly and his wife, Yuko.[20] The film version of their romance adapted their story so that "Yuko" is a beautiful interpreter (Mitsuko Kimura) who introduces O'Reilly (Aldo Ray) to a needy Osaka orphanage run by Catholic nuns, which O'Reilly's Army unit, the "Wolfhounds," adopts as their pet cause.[21] The film quickly establishes Sergeant O'Reilly's credentials as a Pearl Harbor survivor who hates the Japanese, resents being sent to Occupied Japan for active duty, and immediately asks for a transfer out of Japan.[22] His commanding officer (Phil Carey), however, denies O'Reilly's request as small-minded and lectures him that his country needs its servicemen "to act accordingly" so that they can leave the Japanese "as friendly allies" after the Occupation. By the end of the movie, a changed O'Reilly reverses his request to the same commanding officer: he asks to be discharged in Japan and not sent back to the States. The colonel, now a general—a promotion that emphasizes the character's authority, ability, and wisdom—asks O'Reilly if the sergeant is making this request because of his relationship with Yuko. When O'Reilly affirms this, expecting to be praised for his honorable intention to formalize the relationship, the general surprises him by lecturing him and insinuating that the sergeant is guilty of latent racism:

General: O'Reilly, if a man is lucky enough to find himself a good wife and one as lovely and as intelligent as this one seems to be, he should be the happiest man alive and be proud to take her around the world in any company.

Sgt. O'Reilly, emphatically: Sir, I *am* crazy about this girl. I am not ashamed of her and I would take her anyplace.

General: Except home, to the States. That's why you want a discharge here, isn't it?

Sgt. O'Reilly, defensively: Maybe it is, sir. And it's because I am in love with her. I don't want to take her back and have people pushing her around or sneering at her or laughing at her because she's Japanese.

General: You really think the American people are like that, or are you just telling me how you'd react to a man with a Japanese wife? [*with increasing anger*] You're a coward, O'Reilly. In spite of all . . . you're a coward. You haven't given one thought to this girl's feelings, and all you've been thinking about is yourself. You know you could take her back if you really wanted to. You're putting the decision up to me. All right, I'll make it. Request denied, is that what you wanted to hear?

Sgt. O'Reilly, petulantly: No.

General, calmer again: But secretly you're relieved, aren't you? I don't envy you, sergeant. [*Walks away.*][23]

Soon afterward, O'Reilly seems to have an epiphany; he rushes to Yuko to ask her to marry him and go back to the United States to live. Now confident and unwavering, O'Reilly assures her that they and their future children would be able to handle anything that came their way as long as they "had each other." Yuko accepts, deciding to trust him and to depend on him. As they walk into Yuko's house to get her father's blessing, printed words on the screen inform the audience that O'Reilly is currently living out his romance "with his Yuko" at West Point—where indeed, O'Reilly was stationed after Japan.

The message of *Three Stripes in the Sun,* that Americans needed to put aside wartime hatreds and rid themselves of racial prejudice toward the Japanese, won endorsements for the film from the Departments of State, Defense, and Army. All three departments reviewed the film script, which Columbia Pictures had submitted to secure the Army's cooperation during the movie's filming in Japan. The chief of the State Department's Far East Desk wrote that "[our section] has been very much impressed with the potentialities of this film and believes it will contribute greatly to U.S.-Japanese understanding." Improving bilateral understanding required just what the film did: toning down American racism for Japanese sensibilities, touting the good works of American soldiers in Japan, and providing a positive example to stateside audiences. The State Department therefore not only approved the film, but also urged the Defense Department to actively cooperate with Columbia Pictures because of "the extremely helpful theme of this film" to U.S. policy toward Japan. The Army agreed and promised "reasonable Army cooperation" at the movie's premiere and subsequent showings in the United States, as well as coordination with U.S. embassies and USIA representatives for the "exploitation of this picture" overseas.[24]

Sayonara projected a similar "helpful theme," with the male protagonist played by Marlon Brando going through the same transformation as the film character O'Reilly: learning to put aside bitterness, grow up, and overcome racial prejudice through his love of a Japanese woman. The first extended dialogue in *Sayonara* shows Lloyd "Ace" Gruver (Brando), a prejudiced, insensitive, and puerile Air Force fighter pilot, trying to deter Airman Joe Kelly (Red Buttons) from marrying his Japanese fiancée, Katsumi (Miyoshi Umeki). The scene setup emphasizes the distinction between "Ace" and his older-looking subordinate, Kelly. Although in Michener's novel Kelly is a "punk" kid, barely out of his teens, director Logan and producer William Goetz cast a man in his late thirties to play opposite a younger Brando, a decision that made Kelly appear experienced and wise compared to his hotshot superior. Brando played Gruver as an overconfident man, making broad gestures and sitting casually, with knees apart, on top of a desk in an airstrip office where the conversation takes place. As Bosley Crowther observed in his review of the film, Brando's Gruver at the beginning of the film is "as emotionally immature as a teenage boy."[25] In contrast, Buttons' Kelly stands behind another desk for most of the conversation, making little arm movement, with his shoulders and back erect. The scene establishes Kelly as the "adult"—standing his ground, sure of what he wants, unlike his callow superior who does not seem to be in any hurry to marry his own fiancée.[26]

By the end of the film Gruver has matured into an adult, determined to marry his Japanese love, to become a parent, and to face the challenges of an interracial family. He and Hana-Ogi decide to stand up to the regressive, racist forces trying to tear them apart. Before a crowd of fans and some journalists, Hana-Ogi explains their decision and makes a plea for understanding:

> [My fiancé] knows there are people in his country who would be disturbed by this. I know that my people will be shocked, too. But I hope that someday they will understand and approve. We are not afraid. Because we know this is right.
>
> *The Stars & Stripes journalist:* Major, the big brass are going to yell off their heads over this. The Japanese aren't going to like it much, either. Have you got anything to say to them, sir?
>
> *Gruver, pausing to find the right words:* Tell them we said, "Sayonara."[27]

This defiant "sayonara" differs from the spirit of Michener's novel, in which "sayonara" is a bittersweet parting between Gruver and Hana-Ogi. Michener has Gruver deciding to give up Hana-Ogi and to return to the States, where a promotion in the Air Force and marriage to Eileen Webster, a general's daughter, awaits him. According to Logan, the director of *Sayonara,* the changed ending for the film came at Marlon Brando's initiative and insistence. Brando initially refused the role of Gruver because he found the story racist. "I can't do a picture," Brando had declared, "where the American leaves the Japanese girl like the arrogant ending of *Madame Butterfly*." Thus Logan and Goetz met Brando's demand to change the ending in order to sign on their temperamental male lead. To emphasize the transformation of Gruver into a man of tolerance, Brando also affected a bad imitation of a southern accent ("a Texas accent thick as crude oil," wrote one reviewer) to identify Gruver as a southerner—a departure from Michener's characterization of his novel's hero.[28] James Michener corroborated Logan's story about Brando's insistence and remembered agreeing with the filmmakers' decision to change "the doleful ending that I had written." After the movie came out, Brando wrote to Logan—with whom he had a difficult relationship during the shooting—that several Asian friends had praised the film as the first time a Hollywood movie presented an Asian as "a first-class citizen in a Western story."[29]

Despite his attention to racism, Brando lacked a similar sensitivity toward women and demanded in his real life the kingly treatment that Euroamerican men received from Japanese women in mainstream Hollywood movies. Brando, who married a South Asian woman during *Sayonara*'s publicity period, told a movie magazine that he preferred foreign women because American women appeared too strident and independent—too "used to shifting for themselves." While foreign women knew "exactly when to encourage [their men] and when to shut up," the modern American woman, according to *Sayonara*'s male lead, didn't "often give the man a chance to feel and act like a man." Brando liked the way foreign women "wanted to please and entertain *him* and did not demand that he please and entertain them"— rather like the heroine in *Sayonara*.[30] In the film, as Gruver turns from bigotry to tolerance, Hana-Ogi goes through a parallel transformation from being a cross-dressing, mannish celebrity with adoring acolytes catering to her every need to a woman who submits herself to her man's will. Brando's progressive views on race and his regressive views on gender mirrored the way *Sayonara* and other Cold War films on Japan sold racial tolerance by subscribing to conservative gender roles.[31]

Sexual and Racial Politics in Casting

Because the interracial love story was at the heart of *Sayonara*, Logan and the studio made sure to cast a woman who they believed would be attractive to Euroamerican men. The search for the female lead took months. For a short time Warner Brothers and Logan thought of casting Audrey Hepburn in the role before they thought better of it. Hepburn herself refused to consider the part. "I can't possibly play an Oriental. No one would believe me. They'd laugh," she told Logan when he flew to Paris to discuss the role with her.[32] In the end, they decided that casting a "Japanese girl" in a "Japanese role" would appear less "prejudicial." After finding no one suitable in Japan or Hawai'i, the studio contacted the Japan American Citizens League (JACL) for help, and they eventually found a Nisei woman working in a Los Angeles travel agency for the part: Bette Ishimoto, who used the stage name Miiko Taka.[33] Prodding the public to appreciate Taka's beauty, just in case it went unnoticed, the studio advertised her as "universally feminine as Eve" or "almost a universal symbol of femininity and grace." A press release claimed, "Any man who could not respond to her dignified beauty should consult his doctor."[34]

Warner Brothers tried to maintain an attractive mystique about their new star. In Japanese culture, the colorful, long-sleeved kimonos that the studio had Taka wear in her publicity tour signify that the wearer is unmarried, and although the *Sayonara* publicists may not have known about this distinction, they promoted the illusion that Taka was a young, single woman. They broadcast Taka's vital statistics and gave her age as twenty-four, although that would have made her about twelve when she married Dale Ishimoto twelve years earlier.[35] Not surprisingly, the studio publicists omitted Taka's marital status, knowing that the public, especially heterosexual men, would not have responded very enthusiastically if they knew that the "exotically costumed Oriental miss" (to quote Lucy Crockett)[36] of the film was actually the married mother of two preteens. But the studio had Taka showcase her supposed skills in the housewifely arts on an extended publicity tour for the film. Thus a publicity stunt in the nation's capital had Taka serving an "authentic sukiyaki meal for representatives of press, radio, and TV." And the press book for the movie included four photos of Taka preparing and serving a tempura meal (one shows her dipping raw shrimp into a batter), again in a long-sleeved kimono, an outfit completely unsuited for the task.[37]

Even more disruptive to the romantic illusion than Taka's real age and marital status was the fact of her imprisonment in a relocation camp in Arizona during the war. When one reporter asked her about this in a telephone interview, Taka evaded the question by pretending to have a bad connection.[38] The studio may or may not have instructed her to downplay her history. The topic of the Japanese American internment was not taboo in Hollywood; for example, the publicity for *Go for Broke*, which came out six years before *Sayonara*, included a clearly scripted interview in which the star Van Johnson pointed out that the Nisei actors in the film—many of them actual 442nd veterans—had volunteered for the Army "from behind barbed wire."[39] But whether or not the studio explicitly told Taka to erase her recent past, Taka was acting as many Nisei did in the postwar period, seeking to go on with their lives rather than broadcasting their imprisonment because they realized that many of their fellow citizens still viewed them with suspicion. *Sayonara* was Taka's first film, and since she hoped to continue a career in the movies, highlighting a painful past was not on her agenda.[40] As a result, Taka's personal history and career goals as a minority actress inadvertently helped her fit the stereotype of Japanese women—never complaining and eager to please.[41]

Although Warner Brothers and Logan took pains to find a Japanese woman for the role of Hana-Ogi, it did not do likewise for the only significant Japanese male role, that of "Nakamura," the kabuki actor. This role went to actor Ricardo Montalban, whose character served ambiguously as a romantic interest for Gruver's discarded fiancée, Eileen Webster (Patricia Owens).[42] Publicity for the film highlighted this supposed progressivism in showing an attractive Japanese male: "I thought it was high time someone portrayed the Japanese male as something other than a bucktoothed soldier-rapist or owl-eyed detective who uttered guttural sounds," a press release "quoted" Logan as saying. "We hear no end of talk on the charm of Japan's women, and believe it is so, but how about the poor men?" Of course, despite this noble intention, Logan cast a Latino for the role, not a Japanese or even an Asian. Justifying the choice of Montalban for the part, this same press release explained that the director had found numerous Japanese actors who could perform the dancing but none who were "mature enough in appearance."[43] Perhaps perpetuating another ethnic stereotype, Logan later explained that he cast the Latino Montalban because he failed to find in Japan a "virile man who would look romantic to an American girl" and who was also fluent in English.[44] No Japanese man was either "mature" or manly enough for the role, even though the role itself was that of a cross-dresser who excelled at exuding femininity. Among the rejected candidates for the role was the Japanese American and 442nd veteran Dale Ishimoto, co-star Miiko Taka's husband at the time.[45]

Though he did not admit it, Logan may have also found it easier—as did many Americans—to see an Asian woman with a white man than to see an Asian male with a white woman. Hollywood produced at least three films that portrayed a relationship between a nonwhite man and a white woman positively during this era—*Bridge to the Sun, The Crimson Kimono,* and *A Majority of One*—but the plots of all three imparted conflicting messages.[46] In *Bridge to the Sun,* the Japanese male character dies at the end, and so—in ways similar to the earlier films *Broken Blossoms* (1919) and *The Bitter Tea of General Yen* (1933)—*Bridge* carries "the conservative reading that a Caucasian woman's love for a nonwhite male must somehow end in death."[47] Samuel Fuller's *Crimson Kimono* allows Joe Kojaku (James Shigeta) to win the love of an attractive Euroamerican woman, Chris Downes (Victoria Shaw), but presents Kojaku's sensitivity to racism as paranoia rather than as a valid fear.[48] Finally, in *A Majority of One* the widow Bertha Jacoby (Rosalind Russell) learns to overcome her hatred of the Japanese by befriending a Japanese businessman, Koichi Asano (Alec Guinness), but she rejects his marriage proposal. The plea for racial tolerance in this movie is further undermined by having Guinness play Asano in yellowface. The faux epicanthic folds on the heavily made up Guinness made him appear as if he had "two fat little patties of ravioli hanging from his eyebrows," according to one review.[49] Although the intention was otherwise, these three films continued to reinforce a racial hierarchy to greater and lesser degrees.

Hollywood films strongly suggested that Japanese women, like

Hana-Ogi, would readily choose to be with a white man over an Asian man if given a chance. Although some non-Hollywood films defied the stereotype of Japanese women as submissive creatures only too happy to love and serve American men, these films were not widely distributed in the United States. For example, the heroine of Japanese filmmaker Imamura Shōhei's *Pigs and Battleships* (*Buta to Gunkan,* 1961) much prefers her Japanese lover, but she is pressured by her mother and older sister to become an American man's mistress because his gifts would alleviate their grinding poverty. White men are not irresistible to Japanese women in Imamura's films. The long opening sequence of *Pigs and Battleships* is a fast-moving scene of dozens of American men entering a brothel near the naval base in Yokosuka like wolfish predators. Focusing on the American men's huge, muscular thighs and buttocks, Imamura shows their smiles of eager anticipation as they climb into the bunk beds with the sex workers.[50] Josef von Sternberg's *The Saga of Anatahan* (1953) also departed from mainstream Hollywood depictions of submissive, gentle Japanese women. His film, based on the true story of a group of Japanese stranded on an island without knowing that the war had ended, portrayed a forceful Japanese woman. But von Sternberg goes to the other extreme, making his "Keiko" a symbol of women's power to destroy men by their sexual hold on them.[51] Imamura's films remained obscure in the United States, and von Sternberg's *Anatahan,* the last film of the acclaimed director of *The Blue Angel* (1930), was, in his own words, his "most unsuccessful." It failed in Japan and had a very limited showing in the United States.[52] Thus the dominant interpretation of Japanese womanhood in films overwhelmed the alternative portrayals, especially in America where the market for the alternative films appeared to be nonexistent.

Marketing the Ally

There was, however, always a ready market for representations of docile, "exotically costumed misses" or "lotus-beauties" who were prepared to pamper American men. Images such as geishas in jinrikishas under branches of cherry blossoms dated back to the late nineteenth century, inscribed in American culture by iconic performances such as *Madame Butterfly.* These images were popularized even further when a few hundred thousand Americans went to serve in Occupied Japan. Pre-existing Orientalist visions not only sold the postwar Hollywood movies about Japan, but also advertised Japan—its landscape, products, and women—to American consumers. The filmmakers' business objectives to sell their movies thus dovetailed with their government's goal to bolster the Japanese economy, in part by getting Americans (and possibly even an international audience) to overcome their resistance to visiting Japan and buying the products of their former World War II enemy.[53] In other words, Hollywood marketed Japan and the Japanese by reinscribing Orientalism.

The studios heavily exploited the notion of the Japanese women's availability to white men in their publicity for the movies. A poster for *The Barbarian and the Geisha,* a quasi-historical story about the nineteenth-century American envoy Townsend Harris (John Wayne) and his Japanese mistress (Eiko Ando), for example, advertises the ready submission of Japanese women to Euroamerican men. The supine Ando, with a kimono slipping from her shoulder, says: "I was sent to spy upon you . . . to kill you—now I am ready to become whatever you want."[54] Similarly, the submissive charms of Japanese women are advertised in posters for *House of Bamboo, Tokyo After Dark,* and *Cry for Happy.* These depictions of Japanese women leave them without

much self-determination—except for choosing to be with Euroamerican men. Hollywood has played and replayed this presumption that an indigenous, nonwhite woman would always choose a
white man over an indigenous man and might even turn her back
on her people.

In addition to depicting Japanese women as willing partners
for white men, Hollywood—attentive to its large audience of heterosexual white women—appealed to American consumerism. A
publicity item for *Sayonara* released around Christmas compared
the supporting actress, Miyoshi Umeki, to the dolls being stocked
on store shelves for the holidays, calling the actress "a real Japanese doll . . . with slanting eyes that dance with merriment one
moment and swim with tragic emotion the next."[55] By depicting
Umeki and Taka (but especially Umeki) as dolls, the *Sayonara*
press releases drew upon the old stereotype of Japanese women as
ready to be manipulated as plaything or displayed as decoration
by either gender. Comparing them to dolls made the women seem
as if they were available for purchase, like the prewar "Jap dolls"
or the glass-encased, kimonoed Japanese dolls that servicemen
and others took home as souvenirs from Japan.

Studios advertising movies about Japan gave strong pitches to
theater managers with suggestions for commercial tie-ins with actual products. For the films that derived from novels, like *Sayonara* and *Bridge to the Sun,* the studios suggested that the theater
contact a local bookstore to set up a mutually beneficial counter
or window display to publicize the film. Others suggested cooperative ventures with businesses that sold Japanese products, such
as furniture stores carrying shoji doors or the "local sukiyaki restaurant." The most common suggestion, of course, was a tie-in
with Japan Air Lines or a local travel agency to advertise tourist
trips to Japan—a logical outcome since practically all the Cold
War-era films about Japan served as stories within a travelogue.[56]

Hollywood treated the travelogue aspect as a significant part of its movies' attraction to American filmgoers, and its assessment was not wrong. *Life*'s review of *Sayonara* stated with approval: "The movie wanders happily amid Nippon's delights—the rock gardens, bridges and pine groves of the Imperial Palace in Kyoto, the stylized posturings of *bunraku* puppets and traditional dancers, backrubs, tea ceremonies, and oodles of sake and sukiyaki."[57] Scenic shots such as those of Kyoto temples and shrines, Kamakura's enormous *Daibutsu* Buddha statue, Mount Fuji, Zen gardens, and kimonoed women playing "Sakura" on the koto became familiar images to American audiences—so much so that by the 1960s, publicity for *My Geisha* and *A Girl Named Tamiko* both claimed to bring a fresh perspective by portraying Japan as a nation of "warm and breathing people, not as a series of cliché postcards" and bragged that their film did *not* include Mount Fuji.[58] The travelogues of Japan encouraged viewers to forget the brutal war and instead to "wander happily" in the colorful spectacles of a charmingly exotic locale. When filmgoers were inspired to travel to Japan themselves, they added much-needed dollars to the Japanese economy. The Japanese appreciated the way these films advertised their country: *Sayonara* received cooperation from the Japanese Tourist Bureau and "other government agencies," and other films shot on location in Japan presumably did as well.[59]

The Hollywood studios, however, did not know how to market their films on Japan without exoticizing Japan, objectifying Japanese women, or belittling Asians in one way or another. This was especially evident in the studios' "exploitation suggestions" to theater managers. MGM's press book for *The Barbarian and the Geisha* suggested having Japanese American women "decorate" the film's premiere, preferably holding parasols and riding in a jinrikisha "for additional color." Other advertising recommendations from MGM included getting a "coolie" to pull a jinrikisha around town to ballyhoo the film, or hiring a woman to wear a kimono and a geisha hairpiece to pass out flyers at "busy shopping corners or at an entrance of [a] leading department store."[60] Calling for "a coolie" to pull a jinrikisha, needless to say, blunted the filmmakers' expressed purpose to humanize the Japanese, but they nonetheless succeeded in having the proverbial twain meet. Americans and Japanese "met" and could be friendly, but they didn't have to be equals. *Variety* reported in December 1957, for instance, that the films on Japan inspired wealthy New Yorkers to send "rush calls for Nipponese performers, including girls skilled in the art of geisha" to entertain at private parties; one can suppose, however, that the films did not motivate them to befriend some Japanese individuals and invite them into their homes as guests.[61] Having affection, affinity, or a measure of respect for another people and their culture did not mean that one treated them as equally capable to determine the fate of their own countries or lives.

Buying Tolerance

A limited number of sources do indicate that some American moviegoers appreciated the Japan-themed postwar films' overall message of racial tolerance and international friendship. In a letter to studio head Jack Warner, W. Lasiter of Holdenville, Oklahoma, praised *Sayonara:* "What better medium could one employ to promote better relations between our two peoples— Japanese and American—than the motion picture?"[62] Mrs. Eula M. McNabb of Dallas, Texas, also wrote to Warner, praising *A Majority of One:*

> In movies, there is an unlimited opportunity to benefit the easily influenced public. Pictures which degrade and wrongly influence the

public are not to be condoned. Intellectually *immature* thinking in regard to war, (now an archaic and futile method of attempting to determine Right) and regard to snobbery (in any form), or racial tolerance, must be raised to a more intellectually *mature* plane. Thank you for all your worthwhile efforts.[63]

Hollywood's efforts to link racial tolerance with maturity thus resonated with at least some of its audience. Americans often described social problems in terms of "maturity" or "immaturity" in mid-twentieth-century public discourse—indicating, even after the horrors of World War II, the persistence of a modernist faith that societies progressed in a linear fashion to higher levels—in the words of the letter writer, to a "more . . . mature plane." In common with public intellectuals like H. A. Overstreet, this woman depicted racial intolerance—and war—as "immature," a childish state which Americans and others throughout the world needed to outgrow. With their nation now indisputably the leader in what they soon called "the free world," Americans saw that they themselves had some "growing up" to do, but they generally felt comfortable, even destined, to be in the role of global mentor, policeman, and protector. Hollywood reconfirmed and widened this belief with its films on Japan, and continues to do so especially with the appearance of these films on cable television. The postwar films on Japan portrayed the American male hero as growing to understand that racial prejudice is wrong and as gaining insight into himself and the Japanese. With this new wisdom, his and indeed America's role as the "man in charge" was affirmed.

Focusing on racial prejudice rather than racism, the films on Japan attempted to show that prejudice did not spring from a hierarchical system integral to the functioning of American society, but rather reflected the unfortunate beliefs of individual, small-minded people. In *Bad Day at Black Rock*, for example, the racist villain who murdered the Japanese American farmer also coldly kills a young, misguided, and trusting white woman for no apparent reason. Very few in the 1950s audience would have identified with, much less seen themselves in, such a miscreant, and they could feel assured that they were not similarly bigoted. Because the postwar films suggest that racial prejudice can be eliminated with open-minded goodwill—it is simply a matter of changing bigoted minds to become more tolerant, making an "emotionally immature . . . teenage boy" grow up—they did not demand much of their viewers, many of whom already considered themselves full-fledged adults with open minds and goodwill. In the end, *Sayonara* challenged Americans to do nothing more than be accepting of relationships between U.S. servicemen and Japanese women. Toward the end of the movie, the audience learns that the U.S. Congress is getting around to revising the immigration law that prevented servicemen from bringing home their Japanese spouses—which indeed Congress had done in 1952 with the McCarran-Walter Act. The filmmakers thus showed that the U.S. government had already corrected the racist law; the audience needed to do nothing.

The liberal rhetoric of Cold War-era films on Japan thus served to distract Americans from seriously engaging domestic and international racism. By focusing on racial prejudice against the Japanese, the films ignored the more disturbing, deeply entrenched socioeconomic and legal order that systematically denied material opportunities and political rights to Americans based on the color of their skin. Observant Euroamerican viewers admitted and appreciated this. *Sayonara* was "easier than most to take," wrote the reviewer for the *New Yorker*, because it was not as "astringent and forthright" as other films that had portrayed the subject of race relations. Focusing on "charming scenes of traditional home life and arts" in Japan, the films about

Euroamerican relations with the Japanese or Japanese Americans could more easily ignore the long-standing effects of American racism at home and abroad.[64]

Most of these postwar filmmakers had sincere aspirations for goodwill throughout the world and were confident that their nation was acting in the best interest of all peoples. Fostering goodwill meant serving as an informal ambassador—that is, keeping one's national priorities while trying to forge working relationships and friendships abroad. However, the apparent reciprocity of these "friendships" and cultural exchanges left unexamined the American dominance in economic, political, and military power.[65] Like other Cold War liberals, Hollywood filmmakers did not demand that the United States "scale back overseas military bases or remove itself from political alliances with colonial regimes and repressive postcolonial governments, or restrict the flow of foreign trade."[66] They suggested that it was only attitudes, not institutions, that needed to be adjusted for smooth relations with Asians, as in *The Teahouse of the August Moon*. Although they preached racial tolerance, the postwar films failed to profoundly change Orientalist preconceptions about the Japanese, Asians, or Asian Americans. Thus they complemented the U.S. policy on Japan that, in the end, required nothing more than having the American public be willing to accept Japan as an ally and to buy Japanese products. U.S. policy did not call for Americans to reject hierarchies, whether those of race, gender, or geopolitics. Rather, U.S. policy called upon Americans to forget and consume, something for which the Hollywood spectacles on Japan were superbly suited.

The Geisha Boy

Banking on an American fascination with the spectacle of Japan, Paramount Pictures released a comedy at the end of 1958 called

280 Aiiieiiua's Geisha Ally

The Geisha Boy. This Jerry Lewis vehicle concerns the friendship between a failing magician of humble American origins and an upper-class Japanese boy, not a geisha. The movie is a frivolous comedy, but it can instruct us about mid-century American thoughts on weighty issues: the nation's relationship with its former World War II enemy, U.S. abilities to be a world leader, and perplexing domestic social relations.[67] The film reveals not only what concerned Americans about these serious issues, but also how they managed those concerns.

The Geisha Boy shows the development of "The Great Wooley" (Lewis) into a successful entertainer through his friendship with a Japanese boy. Hoping to revive his flagging career by entertaining U.S. troops in Japan, Wooley literally stumbles off the plane into Japan. But he also pulls a huffy blonde starlet down the stairs with him, to the amusement of the crowd waiting below, including 7-year-old Mitsuo Watanabe (Robert Kazuyoshi Hirano) who laughs for the first time since the death of his parents. His aunt, Kimi Sikita (Nobu Atsumi McCarthy), is so amazed by Mitsuo's mirth that she arranges for him to meet Wooley. When he does, Mitsuo asks him quite boldly and rather inexplicably: *"Dōzō boku no otōsan ni natte kudasai"* ("Please become my father").[68] Wooley and Mitsuo then become devoted to each other, although they know that the end of Wooley's tour in Japan will separate them forever. This sad fate is averted when Wooley returns to Japan, apparently to settle there. Mitsuo's esteem for Wooley gives the latter the confidence to turn his life around so that the stateside loser, a self-proclaimed "first-class jerk," becomes a headliner in Tokyo for a happy ending to the movie. Like Lloyd Gruver of *Sayonara,* Wooley becomes a "man" as a result of his relationship with the Japanese. With Wooley, the American, serving as guardian and mentor to the young Japanese boy, the film also presents symbolically the postwar U.S.-Japan bilateral relationship, with Japan as a junior ally needing Amaerican guidance. Director-screenwriter Frank Tashlin based *Geisha Boy* loosely on an original screenplay called *Pete-San,* and like the makers of *Sayonara,* he significantly changed the original script for commercial and artistic purposes. *Pete-San* was a tale about a half-Korean, half-American orphan boy who runs away from an orphanage in the United States and attaches himself to an ineffectual vaudeville actor. The performer's failing show suddenly starts attracting large audiences after he includes "Pete" in his act. In the end, the actor realizes that he must give up his stage career and provide a more stable family life for Pete. His long-suffering girlfriend accepts his proposal on the pledge that they quit show business, and together, they adopt Pete.[69] Tashlin altered the nationality of Pete and the girlfriend to be Japanese and shifted the setting so that most of the action of *Geisha Boy* occurs in Japan, not America.

Notably, Tashlin did not move the story to Korea, although Pete was half-Korean, and his commercial decision to focus on Japan and ignore Korea thus roughly paralleled the U.S. policy to concentrate on making Japan its main ally in the Far East. Rather than making the movie a commentary about the neglected interracial offspring of the Korean War, Tashlin chose for the story of his film the simpler one of international and interracial friendship between an American man and a Japanese boy. This decision allowed Tashlin to completely sidestep any difficult social issues and permitted both the director and Paramount to exploit visual symbols of Japan that were already familiar to Americans—like geishas—and to use Paramount's stock footage of Japan to create a travelogue cheaply.[70] *The Geisha Boy* showed familiar shots of Kyoto temples and shrines, Kamakura's *Daibutsu,* Mount Fuji,

Zen gardens, and even a *geishaya,* a house of geishas. Tashlin also chose to make Mitsuo an upper-class boy so that the film could showcase a beautiful traditional home with a large Japanese garden. Korean culture was less familiar to Americans for a variety of historical reasons, and the war-devastated, divided nation could not be as easily used as Japan to create a consumerist spectacle because it remained economically underdeveloped—in large part as a result of its prior status as a colony of Japan.

As with the other postwar films about Japan, the marketing strategy for *The Geisha Boy* attempted to promote things Japanese to American consumers and resorted to sexist and Orientalist selling angles. Paramount's press book for *Geisha Boy* also urged theater managers to advertise the film by establishing tie-ins with local department or furniture stores: it suggested mounting film stills along with theater and store credits on "the currently popular shoji screens" for mutual promotion.[71] Although not about geishas, the film opens with a succession of shots of coyly smiling, seemingly nude "cute Geisha Girls" (as Tashlin describes them in the script) unfolding fans with screen credits lettered on the fans.[72] The opening, like the film's title, sets up the locale, but it also provided Tashlin with an excuse to create an elaborate spectacle and the studio with a reason to arrange for the presence of kimonoed Japanese women servers at the film's premiere. The jinrikisha-pulling "coolie" for this movie's premiere was the film's star, Jerry Lewis, himself. Lewis donned his idiot "Oriental" persona, complete with coke-bottle glasses, skull cap, fake buck teeth, and a "flaming red" happi coat, to pull the film's co-star, Nobu McCarthy ("Kimi"), to the opening gala in Hollywood.[73]

As in *Sayonara,* the plot of *Geisha Boy* includes a competition for the American man's heart between a Japanese and a Euroamerican woman that the Japanese woman wins. Kimi's rival is

Sergeant Pierson of the Women's Auxiliary Air Forces (Suzanne Pleshette); inexplicably, these two beautiful, seemingly intelligent women are attracted to woolly-headed Wooley. Wooley pays little attention to either of them, but he does note Kimi's beauty. After meeting her, he comments, "Wow! I'd like to chop chopsticks with her anytime! I can see why Marlon Brando dug this place."[74] Sgt. Pierson, a career woman whose first name we never learn, wears only her stiff military uniform during the film, but viewers see Kimi in a variety of more feminine and flattering outfits, including a two-piece bathing suit. And while Sgt. Pierson reprimands Wooley at one point and accuses him at another, Kimi remains supportive, pleasant, and nonjudgmental throughout. Kimi is oblivious to Sgt. Pierson, but Sgt. Pierson immediately sees Kimi as a rival. Jealous of the attention she thinks he is giving to Kimi, Sgt. Pierson demands of Wooley, "What is it you American men see in these girls? What is the big difference between American girls and Oriental girls?" She later apologizes for her outburst, explaining that she had lost a boyfriend to a Japanese woman. But she vows, "Believe me, the next man I meet I'm going to forget that so-called American-emancipated-woman-type of independence and treat him like the girls in Japan do." Sgt. Pierson apparently learned the lesson that Occupation soldiers complaining about "American girls" hoped they would learn; the men in Hollywood who produced these films on Japan seemed to be suggesting that more American women should follow suit. (In terms of pay, however, Euroamerican women still held an advantage over Japanese women. Although the role of Sgt. Pierson was Suzanne Pleshette's film debut, she earned more than Nobu McCarthy, who had already co-starred in three films.)[75]

In Hollywood films, Japanese men offer only a trivial challenge to the affection of Japanese women for Euroamerican men. Wooley, however, has a rival of a sort that Brando's Lloyd Gruver never had—an extremely tall, gruff baseball star who we learn is Kimi's fiancé. The fiancé, Ichiro (Ryuzo Demura), is portrayed as a monster with enormous physical strength but little brainpower. He grunts instead of speaks, and seems set on wreaking havoc whenever he spots Wooley. His character, resembling a gorilla out of control, recalls propaganda posters from the early war years when the Japanese seemed unstoppable in their expansion in Southeast Asia and the Asian mainland.[76] The propaganda posters had implied such reckless action would get the Japanese nowhere, and indeed, this also holds true for the fiancé. Kimi, embarrassed by her fiancé's behavior, breaks off her engagement with him and apologizes to Wooley.

Although Hollywood did not forget the wartime images of fanatical Japanese military men, the postwar movies tended to play down their zealotry by humanizing Japanese men to various degrees. Exploiting and parodying the theme from a different blockbuster film from the previous year, *The Bridge on the River Kwai*, Tashlin cast Sessue Hayakawa, who played the imperious Japanese commandant in *River Kwai*, as Kimi's father and Mitsuo's grandfather. In *Geisha Boy*, we first see him wearing a Japanese army uniform and standing stiffly, fists on hips, while he oversees the building of a small bridge over a pond in his backyard. The crew, meanwhile, whistles the same tune heard in *River Kwai*. When the crew members slack off a bit, Sikita barks at them harshly, causing them to double the pace of their work while whistling "Colonel Bogey's March." Each of Sikita's oddly familiar staccato outbursts makes Wooley wince. Sikita then approaches Wooley and salutes him before shaking his hand warmly, thanking him for bringing joy back to his grandson. The devoted grandfather explains that he was building the small bridge for Mitsuo's amusement, but that only Wooley had succeeded in making his grandson smile again. Referring to the bridge, he says,

"Now I know it was a waste of time"—making another allusion to the ill-fated bridge in *River Kwai*. Upon Wooley's questioning, Sikita admits to his similarity to "the actor," but insists, "I was building bridges long before him." As Wooley follows Sikita toward his house, an image of the actor Alec Guinness as Colonel Nicholson in *River Kwai* flashes across the screen; Wooley tries to shake the image from his head, but resigns himself to whistling "Colonel Bogey's March." Even movie history, to paraphrase Marx, repeats itself as farce; the Japanese commandant is domesticated—he becomes a "family man" like Emperor Hirohito—and the brutality of a Japanese POW camp becomes a joke. The symbol of Imperial Japan is treated similarly: the "Land of the Rising Sun" is now, according to a poster for *Geisha Boy*, the "Land of the Rising Fun."

Despite Wooley's comment about wanting to "chop chopsticks" with Kimi, the real love affair in *The Geisha Boy* is between Wooley and Mitsuo. Wooley largely ignores Kimi's longing looks and focuses on the boy. He does gives Kimi one ardent kiss, but this comes at the end of a long "date" with the boy, not with her. Not looking at her either before or after the kiss, he appears tired and deep in thought about having to leave Japan and the boy the very next day. It is a bittersweet kiss of parting and unfulfilled desire—Wooley deflecting his passion and releasing it in a seemingly appropriate way. Rather than shying away from this homoeroticism, Paramount advised movie theaters to exploit it instead. In the press book for theater managers, the studio suggested a "teaser" that would run four consecutive days:

1st day: "GEISHA It's pronounced GAY-SHA!"
2nd day: "GEISHA It's pronounced GAY-SHA with the accent on GAY!"
3rd day: "GEISHA It's pronounced GAY-SHA with the accent on GAY . . . THE JERRY LEWIS WAY!"

4th day: "GEISHA It's pronounced GAY-SHA with the accent on GAY . . . SEE JERRY LEWIS as 'THE GEISHA BOY' ([name of] THEATRE)."[77]

The studio recognized that this homoerotic, gender-bending trait was one of Lewis's attractions. Offering a visual demonstration of a body utterly lacking in self-control and self-mastery, Lewis's performance as Wooley served to reinforce existing ideas about manliness and maturity—qualities that Americans often saw as inseparable. The "boy" in *Geisha Boy* probably did not refer to the Japanese child—this would have seemed absurd to Japanese sensibilities, given Mitsuo's social class and gender—but most likely alluded to Lewis himself.[78] Director Tashlin explored gender-bending themes in a succession of other films, from *The Lieutenant Wore Skirts* (1956) to *Cinderfella* (1960)—the latter also starred Lewis—and Tashlin's films with Lewis capitalizing on the "Idiot-Kid" persona popularized by the actor in his earlier cabaret, film, and television work with Dean Martin. The "Idiot-Kid" performances allowed Lewis to present "a glaring inversion of acceptable standards governing the body, maturity, and masculinity."[79] To laugh at "gay" Jerry Lewis was like laughing at Jack Benny at an earlier time: both allowed their audiences to laugh at things they "most feared" while reassuring them that even "the most feckless person" could still be lovable.[80] Like Glenn Ford's Fisby in *Teahouse of the August Moon*, Lewis's antics as a well-meaning but blundering American in *The Geisha Boy* can be seen as satirizing Americans' ability to provide firm and wise leadership to Japan, the junior ally.

In the end, however, the film averts the threat of homoeroticism and dysfunctional masculinity and reaffirms Americans' ability to provide patriarchal leadership. Even a feckless American man can become manly by going to Japan and making the right choices.

Two attractive women, after all, see the "man" in Lewis's character. By needing Wooley, the boy also helped Wooley become a "man" in two other ways—as a father and as a success in his career. Mitsuo's convenient orphan status meant that Wooley's role in his life did not violate a father-son relationship. Mitsuo, like Occupied Japan, was there to be guided—and, in the film, he had even asked to be parented. The film's ending, with Wooley, Kimi, and Mitsuo all performing together on stage—with the latter two as helpers—suggests that they have formed a nuclear family with the father firmly in control. Thus by the film's end, Wooley's potentially disruptive and deviant presence is contained: the plot finds a resolution that validates the protocols of 1950s American masculinity and maturity.[81] The blundering American man has grown up to become a global leader.

EPILOGUE

Rising Sun Redux

Fifteen years ago," observed a book reviewer for the *New York Times* in 1960, "most Americans believed that most Japanese were bloody-minded barbarians, fanatical militarists, benighted worshipers of a divine Emperor. Today most Americans who think about the Japanese at all seem to believe that most of them are quaint and charming members of a delightful civilization with esthetic perceptions and traditions rarer and finer than anything the West can claim." Reviewing Elizabeth Gray Vining's *Return to Japan,* a sequel to *Windows for the Crown Prince,* this writer attributed part of "the speed with which hatred . . . changed into admiration" to those thousands of Occupationers who enjoyed their life in Japan and part to the "many books about Japan written by Americans who have lost their hearts to their former foes."[1] By this time a confluence of geopolitical, consumerist, and domestic concerns had helped Americans accept their former enemy as a worthy recipient of their nation's largesse, protection, and guidance. American liberals in the media and government had succeeded in adapting pre-existing ideologies about maturity and gender to create new narratives for promoting amity with the Japanese.

The process of transforming the racial enemy into a valuable junior ally appeared to be complete by 1964. In that year Japan joined the Organization for Economic Co-Operation and Development (OECD), after heavy U.S. lobbying. This event symbolized the fact that MacArthur's "boy of twelve" was now economically developed enough to be a participating "adult" among other "mature" nation-states. 1964 was also the year when Japan became the first Asian nation to host the Olympics. The Japanese government spent $2.8 billion (in 1964 dollars) to build or renovate athletic facilities, subsidize new hotels, and update Tokyo's transportation system, while Japanese businesses invested heavily to showcase their products and their nation as a tourist attraction for a huge international audience. *Business Week* reported that the Japanese government hoped the "principal immediate return on this investment" would be "international prestige"—for Japan to be taken seriously as a thriving modern economy. But the magazine placed this flurry of activity in a familiar gendered framework: "Like a woman who is expecting company, Tokyo is scurrying around trying to make the place presentable for the Olympic Games." Although *Business Week* found it hard to resist the notion of a feminized Japan, its article focused primarily on the maturation of Japan's technological consumer goods industry. The watch company Seiko, the magazine noted, would be supplying the official timing devices for the games and was making "considerable hoopla" about breaking "a virtual Swiss monopoly."[2] Just as the Swiss had managed, in an earlier period, to change a common belief that "Swiss quality" was an oxymoron, so too were the Japanese beginning to shift American perceptions so that "Made in Japan" no longer signified shoddy products.

The Tokyo Olympics became a moment for American liberals to reflect upon the changes since the war's end. Norman Cousins

This image of a geisha bowling served as the cover picture for *Life* magazine's special issue on Japan in September 1964. Getty Images.

revisited Hiroshima in 1964, and reported to *Saturday Review* readers that the Hiroshima Maidens and the moral adoptees were all thriving—some now with children of their own.[3] *Life* magazine sent a group of staff to Japan for nearly a year to prepare an issue completely devoted to the country. Reflecting on the drastic changes since 1945 in that special issue's editorial, Henry Luce wrote: "In all the annals of history, it would be difficult to match the extremes of adulation and hate, treachery and trust, cooperation and terrible violence which have marked the short, intense relationship between Japan and the U.S." The relationship went from friendship to war and back not only to friendship but also to interdependence: "Today Japan and the U.S. are intricately linked by trade, defense policies, and political systems—and are even having somewhat of a cultural love affair." The "Americanization" of Japan continued, while in the United States, Japanese aesthetics influenced a new generation of artists and architects. To epitomize this "cultural love affair," *Life*'s cover photograph showed a "geisha" in traditional dress—symbolizing Japan—throwing a ball down a bowling lane.[4] The Americans were the innovators of modern bowling; the sport was immensely popular in postwar America and was spreading across the globe. The Japanese rarely, if ever, bowled wearing a kimono, but the costume was important to *Life*'s editors because it juxtaposed traditional Japan with modern Japan—a composition perennially favored by photographers, especially since the Occupation. The fact that the "geisha" is caught in middle of an action implies that "Japan" itself was moving and shaking itself up. Americans usually depicted a Japan in movement with images of young Japanese males, but now both the editors' desire to sell magazines and the issue's theme about the "love affair" between America and Japan had called forth a kimonoed Japanese woman.

The juxtaposition between the traditional and the modern showed how Americans continued to see the Japanese as exotic, Orientalized others. Although *Life*'s editors instructed its writers and photographers to avoid "the familiar tourist tracks," the editors selected many recognizable images of cherry-blossom Japan in their special issue. They could not even resist the customary photograph of a bathing Japanese woman (in a spectacular hot spring bath with a full view of *Fuji-san*).⁵ Overall, the images in *Life*'s special issue fell into two types that corresponded with Americans' contradictory feelings about Japan. One type, including the silhouette of a lone monk in a gateway to a forest and the bathing beauty, emphasized what Americans admired about Japanese culture: its meditative, orderly, and aesthetic qualities. The other type reflected Americans' negative beliefs about the Japanese: their lack of individuality, irrationality, and potential enmity. These images generally depicted a group of Japanese people, jumbled together, signifying chaos and evoking repulsion or fear—such as the large color photograph of a writhing mass of naked young male bodies engaged in a poorly explained ritual. This dual view allowed Ambassador Reischauer to argue that Japan and the United States were "inevitable partners" in the same issue in which Luce asserted that Americans still harbored a "bone-deep suspicion of the present friendly state of affairs" between the U.S. and Japan.⁶

Despite the Cold War liberal commitment to racial tolerance, many Americans maintained racialized fears that the enigmatic Japanese and other "Orientals" were essentially different from "the West" and thereby untrustworthy. Thus a decade later, when the Nixon administration presented Japan as the economic enemy who was responsible for America's fiscal woes, the public readily bought it.⁷ It was easier to blame the Japanese than to at-

Now in the same boat: the new, humanized emperor, circa 1964, on an expedition to look at marine biology with his wife and a group of unidentified Japanese men. Getty Images.

tribute economic hardship to the structural changes in the U.S. economy, or to the long, expensive, and disastrous war in Southeast Asia. The Japanese had waged a military war against the United States; now they seemed to be fighting an economic one. And, until the "bubble economy" burst in the early 1990s, it appeared that they were "winning." Supposedly using their powers of imitation, cleverness, and industriousness, the Japanese fought the Americans on their own turf by flooding the American market with cars and electronic equipment and making high-profile purchases of American landmarks and industries. For lessons on how to compete with the Japanese, American MBA students pored over texts such as Ezra Vogel's *Japan as Number One* (1979), William Ouchi's *Theory Z* (1981), and even the premodern samurai classic, *The Book of Five Rings* by Miyamoto Musashi.[8] Although West Germany also emerged as an economic superpower during the same period, its success did not attract as much attention or fear in America.

In popular culture, films like *Rollerball* (1975) and *Brazil* (1985) depicted militaristic "samurai" villains. But these villains were robotic, befitting Japan's new status as a technologically advanced power, yet reminiscent of Frank Capra's line that the Japanese soldiers were "prints off the same negative." Meanwhile, the camera-toting Japanese tourist emerged as a new stereotype. Picture taking now seemed to be a Japanese prerogative, and Americans' discomfort about the positional superiority of this Japanese gaze may be the reason why this derisive stereotype was so pervasive in the 1970s and 1980s. The fear of Japanese economic power—viewed as masculine, perverse, and inscrutable—persisted in American popular culture right up to the Japanese recession, with bestsellers like Clive Cussler's *Dragon* (1990) and Michael Crichton's *Rising Sun* (1992). But since the "war" was metaphoric, not actual, these images were able to coexist with those of a cherry-blossom Japan. Graceful-looking, kimonoed Japan Air Lines stewardesses, for instance, advertised the gentler, feminized vision of Japan on billboards in Los Angeles throughout this period. There was no simple substitution of samurai images for geishas; Americans kept using both tropes to help explain their bilateral relationship with Japan.

In other words, Americans continued to understand the Japanese through binaries: attractive/repulsive, gentle/threatening, good/bad, or junior ally/treacherous foe. These crude oppositions lent themselves to simple, easily comprehensible narratives that explained the postwar alliance, such as the story that the "liberal," peace-loving emperor had faced down the "feudalistic," war-mongering militarists. One side of this view allowed Americans to continue expressing racialized hatred toward the "bad Japs," like the preening Tōjō or the "twisted" and embittered Kawakita. The other side helped them make room for the "good Japanese" in postwar discourse: the Americanized, open-minded Nishiyama, the dutiful Hiroshima Maidens, or the innocent war orphans. This double vision of the Japanese existed before the war and remains readily available for Americans to draw upon to explain the situation at hand. Depending on the political context, one side can quickly dominate the other—for they are opposite sides of the same phenomenon—but in the absence of a crisis, both sides are usually visible simultaneously.

Admittedly the efforts to transform the image of the Japanese did not convince all Americans; some still find the Japanese creepy or suspect.[9] But the effort did reach many—with predictably mixed results. During a 1995 debate on H-Asia about the use of the atomic bombs, a staunch supporter of the bombings wrote in an e-mail to the author: "I admire the Japanese as a basically good and great people . . . They have beautiful women, cute children, and a fascinating culture with neat sports and games." But he felt uneasy about the Japanese because they were "still (technically) an Imperial society and 100 million hyper-competitive people crowded" on a group of relatively unfertile, geologically unstable islands. He was frightened by "this lemminglike Japanese *eagerness* to kill themselves." "I really *don't*," he emphasized, "want someone in Japan activating a 'Doomsday Machine' and terminating life on this planet because they feel they—or humanity—have unforgivably shamed themselves!"[10]

Ruth Benedict's theory about the Japanese culture of shame has entered mainstream American notions of Japan, evident in the views of history buffs like the e-mail correspondent as well as in the writings of Japan experts like Ian Buruma.[11] Benedict believed that her study would contribute toward "a world made safe for differences," but it ended up reifying the differences and thus reinforcing racism.[12] At the time, postwar liberals like Benedict believed that they were making a break with the racist thinking of the past by emphasizing culture over biology and stressing the potential of nonwhites to "mature" into modern societies. But as this book has shown, the postwar liberals, despite their good intentions, ended up reconstructing racism through other categories. Their actions helped to make racism unrecognizable as such to many Americans, and their influence continues even today. By reinforcing rather than challenging notions of essential difference, consensus liberals failed to promote an end to racist thinking.

Sixty years after the war's end, perceived racial and Orientalized "otherness" remains paramount in the American understanding of Japan.[13] Antiracist dialogue and education continue, but today few evoke the language of maturity to encourage Americans to "grow up" and improve their race relations with minorities in the United States or with nonwhites in the larger world. Progressive faith in the ability to produce the "mature mind" among Americans died with the liberal consensus. Many Americans retain the belief that others need to develop and mature; they may even deride others as childish; but they do not currently apply this language to themselves.

In the worldview of the Cold War liberals, the old and powerfully persuasive notions of maturity and development were not only gendered, but also narrowly framed. Today, some may look back at the views of these consensus liberals with nostalgic longing for their genuine impulse and material commitment to make a better world. But it is important to remember how their worldview also undermined their professed goals to create a more equitable and democratic global community.

NOTES

ACKNOWLEDGMENTS

INDEX

Introduction

1. All the preceding quotes are from *Time* magazine: 15 December 1941, 17–19; 22 December 1941, 12–13.
2. John W. Dower, *War Without Mercy: Race and Power in the Pacific War* (New York: Pantheon Books, 1986).
3. For a summary and detailed discussion of such views, see Colleen Lye, *America's Asia: Racial Form and American Literature* (Princeton: Princeton University Press, 2004).
4. "On to Tokyo and What?" *Life*, 21 May 1945, 32.
5. Michael Paul Rogin, *Fathers and Children: Andrew Jackson and the Subjugation of the American Indian* (New York: Knopf, 1975), 7, 11.
6. Dower, 78–79.
7. Lawrence E. Davies, "Leniency to Japan Decried by Halsey," *New York Times* (hereafter *NYT*), 17 October 1945, 5.
8. At the same time, the United States acted similarly toward its main European enemy, focusing on strengthening the West German economy to withstand the communist threat in Europe.
9. Kazuo Kawai, *Japan's American Interlude* (Chicago: University of Chicago Press, 1960); Michael Schaller, *The American Occupation of Japan: The Origins of the Cold War in Asia* (New York: Oxford University Press, 1985); Theodore Cohen, *Remaking Japan: The American Occupation as New Deal*, ed. Herbert Passin (New York: Free

Press, 1987); Howard B. Schonberger, *The Aftermath of War: Americans and the Remaking of Japan, 1945–1952* (Kent: Kent State University Press, 1989); John W. Dower, *Embracing Defeat: Japan in the Wake of World War II* (New York: W. W. Norton, 1999); Eiji Takemae, *Inside GHQ: The Allied Occupation of Japan and Its Legacy,* trans. Robert Ricketts and Sebastian Swan (New York: Continuum, 2002); Yoneyuki Sugita, *Pitfall or Panacea: The Irony of US Power in Occupied Japan* (New York: Routledge, 2003). On the emperor, see: Masanori Nakamura, *The Japanese Monarchy: Ambassador Joseph Grew and the Making of the "Symbol Emperor System," 1931–1991,* trans. Herbert P. Bix, Jonathan Baker-Bates, and Derek Bowen (Armonk, N.Y.: M. E. Sharpe, 1992); Daikichi Irokawa, *The Age of Hirohito: In Search of Modern Japan,* trans. Mikiso Hane and John K. Urda (New York: Free Press, 1995); Herbert P. Bix, *Hirohito and the Making of Modern Japan* (New York: HarperCollins, 2000); Kenneth Ruoff, *The People's Emperor: Democracy and the Japanese Monarchy, 1945–1995* (Cambridge, Mass.: Harvard University Asia Center, 2001).

10. Aaron Forsberg, *America and the Japanese Miracle: The Cold War Context of Japan's Postwar Economic Revival, 1950–1960* (Chapel Hill: University of North Carolina Press, 2000); Sayuri Shimizu, *Creating a People of Plenty: The United States and Japan's Economic Alternatives, 1950–1960* (Kent: Kent State University Press, 2001).

11. Michael E. Latham, *Modernization as Ideology: American Social Science and "Nation-Building" in the Kennedy Era* (Chapel Hill: University of North Carolina Press, 2000); David C. Engerman, Nils Gilman, Mark H. Haefele, and Michael E. Latham, eds., *Staging Growth: Modernization, Development, and the Global Cold War* (Amherst: University of Massachusetts Press, 2003); Nils Gilman, *Mandarins of the Future: Modernization Theory in Cold War America* (Baltimore: Johns Hopkins University Press, 2003).

12. Throughout the twentieth century, U.S. policymakers frequently deemed a people "too immature" to handle democracy and used this perception to justify U.S. support of authoritarian, right-wing dictators who kept countries such as Iran, Guatemala, Chile, the Dominican Republic, and South Korea—to name only a few—safe from

communism and for U.S. investment. See David F. Schmitz, *Thank God They're On Our Side: The United States and Right-Wing Dictatorships, 1921–1965* (Chapel Hill: University of North Carolina Press, 1999).

13. For this definition, Hunt drew from the work of cultural anthropologist Clifford Geertz. Michael H. Hunt, *Ideology and U.S. Foreign Policy* (New Haven: Yale University Press, 1987), xi.

14. Mary L. Dudziak, *Cold War Civil Rights: Race and the Image of American Democracy* (Princeton: Princeton University Press, 2000); Thomas Borstelmann, *The Cold War and the Color Line: American Race Relations in the Global Arena* (Cambridge, Mass.: Harvard University Press, 2003).

15. For example: Emily S. Rosenberg, "'Foreign Affairs' after World War II: Connecting Sexual and International Politics," *Diplomatic History* 18 (Winter 1994): 59–70; Michelle Mart, "Tough Guys and American Cold War Policy: Images of Israel, 1948–1960," *Diplomatic History* 20 (Summer 1996): 357–380; Frank Costigliola, "'Unceasing Pressure for Penetration': Gender, Pathology, and Emotion in George Kennan's Formation of the Cold War," *Journal of American History* 83 (March 1997): 1309–1339; Costigliola, "The Nuclear Family: Tropes of Gender and Pathology in the Western Alliance," *Diplomatic History* 21 (Spring 1997): 163–183; Kristin Hoganson, *Fighting for American Manhood: How Gender Politics Provoked the Spanish-American and Philippine-American Wars* (New Haven: Yale University Press, 1998); Andrew J. Rotter, *Comrades at Odds: The United States and India, 1947–1964* (Ithaca: Cornell University Press, 2000); Robert D. Dean, *Imperial Brotherhood: Gender and the Making of Cold War Policy* (Amherst: University of Massachusetts Press, 2001); Petra Goedde, *GIs and Germans: Culture, Gender, and Foreign Relations, 1945–1949* (New Haven: Yale University Press, 2002).

16. See Jean-Pierre Lehmann, *The Image of Japan: From Feudal Isolation to World Power, 1850–1905* (London: George Allen & Unwin, 1978); Sheila K. Johnson, *The Japanese Through American Eyes* (Stanford: Stanford University Press, 1988); Ian Littlewood, *The Idea of Japan: Western Images, Western Myths* (Chicago: Ivan

Dee, 1996); Charles B. Wordell, *Japan's Image in America, 1800–1941* (Kyoto: Yamaguchi Publishing House, 1998). Works that do relate the images more specifically to power relations are the following: Akira Iriye, ed., *Mutual Images: Essays in American-Japanese Relations* (Cambridge, Mass.: Harvard University Press, 1975); Hiromi Chiba, "From Enemy to Ally: American Public Opinion and Perceptions about Japan, 1945–1950" (Ph.D. diss., University of Hawaii, 1990); James F. Hilgenberg, Jr., *From Enemy to Ally: Japan, The American Business Press, and The Early Cold War* (Lanham, Md.: University Press of America, 1993); Joseph M. Henning, *Outposts of Civilization: Race, Religion, and the Formative Years of American-Japanese Relations* (New York: New York University Press, 2000). See also Traise Yamamoto, *Masking Selves, Making Subjects: Japanese American Women, Identity, and the Body* (Berkeley: University of California Press, 1999), chap. 1, esp. 16–22. Yamamoto points out the infantilization of Japan, but does not give an expanded analysis of this phenomenon.

17. Historians and American Studies scholars who have recently investigated this subject include: Mary A. Renda, *Taking Haiti: Military Occupation and the Culture of U.S. Imperialism* (Chapel Hill: University of North Carolina Press, 2000); Melani McAlister, *Epic Encounters: Culture, Media, and U.S. Interests in the Middle East, 1945–2000* (Berkeley: University of California Press, 2001); Amy Kaplan, *Anarchy of Empire in the Making of U.S. Culture* (Cambridge, Mass.: Harvard University Press, 2002); Christina Klein, *Cold War Orientalism: Asia in the Middlebrow Imagination, 1945–1961* (Berkeley: University of California Press, 2003).

18. Edward W. Said, *Orientalism* (New York: Pantheon Books, 1978); Said, *Culture and Imperialism* (New York: Knopf, 1993).

19. Chalmers A. Johnson, *Blowback: The Costs and Consequences of American Empire* (2000; New York: Metropolitan/Owl Books, 2004), 21.

1. Women and Children First

1. Lucy Herndon Crockett, *Popcorn on the Ginza: An Informal Portrait of Postwar Japan* (New York: William Sloane Associates, 1949), 29.

2. Orville Prescott, *NYT,* 18 April 1945, 21; [Henry Luce], "Editorial: On to Tokyo and What?" *Life,* 21 May 1945, 32.
3. "No Time to Talk Friendship," *Honolulu Advertiser,* 5 September 1945, editorial page.
4. Quotes from: "Fanatic?" *Time,* 24 September 1945, 21; Gerry Burtnett, "Enemy Is Actually Bitter and Hostile Inside," *Honolulu Advertiser,* 5 September 1945, 1. See also "Unregenerate Japan," *The Nation,* 22 September 1945, 273; "MacArthur Cracks Down Hard on Fawning, Unrepentant Enemy," *Newsweek,* 24 September 1945, 52; "Devereux Warns U.S. About Japan: Foe 'Bowing and Scraping,' He Says at Tokyo, but Is Different When 'on Top,'" *NYT,* 17 September 1945, 4.
5. Crockett, 16–17.
6. Frank L. Kluckhorn, "First Impressions of Conquered Japan," *NYT,* 9 September 1945, 89; Ray Coll, Jr., "Surrender of Yokosuka Naval Base," *Honolulu Advertiser,* 15 September 1945.
7. Crockett, 171–172.
8. Robert Shaplen, "Yanks Start Kimono Hunt, Learn What Geisha Doesn't," *Newsweek,* 24 September 1945, 44–45.
9. John W. Dower, *Embracing Defeat: Japan in the Wake of World War II* (New York: W. W. Norton, 1999), 72, 110; Burton Watson, "Recollections of Postwar Japan," *International House of Japan Bulletin* 21:2 (Autumn 2001): 51–52.
10. Shaplen; see also "GI's Begin Survey of Tokyo's Stores," *NYT,* 11 September 1945, 3; Robert Trumbull, "U.S. Sailors Throng Yokosuka Streets," *NYT,* 28 September 1945, 4; "A Sailor Goes on a Shopping Spree in Japan," *NYT,* 3 December 1945, 3.
11. Bernard Perlin, "Tokyo Street Scenes," *Life,* 11 November 1945, 73; Carl and Shelley Mydans, "A Trip to the 'Jap Riviera,'" *Life,* 12 November 1945, 22; Crockett, 112; Margery Finn Brown, *Over a Bamboo Fence: An American Looks at Japan* (New York: William Morrow, 1951), 46–47. See also Watson, 52–53.
12. Crockett, 35.
13. Ibid., 99; Lt. John Ashmead, "The Japs Look at the Yanks," *Atlantic,* April 1946, 88.
14. *Our Job in Japan,* 1946, RG 111, NARA-College Park; John LaCerda, *The Conqueror Comes to Tea: Japan under MacArthur* (New Brunswick, N.J.: Rutgers University Press, 1946), 47–48.

15. U.S. Department of the Army, *Pocket Guide to Japan* (Washington, D.C.: U.S. Government Printing Office, 1950), 58–59. The 1952 version strengthens the original points, giving the section subtitle as "Be a Good American" rather than the previous "Be an American." The cover of the original edition was more neutral: it pictured bamboos.

16. An earlier version of this orientation pamphlet suggested Edwin O. Reischauer's *Japan, Past and Present* and Ruth Benedict's *The Chrysanthemum and the Sword* for "real background information" on Japan, but later revised this recommendation to advocate the Japan Tourist Bureau's inexpensive books on contemporary Japan rather than scholarly works. "CI and E: An Orientation Pamphlet for New Personnel," CIE Section, GHQ, SCAP, revised 15 January 1948, p. 14 and revised 1 February 1949, p. 15 (orig. 22 February 1947), box 5342, folder 2; Record Group (RG) 331, National Archives Records Administration at College Park, Maryland (cited hereafter as NARA-College Park).

17. LaCerda, 47–48.

18. U.S. Department of the Army, *Pocket Guide to Japan,* rev. ed., (Washington, D.C.: U.S. Government Printing Office, 1952). Quotes from pp. 1, 18, 34.

19. Compare this attitude to Japanese views of the Occupation as emasculation or even rape. See Michael S. Molasky, *The American Occupation of Japan and Okinawa: Literature and Memory* (New York: Routledge, 1999).

20. John W. Dower, *War Without Mercy: Race and Power in the Pacific War* (New York: Pantheon Books, 1986).

21. In the late Victorian era, the stereotypes of delicate and obedient Japanese women were used to counteract the images of energetic and liberated modern women, who paradoxically sometimes advanced their careers by portraying Japanese women on the stage, in stories, or in artwork. Eunyoung Cho, "The Selling of Japan: Race, Gender, and Cultural Politics in the American Art World, 1876–1915" (Ph.D. diss., University of Delaware, 1998), chaps. 4, 5; Mari Yoshihara, *Embracing the East: White Women and American Orientalism* (New York: Oxford University Press, 2003).

22. Kevin Nute, *Frank Lloyd Wright and Japan: The Role of Traditional Japanese Art and Architecture in the Work of Frank Lloyd Wright*

Notes to Pages 22–23   305

(New York: Van Nostrand Reinhold, 1993), 10–13; Edward W. Said, *Orientalism* (New York: Pantheon Books, 1978); T. J. Jackson Lears, *No Place of Grace: Antimodernism and the Transformation of American Culture, 1880–1920* (Chicago: University of Chicago Press, 1981); William Eleroy Curtis, *The Yankees of the East: Sketches of Modern Japan,* vol. 1 (New York: Stone & Kimball, 1896); Mae St. John Bramhall, *The Wee Ones of Japan* (New York: Harper, 1894).

23. Other popular stage productions included Sidney Jones's *The Geisha* (1896), Pietro Mascagni's *Iris* (1898), John Luther Long and David Belasco's *Darling of the Gods* (1903), and Lionel Monckton's *The Mousmé* (1911). For Japanese design and aesthetics in magazines, see Jane Converse Brown, "The 'Japanese Taste': Its Role in the Mission of the American Home and in the Family's Presentation of Itself to the Public as Expressed in Published Sources—1876–1916" (Ph.D. diss., University of Wisconsin at Madison, 1987).

24. Nute, 19; Katharine Schuyler Baxter, *In Beautiful Japan* (1895; New York: Hobart, 1904), 376.

25. Curtis, 1; Ernest Satow quoted in Littlewood, 63; Yoshihara; Cho.

26. Ironically, the Japanese themselves exploited the attraction of traditional Japan to help raise capital for their modernization efforts, producing curios for foreign consumption that perpetuated stereotyped, romantic visions of their land and society. William Hosley, *The Japan Idea: Art and Life in Victorian America* (Hartford, Conn.: Wadsworth Atheneum, 1990), 42–45, 116–117; Yoshihara, chap. 1; Cho, chap. 3; Clay Lancaster, *The Japanese Influence in America* (New York: Walton H. Rawls, 1963); Julia Meech and Gabriel P. Weisberg, *Japonisme Comes to America: The Japanese Impact on the Graphic Arts, 1876–1925* (New York: Harry N. Abrams, 1990).

27. Isabella L. Bird, *Unbeaten Tracks in Japan* (New York: G. P. Putnam's Sons, 1881), 29.

28. Yoshihara, 33–35.

29. See images of period advertisements at Judy Shoaf's remarkable website on Japanese dolls: "How Japanese Dolls Came to Europe and America: A 'Prehistory' of Japanese Dolls in the West," *www.clas.ufl.edu/users/jshoaf/Jdolls/jdollwestern/* (accessed 17 November 2004).

30. Ibid.

31. Pierre Loti [Louis-Marie-Julien Viaud], *Madame Chrysanthème*, trans. Robert Arnot (1887; New York: Current Literature, 1910), 35, 40, 46, 186, 193.

32. Quoted in Littlewood, 92–93. For similar references about Japan being "dainty," "toy-like," "child-size," or a "doll's house," see Holland, *My Japanese Wife* (1902) and primary sources at Shoaf's website.

33. Part of the attempt to denigrate the Japanese as childish and feminine thus spoke to western fears about Japan as a potential rival and to the West's own discomfort with the fussy, effeminate, and infantile features in its culture and society. See Hugh Cortazzi and George Webb, *Kipling's Japan: Collected Writings* (London: The Althlone Press, 1988), 73–74, 92.

34. "Tokyo Street Scene," *Saturday Evening Post*, 28 February 1946, 28. See also Russell Brines, *MacArthur's Japan* (Philadelphia: J. B. Lippincott, 1948), 28; Clark Lee, *One Last Look Around* (New York: Duell, Sloan and Pearce, 1947), 9.

35. Shaplen; "Tokyo Street Scene"; Honor Tracy, *Kakemono: A Sketch Book of Post-War Japan* (London: Methuen, 1950), ix. See also Edward Seidensticker, "Remembrances," *International House of Japan Bulletin* 21:2 (Autumn 2001): 35; Coll; Brines, 28; Lee, 9.

36. F. D. Morris, "Seventy Million Problem Children," *Collier's*, 1 December 1945, 22–23, 53–54; "Rise and Fall of Japan's Empire," *Senior Scholastic*, 17 September 1945, 3; Frank Kelley and Cornelius Ryan, *Star-Spangled Mikado* (New York: Robert M. McBride, 1947), 233. In Japan, Ryan wrote for the *London Daily Telegraph.*

37. Noel F. Busch, *Fallen Sun: A Report on Japan* (New York: D. Appleton-Century, 1948), 21–22, 25–26; Bernadine V. Lee, "Army Wife in Tokyo," *Army Information Digest*, December 1945, 14–22.

38. "Okinawa," *Life*, 88; "Our Fighting Men Turn Tourist in Tokyo," *NYT*, 9 September 1945, 5; "Yank Sightseers in Tokyo," *Senior Scholastic*, 29 October 1945, cover.

39. See Dower, *War Without Mercy.*

40. Lisa Yoneyama notes that the *New York Times* switched in depictions of the Japanese from "women warriors" during the war to "the unhappiest women in the world" after it. Yoneyama, "Liberation Un-

der Siege: U.S. Military Occupation and Japanese Women's Enfranchisement," *American Quarterly* 57:3 (September 2005): 890–892.

41. "Life in Tokyo," *Life*, 3 December 1945, 105–113; "Tokyo's GI Tunesmith," *Life*, 7 October 1946, 6–7. See also identical Associated Press photos used in *Newsweek*, 24 September 1945, 44 and 52, and *Time*, 24 September 1945, 22. The captions for the flag-waving children were remarkably different, illustrating how much editors tried to shape public opinion. *Time:* "Japanese Children and U.S. Flags: The grown-ups, too, seemed sincerely submissive." *Newsweek:* "Forgetting Pearl Harbor: A Jap woman prompts her children to wave Allied flags."

42. Carl Mydans, Shelley Mydans, and Shinpei Ishii, *Makkāsā no Nihon: Karu Maidansu shashinshū, 1945–1951* (Tokyo: Kodansha, 1995).

43. Shelley Mydans, letters to the author, 29 January 1996, 8 July 1996, and 2 August 1996.

44. Mydans, letter to the author, 29 January 1996.

45. Coll; see also Kluckhorn, "GI's in Japan Obey Fraternizing Ban," *NYT*, 21 September 1945, 3.

46. Lieutenant Doris Schwartz, A.N.C., "Letters from an Army Nurse in Japan," *NYT Magazine*, 14 April 1946, 57; Mark Gayn, "Our Balance Sheet in Japan," *Collier's*, 23 March 1946, 12; Harold J. Noble, "We're Teaching the Children to Lead Japan," *Saturday Evening Post*, 27 July 1946, 9. See also Edwin M. Zimmerman, "'Herro' and 'Goomby,'" *NYT Magazine*, 22 December 1946, 118; Ashmead, 91.

47. William L. Worden, "The GI is Civilizing the Jap," *Saturday Evening Post*, 15 December 1945, 103–104; Schwartz, 57; "Children of Koga See First GIs, Koga, NW of Tokyo Japan," unedited film, 16 September 1945, RG 111 ADC 5329, NARA-College Park.

48. Letter from Hisashi Kubota to Donald Keene, 24 November 1945, in Otis Cary, ed., *War-Wasted Asia: Letters, 1945–46* (Tokyo: Kodansha International, 1975), 194.

49. Crockett, 176–177.

50. Lindesay Parrott, "GI's Are Great Guys," *NYT Magazine*, 17 May 1946, 15.

51. Interview with Hugh O'Reilly, 22 June 2004.

52. Ibid.; "A G.I. 'Father' Greeted by His Happy 'Family," *NYT*, 27 February 1951, 3; Gertrude Samuels, "O'Reilly's Mission," *NYT Maga-*

zine, 3 June 1951, 187; L. O. Maroney, "The Wolfhounds and the Children," *Catholic World,* September 1951, 435–440; E. J. Kahn, Jr., "The Gentle Wolfhound," *New Yorker,* 9 May 1953, 75–90; "The Good Sergeant's Return," *Life,* 31 October 1955, 101.

53. The movie was *Three Stripes in the Sun* (1955); see Chapter 7 for further discussion. James A. Michener, "Japan," *Holiday,* August 1952, 77–78; Kahn.

54. See Nosaka Akiyuki, "American Hijiki," trans. Jay Rubin, in Howard Hibbett, ed., *Contemporary Japanese Literature: An Anthology of Fiction, Film, and Other Writings Since 1945* (New York: Alfred A. Knopf, 1977).

55. See photographs in Parrott, "We Bring a Revolution to the Japanese"; Gayn; "How a 25¢ Christmas Gift can help build a permanent peace," *NYT* display ad, 1 December 1946, B9; "Our Record in Japan," *Senior Scholastic,* 13 April 1949, 5.

56. William L. Worden, "These Japs Took to Conquest," *Saturday Evening Post,* 9 May 1945, 24. It also explains why the United States censored photos of *Japanese* soldiers with children. See George H. Roeder, Jr., *The Censored War: American Visual Experience during World War II* (New Haven: Yale University Press, 1993).

57. Ashmead, 91. The other question most requested by servicemen to have Ashmead translate into Japanese was: "Have you any kimonos?"

58. Quoted in Maroney, 435.

59. At the same time, however, GIs' generosity came from their privileged position, a language officer admitted. All smiles and full of generosity in a second-class train car, he became quickly sullen and unwilling to give candy or make contact with the Japanese in crowded third-class cars. Ted DeBary to Donald Keene, 12 November 1945, in Cary, 144–145.

60. For a recent example, see the photo essay on George W. Bush's White House website of GIs either giving food and supplies to Iraqis or posing with smiling Iraqi children and adults. Three of the twenty photos in this essay depict an American soldier giving candy to children: *www.whitehouse.gov/infocus/iraq/photoessay/essay1/19.html* (accessed 28 December 2004).

61. Ashmead, 90.
62. Harold Wakefield, *New Paths for Japan* (New York: Oxford University Press, 1948), 76.
63. Crockett, 131.
64. Ibid., 148–149; M. Brown, 140; Kelley and Ryan, 160–161.
65. Bill Hume and John Annarino, *Babysan: A Private Look at the Japanese Occupation* (Columbia, Mo.: American Press, 1953); Hume and Annarino, *Babysan's World: The Hume'n Slant on Japan* (Rutland, Vt.: Tuttle Books, 1956); Ray Falk, "What the GIs in Korea Are Reading," *NYT Book Review,* 27 June 1954, 19.
66. Kelley and Ryan, 146.
67. Ibid., 36. Hume drew all young women in this manner. See his cartoons of young American wives in Bill Hume and John Annarino, *When We Get Back Home from Japan* (Tokyo: Kyoya, 1953), and Hume and Annarino, *Anchors Are Heavy* (Rutland, Vt.: Tuttle Books, 1955).
68. Hume and Annarino, *Babysan,* 16, 20, 32–33. Extract from p. 20.
69. "Life in Tokyo," 108–109.
70. Eiji Takemae, *Inside GHQ: The Allied Occupation of Japan and Its Legacy,* trans. Robert Ricketts and Sebastian Swan (New York: Continuum, 2002), 580, note 28; 69–71.
71. Hume and Annarino, *Babysan,* 5, 7, 50–53, 123.
72. Kelley and Ryan, 145–146; Crockett, 107–108; Harry Emerson Wildes, *Typhoon in Tokyo: The Occupation and Its Aftermath* (New York: MacMillan, 1954), 327.
73. Martin Bronfenbrenner, *Fusako and the Army: An Episode of Occupation* (Tokyo: Hokuseido Press, 1952), 40, 42; italics in the original. Bronfenbrenner, an economist, wrote the story in 1946 and published it in 1952 when SCAP censorship was lifted. *Fusako* was republished in his *Tomioka Stories: From the Japanese Occupation* (Hicksville, N.Y.: Exposition Press, 1975).
74. Quoted in Takemae, 68. See also Yuki Tanaka, *Japan's Comfort Women: Sexual Slavery and Prostitution during World War II and the US Occupation* (London: Routledge, 2002).
75. Crockett, 145–146.
76. Elliott Chaze, *The Stainless Steel Kimono* (New York: Simon &

Schuster, 1947), vii, 204. For another, extremely vivid narrative of GIs behaving badly, see Bronfenbrenner, "Porky the Nympho," in *Tomioka Stories*, 47–61.

77. Occupation servicemen who had temporary liaisons did not leave much of a paper trail. The attitudes described in the text came from fictionalized accounts of GIs in the Occupation by two veterans: Chaze, 168–174; Bronfenbrenner, *Fusako*, 41. Bronfenbrenner's stories were endorsed as a "charming collection of tales of the Occupation" by a fellow language-officer in his own memoir. Herbert Passin, *Encounter With Japan* (Tokyo and New York: Kodansha International Ltd., 1982), 127.

78. Yukiko Koshiro, *Transpacific Racisms: The U.S. Occupation of Japan* (New York: Columbia University Press, 1999), 59–62.

79. Petra Goedde, *GIs and Germans: Culture, Gender, and Foreign Relations, 1945–1949* (New Haven: Yale University Press, 2002); Maria Höhn, *GIs and Fräuleins: The German-American Encounter in 1950s Germany* (Chapel Hill: University of North Carolina Press, 2002).

80. Koshiro, 156–158.

81. Bronfenbrenner, 49–53; Elfrieda Berthiaume Skukert and Barbara Smith Scibetta, *War Brides of World War II* (Novato, Calif.: Presidio Press, 1988), 206–207.

82. The Japanese, on the other hand, did nothing for the estimated 70,000 to 100,000 illegitimate children fathered by Japanese soldiers in Southeast Asia. Koshiro, chap. 5.

83. LaCerda, 52.

84. See, for example, Karen Anderson, *Wartime Women: Sex Roles, Family Relations, and the Status of Women During World War II* (Westport, Conn.: Greenwood Press, 1981); Sherna Berger Gluck, *Rosie the Riveter Revisited: Women, the War, and Social Change* (Boston: Twayne, 1987); Susan Hartmann, *The Homefront and Beyond: American Women in the 1940s* (Boston: Twayne, 1984); Elaine Tyler May, *Homeward Bound: American Families in the Cold War Era* (New York: BasicBooks, 1988).

85. Irene Corbally Kuhn, "Women Don't Belong in Politics," *American Mercury*, August 1953, 3–6.

86. Joanne Meyerowitz, ed., *Not June Cleaver: Women and Gender in*

Postwar America, 1945–1960 (Philadelphia: Temple University Press, 1994); Stephanie Coontz, *The Way We Never Were: American Families and the Nostalgia Trap* (New York: BasicBooks, 1992).

87. Mari Jo Buhle, *Feminism and Its Discontents: A Century of Struggle with Psychoanalysis* (Cambridge, Mass.: Harvard University Press, 1998), chaps. 4, 5.

88. Earnest Hoberecht, *Asia Is My Beat* (Rutland, Vt.: Charles E. Tuttle, 1961), 167. For unflattering depictions of top officers' wives, see J. Malcolm Morris's memoir as the manager of the Imperial Hotel billet. J. Malcolm Morris, *The Wise Bamboo* (Philadelphia: J. B. Lippincott, 1953), 56–61, 96–105, 112.

89. Carl Mydans, "The White Man's Burden," *Life*, 10 May 1948, 4–13.

90. M. Brown, 230.

91. Crockett, 148, 93, 71–72, 41–42; italics in the original.

92. Kelley and Ryan, 145, 161–162.

93. LaCerda, 41–43, 89.

94. Crockett, 168–169.

95. The exception was Margery Brown, who found that her group of Japanese friends envied her wealth and conveniences but did not see themselves as slaves, were proud to be Japanese, and would not have traded places with her "for all the salt in the sea." She also pointed out that the Japanese suffrage movement dated back to the nineteenth century, and she observed Japanese women getting irritated at the pomposity of a Japanese male speaker. M. Brown, 148, 152, 172, 179.

96. For example, see Parrott, "Out of Feudalism: Japan's Women," *NYT Magazine*, 28 October 1945, 10, 44–46.

97. Kelley and Ryan, 160–161, 164–165; LaCerda, 54.

98. Reina Lewis, *Gendering Orientalism: Race, Femininity, and Representations* (London: Routledge, 1996), 22; Cynthia Enloe, *Bananas, Beaches, and Bases: Making Feminist Sense of International Politics* (1989; Berkeley: University of California Press, 2000), chap. 3.

99. Crockett, 148–151.

100. Kathleen S. Uno, "Death of 'Good Wife, Wise Mother?'" in Andrew Gordon, ed., *Postwar Japan as History* (Berkeley: University of California Press, 1993), 296–297.

101. See Ray Falk, "G.I. Brides Go to School in Japan," *NYT Magazine*, 7 November 1954, 54–56; Yo Tajiri, "Practical Democracy: Japanese Wives of U.S. GIs Prepare for Life in America," *Pacific Citizen*, 25 September 1948, 5; Janet Wentworth Smith and William L. Worden, "They're Bringing Home Japanese Wives," *Saturday Evening Post*, 19 January 1952, 26–27, 79–81; and a series of unedited films at the NARA-College Park: "Japanese War Brides School, Tokyo, Japan," 6 June 1952, RG 111, LC 30177; "American Red Cross Brides' School, Tokyo Japan," 10 November 1955, RG 111, LC 39278-39283; "Japanese Bride School," March 1956, RG 428, NPC, Item 74; "Japanese Bride School, Yokosuka, Japan," March 1956, RG 428, NPC 46; "Japanese Bride School, Yokosuka, Japan," March 1956, RG 428, NPC 73; "Japanese Bride School, Yokosuka, Japan," March 1956, RG 428, NPC 95; "Japanese Bride School, Yokosuka, Japan," March 1956, RG 428, NPC 117.

102. Quoted in Falk, "G.I. Brides," 55.

103. Earnest Hoberecht, *Tokyo Romance* (New York: Didier, 1947), 144. Hoberecht received national coverage for his novel. See "Nipponese Best-Seller," *Time*, 28 October 1948, 56; W. James, "$80,000 Kiss," *Colliers*, 8 March 1947, 58; "Japanese Best-Seller," *Life*, 7 April 1947, 107–111.

104. Wentworth and Worden, 26–27, 79–81. Quote on p. 81. For responses, see n. 103 above.

105. The *Post* published no letters, positive or negative, in response to this second article. See Worden, "Where are Those Japanese Brides?" *Saturday Evening Post*, 20 November 1954, 38–39, 133–134. Compare Worden, "The Japs' Last Bite," *Saturday Evening Post*, 27 October 1945, 23.

106. James A. Michener, "Sayonara Means Good-Bye," serialized in *McCall's*, October, November, December 1953; Michener, "Pursuit of Happiness by a GI and a Japanese," *Life*, 21 February 1955, 124–141, esp. boxed insert on p. 126; "Letters to the Editors: Pursuit of Happiness," *Life*, 14 March 1955, 15; "Michener Will Marry a Japanese-American," *NYT*, 20 October 1955, 9; "James Michener Marries," *NYT*, 24 October 1955, 48.

107. Hugh F. O'Reilly, "Our East-West Marriage Is Working," *American Mercury,* December 1955, 17–19.
108. Interview with Hugh and Yuko O'Reilly, 22 June 2004. The couple still banter back and forth with playful affection. "She pushes me around," hooted the 90-year-old, wheelchair-bound O'Reilly.
109. Caroline Chung Simpson, *An Absent Presence: Japanese Americans in Postwar American Culture, 1945–1960* (Durham: Duke University Press, 2001), 151–152.
110. In 1947 President Truman signed a bill, Public Law No. 126, which gave American men in Occupied Japan a brief window of opportunity—thirty days—to marry Japanese women who would then be allowed to enter the United States on a non-quota basis. At the end of this period, the Associated Press reported that 823 marriages had occurred between American men and Japanese women: 597 of the men were Nisei, 211 were Euroamerican, and 15 were African American. Koshiro, 157.
111. Crockett, 21–22.
112. The role of tourism in rebuilding the Japanese economy had become increasingly important to SCAP after the "reverse course" of 1947–1948. SCAP helped the Japanese tourist industry most by making Japan the rest and recreation destination for U.S. soldiers fighting in the Korean War, but it also tried to promote tourism to civilians. The Japan Tourist Bureau announced its efforts to revive a tourist trade, and SCAP began permitting package tours of Occupied Japan for a limited number of visitors not on official business in the summer of 1948. In May 1950, *Newsweek* announced, "Japan: A Pacific Tourist Paradise Opens for Business Again," and noted that by the end of 1950, visitors were expected to bring about $15 million "badly needed dollars" into the Japanese economy. Ray Falk, "Seven Days in Japan," *NYT,* 22 August 1948, X15; Falk, "Five Tours of Japan," *NYT,* 1 May 1949, X15; "Japan: A Pacific Tourist Paradise Open for Business Again," *Newsweek,* 15 May 1950, 88; "Japan: Tourists Accommodated," *Newsweek,* 28 March 1949; Ray Falk, "Japanese Comeback," *NYT,* 30 March 1947.
113. Willard Price, "A Million Americans Will Visit Japan," *Travel,* De-

cember 1945, 5–9, 33; Falk, "Japanese Comeback," X11; Crockett, 99, 109–110; Kelley and Ryan, 11.

114. Crockett, 40, 44–46, 54–55.

115. Passin, 126.

2. "Like a Boy of Twelve"

1. U.S. Senate Committee on Armed Services and Committee on Foreign Relations, Military Situation in the Far East, *Hearings to Conduct an Inquiry into the Military Situation in the Far East and the Facts Surrounding the Relief of General of the Army Douglas MacArthur from His Assignment in the Area,* 82nd Congress, 1st sess., pt. 1, 3 May 1951, 312–313.

2. On Japanese reactions to MacArthur's statements, see John W. Dower, *Embracing Defeat: Japan in the Wake of World War II* (New York: W. W. Norton, 1999), 551. For Japanese uses of the immaturity trope, see Dower, *War Without Mercy: Race and Power in the Pacific War* (New York: Pantheon Books, 1986), chap. 10, esp. p. 284; see also the Japanese cartoon reprinted as the frontispiece of W. Petrie Watson, *Japan: Aspects and Destinies* (London: Grant Richards, 1904).

3. Gail Bederman, *Manliness and Civilization: A Cultural History of Gender and Race in the United States, 1880–1917* (Chicago: University of Chicago Press, 1995), 20–31. See also Dower, *War Without Mercy;* Michael H. Hunt, *Ideology and U.S. Foreign Policy* (New Haven: Yale University Press, 1987); Reginald Horsman, *Race and Manifest Destiny: The Origins of American Racial Anglo-Saxonism* (Cambridge, Mass.: Harvard University Press, 1981).

4. For an example in a different era, see how American revolutionaries called England a "haggard mother." Gordon Wood, *The Creation of the American Republic, 1776–1787* (New York: W. W. Norton, 1969), 42. See also Michael Kimmel's definition of "hegemonic masculinity." Michael Kimmel, *Manhood in America: A Cultural History* (New York: Free Press, 1996), 5–6, 18–20.

5. Nils Gilman, "Paved with Good Intentions: The Genesis of the Modernization Theory" (Ph.D. diss., University of California at Berkeley,

2000), 21. For discussion of modernization theory as it related to Japan, see Laura E. Hein, "Free-Floating Anxieties on the Pacific: Japan and the West Revisited," *Diplomatic History* 20 (Summer 1996): 411–437.

6. Honor Tracy, *Kakemono: A Sketch Book of Post-War Japan* (London: Methuen, 1950), 15.
7. Bederman, 92–94.
8. Dower, *War Without Mercy,* chaps. 5–6; Mari Yoshihara, *Embracing the East: White Women and American Orientalism* (New York: Oxford University Press, 2003), chap. 7 and notes 22 and 60 on pp. 215, 218; Clifford Geertz, *Works and Lives: The Anthropologist as Author* (Stanford: Stanford University Press, 1988), chap. 5; essays in *Dialectical Anthropology* 24 (1999); Adrian Pinnington, "Yoshimitsu, Benedict, Endō: Guilt, Shame and the Post-War Idea of Japan," *Japan Forum* 13:1 (2001): 91–105; John Lie, "Ruth Benedict's Legacy of Shame: Orientalism and Occidentalism in the Study of Japan," *Asian Journal of Social Science* 29:2 (2001): 249–261; Christopher Shannon, "A World Made Safe for Differences: Ruth Benedict's *The Chrysanthemum and the Sword,*" *American Quarterly* 47:7 (December 1995): 659–680.
9. Yoshihara, 187.
10. Ruth Benedict, *The Chrysanthemum and the Sword: Patterns of Japanese Culture* (1946; New York: Mentor, 1974), 160.
11. Compare Erik H. Erikson's influential *Childhood and Society* (1950). Erikson is best known for his work on identity crises and for adapting and expanding Freud's five stages of psychosexual development into eight stages of psychosocial development (1956).
12. Helen Mears, *Mirror for Americans: Japan* (Boston: Houghton Mifflin, 1948), 6, 321.
13. Richard H. Minear, "Cross-Cultural Perception and World War II: American Japanists of the 1940s and Their Images of Japan," *International Studies Quarterly* 24:4 (December 1980): 572–574.
14. Ibid., 560; Mears, 39–40.
15. Mears described her 1935 sojourn in Japan in *Year of the Wild Boar: An American Woman in Japan* (Philadelphia: J. B. Lippincott, 1942). She also wrote a children's book on Japan.

16. Mears, 37–44.
17. Bruce Cumings, *Parallax Visions: Making Sense of American–East Asian Relations* (Durham: Duke University Press, 2002), 4.
18. Minear, 575; Ruth Benedict, *The Chrysanthemum and the Sword: Patterns of Japanese Culture* (1945; New York: Houghton-Mifflin, 2005).
19. Lucy Herndon Crockett, *Popcorn on the Ginza: An Informal Portrait of Postwar Japan* (New York: William Sloane Associates, 1949), 31.
20. Noel Busch, "A Report on Japan," *Life,* 2 December 1946, 127.
21. After the Civil War, Northerners also feminized Southerners as nostalgic, stagnated, and enervated, while the Northerners were viewed as forward-looking, moving, and energized. They labeled Southerners as women, the antiquarians, the preservationists of history, while the Northerners saw themselves as men, the agents, the makers of history. Nina Silber, *The Romance of Reunion: Northerners and Southerners, 1865–1900* (Chapel Hill: University of North Carolina Press, 1993).
22. Russell Brines, *MacArthur's Japan* (Philadelphia: J. B. Lippincott, 1948), 123.
23. Noel F. Busch, *Fallen Sun: A Report on Japan* (New York: D. Appleton-Century, 1948), 173–175.
24. Crockett, 254–255, 47.
25. This idea that the Japanese feel no individual personal guilt but feel chastised only when shamed in front of a group still persists in American and western discourse. For an example, see Ian Buruma, *The Wages of Guilt: Memories of War in Germany and Japan* (New York: Farrar, Straus, Giroux, 1994).
26. Busch told this story both in his *Life* article and in *Fallen Sun* (15–16). Versions of the story appeared in LaCerda (1946), 31; Frank Kelley and Cornelius Ryan, *Star-Spangled Mikado* (New York: Robert M. McBride, 1947), 205; and Crockett (1949), 98.
27. Kelley and Ryan, 140.
28. Ibid., 163–164; Crockett, 204, 267–269.
29. See, among others, Ray Falk, "Teaching 'Demokratzi' to the Japanese," *NYT Magazine,* 12 June 1949, 12.

30. Michael Adas, "Modernization Theory and the American Revival of the Scientific and Technological Standards of Social Achievement and Human Worth," in David C. Engerman, Nils Gilman, Mark H. Haefele, and Michael E. Latham, eds., *Staging Growth: Modernization, Development, and the Global Cold War* (Amherst: University of Massachusetts Press, 2003), 36.

31. Stoddard mission report quoted in Lindesay Parrott, "Educating Japan's Children for Democracy," *NYT Magazine,* 10 November 1946, 10; Harold Noble, "We're Teaching the Children to Lead Japan," *Saturday Evening Post,* 27 July 1946, 9.

32. Eiji Takemae, *Inside GHQ: The Allied Occupation of Japan and Its Legacy,* trans. Robert Ricketts and Sebastian Swan (New York: Continuum, 2002), 350–371.

33. Julianne Burton, "Don (Juanito) Duck and the Imperial-Patriarchal Unconscious: Disney Studios, the Good Neighbor Policy, and the Packaging of Latin America," in Andrew Parker, Mary Russo, Doris Sommer, and Patricia Yaeger, eds., *Nationalisms and Sexualities* (New York: Routledge, 1992), 36. For an example involving Japan, see Shelley Mydans, "The Conquerors," *Life,* 5 May 1947, 19–22.

34. Brines, 305; Kelley and Ryan, 215.

35. See Matthew Frye Jacobson, *Barbarian Virtues: The United States Encounters Foreign Peoples at Home and Abroad, 1876–1917* (New York: Hill and Wang, 2000); Jacobson, *Whiteness of a Different Color: European Immigrants and the Alchemy of Race* (Cambridge, Mass.: Harvard University Press, 1998); Gary Gerstle, *American Crucible: Race and Nation in the Twentieth Century* (Princeton: Princeton University Press, 2001).

36. Hunt; Gilman; Olivier Zunz, *Why the American Century?* (Chicago: University of Chicago Press, 1998), esp. chap. 8.

37. Sigmund Freud, *Civilization and Its Discontents,* trans. and ed. James Strachey (1930; New York: W. W. Norton, 1961, 1989), 59.

38. Vernon J. Williams, *Rethinking Race: Franz Boas and His Contemporaries* (Lexington: University Press of Kentucky, 1996), 16.

39. Freud, 70–71. Freud spoke against homophobia in the same book (p. 60), but this was largely ignored during the era.

40. H. W. Brands, *The Strange Death of American Liberalism* (New Ha-

ven: Yale University Press, 2001); Alan Brinkley, *Liberalism and Its Discontents* (Cambridge, Mass.: Harvard University Press, 1998); Alonzo L. Hamby, *Liberalism and Its Challengers: From F.D.R. to Bush*, 2nd ed. (New York: Oxford University Press, 1992).

41. Fritz Fischer, *Making Them Like Us: Peace Corps Volunteers in the 1960s* (Washington, D.C.: Smithsonian Books, 1998).

42. Hunt, chap. 2; Anders Stephanson, *Manifest Destiny: American Expansion and the Empire of Right* (New York: Hill and Wang, 1995).

43. [Henry Luce], "How to Think About 'Civilization,'" *Life*, 23 February 1948, 34–35, italics in the original; [Luce], "The American Century," *Life*, 17 February 1941, 61–65; [Luce], "The Challenge," *Time*, 17 March 1947, 71; Stephen Duggan, "Education Under the New Order," *Saturday Review of Literature*, 15 September 1945, 7–9.

44. "Are You Smart Enough to Be a Citizen?" *Saturday Evening Post*, 21 September 1946, 19, 98, 102.

45. "Western Culture: America is Heir and Hope of the West's Civilization," *Life*, 22 March 1948, 73–101.

46. Glowing reviews included the following: "The Challenge," *Time*, 17 March 1947, 71–81; "A Study of History," *Life*, 23 February 1948, 118–133; "Toynbee's Decline and Fall," *Newsweek*, 24 March 1947, 96–98; Granville Hicks, "Encounters Between Civilizations," *Harper's*, April 1947, 289–294.

47. "A Study of History," *Life*, 118.

48. The scholar wrote the magazine a letter congratulating and thanking them for explaining his ideas so well in a shortened form. "Toynbee," *Life*, 15 March 1948, 23.

49. M. F. Ashley Montagu, ed., *Toynbee and History: Critical Essays and Reviews* (Boston: Porter Sargent, 1956), vii. *A Study of History* eventually became a twelve-volume work that Toynbee wrote over almost three decades. The first three volumes came out in 1934, and the last volume, *Reconsiderations: A Study of History, Vol. XII*, was published in 1961.

50. "A Study of History," *Life*, 133. Likewise, in Paul Kennedy's *Rise and Fall of the Great Powers* (1987), a bestseller at the *end* of the Cold War, Americans zeroed in on the chapter titled "The United States: The Problem of Number One in Relative Decline." A reviewer

praised Kennedy's study as "a work of almost Toynbeean sweep" that should have "a great and beneficent impact . . . at [this] potentially decisive moment in America's history." Michael Howard, "Imperial Cycles: Bucks, Bullets, and Bust," review of *Rise and Fall of the Great Powers* by Paul Kennedy, *NYT Book Review*, 10 January 1988, A1. See also Richard Crockatt, "Challenge and Response: Arnold Toynbee and the United States during the Cold War," in Dale Carter and Robin Clifton, eds., *War and Cold War in American Foreign Policy, 1942–62* (New York: Palgrave, 2002).

51. Rebecca Jo Plant, "The Repeal of Mother Love: Momism and the Reconstruction of Motherhood in Philip Wylie's America" (Ph.D. diss., Johns Hopkins University, 2001); Philip Wylie, *A Generation of Vipers*, rev. ed. (New York: Rinehart & Co., 1955), 201; Edward A. Strecker, *Their Mother's Sons: The Psychiatrist Examines an American Problem* (Philadelphia: J. B. Lippincott, 1946), 31.

52. Ellen Herman, *The Romance of American Psychology: Political Culture in the Age of Experts* (Berkeley: University of California Press, 1995); Elaine Tyler May, *Homeward Bound: American Families in the Cold War Era* (New York: BasicBooks, 1988); Mari Jo Buhle, *Feminism and Its Discontents: A Century of Struggle with Psychoanalysis* (Cambridge, Mass.: Harvard University Press, 1998); Jennifer Terry, "'Momism' and the Making of Treasonous Homosexuals," in Molly Ladd-Taylor and Lauri Umansky, eds., *"Bad Mothers": The Politics of Blame in Twentieth-Century America* (New York: New York University Press, 1998), 169–190; David K. Johnson, *The Lavender Scare: The Cold War Persecution of Gays and Lesbians in the Federal Government* (Chicago: University of Chicago Press, 2004).

53. May; see also sociologist Ferdinand Lundberg and psychoanalyst Marynia F. Farnham's *Modern Women: The Lost Sex* (New York: Harper & Brothers, 1947).

54. The perception of juvenile delinquency did not match the number of crimes committed by youth. See James Gilbert, *A Cycle of Outrage: America's Reaction to the Juvenile Delinquent in the 1950s* (New York: Oxford University Press, 1986), 62–80. For a contemporary example, see Dorothy Thompson, "What Juvenile Crime Reflects," *Ladies Home Journal*, October 1946, 24–26. For an analysis of the

depictions of j.d. in 1950s films, see Thomas Doherty, *Teenagers and Teenpics: The Juvenilization of American Movies in the 1950s* (Boston: Unwin Hyman, 1988), 245–261.

55. The near-universal enrollment of youth in high school meant that the postwar generation had more unstructured time to "make trouble" than previous generations. Grace Palladino, *Teenagers: An American History* (New York: BasicBooks, 1996), xiii–xxi. See also "The Small Fry Take Over: For some reason the world suddenly seems full of kids who are active, attractive, and less than 42 inches high," *Life,* 12 September 1949, 101–104; "The War Babies Hit the First Grade," *Life,* 19 September 1949, 45–51.

56. For example, see Harry J. Carman, "Setting Our Sights for Tomorrow," *Saturday Review of Literature,* 15 September 1945, 16–18. The *Saturday Review* published reviews of more than twenty books on the state of American education from early 1945 to early 1947 alone. Note the post–Cold War concerns about education—especially from conservatives like Lynne Cheney and William Bennett.

57. Cited in Harry D. Gideonse, "The Coming Showdown in the Schools: A Report on the Battle of Educators," *Saturday Review of Literature,* 3 February 1945, 5.

58. The original edition of *Liberal Education* came out in 1943, and the second edition in 1948. The third edition, published in 1959, and attesting to the book's popularity, had its third printing in 1962.

59. Gideonse, 5, 7.

60. Benjamin Fine, however, attacked the great books approach as aristocratic and advocated a future that might see college for all. Benjamin Fine, *A Report on Colleges* (New York: Thomas W. Crowell, 1945).

61. Adler oversaw the revised and expanded version of *Great Books* in 1990. He died in 2001, at age 98.

62. With his writer wife, Bonaro, Overstreet also traveled widely and often on a lecture circuit, promoting adult education and talking about his "maturity concept." From 1950 to 1958, the Overstreets gave "an estimated 600 lectures, symposia, colloquies, and workshops" in thirty-seven states, the District of Columbia, and Canada at churches, synagogues, town halls, PTA conventions, YMCAs, YWCAs, business and management conferences, Men's Clubs,

Women's Clubs, large corporations, and universities. Yvonne Rappaport, "The Whole World Was Their Classroom: The Contributions of Harry and Bonaro Overstreet to the Field of Adult Education" (E.D. diss., Virginia Polytechnic Institute and State University, 1998), 133, 146; James Patrick Brennan, "Harry Allen Overstreet's Concept of the Mature Mind" (Ph.D. diss., University of Wyoming, 1996), 60.

63. H[arry] A[llen] Overstreet, *The Mature Mind* (New York: W. W. Norton, 1949), 42–75.

64. Bucklin Moon, ed., *Primer for White Folks* (Garden City, N.Y.: Doubleday, Doran, 1945), xii.

65. Southern whites, of course, have employed the rhetoric of paternalism to justify white privilege since the age of slavery. For a study attentive to paternalism and gender, see Kathleen M. Brown, *Good Wives, Nasty Wenches, and Anxious Patriarchs* (Chapel Hill: University of North Carolina Press, 1996), esp. 322–324.

66. H. A. Overstreet, "Some Things Adults Ought to Know," *Saturday Review of Literature*, 29 September 1945, 34.

67. Other chapter titles in Gunther's bestseller were less judgmental, even flattering—"California the Golden," "Stop Roaming, Try Wyoming"—or neutrally stated: "Oklahoma and the Indians." John Gunther, *Inside U.S.A.*, rev. ed. (1946, 1947; New York: Harper & Row, 1951).

68. Eugene V. Rostow, "Our Worst Wartime Mistake," *Harper's*, September 1945, 193–201, quotes on 193, 199; Rostow, "The Japanese American Cases—A Disaster," *Yale Law Journal* 54:3 (June 1945): 489–533, quotes on 489.

69. As Brian Hayashi has recently argued, the internment decision came from a confluence of factors—especially the notion that the internees could be exchanged for American POWs. The decision did not, he maintains, result from racist "mass hysteria"—the most common explanation even among scholars for the internment since the war's end. Brian Masaru Hayashi, *Democratizing the Enemy: The Japanese American Internment* (Princeton: Princeton University Press, 2004), introduction, chap. 3.

70. For a small sampling see T. B. Clark et al., "Japanese-American Soldiers Make Good," *American Mercury*, June 1945, 698–703; "Ku-

Kluxism on the West Coast," *Colliers*, 14 July 1945, 74; "$1,000 Reward," *Colliers*, 21 September 1945; "Go for Broke," *Time*, 22 July 1946, 22; R.C.L, "Our Japanese Americans Now," *Survey Midmonthly*, November 1946, 291–294; R. F. Martin, "Hood River Odyssey," *New Republic*, 16 December 1946, 814; W. L. Worden, "The Hate that Failed," *Saturday Evening Post*, 4 May 1946, 22–23; "Wallace Condemns Evacuation as 'Un-American' in Meeting with Nisei Supporters in Group," *Pacific Citizen*, 3 October 1948, 2; "More Signs of Recovery from War Hysteria," *Christian Century*, 4 May 1949, 547.

71. Rostow, "Japanese American Cases," 531.

72. See also Adler and Kelso, *The Capitalist Manifesto* (1958). Louis Kelso is best known today for creating ESOPs, Employee Stock Ownership Plans, an innovation that would spread stock ownership more broadly and give more people a stake in the capitalist system.

73. Overstreet, *Mature Mind*, 292.

74. X [George Kennan], "The Sources of Soviet Conduct," *Foreign Affairs* 25 (July 1947), 581–582.

75. John Foster Dulles, "How to Take the Offensive for Peace," *Life*, 24 April 1950, 134–135.

76. Kimmel.

77. William Franklin Sands, "*Japan and the Son of Heaven* [by] Willard Price," *Commonweal*, 26 October 1945, 49; LaCerda, 13.

78. Quoted in Clark Lee, *One Last Look Around* (New York: Duell, Sloan and Pearce, 1947), xii; see also Gerald Horne, *Race War! White Supremacy and the Japanese Attack on the British Empire* (Chapel Hill: University of North Carolina Press, 2004).

79. For a cultural view of senescence—specifically, retirement—as the loss of manhood at mid-century, see Gregory Wood, "The Problem of the Old Man: Manhood, Work, and Retirement in the United States, 1910–1950s" (Ph.D. diss, University of Pittsburgh, 2006).

80. Petra Goedde, *GIs and Germans: Culture, Gender, and Foreign Relations, 1945–1949* (New Haven: Yale University Press, 2002).

81. Hans W. Gatzke, *Germany and the United States: A "Special Relationship"?* (Cambridge, Mass.: Harvard University Press, 1980), 168.

82. [Henry Luce], "Japan," *Life*, 6 August 1945, 24.

83. This perception continues in American studies of the Bataan cam-

paign. John Whitman's study lumps together the number of American and Filipino deaths at 21,000, although other statistics he provides suggest that the number of Filipinos in the Luzon Force outnumbered Americans about five to one. He does not state otherwise, so presumably the number of deaths were proportional, with the Filipinos accounting for a much larger share of the deaths. John W. Whitman, *Bataan: Our Last Ditch: The Bataan Campaign, 1942* (New York: Hippocrene Books, 1990), 605.

84. See the following articles by philosopher-writer Lewis Mumford in the *Saturday Review of Literature:* "German Apologists and the German Record," 11 August 1945, 6; "The Voice of Prussia," 22 September 1945, 9–10; "A Letter to a German Writer," 8 December 1945, 7–8; "Letter to a German Professor," 19 January 1946, 5–6; "The Case Against Germany," 16 March 1946, 13–14. The fact that Mumford's teenage son died fighting the Germans partly explains his fury. Donald L. Miller, *Lewis Mumford: A Life* (New York: Weidenfeld & Nicolson, 1990), 437.

85. The theme of the Germans' lack of repentance persisted for years. See negative responses to the article by two German émigrés who returned to their hometown for the first time since the war: Hansel Mieth and Otto Hagel, "We Return to Fellbach," *Life,* 26 June 1950; "We Return to Fellbach," *Life,* 1 July 1950, 9.

86. "Displaced Germans," *Life,* 15 October 1945, 107–115, quote on 106. Contrast with "Japanese Come Home from Lost Empire," *Life,* 2 February 1946, 17–23.

87. For example, when *Life* published an unsympathetic feature on Nazi "super babies," one reader chastised the magazine, declaring, "There are no Nazis. *Nazis are made, not born*" (italics in the original); while five others suggested that the babies ought to be adopted by American or Allied families, with two writers offering to adopt one personally. "'Super Babies': Illegitimate Children of S.S. are Housed in German Chateau," *Life,* 13 August 1945, 37–40; "Super Babies," *Life,* 3 September 1945, 2–4.

88. "Displaced Germans," *Life,* 5 November 1945, 4–6. Among the nine letters published, only servicemen seemed to show sympathy for the Germans.

89. In fact, American media coverage of the Japanese massacre of Nan-

jing dropped off precipitously after 1948–1949, as Japan became an important Cold War ally. Discussion of the massacre did not reappear in American public discourse until the 1970s, as Japan became a rival economic superpower. The first popular, book-length narrative of the massacre did not appear in the United States until Iris Chang's *The Rape of Nanking: The Forgotten Holocaust of World War II* (1997). See Kate Brandt, "The Rape of Nanjing in American Discourse: From Front Page to 'Oblivion' and Back Again," unpublished paper, December 2005, in the author's files.

90. U.S. Senate Committees on the Army and Foreign Relations, 113.

3. Sunday at Hirohito's

1. Douglas MacArthur, *Reminiscences* (New York: McGraw-Hill, 1964), 287.
2. "MacArthur Arrives," *Life*, 10 September 1945, 30–31; "Japan Signs the Surrender," *Life*, 17 September 1945, 27.
3. Clark Lee, *One Last Look Around* (New York: Duell, Sloan and Pearce, 1947), 46–47.
4. "Ex-God Descends," *Life*, 22 October 1945, 40; see also Lindesay Parrott, "Hirohito Calls on MacArthur in Precedent-Shattering visit," *NYT*, 27 September 1945, 1.
5. "Ex-God Descends," *Life*, 22 October 1945.
6. *Life*'s account of the surrender ceremony on the *Missouri* also conveyed this impression of masculinized Allied power versus Japanese weakness, stressing the contrast between the "small delegation" and "the world's biggest battleship"; the "purse-mouthed" Mamoru Shigemitsu and the firmness in General "Vinegar Joe" Stilwell's "flexed" cheek muscles; and the passive, "expressionless" Japanese and "tough-talking, tough-fighting" "Bull" Halsey. A portfolio-sized aerial shot shows hundreds of Allied forces on a huge, phallic ship and a tiny group of Japanese delegates with a leader who, readers learn, not only wears the stereotypical Coke-bottle glasses but also limps around on an artificial leg. "Japan Signs the Surrender," 27–29.
7. Halsey's comment, in turn, served as the inspiration for a war loan ad that blared, "LET'S GET THE ADMIRAL HIS HORSE!" The ad

went on, "High time we got the Emperor off his high horse, and gave Admiral Halsey his ride." U.S. Treasury ad for the 7th War Loan, *Life*, 4 June 1945, 107.

8. Associated Press report: "Rides on Tojo's White Horse," *NYT*, 10 March 1946, 12.

9. Masanori Nakamura, *The Japanese Monarchy: Ambassador Joseph Grew and the Making of the "Symbol Emperor System," 1931–1991*, trans. Herbert P. Bix, Jonathan Baker-Bates, and Derek Bowen (Armonk, N.Y.: M. E. Sharpe, 1992; John W. Dower, *Japan in War and Peace: Selected Essays* (New York: New Press, 1993), 342–343.

10. Rudolf V. A. Janssens, *"What Future for Japan?" U.S. Wartime Planning for the Postwar Era, 1942–1945* (Amsterdam: Rodopi, 1995), 301–304; 323.

11. Ibid., 302; Dower, *Japan in War and Peace*, 342. During the war, policymakers and advisers, notably Edwin O. Reischauer, recommended separating the emperor from the "militarists" because of his potential usefulness to the U.S. after the war. T. Fujitani, "The Reischauer Memo: Mr. Moto, Hirohito, and Japanese American Soldiers," *Critical Asian Studies* 33:3 (2001): 379–402; Akira Iriye, *Power and Culture: The Japanese-American War, 1941–1945* (Cambridge, Mass.: Harvard University Press, 1981), 59.

12. See the following books published on this subject in 1945: Otto D. Tolischus, *Through Japanese Eyes* (New York: Reynal & Hitchcock, 1945), 49–55; Andrew Roth, *Dilemma in Japan* (Boston: Little, Brown, 1945), 99–122; Wilfrid Fleisher, *What To Do With Japan* (Garden City, N.Y.: Doubleday, Doran, 1945), 15–36; William C. Johnstone, *The Future of Japan* (New York: Oxford University Press, 1945); Willard Price, *Japan and the Son of Heaven* (New York: Duell, Sloan and Pearce, 1945).

13. Janssens, 375.

14. For an example of the completed transmogrification, see "The Emperor: A gentle ruler and his wife go on a search for shellfish," *Life*, 11 September 1964, 45–47.

15. John W. Dower, *Empire and Aftermath: Yoshida Shigeru and the Japanese Experience, 1878–1954* (Cambridge, Mass.: Council on East Asian Studies, Harvard University, 1979).

16. Some Americans appeared aware of the similarity at the time. Along with twenty other prominent Americans, Albert Einstein protested the spread of military influence into science, education, industry, and even the Boy Scouts. See "The Militarization of America" (Washington, D.C.: National Council Against Conscription, 1948). See also Michael S. Sherry, *In the Shadow of War: The United States Since the 1930s* (New Haven: Yale University Press, 1995).

17. See Iriye.

18. John W. Dower, *Embracing Defeat: Japan in the Wake of World War II* (New York: W. W. Norton, 1999), 282–283.

19. Janssens, 387–395; Dower, *Embracing Defeat,* 280–286.

20. Kenneth Ruoff, *The People's Emperor: Democracy and the Japanese Monarchy, 1945–1995* (Cambridge, Mass.: Harvard University Asia Center, 2001), 205–207; Lindesay Parrott, "Japanese Feel Closer to Hirohito Now That Divinity Fence Is Down," *NYT,* 3 January 1946, 3.

21. For an example of a Hiroshima survivor's anger toward the emperor for prolonging the war, see Rodney Barker, *The Hiroshima Maidens: A Story of Courage, Compassion, and Survival* (New York: Viking Penguin, 1985), 45.

22. For a sample of Japanese views on the emperor in 1945, see Rinjirō Sodei, *Dear General MacArthur: Letters from the Japanese during the American Occupation,* trans. Shizue Matsuda (Lanham, Md.: Rowman & Littlefield, 2001), chaps. 4, 5. See also Daikichi Irokawa's analysis of a Hirohito poem released to the public: "Whatever may happen to me / I put a stop to the war / Thinking only of the people who were dying." Daikichi Irokawa, *The Age of Hirohito: In Search of Modern Japan,* trans. Mikiso Hane and John K. Urda (New York: Free Press, 1995), 98–99.

23. MacArthur, 288.

24. Dower, *Embracing Defeat,* 295–297.

25. Herbert P. Bix, *Hirohito and the Making of Modern Japan* (New York: HarperCollins, 2000), chap. 13; Eiji Takemae, *Inside GHQ: The Allied Occupation of Japan and Its Legacy,* trans. Robert Ricketts and Sebastian Swan (New York: Continuum, 2002), chap. 5.

26. Bonner Fellers, "Hirohito's Struggle to Surrender," *Reader's Digest,* July 1947, 90–95. Quotes on pp. 92, 95.

27. Paul Fussell, *Thank God for the Atom Bomb and Other Essays* (New York: Summit Books, 1988).

28. Frank Kelley and Cornelius Ryan, *Star-Spangled Mikado* (New York: Robert M. McBride, 1947), 9.

29. Ibid., 5; see also John LaCerda, *The Conqueror Comes to Tea: Japan Under MacArthur* (New Brunswick, N.J.: Rutgers University Press, 1946), 47–48, 70. The Japanese also made fun of him as "Emperor Ah-sō." Dower, *Embracing Defeat*, 337.

30. Lucy Herndon Crockett, *Popcorn on the Ginza: An Informal Portrait of Postwar Japan* (New York: William Sloane Associates, 1949), 123–128.

31. See *The Mikado* page of the Gilbert and Sullivan web archive: *http://math.boisestate.edu/gas/mikado/html/index.html* (accessed 6 March 2005).

32. The writer seemed unsure of which metaphor to stick to; just a few lines later, he or she alluded to a classroom: "And the so-called 'God-Emperor' Hirohito is reduced to a position as a sort of 'monitor.'" "Rise and Fall of Japan's Empire," *Senior Scholastic,* 17 September 1945, 3.

33. LaCerda, 70; Kelley and Ryan, 67.

34. LaCerda, 16–17.

35. Lee, 39–47; LaCerda, 70; Kelley and Ryan, 67–69.

36. Crockett, 13.

37. Noel F. Busch, *Fallen Sun: A Report on Japan* (New York: D. Appleton-Century, 1948), 48–49.

38. Crockett, 128.

39. Ibid., 12–13.

40. See the following *Life* articles: Wilfrid Fleisher, "What to Do with Japan," 16 April 1945, 88–89; "The Japanese Emperor Is Japan," 20 August 1945, 38D; "The Meaning of Victory," 27 August 1945, 34; "The Japanese Nation," 17 September 1945, 110.

41. "Sunday at Hirohito's," *Life,* 4 February 1946, 75–79, extract quoted from p. 78; "Sunday at Hirohito's," *Life,* 25 February 1946, 10.

42. "People," *Life,* 15 September 1947, 53.

43. "Democratic Nuptials," *Life,* 5 June 1950, 28–29. See Crockett,

165–166. Fifty-six years earlier, missionaries in Japan saw the public celebration of the twenty-fifth wedding anniversary of the Meiji emperor and his wife as a repudiation of polygamy and a sign of their modernity and civilization. Joseph M. Henning, *Outposts of Civilization: Race, Religion, and the Formative Years of American-Japanese Relations* (New York: New York University Press, 2000), 325–326.

44. Richard E. Lauterbach, "Secret Jap War Plans," *Life*, 4 March 1946, 16–22, quote on p. 22.

45. Hirohito, however, did try to explain himself in a dictation taken by imperial adviser Terasaki Hidenari. Terasaki's daughter found what is now known as the "Emperor's Monologue" in 1989 among her late father's papers.

46. For example, see Carl Mydans, "Jap Admiral Hides," *Life*, 1 October 1945, 22.

47. Lindesay Parrott, "At Long Last Hirohito Begins to Enjoy Life," *NYT Magazine*, 12 May 1946, 12–13; Parrott, "Mr. Hirohito Is Still the 'Sun God,'" *NYT Magazine*, 22 May 1949, 15, 48, 50–51. In the latter article, Parrott describes the continued Japanese reverence for the "Sun God" in a wholly positive manner.

48. *Life*, 4 August 1947, 42; *NYT*, 4 August 1947, 19; *Life*, 9 June 1947, 48.

49. Lee Hills, "Elizabeth and the Crown Prince of Japan," *Reader's Digest*, January 1948, 129–131; "Elizabeth and the Prince," *NYT*, 29 August 1946, 19. See also John Gunther's glowing review: "A Quaker and the Prince of Japan," *NYT Book Review*, 11 May 1952, 1.

50. Not all readers were charmed. The *New Yorker*, for example, complained about Vining's "unflaggingly" "rose-colored" view of the Japanese she met. "Windows for the Crown Prince," *New Yorker*, 17 May 1952, 145.

51. Elizabeth Gray Vining, *Windows for the Crown Prince* (Philadelphia: J. B. Lippincott, 1952), 229, 219.

52. Ibid., 123. For more praise on Akihito, see Orville Prescott's review of Vining's book: *NYT*, 12 May 1952, 23.

53. Vining also provided good publicity for the imperial family as she promoted her book. Harvey Breit, "Talk with Mrs. Vining," *NYT Book Review*, 8 June 1952, 18.

54. Ruoff makes brief mention of the fact that the idea to hire Vining originated with SCAP. Ruoff, 212. A brief foray into the National Archive's SCAP documents about this issue yielded nothing illuminating.
55. The emperor's role in selecting her was even emphasized in print ads for the book. See "Display Ad 28," *NYT*, 22 April 1953, 27.
56. For examples of Akihito's independent thinking, see Vining, 185–187, 267–269; quote on p. 17.
57. Ibid., 13–14, 31, 167.
58. Kido, in turn, was instructed by the Imperial Household Ministry, who was instructed by U.S. chief prosecutor, Joseph Keenan, who was instructed by the Truman administration. Dower, *Embracing Defeat*, 468, 631–632, n. 62.
59. Vining, 299, 310–311, 308.
60. Vining wrote a sequel, *Return to Japan* (1960), describing her visit back to Japan for the occasion of Akihito's wedding. This book did not sell nearly as well, suggesting that Americans' fascination with the imperial family had passed. Perhaps the narrative about the peace-loving imperial family had been well-established and needed no further explication. Prescott, *NYT*, 27 April 1960, 35; Daniel Ramsdell, "Asia Askew: U.S. Bestsellers on Asia, 1931–1980," *Bulletin of Concerned Asian Scholars* 15:4 (1983): 2–25.
61. See, for example, articles by Tolischus in the *New York Times*. See also his article on Tōjō, "Leader of the Gang," *NYT Magazine*, 13 September 1942, 8, 61–63.
62. Lee, 95–96; "Hull Assails Hitler, Tojo," *NYT*, 21 April 1943, 8.
63. For example, see "Snafu Suicide," *Life*, 24 September 1945, 36–37.
64. Lee, 39–47; LaCerda, 70; Kelley and Ryan, 67–69.
65. Although some cartoons clearly label the Japanese enemy as Tōjō, in many others it was unclear whether the figure—usually a bespectacled, slant-eyed, buck-toothed character in military uniform—was Tōjō, the emperor, or some other "Jap militarist." This ambiguity resulted not only from an old stereotype that all Asians look alike, but also from confusion as to where the base of power in Japan resided. Today, the bespectacled "Jap" figure seen with Mussolini and Hitler in vintage World War II propaganda posters is often identified as Tōjō even when it is not clear from the image who the Japanese figure

is supposed to be. The portrayal of Tōjō as the main enemy of the U.S. has thus influenced how individuals today are interpreting the World War II images. For an example, see "Honorable Spy Says" at *http://bss.sfsu.edu/internment/posters.html* (accessed 14 December 2004).

66. "How to Tell Japs from Chinese," *Life,* 22 December 1941, 81–82; "How to Tell Your Friends from the Japs," *Time,* 22 December 1941, 33.

67. See Fujitani. The OWI effort was not completely successful. Frank Capra's propaganda film, *Know Your Enemy: Japan,* however, focuses on the emperor as the *raison d'être* of the Japanese war effort.

68. "A Dead Man Speaks," *Life,* 26 January 1948, 87–91.

69. Quoted in Robert G. Lee, *Orientals: Asian Americans in Popular Culture* (Philadelphia: Temple University Press, 1999), 114.

70. Ibid., 116–117. See also Jachinson Chan, *Chinese American Masculinities: From Fu Manchu to Bruce Lee* (New York: Routledge, 2001), esp. chap. 2.

71. An example from a later film is the pompous commandant (Sessue Hayakawa) in *The Bridge on the River Kwai* (1957), who throws hysterical temper tantrums and cries when frustrated.

72. Sometimes they were depicted as emotional and hysterical in victory as well. The "banzai" victory scene in *Purple Heart* has to be seen to be believed—with the Japanese raising their swords and prancing about, well, hysterically.

73. Kelley and Ryan, 19.

74. *The Cheat* (1915, dir. Cecil B. DeMille), starring Sessue Hayakawa, was a previous expression of the motif that one only had to scratch the surface of Japanese modern cosmopolitanism to see the savagery beneath. The Japanese government protested this portrayal, and Tori's character became Burmese in later releases of the film. R. Lee, 120–126; Gina Marchetti, *Romance and the "Yellow Peril": Race, Sex, and Discursive Strategies in Hollywood Fiction* (Berkeley: University of California Press, 1993), 18–27; Sumiko Higashi, *Cecil B. DeMille and American Culture: The Silent Era* (Berkeley: University of California Press, 1994), 100–112.

75. Johnstone, 4; see also Fleisher, 36.

76. James McGlincy, "Japan's Plea—The Occupation: The Emperor's Spokesman (A Harvard Man) Puts in a Bid for American Friendship," *SF Chronicle*, 1 September 1945, 1.

77. C. Lee, 47.

78. Nina Silber, *The Romance of Reunion: Northerners and Southerners, 1865–1900* (Chapel Hill: University of North Carolina Press, 1993); "Herr Göring Talks," *Life*, 28 May 1945, 30–31.

79. Kelley and Ryan, 46–47; ellipses in the original.

80. "Snafu Suicide"; ellipses in the original.

81. Kelley and Ryan, 53. For examples of more sanitized versions of events, see George E. Jones, "His Suicide Foiled," *NYT*, 12 September 1945, 1, 2; "The Ridiculous Tojo," *Newsweek*, 24 September 1945, 54–58.

82. C. Lee, 103–104; Harry T. Brundidge, "Tojo Tried to Die," *American Mercury*, August 1953, 8–9.

83. Kelley and Ryan, 53; C. Lee, 106; Brundidge, 10–12.

84. The *New York Times* editorial the next day also implied that he was a coward: for waiting to the last minute before his arrest and for opting to use a pistol even though he "had laid out his hara-kiri knives." "Tojo," *NYT*, 12 September 1945, 24.

85. C. Lee, 105–108, extract quoted from p. 108.

86. Kenneth Lewes, *The Psychoanalytic Theory of Male Homosexuality* (New York: Simon & Schuster, 1988), 97, 149, 232.

87. Quoted in Janssens, 242.

88. Takemae, 247–250; Dower, *Embracing Defeat*, 461–474; see Richard H. Minear, *Victor's Justice: The Tokyo War Crimes Trial* (Princeton: Princeton University Press, 1971).

89. An Associated Press report published on the day of his attempted suicide stated that he "was roundly hated by the Japanese public because he had thus far failed to commit suicide" and that his family got anonymous phone calls demanding when he was going to do so. "Tojo Sees Time Vindicating Japan," *NYT*, 11 September 1945, 1–2; Robert Trumbull, "Transfusion Aids Tojo," *NYT*, 12 September 1945, 1, 3.

90. LaCerda, 14–15.

91. "How Beaten Japs Feel: It Was Tojo's Fault," *Newsweek*, 17 Septem-

ber 1945, 42; "Japanese Lay Ills to Tojo Blunders," *NYT*, 2 September 1945, 13.

92. Edwin M. Zimmerman, "'Herro' and 'Goomby,'" *NYT Magazine*, 22 December 1946, 118.
93. The article, however, indicated a grudging admiration and sympathy for the old general. "Jap War Criminals Await Trial," *Life*, 12 November 1945, 32–33.
94. Crockett, 20.
95. Naoki Sakai, "'You Asians': On the Historical Role of the West and Asia Binary," *South Atlantic Quarterly* 99:4 (Fall 2000): 804–810; Dower, *Embracing Defeat*, chap. 9.
96. "Japanese Cannibals," *Life*, 10 November 1947, 155–156.
97. "Jap Surrenders Are Increasing," *Life*, 19 July 1945, 67–70; S. Mydans, "Guam Holdouts Give Up," *Life*, 9 July 1945, 70.
98. John Hersey, "Kamikazes," *Life*, 30 July 1945, 72.
99. C. Lee, 21; see also Associated Press article reprinted in the *New York Times*: "Japanese Pilots Balked At Service as Kamikazes," *NYT*, 7 September 1945, 4.
100. "Tokyo Street Scenes," *Life*, 19 November 1945, 74–75. For another early sympathetic look at war-weary and repressed Japanese, see Lindesay Parrott, "Prestige of Emperor Among Japanese Rises," *NYT*, 28 October 1945, E5.
101. "Japanese Farmer," *Life*, 24 December 1945, 67–73. For a sympathetic portrayal of Japanese imprisoned by the Russians in Manchuria after World War II—with no mention of Manchukuo—see "A Japanese Prisoner in Siberia," *Life*, 6 November 1950, 65–67.
102. LaCerda, 125.
103. Lee, 68; John Dower corroborates this assertion in *War Without Mercy*.
104. During the Sino-Japanese War, the Japanese depicted their enemies in a similar manner—as corrupt and womanly. See Donald Keene, *Dawn to the West: Japanese Literature of the Modern Era* (New York: Holt, Rinehart & Winston, 1984.)
105. Iriye, 265.
106. H. D. Harootunian, "America's Japan/Japan's Japan," in Masao

Miyoshi and H. D. Harootunian, eds., *Japan in the World* (Durham, N.C.: Duke University Press, 1993).

107. George Lakoff, *Moral Politics: How Liberals and Conservatives Think,* 2nd ed. (Chicago: University of Chicago Press, 2002).

108. Ambrose was explaining the national perspective on the war, not necessarily his own view. Interview of Stephen Ambrose on *All Things Considered,* National Public Radio, aired 1 January 1998.

4. A Transpacific Treason Trial

1. "L.A. Jap Arrest as Horror Camp Leader," *LA Times,* 6 June 1947, 1; "Man Who Recognized Kawakita Takes the Stand," *LA Times,* 22 July 1948, 8; "Government Witnesses Testify on Acts of Brutality Charged to Prison Camp Interpreter," *Pacific Citizen,* 3 July 1948, 2; "Government Witnesses Tell of Alleged Brutalities in Trial of Tomoya Kawokita [*sic*]," *Pacific Citizen,* 10 July 1948, 2.

2. The third American tried for collaborating with the Japanese during World War II was John David Provoo. His trial conjured up fears that the dangerous "Orient" could weaken or emasculate the "western" man. See Naoko Shibusawa, "America's Geisha Ally: Race, Gender, and Maturity in Refiguring the Japanese Enemy, 1945–1964" (Ph.D. diss., Northwestern University, 1998).

3. The basic facts about Toguri's story can be found in numerous secondary sources, including Masayo Duus, *Tokyo Rose: Orphan of the Pacific,* trans. Peter Duus (Tokyo: Kodansha International, 1979); Russell Warren Howe, *The Hunt for "Tokyo Rose"* (Lanham, Md.: Madison Books, 1990); David A. Ward, "The Unending War of Iva Ikuko Toguri d'Aquino," *Amerasia* 1:2 (1971): 26–35; Isami Arifuku Waugh, "The Trial of 'Tokyo Rose,'" *Bridge* 3:1 (1974): 5–12, 40–46; Raymond Okamura, "Iva Ikuko Toguri: Victim of an American Fantasy," in Emma Gee, ed., *Counterpoint: Perspectives on Asian America* (Los Angeles: Asian American Studies Center, UCLA, 1976), 86–96; Clifford I. Uyeda, "The Pardoning of 'Tokyo Rose,'" *Amerasia* 5:2 (1978): 69–84; Stanley I. Kutler, *The American Inquisition: Justice and Injustice in the Cold War* (New York: Hill & Wang,

1982), chap. 1; Caroline Chung Simpson, *An Absent Presence: Japanese Americans in Postwar American Culture, 1945–1960* (Durham: Duke University Press, 2001), chap. 3.

4. Kay Kokubun, son of the pastor of Calexico Union Church, telephone interview, January 29, 1997.
5. The other Americans convicted of treason for the war in Europe included Douglas Chandler, who was sentenced to life imprisonment for broadcasting for the Nazis, and Robert H. Best, who received the same sentence as Chandler for the same crime. Gillars received a sentence of ten to twenty years; Burgman was given six to twenty years; and Monti, a deserter turned Nazi propagandist, got a sentence of twenty-five years in prison.
6. Gillars and Burgman were released from an Army prison in Berlin in December 1946 with no pending charges against them, and Monti, who was court-martialed for deserting and stealing a plane, had been released by the Army by January 1946. "An 'Axis Sally' Released," *NYT,* 25 December 1946, 6; "Ex-Army Officer Held for Treason," *NYT,* 15 October 1948, 6.
7. R. Danielle Egan, "Cowardice," in John Collins and Ross Glover, eds., *Collateral Language: A User's Guide to America's New War* (New York: New York University Press, 2002), 54.
8. Reporter's Transcript of Proceedings *United States v. Tomoya Kawakita,* criminal case 19665, RG 21 Records of the District Court of the United States, Southern District of California, NARA-Laguna Nigel (hereafter cited as Kawakita transcript), 5041, 5217; "Defense Testimony Initiated in Kawakita Case as Move for Dismissal Denied by Judge," *Pacific Citizen,* 31 July 1948, 3; Federal Jury Deliberates Verdict in Kawakita Case," *Pacific Citizen,* 28 July 1948, 1.
9. Kawakita transcript, 5418, 5003, 5028.
10. It is hard to determine, especially after so many years, if the story about the beating is true or accurate. According to Tucker's narrative, he and another prisoner had been working "six feet deep in snow" when Kawakita and a Japanese guard found them and started to beat them with sticks. The prisoners had not heard the whistle to stop work at their site and were missing from formation. Tucker luckily

ran away from Kawakita and into formation, Tucker recalled, but his co-worker received such a beating from the other guard that he had to be hospitalized. Although it seems implausible that there could have been six feet of snow in Kyoto prefecture "shortly before liberation" in mid-August 1945, Oeyama is near the coast of the Sea of Japan and a ski resort today, and the former prisoners testified in 1948 that there was still snow on the ground in April 1945. Tucker did not specify if "shortly before" meant months or weeks before "liberation." Walter Tucker, telephone interview, 14 March 1997; Kawakita transcript, 4982.

11. "Kawakita Will Face Federal Treason Charge for Alleged Mistreatment of U.S. POWs," *Pacific Citizen,* 7 June 1947, 1.

12. Kawakita transcript, 5009; "Curse Hurled at Japs Repeated at Nisei's Trial," *LA Times,* 15 July 1948, II:8.

13. "Soldier's Memories," letter from Charles J. Cushing of Los Angeles, *LA Times,* 14 June 1947, II:4.

14. "L.A. Jap Arrested as Horror Camp Leader," *LA Times,* 6 June 1947, 1; "'Nisei' Convicted in Treason Trial," *NYT,* 3 September 1948, 40; "Nisei Is Ordered to Die for War Treason," *NYT,* 6 October 1948, 15; "Jap Camp Boss Indicted Here," *LA Times,* 12 June 1947, 6; "Nisei Accused of Treason in Atrocity Case," *SF Chronicle,* 6 June 1947, 4; *Oregonian* editorial, 7 June 1947, quoted in "Comment on Kawakita," *Pacific Citizen,* 14 June 1947, 4; "Government Lines up Fifty Witnesses as Kawakita Trial Set to Open in L.A. June 15," *Pacific Citizen,* 29 May 1948, 2.

15. "Nisei Is Accused in Los Angeles of Abusing GI Prisoners in Japan," *NYT,* 6 June 1947, 10; "Meatball," *Time,* 13 September 1948, 25; "Not Worth Living," *Time,* 18 October 1948, 28; "Tomoya Kawakita Will Face Treason Charge as Case Opens in Los Angeles Court," *Pacific Citizen,* 19 June 1948, 2.

16. Admittedly, though, Dr. Lemoyne C. Bleich's diary ceased in November 1944 when the Japanese forbade it, but Bleich said nothing negative about Kawakita. "Doctor Confirms Cruel Penalties in Jap Camp," *LA Times,* 29 July 1948, 5; "Diary Reveals Jap 'Barbarism' in Prison Camp," *LA Times,* 30 July 1948, II:8.

17. Kawakita transcript, 4153–4155; 4213.
18. "Kawakita Will Face Federal Treason Charge for Alleged Mistreatment of U.S. POWs," *Pacific Citizen*, 7 June 1947, 1.
19. "Government Witness Testifies Regarding Alleged Brutalities as Kawakita Trial Opens," *Pacific Citizen*, 26 June 1948, 3. Another claimed that he said, "You are not here at a damn bingo game, you are not here for your damn health."
20. "Nisei Is Accused in Los Angeles of Abusing GI Prisoners in Japan," *NYT*, 6 June 1947, 10; "Kawakita's Bitterness About Boyhood Told," *LA Times*, 8 July 1948, II:2; *United States v. Tomoya Kawakita*, 190 F2d 506, 515, n. 13.
21. "Federal Jury Deliberates Verdict in Kawakita Case," *Pacific Citizen*, 28 July 1948, 1.
22. "Government Witness Testifies Regarding Alleged Brutalities as Kawakita Trial Opens," *Pacific Citizen*, 26 June 1948, 3.
23. "Kawakita Will Face Federal Treason Charge for Alleged Mistreatment of U.S. POWs," *Pacific Citizen*, 7 June 1947, 1.
24. Walter Tucker, telephone interview, 14 March 1997.
25. This document was cited in *Fujizawa v. Acheson*, 85 F.Supp. 674 (S.D.Cal. 1949). Fujizawa successfully fought to have his U.S. citizenship restored. See 85 F.Supp. 674, 676.
26. Kawakita transcript, 4974; "Nisei Treason Verdict Asked but Jury Warned on Prejudice," *LA Times*, 20 August 1948, 1.
27. Quote from Edward K. Strong's 1934 work cited in Harry H. L. Kitano, *Generations and Identity: The Japanese American* (Needham Heights, Mass.: Ginn Press, 1993), 28.
28. Taishi Matsumoto, "The Protest of a Professional Carrot Washer," *Kashu Mainichi*, 4 April 1937, cited in Roger Daniels, *Coming to America: A History of Immigration and Ethnicity in American Life* (New York: HarperCollins, 1990), 178. For further description of circumscribed career opportunities for Nisei, see John Modell, *The Economics of Racial Accommodation: The Japanese of Los Angeles, 1900–1942* (Urbana: University of Illinois Press, 1977); Brian Masaru Hayashi, *For the Sake of Our Japanese Brethren: Assimilation, Nationalism, and Protestantism Among the Japanese of Los Angeles* (Stanford: Stanford University Press, 1995); Jere Takahashi,

Nisei/Sansei: Shifting Japanese American Identities and Politics (Philadelphia: Temple University Press, 1997); David K. Yoo, *Growing Up Nisei: Race, Generation, and Culture among Japanese Americans of California, 1924–49* (Urbana: University of Illinois Press, 2000); Lon Kurashige, *Japanese American Celebration and Conflict: A History of Ethnic Identity and Festival in Los Angeles, 1934–1990* (Berkeley: University of California Press, 2002).

29. Larry Tajiri, "Nisei USA: New Post-War Jobs for Nisei," *Pacific Citizen,* 18 June 1949, 4.
30. For a fuller discussion about Nisei seeking opportunity outside of America, see John J. Stephan, "Hijacked by Utopia: American Nikkei in Manchuria," *Amerasia Journal* 23:3 (Winter 1997–98): 1–42.
31. Kitano, 27–30.
32. See Eriko Yamamoto, "Miya Sannomiya Kikuchi: A Pioneer Nisei Woman's Life and Identity," *Amerasia* 23:3 (Winter 1997–98): 73–101.
33. Yuji Ichioka, "The Meaning of Loyalty: The Case of Kazumaro Buddy Uno," *Amerasia* 23:3 (Winter 1997–98): 58–60. Unlike Kawakita, Uno was never tried for his wartime actions because he relinquished his U.S. citizenship and never tried to return to the United States. After capture in the Philippines, Uno was repatriated to Japan, where he lived until his death in 1954.
34. Kawakita transcript, 4047–4196.
35. Kawakita transcript, 4098–4099; "Kawakita Asserts Innocence in Note to News Reporters," *Pacific Citizen,* 9 October 1948, 2; "Disclose Contents of Mother's Letter to Judge, Pleading for Life of Son in Treason Case," *Pacific Citizen,* 16 October 1948, 2.
36. Kawakita transcript, 4115–4146.
37. Fujizawa, however, also remembered it as a wooden sword.
38. Kawakita transcript, 4081–4084; "Defense Witness Presents Alibi for Tomoya Kawakita in Seventh Week of Trial," *Pacific Citizen,* 7 August 1948, 2.
39. Kawakita transcript, 4092–4093, 4240.
40. "Government Witness Testifies Regarding Alleged Brutalities As Kawakita Trial Opens," *Pacific Citizen,* 26 June 1948, 3.
41. Kawakita transcript, 3639–3645, 3716.

42. Kawakita transcript, 3621, 3670–3675; "Witness Flown From Japan Gives Alibi for Nisei at Treason Trial," *LA Times*, 4 August 1948, 2; Meiji Fujizawa, telephone interview, 14 March 1997.

43. *United States v. Tomoya Kawakita*, 96 F.Supp. 824, 853–857.

44. "Kawakita Found Guilty on 8 of 13 Treason Charges," *SF Chronicle*, 3 September 1948, 3; "Kawakita Given Sentence of Death in U.S. Court," *Pacific Citizen*, 9 October 1948, 1; statistic from "Mrs. D'Aquino Await[s] Arrest by U.S. Occupation Officers," *Pacific Citizen*, 21 August 1948, 1.

45. 96 F.Supp. 824, 837.

46. Ibid., 824, 860. The *New York Times* quoted Judge Mathes's contrast between Kawakita and the men of the 442nd. See "Nisei Is Ordered to Die for War Treason, Kawakita Was Japanese Camp Interpreter," *NYT*, 6 October 1948, 15.

47. 96 F.Supp. 824, 836.

48. "Thousands of Reds Holding Government Jobs, Witness Says," *LA Times*, 3 August 1948, 1; "Four New Dealers Linked to Spy Ring by Ex-Red," *LA Times*, 4 August 1948, 1.

49. 96 F.Supp. 824, 836, 860.

50. "High Court Backs Treason Verdict," *NYT*, 3 June 1952, 25. Justice William O. Douglas wrote the majority opinion; Chief Justice Fred M. Vinson, Justice Hugo L. Black, and Justice Harold H. Burton dissented; and Justices Tom C. Clark and Felix Frankfurter did not participate. *United States v. Tomoya Kawakita*, 343 U.S. 717, 737.

51. "Why Tomoya Kawakita Is a Traitor to the U.S.," *LA Times*, 4 September 1948, II:4.

52. *LA Times*, 24 June 1948, 1.

53. "Kawakita Writes to His Mother," *Pacific Citizen*, 16 October 1948, 2; "VJ-Day Parade Has 3000 Marchers," *LA Times*, 15 August 1948, 1, 3.

54. "Forget Traitor But Remember Nisei Patriot, Imperial Valley Newspaper Urges in Editorial," *Pacific Citizen*, 15 October 1949, 5; *San Diego Tribune-Sun*, 4 September 1948, reprinted in "Democracy Failed with Kawakita, Newspaper Says," *Pacific Citizen*, 18 September 1948, 3.

55. Kawakita transcript, 4971–4972.

56. Japanologist John J. Stephan was one of the first to challenge this binary of Nikkei loyalty versus disloyalty in 1984, but Nikkei loyalty to Japan still remains a subject understudied in Asian American history. John J. Stephan, *Call of Ancestry: American Nikkei in Imperial Japan, 1895–1945* (Stanford: Stanford University Press, forthcoming).

57. Jeanne Wakatsuki Houston and James D. Houston, *Farewell to Manzanar* (1973; New York: Houghton-Mifflin, 2002), 58.

58. "Report 7,000 Stranded Nisei in Japan Have Forfeited American Citizenship Rights," *Pacific Citizen*, 7 February 1948, 2; "59 More Nisei Return Home from Japan," ibid., same page.

59. "Taihei Tsuda Gets Jail Term for Slapping POWs," *Pacific Citizen*, 8 May 1948, p. 3.

60. Bill Hosokawa, "The Kawakita Case," *Pacific Citizen*, 21 June 1947, 5.

61. "Editorials: Treason Case," *Pacific Citizen*, 12 July 1947, 4.

62. "Five Thousand Stranded Nisei in Japan Have Lost American Nationality, Says Baldwin," *Pacific Citizen*, 19 June 1948, 3. As the trial wore on, however, the paper pointed out that if the Justice Department was insisting that Kawakita was still an American citizen despite his wartime activities, then the State Department should hold the same standard for the stranded Nisei—a logic that did not persuade the State Department or Congress. See "Kawakita Case By-Product," *Pacific Citizen*, 7 August 1948, 4.

63. "Treason Trials . . .," *Pacific Citizen*, 10 September 1949, 5.

64. Paul K. Oda to JFK, 16 June 1962, Kawakita file, John F. Kennedy Library, Boston, Mass. (hereafter JFKL). Similarly, U.S. servicemen in Japan were upset about the William Girard case in 1957. The 23-year-old sentry was accused of killing a Japanese woman, and news of the murder caused a huge uproar in Japan. The *New York Times* reported: "Many servicemen are deeply interested in good relations between the United States and Japan, and are more than a little annoyed with Specialist Girard for being the cause of a possible crisis in what has hitherto been an exceptionally amicable partnership." Robert Trumbell, "How Other U.S. Servicemen View the Case of Girard," *NYT*, 16 June 1957, E4.

65. "Editorials: Treason Case," *Pacific Citizen*, 12 July 1947, 4; for a photograph of flag-draped coffins carrying dead Nisei, see *Pacific Citizen*, 8 May 1948, 3

66. "Editorials: Kawakita on Trial," *Pacific Citizen*, 17 July 1948, 4.

67. Larry Tajiri, "Nisei USA: RKO and Tomoya Kawakita," *Pacific Citizen*, 2 October 1948, 4. This movie, *The Clay Pigeon*, came out in 1949, but Hollywood also released a film on the 442nd, *Go For Broke*, in 1951.

68. "Nisei Veterans Urge Strict Jap Screening," *LA Times*, 10 June 1947, 7.

69. For a fictional depiction of this sentiment, see John Okada, *No-No Boy* (1957; Seattle: University of Washington Press, 1976).

70. Kawakita transcript, 5166.

71. Editorial from the *Washington Post*, 25 July 1948, reprinted in "Citizenship Restored," *Pacific Citizen*, 7 August 1948, 4.

72. "Mayor Bowron," *Pacific Citizen*, 8 May 1948, 4. Later that year, Bowron—who now called the Japanese Americans among the "best citizens of Los Angeles"—stated that he supported legislation allowing the Issei to become naturalized citizens. "Mayor Bowron Supports Issei Citizen Move," *Pacific Citizen*, 7 August 1948, 1.

73. "Japanese Americans Achieve Results in Attempt to Remove Discrimination, Says ACLU," *Pacific Citizen*, 16 October 1948, 3; "Drew Pearson Notes Changes in Coast Attitude Toward Nisei," *Pacific Citizen*, 12 February 1949, 5.

74. "Oyama Decision Upholds Nisei Rights," *Pacific Citizen*, 24 January 1948, 1.

75. "Hood River Plans Tribute to Nisei Killed on Leyte," *Pacific Citizen*, 4 September 1948, 1; "Hood River Community Holds Services for Nisei Solider," *Pacific Citizen*, 11 September 1948, 12.

76. Hisaye Yamamoto, "Fire Hose Used by Swimming Pool to Stress Ban Against Nisei, Other Non-Caucasians," *Pacific Citizen*, 5 June 1948, 6.

77. Frank F. Chuman, *The Bamboo People: The Law and Japanese-Americans* (Del Mar, Calif.: Publisher's Inc., 1976), 336–340.

78. "Mysterious Fire Razes Home for Rent to Nisei Family," *Pacific Citizen*, 30 July 1949, 2.

79. Yukiko Koshiro, *Transpacific Racisms: The U.S. Occupation of Japan* (New York: Columbia University Press, 1999), 142–151.

80. I. H. Gordon, "Nisei and Employment: 'Any Openings Today?'" *Pacific Citizen,* 24 December 1949, 26.

81. "Amvets Commander Hails Death Decree for Kawakita," *Pacific Citizen,* 9 October 1948, 3.

82. Angela Riggs to Eisenhower, 1 September 1960, File GF 6-X Amnesty & Pardons (22), Box 151, General File, White House Central Files, Dwight D. Eisenhower Library, Abilene, Kansas (hereafter DDEL). Riggs may have seen a news item about Kawakita seeking a pardon; Eisenhower received new petitions for Kawakita's clemency in 1959 and 1960.

83. Rubie Kawakita and Dorothy Orida to Maxwell Raab, 11 January 1956, File OF 101-R "K" Amnesty-Pardons (I), Official File, White House Central Files, DDEL. His sisters were correct; the author received from the Pardon Attorney's Office a one- by two-foot box full of petitions in Japanese.

84. Route Slip to the State Department from Office of the President, 7 November 1953, and Cozart to Koro, 20 July 1960, copy in File GF 6-X Amnesty & Pardons (22), Box 151, General File, White House Central Files, DDEL.

85. Fujizawa, telephone interview, 14 March 1997.

86. In two separate trials, juries found Haupt guilty of aiding and sheltering a failed German saboteur—his own son, who had slipped out and then back into the United States after completing an intensive course on sabotage in Germany. The younger Haupt and seven other saboteurs were to disrupt U.S. aluminum production, but they were caught, quickly tried, and electrocuted in the summer of 1942. Although Haupt's son was German-born, he had spent most of his life in America; he and his parents, however, seem to have been active in the German American Bund. See Shirley J. Burton and Kelle Green, "Oaths of Allegiance, Acts of Treason: The Disloyalty Prosecutions of Max Stephan and Hans Haupt," *Prologue* (Fall 1991): 236–247.

87. Kichiro Sasaki to JFK, Kawakita file, JFKL; see also the letter from the students of Nagoya to JFK, received 27 June 1961, JFKL.

88. Memorandum from Andrew F. Oehmann, Executive Assistant to the Attorney General, to Lee C. White, Assistant Special Counsel to the President, 9 October 1963, in Subject File JL1-1, Approved Applica-

tions 08/15/1963–11/1963, Box 450, White House Central Subject File, JFKL.

89. Route Slip to Mr. White from the Special Assistant to the President, 19 October 1961, and Lee C. White to Judge James M. Carter, 13 November 1961, White House Central Subject File, JFKL.

90. Memorandum from RFK to JFK, 9 October 1963, In the Matter of the Application for Executive Clemency of Tomoya Kawakita in Subject File JL1-1, Approved Applications 08/15/1963–11/1963, Box 450, White House Central Subject File, JFKL.

91. "Kawakita, War Criminal, In Tokyo as a Japanese," *NYT*, 13 December 1963, 11.

92. Toguri's trial cost $700,000. Provoo's cost even more: $1,000,000. Given the length of Kawakita's trial, it also must have cost hundreds of thousands of dollars.

93. For example, see "Un-American House Group," *SF Chronicle*, 14 July 1949, 1: "A Negro investigator and a Jewish rabbi today assured Congress their people have a deep loyalty to their country but that communists are trying relentlessly to destroy it." See also Brenda Gayle Plummer, *The Rising Wind: Black Americans and U.S. Foreign Affairs, 1935–1960* (Chapel Hill: University of North Carolina Press, 1996); Penny Von Eschen, *Race against Empire: Black Americans and Anticolonialism, 1937–1957* (Ithaca: Cornell University Press, 1997); Mary L. Dudziak, *Cold War Civil Rights: Race and the Image of American Democracy* (Princeton: Princeton University Press, 2000); Thomas Borstelmann, *The Cold War and the Color Line: American Race Relations in the Global Arena* (Cambridge, Mass.: Harvard University Press, 2003).

94. In recent decades, however, some Asian Americans—by no means all—have started to see the "no-no boys" as brave conscientious objectors and the ones who answered "yes-yes" as lacking backbone.

95. [Henry Luce], "Negroes are Americans," *Life*, 1 August 1949, 22–23.

96. Other than brief references in studies on Toguri and a section in Chuman's *Bamboo People*, secondary sources on Kawakita remain almost nonexistent in English. There is, however, one book-length treatment of Kawakita in Japanese: Tetsuo Shimojima, *Amerika*

Kokka Hangyakuzai [lit. *American National Treason*] (Tokyo: Kodansha, 1993.

5. A Kamikaze Goes to College

1. "A Guy Named Mickey," a videorecording of the ABC television series *Navy Log*, was aired on 26 December 1956, UCLA-Film/TV. *Navy Log* was shown on CBS for one season, 1955–56, and on ABC from 1956 to 1958. At the beginning and end of each episode, the sentence "This program was produced with the full cooperation of the Department of Defense and the Department of the Navy" flashed across the screen. The last image of each episode was a naval insignia, bolstering the program's authoritative claims. For another analysis of this episode, see Darrell Y. Hamamoto, *Monitored Peril: Asian Americans and the Politics of TV Representation* (Minneapolis: University of Minnesota Press, 1994).

2. The screen credits name the actor as "Lane Nakano," but Nakano states that this was a mistake. At the time, Nakano was a Nisei actor well known for his role in Robert Pirosh's *Go For Broke!* (1951). This and other errors suggest that the screen credits were inserted at a later point by an individual who did not bother to get the correct names of either the Asian actors or the characters. Lane Nakano, telephone interview, 8 July 1997.

3. Theodore Cohen, *Remaking Japan: The American Occupation as New Deal,* ed. Herbert Passin (New York: Free Press, 1987); William H. Chafe, *The Unfinished Journey: America Since World War II* (New York: Oxford University Press, 1995), esp. pp. 104–105; William Appleman Williams, *The Tragedy of American Diplomacy,* rev. ed. (New York: W. W. Norton, 1972), esp. chaps. 3, 4.

4. Dulles to Acheson, 7 June 1950, quoted in Cumings, "Japan in the World System," in Andrew Gordon, ed., *Postwar Japan as History* (Berkeley: University of California Press, 1993), 45.

5. George F. Kennan, *Memoirs, 1925–1950* (Boston: Little, Brown, 1967), 374.

6. On 30 July 1947, the 80th Congress had passed this stopgap measure to pay for additional expenses to help Occupation authorities in Ja-

pan, as well as in Germany, "prevent starvation, disease, or unrest" and ensure political stability in both countries. The Occupation authorities took advantage of GARIOA's loosely defined mandate to commence in 1949 a scholarship program that sent fifty-three Japanese students to American campuses that year. The GARIOA scholarships were precursors to the Fulbright scholarships, which began in 1952. *United States Statutes at Large, 80th Congress, 1st Session 1947, Volume 1, Part 1: Public Laws, Reorganization Plans, Proposed Amendments to the Constitution* (Washington, D.C.: Government Printing Office, 1948), 625.

7. Intrasection Memorandum, GHQ, SCAP, Civil Information and Education Section, 6 September 1951; "Basic Information for Interviewers' Guide," in folder "GARIOA Student Interview Guide," RG 331 UD 1678, box 5483, item 49, NARA-College Park.

8. "The Truman Doctrine: President Harry S. Truman's Address before a Joint Session of Congress, 12 March 1947," transcribed at *www.fordham.edu/halsall/mod/1947TRUMAN.html* (accessed 11 April 2002).

9. Mary L. Dudziak, *Cold War Civil Rights: Race and the Image of American Democracy* (Princeton: Princeton University Press, 2000), 8–9.

10. Technically, the first Japanese student to enroll at an American college after the war was Sawada Mitzi, who registered at Reed College on 20 September 1948. Nishiyama registered at Lafayette about a week later. "First Japan Student Since War Registers," *Pacific Citizen,* 25 September 1948, 1.

11. Bruce V. Johnstone (Robert's younger brother), telephone interview, 22 April 1997.

12. Wilma Johnstone, telephone interview, 16 April 1997; B. Johnstone, telephone conversation; Ralph C. Hutchinson to Robert McC. Johnstone, 30 October 1945, and Hutchinson to Johnstone, 1 October 1945, Johnstone Scholarship Folder, President's Files, David Bishop Skillman Library, Lafayette College, Easton, Pa. (this file cited hereafter as Johnstone-DBSL).

13. "Parents of Soldier Benefactor," *Philadelphia Bulletin,* 10 January 1946, clipping from Johnstone-DBSL.

14. Hutchinson to [given name missing] Bell, 30 October 1945, Johnstone-DBSL.

15. R. Johnstone to Hutchinson, 4 October 1945, Johnstone-DBSL.

16. See Hiromi Chiba, "From Enemy to Ally: American Public Opinion and Perceptions about Japan, 1945–1950" (Ph.D. diss., University of Hawaii, 1990). Chiba's study focused on the Christian majority and did not examine non-Christian Americans who made concerted efforts to rebuild relationships with their former enemies.

17. "Education and War," *Easton Express* (Easton, Pa.), editorial, 10 January 1946; "The Other Cheek," *Blade* (Toledo, Ohio), editorial, 14 January 1946; "A Steadier Flame," *The Messenger* (New York), 22 January 1946. Clippings from Johnstone-DBSL.

18. Robert Yukimasa Nishiyama, letter to author, 2 March 1997; Nishiyama, e-mail to author, 6 April 1997; ibid., 12 April 1997; Alvin Spivak, "'Exchange Student' Japanese Gets Lafayette Scholarship from Parents of Boy Killed in Pacific," *Philadelphia Bulletin*, 3 January 1947; "Jap Suicide Bomber Awarded Johnstone, '46, Scholarship," *The Lafayette Alumnus*, February 1947, 5–6; Nishiyama, "What America Means to Me," *The American Magazine* (November 1949), 129.

19. "I would hate to think my son died in vain," wrote a New Jersey man with no connection to the college. It seems likely that Lafayette received letters of protest from irate alumni, but if such letters exist, the college archivists would not permit the author to see them. James E. Corbett (Camden, N.J.) to Dean of Lafayette, n.d. (sometime in January 1946, judging by Hutchinson's reply). Hutchinson to Corbett, 16 January 1946, Johnstone-DBSL.

20. Corporal Frank J. Rohosky (Pittsburgh, Pa.) to the Dean of Lafayette, n.d. (sometime in late December 1946 or January 1947, based on Hutchinson's reply of 9 January 1947), Johnstone-DBSL.

21. "Letters to the Editors: A Christian Act," *Time*, n.d., press clippings in Johnstone-DBSL.

22. Hutchinson to Frank J. Rohosky (Pittsburgh, Pa.), 9 January 1947, Johnstone-DBSL.

23. "Letters to the Editors: A Christian Act," *Time*, n.d., press clippings in Johnstone-DBSL.

24. W. Johnstone; B. Johnstone; Nishiyama, e-mail message to author, 21 April 1997.
25. "Noble Act, Bad Timing," *Philadelphia Record*, 11 January 1947; "Good Will Personified," *The Stars and Stripes*, 30 September 1948.
26. Editorial, "Beyond Victory," *Denver Post*, 15 February 1947. Johnstone-DBSL.
27. Ellipses in the original. Paul L. Hunsberger (Reading, Pa.), "Letters to the editors: 'Kamikaze Controversy,'" *Life*, 15 November 1948, 16. McFayden, an ex-infantryman, admitted that he retained "a piercing hatred of the Jap." Buchanan, another veteran, had simply protested, "That Kamikaze story is too much!" John W. McFayden (Yale University, New Haven, Conn.) and Robert C. Buchanan (Philadelphia, Pa.), "Kamikaze," *Life*, 25 October 1948, 11–12.
28. Harvey H. Hunerberg, "Kamikaze," *Life*, 25 October 1948, 11–12. Hunerberg had been a writer for the school newspaper the previous year when Hutchinson announced news of Nishiyama winning the scholarship.
29. In her *Daily Northwestern* column, Mary Ellen Munger reflected, "True, we are at war with Japan, and Northwestern has it's [*sic*] full share of defense projects [the ostensible "security" reason for excluding Nisei]. But there is a delicate line to be drawn between the Japanese militaristic government and its policies, and [an] American student who may have the current misfortune to be of Japanese extraction." Several months later, the university administration retracted the policy and allowed the admission of Nisei. "Synder Refuses Jap-American Enrollments," *Daily Northwestern*, 30 April 1942; Lu Himes, "We should accept Nisei," *Daily Northwestern*, 1 May 1942; Mary Ellen Munger, *Daily Northwestern*, 13 May 1942; "Jap-Americans to be accepted at NU," *Daily Northwestern*, 16 October 1942.
30. Fred N. Shimizu to Lafayette College, 1 March 1946; Mr. and Mrs. Isao Tanaka to the Johnstones, 19 January 1946. Both letters in Johnstone-DBSL.
31. During the war, however, the National Japanese American Student Relocation Council—an organization led by the Quakers in conjunction with private and public organizations—helped approximately

4,000 Japanese Americans relocate from the internment camps to college campuses away from the west coast. See Gary Y. Okihiro, *Storied Lives: Japanese American Students and World War II* (Seattle: University of Washington Press, 1999); Allan W. Austin, "From Concentration Camps to Campus: A History of the Japanese American Student Relocation Council, 1942–1946" (Ph.D. diss., University of Cincinnati, 2001).

32. Letters to the Johnstones from the following: Cyrus Martinez, 14 January 1946; Ceferino Canlas, 14 January 1946; Rosario Bobila, 10 January 1946; Florentino F. Fuentes, 14 January 1946; Leonardo G. Alfuente, 15 January 1946; and Jesus V. Peroy, 28 March 1946. The *Manila Times* clipping attached to letter by Patricio G. Jacoba, 19 January 1946. All letters in Johnstone-DBSL.

33. Unfortunately, neglect of the Filipino veterans—who were drafted by the U.S. Army—continues today, sixty years after the end of World War II. In December 2003, President George W. Bush signed H.R. 2297, which gave the Filipinos some, but not all, of the benefits given to other veterans. At this writing, H.R. 4574, the Filipino Veterans Equity Act of 2006, which would give these veterans their long-overdue benefits, is once again before Congress.

34. Thomas J. McCormick, *America's Half-Century: United States Foreign Policy in the Cold War and After,* 2nd ed. (Baltimore: Johns Hopkins University Press, 1995), 110. Before the stalemate in Korea in 1953, the United States had also planned to relegate Manchuria and North Korea to colonial status as the suppliers of raw goods to Japan. Cumings in Gordon, 41–42.

35. Positive articles and editorials include the following: Alvin Spivak, "Johnstone Scholarship: 'Exchange Student' Japanese Gets Lafayette Scholarship from Parents of Boy Killed in Pacific," *Philadelphia Bulletin,* 3 January 1947; "A Case of Vision," *Baltimore Evening Sun,* 4 January 1947; "A Fitting Memorial," *Philadelphia Bulletin,* 6 January 1947; "A Soldier Sets a Welcome Example," *Arizona Daily Star,* quoted in Elyria [Ohio] *Chronicle-Telegram,* 15 January 1947; "Beyond Victory," *Denver Post,* 15 February 1947; "Johnstones Call Asiatic Scholarship an Experiment in Understanding," *The Archive,* n.d. Clippings in Johnstone-DBSL.

36. "Storm Brewing over Jap Getting College Scholarship," *The Pittsburgh Press,* 2 February 1947; "Editorial," *The Lafayette,* 17 January 1947.

37. President Hutchinson turned down the request of a progressive Methodist publication to do a feature on the scholarship, explaining that the college was "not eager for publicity" because "it is beginning to rouse up opposition." Hutchinson to Richard Schisler, Editorial Assistant, *motive* (Nashville, Tenn.), 20 January 1947, Johnstone-DBSL.

38. "Kamikaze Goes to College," *Life,* 4 October 1948, 126. See also "Lafayette Enrolls Japanese Student," *McKeesport News* (Pa.), 18 September 1948; "Japanese Vet Praises US," *San Francisco Examiner,* 14 September 1948; "Dead GI Assures Ex-Foe Study of US Way of Life," *Denver Post,* 11 September 1948. Clippings in Johnstone-DBSL.

39. Kathleen I. Smith, Special Collections Assistant, DBSL, e-mail message to author, 29 January 1996; Mark A. Staples, "A Most Unassimilated Bunch," *Lafayette College Alumni Quarterly,* 58:3 (Spring 1987), 16–17.

40. John Leming, "A Cloud over the Sun Bowl," *Lafayette Alumni News,* September 1998, 7; Nishiyama, e-mail to author, 21 April 1997. *Life* also covered this incident briefly: "Prejudice in Texas," *Life,* 6 December 1948, 64.

41. Totals derived from Lafayette yearbooks, 1948–1952. Phone conversation with Diane Windham Shaw, Special Collections Librarian and College Archivist, 7 June 2002; Nishiyama, e-mail to author, 28 June 2002; Emelie George, Collections Assistant, DBSL, e-mail to author, 11 July 2002.

42. Nishiyama, "What America Means to Me," *American Magazine,* 148 (November 1949), 21, 129–132.

43. Nishiyama, e-mail to author, 2 March 1997.

44. Lauri Rice, "Japanese Man Recalls War, Lafayette Days," *The Morning Call* (Easton, Pa.), 14 September 1989. Clipping in Johnstone-DBSL.

45. Nishiyama appeared in a newsreel for Paramount Pictures, a popular TV show called "We, the People" on NBC, a talk show in Philadel-

phia, and a local Easton radio station, WEST, hosted by Lloyd Moss. Nishiyama, e-mail to author, 6 July 1997.

46. Nishiyama, e-mail to author, 21 April 1997.

47. Mitsuya Gotō, "Commencement Address: 'The Frog in the Well,'" *Wabash Bachelor,* June[?] 1955, 3; Gotō, "The Bridge of Understanding," *The Wabash Bulletin* 49 (June 1953): 12–14. Both articles from the collection of Mitsuya Gotō, Yokohama, Japan.

48. Robert S. Harvey, "Dedicated to Peace," *The Indianapolis Star Magazine,* [1954? 1955?], Gotō collection.

49. Nishiyama, e-mail to author, 21 April 1997.

50. Shigemitsu Kuriyama, "U.S. Educational Grant Programs in Japan," in Arthur Power Dudden and Russell R. Dynes, eds., *The Fulbright Experience, 1946–1986: Encounters and Transformations* (New Brunswick: Transaction Books, 1987), 256. Kuriyama, who became an executive for IBM-Japan (U.S.A.), also minimized racism.

51. Gotō, letter to author, 8 March 1997; Nishiyama, e-mail to author, 7 July 1997; Azumi Koya, letter to author, 3 May 1997.

52. "Basic Information for Interviewers' Guide"; "Acceptance of Applications for 1952 SCAP Scholarships," press release by General Headquarters, SCAP, Civil Information and Education Section, 27 October 1951. RG 331 UD 1678, box 5484 item 21, NARA-College Park.

53. See files relating to Torao Miyamori in "Students Special Cases" in RG 331 UD 1678, boxes 5484 and 5486, NARA-College Park. Quotations from Torao Miyamori, c/o Immigration Station Ellis Island, New York Harbor, New York, letter to the president of IIE (Institute of International Education), 1 March 1951. The IIE was the civilian organization the Army used to administer the placement of GARIOA scholarship recipients.

54. See files relating to Torao Miyamori. Quotations from "M/E Report on Torao Miyamori, Returned GARIOA Student," 28 March 1951; "Excerpts from Letters from Two Japanese at Iowa State College, Ames, Iowa," Testuo Eguchi to Mrs. A. D. Bowles, 9 February 1951.

55. John W. Dower, *Embracing Defeat: Japan in the Wake of World War II* (New York: W. W. Norton, 1999).

56. Nishiyama, letter to author, 2 March 1997; Gotō, letter to author, 8

March 1997; Yamamoto, e-mail to author, 29 April 1997; Azumi Koya, letter to author, 3 May 1997.

57. Kimie Gilbertson, telephone interview, 5 July 2001. While Yamamoto Chiyoko attended college in the Boston area from 1961 to 1965, she knew only one other Japanese female student, a woman from a wealthy family whose brother was also attending college in Boston. Ebihara Harumi, a student at the University of New Hampshire in 1959–60, recalls no other Japanese female student during her year in Durham. Yamamoto Chiyoko, e-mail to author, 9 July 2001; Ebihara Harumi, facsimile to author, 13 July 2001.

58. Gotō, telephone interview with author, 22 May 1997. Gotō and his wife are friends with this daughter of Japan's wartime premier.

59. *Lancaster New-Era*, 18 September 1948, newspaper clipping in Johnstone-DBSL.

60. Nishiyama, letter to author, 2 March 1997; Nishiyama, e-mails to author, 17 June 2002, 12 February 2006.

61. For an elaboration of this argument as it relates to the Peace Corps, see Fritz Fischer, *Making Them Like Us: Peace Corps Volunteers in the 1960s* (Washington, D.C.: Smithsonian Books, 1998).

6. Channeling Atomic Guilt

1. Rodney Barker, *The Hiroshima Maidens: A Story of Courage, Compassion, and Survival* (New York: Viking Penguin, 1985), 56–58; Marvin W. Green, "A Bird's-Eye View of a Short History of the Hiroshima Peace Center Associates," unpublished typescript, n.d. (references indicate that Green wrote it in mid-1955 or later); taped interview of Green by Rodney Barker, n.d. (Barker remembers the date as the late 1970s or about 1980); "Marvin Green," typed notes of an interview with Green by Barker in 1979 or 1980. The latter three documents can be found among those that Barker collected to research his book, including the personal papers of the late Reverend Green. Barker entrusted the documents to me, and I in turn sent them for safekeeping to the archives of the Peace Resource Center at Wilmington College in Wilmington, Ohio (hereafter cited as RB Collection).

2. R. Lane Fenrich, "Mass Death in Miniature: How Americans Became Victims of the Bomb," in Laura E. Hein and Mark Selden, eds., *Living with the Bomb: American and Japanese Cultural Conflicts in the Nuclear Age* (Armonk, N.Y.: M. E. Sharpe, 1997), chap. 6.

3. "America's Atomic Atrocity," *Christian Century,* 29 August 1945, 974–976.

4. See Barker; Virginia Naeve, *Friends of the Hibakusha* (Denver: Allan Swallow, 1964); Michael J. Yavenditti, "The Hiroshima Maidens and American Benevolence in the 1950s," *Mid-America* 64 (1982): 21–39; Kazuo Chujō, *Hiroshima Maidens: The Nuclear Holocaust Retold*, trans. Asahi Evening News (Tokyo: Asahi Shimbun, 1984); Anne Chisholm, *Faces of Hiroshima: A Report* (London: Cape, 1985); Lawrence Wittner, "The Menace of the Maidens: Japanese Atomic Bomb Victims and the U.S. Government, 1954–1956," paper presented at the Conference of the International Peace Research Association, Valleta, Malta, 2 November 1994; *Hiroshima Maiden* (WonderWorks/PBS video, directed by Joan Darling, 1988); Alan Nadel, *Containment Culture: American Narratives, Postmodernism, and the Atomic Age* (Duke University Press, 1995); Diane Fujino, "Revolutions from the Heart: The Making of an Asian American Woman Activist," in Sonia Shah, ed., *Dragon Ladies: Asian American Feminists Breathe Fire* (Boston: South End Press, 1997); Caroline Chung Simpson, *An Absent Presence: Japanese Americans in Postwar American Culture, 1945–1960* (Durham: Duke University Press, 2001), chap. 4; Christina Klein, *Cold War Orientalism: Asia in the Middlebrow Imagination, 1945–1961* (Berkeley: University of California Press, 2003), chap. 4. Among these works, only Yavenditti and Klein offer a substantial analysis of the moral adoptions program.

5. American Studies scholar Christina Klein calls these "people-to-people narratives." By telling stories of "politically engaged individuals communicating across racial and national boundaries," these "people-to-people narratives" spun a "global imaginary of integration" during the Cold War that celebrated pluralist inclusion and condemned the exclusion of racialized others. According to Klein, this sentimental construction permitted Americans to achieve "some of

the ends of imperialism through non-imperial means." Klein, 83–85, 208.

6. Cynthia Franklin, "Recollecting *This Bridge* in an Anti-Affirmative Action Era: Literary Anthologies, Academic Memoir, and Institutional Autobiography," in Gloria E. Anzaldúa and Analouise Keating, *This Bridge We Call Home: Radical Visions for Transformation* (New York: Routledge, 2002), 429.

7. *Saturday Review of Literature* (hereafter *SRL*): "Modern Man Is Obsolete," 18 August 1945, 5–9, quote on p. 7; "Sovereignty in an Atomic Age," 13 October 1945, 22–24.

8. Kiyoshi Tanimoto, "Hiroshima's Idea," *SRL*, 5 March 1949, 20–21.

9. For excerpts of the speech he made at the ceremony, see N[orman] C[ousins], "Regeneration for What?" *SRL*, 3 September 1949, 22–23.

10. Norman Cousins, taped interview by Rodney Barker, 9 May 1980, RB Collection; Norman Cousins, "Hiroshima Four Years Later," *SRL*, 17 September 1949, 9–10.

11. Eleanor (Ellen) Cousins, telephone interview, 11 September 1996.

12. Shigeki Hata, "With Thanks and Hopes for All," in Naeve, 19; Cousins, "Hiroshima Four Years Later."

13. "Hiroshima 'Moral Adoptions,'" *SRL*, 15 October 1949, 23; italics in the original.

14. "*SRL* Readers and 'Moral Adoptions,'" 5 November 1949, 23; "Letters to the Editor: Hiroshima Orphans," *SRL*, 3 June 1950, 24.

15. Percentages were calculated from the following figures: 93 women, 38 men, 15 married couples, and 5 whose gender could not be determined by their names. Figures derived from list in preceding citation.

16. Kathleen Sproul, "Genus: Parent—Species: Moral," *SRL*, 23 December 1950.

17. "Hiroshima 'Moral Adoptions,'" *SRL*, 8 October 1949, 26.

18. Letter excerpt from Lawrence L. Malis of Philadelphia in "Guilt of Hiroshima," 22 October 1949, 20.

19. Both letters appeared in "Concerning Hiroshima," *SRL*, 19 November 1949, 27–28.

20. Cousins, "On Being a Softie," *SRL*, 1 October 1949, 20.

21. Ibid. Cousins, however, was not free of questionable ideas about the

Japanese. He later told State Department officials that "the Japanese have a strong sense of obligation in definite situations, as to the family or to the Emperor, but they are largely lacking in a feeling of altruism." DOS memorandum of [telephone] conversation among Cousins, Walter S. Robertson (Assistant Secretary for Far Eastern Affairs), William J. Sebald (Deputy Assistant Secretary for Far Eastern Affairs), and Richard B. Finn (Acting Officer in Charge, Japanese Affairs); Cousins to William J. Sebald, 20 June 1955, RB Collection.

22. By June the following year, Yamashita Orphanage was caring for seventy-one children, all of whom had been morally adopted. But this increased number may be a result of the success of the program. See letter from Teiko Yamashita in "Letters to the Editor: Hiroshima Orphans," *SRL*, 3 June 1950, 26.

23. Letter to Mayor Shinzo Hamai from Norman Cousins, 11 October 1949, Box 96, Folder 4 ("Japanese Matters—1950"), Collection 1385, Norman Cousins Papers, UCLA Library of Special Collections (cited hereafter as NC Papers).

24. Barker, 67. Glenn Everett, a journalist with the Religious News Services who became involved in both projects, gave an inflated amount—$470,000—that does not seem possible, given the other known statistics. According to his widow, Everett, who passed away in 1996, wrote his book mostly from memory and without notes nearly forty years after the events. Glenn D. Everett, *Hope from the Horror of Hiroshima: The Story of the Japanese Christians Who Survived the Bomb and Their Prayers for Forgiveness, Reconciliation and Lasting World Peace* (Rutland, Vt.: Academy Books, 1995), 151; Helen Reynolds Everett, telephone interview, 19 January 1998.

25. "Hiroshima Orphans Adopted by *SRL* Readers," 3 June 1950, 25, and "Hiroshima Orphans" in the same issue, 24 and 26.

26. Sproul, 26.

27. As historian Michael Yavenditti has suggested, the program "had the merits of foster parenthood without its responsibilities." Yavenditti, "Hiroshima Maidens," 24.

28. Tanimoto, 20.

29. Green, "A Bird's-Eye View"; Barker, 57–58; and "Declaration of Intent and Request for Detailed Advice in Bringing to the United States

Approximately 12 Victims of the Atomic Bomb" to Frank Hawley, Japanese Desk, State Department, n.d., RB Collection. (Cross-reference with Marvin W. Green, "Brief Outline of Steps to Be Taken to Bring Keloid Girls to America," 2 January 1954, also in RB Collection, suggests that Green wrote the "declaration of intent" sometime after this memo.)

30. Green, taped interview. Green also recalled that the Methodist bishop who agreed to join the organization never attended a single HPCA meeting, but his name appeared on the HPCA letterhead for several years.

31. Green, "A Bird's-Eye View"; Barker, 58–61.

32. Miyoko Matsubara, interview, spring 1996. Matsubara, a member of Tanimoto's group, was not one of the women chosen to receive surgery in the United States.

33. An interview of the group and Tanimoto conducted by Masugi for a Japanese women's magazine focused in part on the *Shion-kai* women's "dreams of love and marriage." See "Sad Are the Dreams of the Atomic Bombed Maidens," translated from *Fujin Kurabu* (lit. *Women's* or *Matrons' Club*) and included in a letter to Norman Cousins by Kiyoshi Tanimoto, 1 October 1952, RB Collection.

34. See letter to Norman Cousins, ibid; Barker, 63.

35. Matsubara interview.

36. Letter to Pearl Buck from Shizué Masugi, Tokyo, Japan, 11 August 1952; letter to Cousins from Mrs. Richard Walsh (Pearl Buck), 29 July 1952; letter from Bernice Frankel [Cousins' assistant] to Walsh [Buck], 31 July 1952; copy of letter to Buck from Masugi, 11 August 1952; and letter to Cousins from Walsh [Buck], 20 August 1952. All letters in Box 1386, NC Papers.

37. Description of injuries and quoted remarks from Barker, 65–66.

38. Letter to Cousins from Helen H. Yokoyama, 13 April 1955, RB Collection.

39. Rodney Barker, telephone interview, 3 February 1998.

40. For a book-length treatment of the irradiated fishermen of the *Lucky Dragon*, see Ralph E. Lapp, *Voyage of the Lucky Dragon* (New York: Harper & Brothers, 1958). The episode was so embarrassing to the United States that some U.S. officials initially believed that

communists intentionally sailed the boat close to the testing site to humiliate the United States. Walter LaFeber, *The Clash: A History of U.S.-Japan Relations* (New York: W. W. Norton, 1997), 311.

41. C. Frank Ortloff, Chairman Special Committee, New York Friends Center Association, 5 April 1955, and attached "An Abbreviated Fact Sheet About the Hiroshima Maidens," Hiroshima Maidens file, New York Friends Center, Wilmington-Peace.

42. Green, taped interview.

43. Wittner, 4.

44. Klein, 73, 79–80, 84.

45. Cousins, taped interview.

46. Description of Tanimoto's appearance on *This Is Your Life* in Barker, 3–12. *This Is Your Life* also helped fund the Arizona Memorial. Congress authorized building a memorial in 1958, but gave it no funding. The largest sources of funding were the following: Elvis ($64,000); *This is Your Life* ($95,000); toy kits of the *Arizona* ($40,000). Emily S. Rosenberg, *A Date Which Will Live: Pearl Harbor in American Memory* (Durham: Duke University Press, 2003), 72.

47. Letter to Sebald from Cousins, 20 June 1955.

48. DOS memorandum, 2 June 1955.

49. Yavenditti, "The Hiroshima Maidens," 27; Cousins, taped interview.

50. Copy of declassified letter to Walter Robinson, Assistant Secretary of State, from Dr. Grant Taylor, Dean of the Postgraduate School of Medicine, University of Texas, 14 May 1955, RB Collection.

51. Copy of declassified letter to William J. Sebald (Deputy Assistant for Far Eastern Affairs) from Cousins, 20 June 1955, RB Collection.

52. "An apologist for the State Department" from an angry letter written in response to Cousins' speech before the Cultural and Scientific Conference for World Peace. See N[orman] C[ousins], "Tell the Folks Back Home," *SRL*, 9 April 1949, 20–22; "Letters to the Editor: Tell the Folks Back Home," *SRL*, 7 May 1949, 22.

53. LaFeber, 289–324.

54. Barker, 82; Cousins, taped interview.

55. DOS memorandum to [?] McCardle and [Walter] Robertson from Max Bishop, Under Secretary of State Office, 1 August 1955; DOS memorandum, 2 June 1955, RB Collection.

56. Letter to Bishop G. Bromley Oxnam from A. Carl Adkins, minister of the Dauphin Way Methodist Church of Mobile, Alabama, 9 July 1955; letter to John Foster Dulles from G. Bromley Oxnam, 20 July 1955. Copies of both letters in RB Collection.

57. DOS memorandum, 2 June 1955; DOS memorandum, 1 August 1955, RB Collection.

58. DOS memorandum, 1 August 1955.

59. Letter to G. Bromley Oxnam from Walter Robertson, 15 August 1955; DOS memorandum of conversation among Dr. A. Carl Adkins (Minister, Dauphin Way Methodist Church, Mobile, Ala.), Robertson, and Finn, 22 September 1955; DOS memorandum, 2 June 1955. Copies of documents in RB Collection.

60. DOS memorandum, 2 June 1955. Later, the Department changed its line slightly to claim that the United States made "no distinction . . . regarding the means by which the injury was inflicted." DOS memorandum, 22 September 1955, RB Collection.

61. Cousins, taped interview by Barker, 9 May 1980.

62. Chujō, 36, 108. See also pp. 41, 63, 104, 107.

63. Mickey Hoffman, "Jap Minister [illegible] Atom War [illegible]," *Dallas Morning News*, 4 July 1955, clipping in RB Collection.

64. Cousins pointed to this visit to demonstrate to State Department officials that the "girls" did not intend to make Americans feel guilty. DOS memorandum, 2 June 1955.

65. Paul Tobenkin, "Hiroshima Girls Here for Surgeries," *New York Herald Tribune*, 10 May 1955. Quote also repeated in Emma Harrison, "Hiroshima Girls Here for Surgery," *NYT*, 10 May 1955. Clippings in RB Collection.

66. Joe Miller, "Hiroshima Maiden Happy She's Never Been Bitter About A-Bomb," *Columbus Sunday Dispatch* (Columbus, Ohio, from an AP dispatch), 31 July 1955. See also "25 Hiroshima Maidens on Way to New York," *Honolulu Advertiser*, n.d. Both clippings in RB Collection.

67. DOS memorandum from Hemmendinger to Sebald re: "Proposal that President Receive Hiroshima Maidens," 6 March 1956, RB Collection.

68. Tanimoto as told to Everett, "A Hiroshima Survivor Testifies," 5–6, in RB Collection.

69. For discussion of Hiroshiman hostility and resentment toward Americans, see Robert Jay Lifton, *Death in Life: Survivors of Hiroshima* (1967; New York: Basic Books, 1982), 242, 298, 317–326, 414–426.

70. Clark Lee, *One Last Look Around* (New York: Duell, Sloan and Pearce, 1947), 76–83.

71. Ibid., 117. Even Cousins resorted to circuitous questioning. See Cousins, "On Acquiring a Soul," *SRL*, 17 April 1948, 31.

72. Green, taped interview. Cousins, however, maintained that he never noticed much hostility when he visited Hiroshima. Cousins, taped interview.

73. Marvin W. Green, Ph.D., Executive Director, The Koko Tanimoto Scholarship Fund (East Orange, N.J.), "A Power Greater Than the Atom Bomb," pamphlet, n.d., in RB Collection. The pamphlet's text indicates that Green wrote it in 1963.

74. Ibid. Tanimoto, however, irritated Cousins by becoming more blunt in his requests for money. Tanimoto was becoming frustrated by the way Cousins controlled the money. Carbon copy of letter to Norman Cousins from Kiyoshi Tanimoto, 16 September 1956; carbon copy of letter to Kiyoshi Tanimoto from Norman Cousins, 27 September 1956. Both documents in RB Collection.

75. Nanjing, as a victim of Japanese aggression, could perhaps have served as an alternative symbol for the Pacific War, but under communist control soon after the war, it was closed to American charity. Moreover, the idea of "original sin" in dropping the first atomic bomb weighed heavily on Americans with humanitarian impulses, as the letters quoted above demonstrate.

76. Cousins, "An Apology for Living," *SRL*, 9 October 1948, 9–12, 54–58.

77. Hersey wrote about troops in the Pacific in the nonfiction work *Into the Valley: A Skirmish of the Marines* (New York: Alfred A. Knopf, 1943), and about soldiers in Italy in his Pulitzer Prize–winning novel *A Bell for Adano* (New York: Alfred A. Knopf, 1944). His novel *The Wall* appeared in 1950, four years after *Hiroshima*. John Hersey, *The Wall* (New York: Alfred A. Knopf, 1950).

78. "Hiroshima 1945; New York 1955," *New York Daily News*, 5 May 1955, clipping in scrapbook, Box 1300, NC Papers. Many other clippings in the same scrapbook contrasted sharply to the *Daily News*'s irreverent view.

79. "For Jap Bomb Victims," *Savannah News* (Ga.), 10 May 1955, clipping in Box 1300, NC Papers. See other clippings in this collection for further examples.

80. "Acme of Brotherhood," *Dayton News* (Ohio), 10 May 1955, Box 1300, NC Papers.

81. Thomas W. Ennis, "Alfred L. Rose, 95," *NYT*, 26 November 1981, sec. D14; telephone conversation with William R. Rose II, 24 January 1995.

82. Israel later designated Sugihara as a "Righteous Gentile," and Sugihara has been a subject of a recent exhibit, "Visas for Life," first shown at the Simon Wiesenthal Museum of Tolerance in Los Angeles in 1995, and a new book: Hillel Levine, *In Search of Sugihara: The Elusive Japanese Who Risked His Life to Save 10,000 Jews* (New York: Free Press, 1996). The more conservative statistic came from the Holocaust Memorial Center's website: *www.holocaustcenter.com/sugihara.shtml* (accessed 8 June 2003).

83. "Hiroshima and Sinai," *Kansas City Jewish Chronicle,* 20 May 1955, clipping in RB Collection. The Jewish gratitude mentioned here toward the Japanese had some truth. The author's father, when he arrived in New York City in the late 1960s, met a Jewish landlord who stated that he always tried to rent to Japanese tenants because a Japanese man had saved his life by giving him a visa.

84. "America's Atomic Atrocity," 974; "Some Scars Will Never Be Erased," *Christian Century,* 25 May 1955, 613.

85. See, for an example, a letter from Ruth F. Kavesh, "HPCA/SR contribution" folder, Box 330, NC Papers.

86. Lois P. Munroe to HPCA, 18 December 1957. See also Hans A. Iling (Los Angeles) to HPCA, 5 November 1957; Mabel Danuser (Washington, D.C.) to HPCA, 14 November 1957. In addition to her first contribution, Danuser sent $25 that she had received as a Christmas gift. "I can think of no better way to use it than to send it to the Hiroshima Peace Center," Danuser explained. Danuser to HPCA, 3 February 1958. All four letters in "HPCA/SR contribution" folder, Box 330, NC Papers.

87. Mrs. Roland Borchers (Mother Seton Residence, Montclair, N.J.) to Cousins, 27 September 1983, "Hiroshima Maidens, Corres., 1983" folder, Box 1386, NC Papers; emphasis in the original.

88. Yuri Kochiyama, telephone interview, 15 January 2004; letter from Yuri Kochiyama, 24 January 2004; Haruko Akamatsu, telephone interview, 6 November 2004. For more on Kochiyama, see Diane C. Fujino, *Heartbeat of Struggle: The Revolutionary Life of Yuri Kochiyama* (Minneapolis: University of Minnesota Press, 2005).
89. Sheila K. Johnson, *The Japanese Through American Eyes* (Stanford: Stanford University Press, 1988), 48–49.
90. Letter to Cousins from Tanimoto, 1 October 1952, Box 1386, NC Papers.
91. Quoted in Yavenditti, "Hiroshima Maidens," 29. Dr. William Hitzig also clearly expressed this sentiment in reference to the Ravensbrueck Lapins, HPCA's project following the Hiroshima Maidens; he described one of the "Lapins" as being "deprived of her right to womanhood" and denied "the possibility of a complete life" because the Nazis had sterilized her. Letter to Cousins from William Hitzig, 20 October 1958, p. 23, Folder 1, Box 272, NC Papers.
92. One report by an American stationed in Japan claimed that the Japanese were "very disturbed" by the exclusion of men from the project and suggested that steps be taken to "definitely establish that no discrimination was intended." Declassified copy of letter from U.S. Representative Cecil King (Calif.) to Assistant Secretary of State Thurston B. Morton, 6 June 1955, RB Collection.
93. "List of Hiroshima Maidens," Box 2 "Japan T.H. 1953" in Box 1272, NC Papers. This list appears to be a 1969 update, since someone penned "Dec. 69" on the document.
94. "Hiroshima Maidens Project Pleasing to All Americans," *Ann Arbor News* (Mich.), 7 May 1955, 1300, NC Papers.
95. Matsubara interview. Matsubara believed that Tomoko Nakabayashi's death (a heart attack during surgery) canceled these plans, but evidence in the NC and RB collections indicates that a lack of interest among potential sponsors stopped the other plans.
96. Yavenditti, "Hiroshima Maidens," 28.
97. Chujō, 70–72.
98. Barker, telephone interview.
99. Chujō, 72.
100. See letters in Hiroshima Maidens file at Wilmington-Peace Center.
101. Letter to Cousins from William Hitzig, 20 October 1958, p. 23,

Folder 1, Box 272, NC Papers; telephone conversation with Jeanne Benenson Lewisohn, 26 January 1998; Green, taped interview by Barker, RB Collection. See also a rough draft of Cousins' essay on the Ravensbrueck Lapins in his papers at UCLA. Box 272, NC Papers.

102. Cousins, taped interview; Barker, telephone interview. See also correspondence between Jack Penn and Cousins in the RB and NC collections.

103. Green, Benenson, and Dittler had been directing HPCA activities on a volunteer basis, and either grew away from it (Benenson remarried in 1964) or could no longer afford to volunteer their services (Dittler and Green) since they were not relatively wealthy like Cousins and Ida Day, a Quaker heavily involved with the "Maidens" project. "Contributors of $100 or More to the HPCA During Fiscal Year of April 1, 1957 to March 31, 1958," Folder "Lists of Donors of $100 or More," Box 330, NC Papers; Jeanne Benenson Lewisohn, telephone interview, 26 January 1998; memorandum Edna [Dittler] to Jeanne [Benenson], 2 January 1957; Marvin [Green] to Cousins, 11 May 1955, Box 1386, NC Papers.

104. Green, taped interview.

105. Green, treasurer, "Newsletter: The Orphanage Program, Hiroshima Peace Center Associates, Inc., 62 Burchard Avenue, East Orange, NJ—Orange 3-0537," July 1956, RB Collection. Green cited 227 "active parents" versus 264 "inactive" ones.

106. Exactly how long the program lasted is hard to determine. Existing papers show no firm end date, and surviving participants of the program do not remember or do not know. Telephone conversation with Lewisohn, 26 January 1998; telephone interview with Herbert Dittler, aged 90, whose wife, Edna, resided in a nursing home, 23 January 1998; letter from Sallie Lou Coyle to the author, 30 January 1998.

107. Memorandum, [Edna] Dittler to [Jeanne] Benenson, 28 March 1957, and memorandum, Edna Dittler to Jeanne [Benenson], 11 August 1958, both memoranda in "Orphans Correspondence '57, '58, '59," Box 1386, NC Papers; telephone conversation with Jeanne Benenson Lewisohn, 26 January 1998; report by Cousins in "Hiroshima Peace Center Newsletter," a pamphlet published by the Hiroshima Peace Center Associates, April 1954, RB Collection.

108. "The Story of the Hiroshima Peace Center Foundation," pamphlet in RB Collection.

109. On "life-time commitments," see letter to Mayor Shinzō Hamai from Norman Cousins, 11 October 1949, Box 96, Folder 4 ("Japanese Matters—1950"), NC Papers.

110. The McCarran-Walter Act of 1952 made Japanese immigration legal on a strict quota basis and was designed to allow elderly Japanese immigrants already in the country—especially the Issei parents of Nisei veterans—to finally gain U.S. citizenship. The bill's proponents tried to reassure their opponents that its tight quota restriction would prevent a flood of Japanese immigration and that the Issei, the primary beneficiaries of the bill, were no longer reproductive. See Yukiko Koshiro, *Transpacific Racisms: The U.S. Occupation of Japan* (New York: Columbia University Press, 1999).

111. See pages 6–7 of a report by Norman Cousins in "Hiroshima Peace Center Newsletter," a pamphlet published by the HPCA, April 1954, RB Collection.

112. Carbon copy of letter to Norman Cousins from Kiyoshi Tanimoto, 16 September 1956, RB Collection; see also Lifton, 253–69.

113. Retired in Hawai'i and 90 years old as of August 2004, Hugh O'Reilly still greets the children from the Holy Family orphanage at the welcoming ceremony every year.

114. DOS memorandum from [given name missing] McClurkin to Robertson re: "Reply to Norman Cousins' letter of December 8, 1955," 16 December 1955, RB Collection. Cousins wrote asking for continuing authorization for the transportation of doctors for the project. The State Department referred Cousins to the Defense Department.

115. Letter to G. Bromley Oxnam from Walter Robertson, 15 August 1955, RB Collection.

116. Klein, 83–85.

117. John Fousek, *To Lead the Free World: American Nationalism and the Cultural Roots of the Cold War* (Chapel Hill: University of North Carolina Press, 2000), 7.

118. "Hiroshima Maidens Project Pleasing to All Americans," *Ann Arbor News* (Mich.), 7 May 1955, Box 1300, NC Papers.

119. Cousins, taped interview.

7. Hollywood's Japan

1. Folder "Sayonara" 706, book 2, Warner Brothers Archives, Doheny Library, University of Southern California (hereafter cited as WBA).
2. Susan Sackett, *The Hollywood Reporter Book of Box Office Hits*, rev. ed. (New York: Billboard Books, 1996), 9–10, 128–129, 131.
3. Other English-language films with a Japanese theme that were screened in the United States at this time included *Tokyo Joe* (1949), *Oriental Evil* (1950, 1952), *Japanese War Bride* (1952), *Geisha Girl* (1952), *Forever My Love* (a.k.a. *Itsu Itsu Made Mo,* 1952), *Three Stripes in the Sun* (1955), *House of Bamboo* (1955), *Navy Wife* (1956), *Joe Butterfly* (1957), *The Geisha Boy* (1958), *Bridge to the Sun* (1961), *A Majority of One* (1961), *Operation Bottleneck* (1961), *A Girl Named Tamiko* (1962), *My Geisha* (1962), *Walk, Don't Run* (1966), and *You Only Live Twice* (1967). Two other important films of the fifties that promoted racial tolerance toward Asians, albeit on superficial terms, were *South Pacific* (1958) and *The King and I* (1956). For an illuminating historical analysis of *The King and I* and similar productions see Christina Klein, *Cold War Orientalism: Asia in the Middlebrow Imagination, 1945–1961* (Berkeley: University of California Press, 2003), Introduction and chap. 5.
4. Only the Philippines were neglected, perhaps reflecting the way U.S. policy prioritized Japan over its former Asian colony in the postwar period. Americans liked and still like stories about Americans as brave fighters for freedom and democracy, but any story about Americans' interactions with the Filipinos would be overshadowed by the Americans' denial of political freedom to Filipinos for nearly fifty years. See Daniel B. Ramsdell, "Asia Askew: US Bestsellers on Asia, 1931–1980," *Bulletin of Concerned Asian Scholars* 15 (1983): 2–25.
5. As racial tensions mounted in postwar America, Broadway confronted black-white race issues in productions such as *Deep Are the Roots, Anna Lucas,* and *Strange Fruit,* which were all staged in 1945. Before turning to the more volatile subject of black-white relations, Hollywood produced two pathbreaking films on anti-Semitism in 1947, *Crossfire* and *Gentlemen's Agreement.* Then in 1949 came a spate of movies on white racism toward African Americans: *Home of*

the Brave, Pinky, Lost Boundaries, and an adaptation of William Faulkner's *Intruder in the Dust.* They were followed a year later in 1950 with *No Way Out,* which featured Sidney Poitier in his screen debut. All of these movies got positive reviews in *Life* magazine: see issues of 30 June 1947, 71–74 (*Crossfire*); 1 December 1947, 95–100 (*Gentlemen's Agreement*); 23 May 1949, 143–146 (*Home of the Brave*); 17 October 1949, 112–115 (*Pinky*); 4 July 1949, 64–66 (*Lost Boundaries*); 12 December 1949, 149–153 (*Intruder in the Dust*); 4 September 1950, 44–46 (*No Way Out*).

6. E. G. D[oughtery], "Memo for the Files In Re: WIND BLOWS FREE-MGM," 10 August 1953; copy of letter to Dore Schary, MGM, from Joseph I. Breen, "re: 34 page synop of WIND BLOWS FREE," 11 August 1953 [*Wind Blows Free* appears to be the title MGM used to submit *Sayonara,* although *Wind Cannot Read* was the 1958 British film based on a novel with the same title]; E. G. D., "Memo for the Files In Re: Sayonara, [conversation with William Gordon acting for William Goetz Productions]," 1 September 1953; copy of letter to Frank McCarthy of Fox from Joseph I. Breen, "re: 50-page synop, dated 16 August 1953 of forthcoming novel SAYO-NARA," 1 September 1953; E.G.D, "Memo for the Files in re: SA-YONARA" [conversation with David O. Selznick of Fox], 2 September 1953. All documents in Sayonara production code file, Margaret Herrick Library at the Academy of Motion Picture Arts and Sciences, Los Angeles (hereafter cited as AMPAS).

7. The Irish Catholic and anti-Semitic Breen referred to the Jewish studio heads as "lice" or "vermin" in letters to other Catholics, and neither his office nor the Legion of Decency cared much about defending or fighting racism.

8. "Special for Armand Marcherd, King Features," press release by "carlile," Sayonara #706 book 1, WBA.

9. During the war, the economy and social mores discouraged conspicuous consumption, and the long workdays left just enough time to squeeze in a 90- or 100-minute movie for many Americans longing for diversion. After the war, the greater consumer choices, the housing boom, and shorter working hours gave Americans more time to spend their money in a wider variety of activities. Although movie at-

tendance began declining before most Americans owned televisions, the film industry saw television as its primary competition. By the early 1950s the studios were using new technologies to make movies more spectacular than television, with color, better sound, and larger screens, to try to reverse the postwar dip in movie attendance rates. John Belton, *Widescreen Cinema* (New York: Cambridge University Press, 1992), 69–75; John Izod, *Hollywood and the Box Office, 1895–1986* (New York: Columbia University Press, 1988), 134, 138–141; David Bordwell, Janet Staiger, and Kristin Thompson, *The Classical Hollywood Cinema: Film Style and Mode of Production to 1960* (New York: Columbia University Press, 1985), 331–332, 358–361.

10. *The Purple Heart,* directed by Lewis Milestone (Twentieth Century-Fox, 1944). For discussion on Hollywood's cooperation with the war effort, see Thomas Doherty, *Projections of War: Hollywood, American Culture, and World War II* (New York: Columbia University Press, 1993); Clayton R. Koppes and Gregory D. Black, *Hollywood Goes to War: How Politics, Profits, and Propaganda Shaped World War II Movies* (New York: Free Press, 1987).

11. *The Bridge on the River Kwai* earned 39 percent more than *Sayonara,* bringing in $17.2 million for Columbia Pictures. *The Bridge on the River Kwai,* directed by David Lean (Columbia Pictures, 1957); Sackett, 9–10, 128–129, 131. *River Kwai* also swept the major categories at the Academy Awards, winning seven of its eight Oscar nominations, including Best Picture, Best Actor (Alec Guinness), and Best Director (David Lean). Although the River Kwai is located in modern-day Thailand, the Thais are missing from this story. The film thus parallels the erasure of the Asian victims of Japanese imperialism.

12. In 1965, Hollywood produced a war film that humanized Japanese enemy soldiers and portrayed them sympathetically. Frank Sinatra's directorial debut, *None But the Brave,* was co-written by a Japanese screenwriter and co-produced by another Japanese. This antiwar war film depicted the Japanese soldiers as patriotic, but eager to go back home to their families. *None But the Brave,* directed by Frank Sinatra (Warner Brothers, 1965).

13. The U.S. occupation governments, however, censored films going into Japan and Germany and even tried, with mixed results, to encourage Hollywood to produce popular, commercial films with pro-American messages for audiences in the two defeated nations. On SCAP's attempts to control the Japanese film industry and capture the Japanese film market for American filmmakers, see Kyoko Hirano, *Mr. Smith Goes to Tokyo: Japanese Cinema under the Occupation, 1945–1952* (Washington, D.C.: Smithsonian Press, 1992); Susan Smulyan, *Film as Propaganda: Reorientation versus Entertainment during the Occupation of Japan,* forthcoming.

14. See the large spread on Japan in *Life:* "BULWARK IN THE FAR EAST," 28 August 1950, 84–90 (caps in the original).

15. DOS memorandum, dated 18 January 1951, by John M. Allison, summarizing opinions expressed in a meeting with Secretary of State John Foster Dulles prior to his trip to Japan. *Foreign Relations of the United States (FRUS), 1951,* vol. VI, 805. For more detailed discussion of U.S. economic policy toward Japan, see William S. Borden, *The Pacific Alliance: United States Foreign Economic Policy and Japanese Trade Recovery, 1947–1955* (Madison: University of Wisconsin Press, 1984); Aaron Forsberg, *America and the Japanese Miracle: The Cold War Context of Japan's Postwar Economic Revival, 1950–1960* (Chapel Hill: University of North Carolina Press, 2000); Sayuri Shimizu, *Creating a People of Plenty: The United States and Japan's Economic Alternatives, 1950–1960* (Kent: Kent State University Press, 2001). The oft-cited "workshop" comment came from a well-publicized speech by Under Secretary of State Dean Acheson before the Delta Council in Cleveland, Mississippi, in spring 1947. The entire address is reprinted in U.S. Department of State, *Bulletin* 61 (18 May 1947): 991–994.

16. Michael Paul Rogin, "'Make My Day!': Spectacle as Amnesia in Imperial Politics," *Representations* 29 (Winter 1990): 99–123, esp. 106–108. See also Teresa De Laurentis, *Technologies of Gender: Essays on Theory, Film, and Fiction* (Bloomington: Indiana University Press, 1987); Gina Marchetti, *Romance and the "Yellow Peril": Race, Sex, and Discursive Strategies in Hollywood Fiction* (Berkeley:

University of California Press, 1993); Molly Haskell, *From Reverence to Rape: The Treatment of Women in the Movies,* 2nd ed. (Chicago: University of Chicago Press, 1998).

17. *The Teahouse of the August Moon,* directed by Daniel Mann (Warner Brothers, 1956).

18. On another level, American audiences understood that the most knowing character in the story, "Sakini," was a white man in yellow face. Marlon Brando tried hard to impart an authentic-sounding accent and to accurately affect the postures of a rural Okinawa male. Memorizing his Japanese lines by rote, he copied the inflections of the Japanese language by listening to a tape of a native speaking his lines and repeating the lines with his Japanese teacher. Despite this effort, Brando could not prevent his characterization from being a slightly simian caricature of Okinawan or Japanese males. Ray Falk, "Bivouac at an Okinawan 'Teahouse' in Japan," *NYT,* 10 June 1956, 125.

19. See Julianne Burton, "Don (Juanito) Duck and the Imperial-Patriarchal Unconscious: Disney Studios, the Good Neighbor Policy, and the Packaging of Latin America," in Andrew Parker, Mary Russo, Doris Sommer, and Patricia Yaeger, eds., *Nationalisms and Sexualities* (New York: Routledge, 1992), 21–40.

20. The "three stripes" referred to the stripes of a U.S. sergeant, and the "sun" was the rising sun of Japan. The opening shots of the film superimposed, amazingly, the sergeant stripes onto Japan's rising sun icon.

21. Mitsuko Kimura starred in a similar role in screenwriter and director Paul H. Sloane's *Itsu Itsu Made Mo* (a.k.a. *Forever My Love*) in 1952. She plays another Japanese woman who falls in love with an American G.I., played by Chris Drake.

22. The real Hugh O'Reilly was and is quite different from his film portrayal by World War II Navy veteran Aldo Ray. Ray, a husky man with a raspy voice, made a career playing working-class guys who, despite their rough mannerisms, have a heart of gold under their tough exteriors. Although O'Reilly is a Marine combat veteran who claims to have been a troublemaker as a teenager in the Bronx, he is quite unlike Ray's tough sergeant. Now over 90 years old, O'Reilly is

no longer the lean and tall man that Saitō Yuko married, but he remains urbane, gracious, and witty. Far from being a verbally awkward tough guy, O'Reilly is smooth-talking, as one would expect of a man who spent most of his career, both in and out of the military, in public relations and marketing. O'Reilly is not a Pearl Harbor survivor, and neither was the general who served as the model for Phil Carey's character. Nor did the real-life general criticize O'Reilly for his racial intolerance; they actually met after O'Reilly started his program for the Holy Family Orphanage. Furthermore, O'Reilly understood the importance of grassroots organizing and interracial accord before going to Osaka. As a union activist before rejoining the Army in 1949, O'Reilly had helped New York City bus workers to elect their first African American union president in the mid-1940s. Hugh O'Reilly, interview, 22 June 2004.

23. Dialogue from the film. *Three Stripes in the Sun*, directed by Richard Murphy (Columbia Pictures, 1955).

24. Memorandum from Donald E. Baruch, Chief, Motion Picture Section, Pictorial Branch, DOD, to John L. Steigmaier, Chief, Far East Desk, Department of State, 5 October 1954; memorandum from Lt. Colonel James G. Chestnut, Acting Chief, Public Information Division, DA, to Director, Office of Public Information, DOD, 8 October 1954; memorandum, Steigmaier to Baruch, 11 October 1954; routine message, Staff Communications Office, DA, 14 October 1955. All four documents in box 5, folder 7, DOD Film Collection, Special Collections, Georgetown University Library.

25. Bosley Crowther, "Sayonara," *NYT*, 6 December 1957.

26. As Michener's novel made more clear than the movie did, Kelly had also been transformed through his wife. Katsumi Kelly domesticated and calmed the self-described "no-good punk," and thus Kelly protested, "And if I lose Katsumi, I'll be no damned good again." Hence his desperate act of double suicide when he fails in his efforts to reverse his orders to go back to the U.S. or to take Katsumi back to the U.S. with him. James A. Michener, *Sayonara* (1953, 1954; New York: Fawcett Crest, 1990), quote on p. 196.

27. Dialogue from the film. *Sayonara*, directed by Joshua Logan (Warner Brothers, 1957).

28. "Romance in the Orient," *Newsweek,* 9 December 1957, 96, clipping of movie review in Sayonara #14587A, WBA.

29. Joshua L. Logan, *Movie Stars, Real People, and Me* (New York: Delacorte Press, 1978), 96–98, 120; James A. Michener, letter to author, 28 March 1996.

30. Clair Primus, "Marlon Brando: Why He Prefers Foreign Girls," *Movie Mirror* [month missing], 1957, 28–33, 52–3, clipping in Sayonara #14587A, WBA.

31. See Marchetti's extended analysis of *My Geisha* (1962); other films from the 1950s and 1960s suggesting that Japanese women made better companions than American women included *House of Bamboo* (1955), *The Geisha Boy* (1958), *The Barbarian and the Geisha* (1958), *Tokyo After Dark* (1959), *Cry For Happy* (1961), *A Girl Named Tamiko* (1962), and *You Only Live Twice* (1967).

32. Logan, *Movie Stars,* 97.

33. Memorandum to Wolfe Cohen (W[arner]B[rothers]-New York) from J. E. Dagal (W[arner]B[rothers]-Japan), 24 July 1956; letter to Col. Jack Warner from Solly Baiano from Japan, 23 July 1956; letter to Mr. Hagiwara (JACL-Chicago) from S[olly].J. Baiano, Talent Executive, 6 November 1956; inter-office communication (cable) to [Jerry] Orbringer from Baiano, 24 December 1956. All four documents in Sayonara file #2752, WBA.

34. Press release, "For Mort Licketer, Special Services," by "Carlile," Sayonara #706, book 1; press release "Special for Armand Marcherd, King Features," by "Carlile," Sayonara #706, book 1, WBA.

35. It is quite possible that Taka herself falsified her age to the studio. Press release by "Ferrero," Sayonara #706, book 1; "Actress Miiko Taka Files Divorce Suit," *LA Examiner,* 8 September 1958; "Actress Miiko Taka of Movies Wins Divorce," *LA Herald* [?], 18 November 1958, clippings in Taka, Miiko file at AMPAS.

36. Lucy Herndon Crockett, *Popcorn on the Ginza: An Informal Portrait of Postwar Japan* (New York: William Sloane Associates, 1949), 146.

37. Press release by "Gersdorf," Sayonara #706, book 1, WBA; "presenting Miss Miiko Taka . . . ," in press book, Sayonara #715, WBA.

38. Kaspar Monahan, "Globaloney Gab Session: Miiko vs. Monahan,"

The Pittsburgh Press, 22 September 1957, p. 9, sec. 5, clipping in Sayonara #14587A, WBA.

39. "Transcribed Radio Interview with Van Johnson for 'Go for Broke,'" Go for Broke folder 2 of 2, MGM collection, WBA.

40. Besides *Cry for Happy* (1961), however, *Sayonara* seems to have been the only starring role that Taka obtained in a Hollywood film.

41. "What's next for me? A beautiful, talented actress wonders if there will be a permanent future in acting for a Japanese-American or if, instead, it'll be a one-role career for her," *Movie Fan,* February 1958, 20–21, clipping in Sayonara #14587A, WBA.

42. By departing from Michener's novel, which featured neither kabuki nor the character Nakamura, Logan highlighted this Japanese theatrical form and presented Japan as a place of intrigue and adventure for American women, too. Rather than pining for her unfaithful fiancé in the film version, Eileen Webster goes on a Japanese adventure of self-discovery of her own with the help of a "Japanese" male.

43. Press release by "Ferrero," Sayonara #706, book 1, WBA.

44. Logan, *Movie Stars,* 98.

45. List for possible casting for "Nakamura," dated 26 November 1956, Sayonara S-196, Box 2271, WBA.

46. *The Crimson Kimono,* directed by Samuel Fuller (Columbia Pictures, 1959); *Bridge to the Sun,* directed by Etienne Perier (MGM, 1961); *A Majority of One,* directed by Mervyn LeRoy (Warner Brothers, 1961).

47. Marchetti, 165.

48. A poster for the movie, however, does show the unusual image of a nonwhite man kissing a white woman, but the picture is small and is shown under the much larger words that were meant to titillate rather than educate, "What was the irresistible appeal that led her into the arms of a Japanese Boy!" Press book for *The Crimson Kimono,* AMPAS.

49. "Alec's Irish Roz," *Time,* 19 January 1962, clipping in Majority #2953, WBA.

50. Toichi Nakata, "[Interview of] Shohei Imamura," in James Quandt, ed., *Shohei Imamura* (Toronto: Toronto International Film Festival Group, 1997), 116–117.

51. *The Saga of Anatahan,* directed by Josef von Sternberg (Daiwa Productions-Twa/Pathé Contemporary, 1953); Blaine Allan, "The Only Voice in the World: Telling *The Saga of Anatahan,*" in Peter Baxter, ed., *Sternberg* (Tonbridge, Kent, U.K.: British Film Institute, 1980), 119–129.

52. Allan, "The Only Voice," 119.

53. The Japanese also showcased their female stars to sell their own films. For the New York Film Fest in January 1958, the Japanese film industry planned to send eight actresses, but no male stars. "Learning From Last Yr.'s N.Y. Fest, Japanese Face January Test Hopeful Commercial Outlook Will Improve," *Variety,* 11 December 1957, 5, 70.

54. Press kit for *The Barbarian and the Geisha,* WBA.

55. Press release by "Watt," Sayonara #706, book 1 (on Taka); press release by "Gersdorf," Sayonara #706, book 1, WBA. The latter short piece on Umeki referred to her as a "doll" or a "dolly" six times.

56. Press books for *Sayonara, The Barbarian and the Geisha,* and *Bridge to the Sun,* WBA; press books for *House of Bamboo, The Geisha Boy,* and *A Girl Called Tamiko,* AMPAS.

57. "Warriors on Leave in a Lovely Land," *Life,* 2 December 1957, 69.

58. "Production Notes and Synopsis for 'My Geisha' (A Steve Parker Production for Paramount)," *My Geisha* file, AMPAS; press release by "Boutyette," Tamiko Folder 11 of 11, Paramount Production and Budget Records, AMPAS.

59. Press release by "Gersdorf," Sayonara #706, book 1, WBA.

60. Press books for *The Barbarian and the Geisha* and *Bridge to the Sun,* WBA. MGM liked this idea with an "Oriental" woman in a jinrikisha so much (or simply lacked imagination) that it pushed the scheme to advertise *Bridge to the Sun,* a love story between a Euroamerican woman and a Japanese man.

61. After scheduling a "Nipponese talent," the booker arranged a tie-in with a local Japanese restaurant to provide the food. "'Have Kimono, Will Travel,'" *Variety,* 11 December 1957, 1, 70.

62. W. Lasiter to Jack Warner, 8 May 1958, Sayonara #2953, WBA.

63. Mrs. Eula M. McNabb of Dallas, Texas, to Jack Warner, 23 June 1962, Majority #2953, WBA; emphasis in the original.

64. John McCarten, "The Current Cinema: Variation on the Puccini Ca-

per," *New Yorker,* 14 October 1957, 89–90; Arthur Knight, "Sayonara," *Saturday Review of Literature,* 4 January 1958. But *Newsweek* judged *Sayonara* as a "dull tale of the meeting of the twain . . . [that] belabors a series of now-defunct Oriental Exclusion Acts." "Romance in the Orient," *Newsweek,* 9 December 1957. The latter two reviews found in Sayonara #14587A, WBA.

65. Putting on America's best face, of course, meant that the filmmakers did not address resentment of the continued presence of U.S. troops in Japan after the Occupation. This resentment was revealed in a famous case in 1957—the same year *Sayonara* premiered. William S. Girard, a 23-year-old enlisted man from Ottawa-LaSalle, Illinois, shot and killed a 46-year-old Japanese mother as she was scavenging spent brass artillery shells at a U.S. Army firing range in Japan. The murder, which Girard claimed was accidental, provoked outrage in Japan and sparked an international controversy about whether Girard should be tried by a Japanese or an American court. In the end, Girard was tried by a Japanese court and given a light sentence. To prevent the Girard case from souring views of the bilateral relationship, the *New York Times* tried to minimize the Japanese uproar, insisting that it stemmed not from a felt grievance about the presence of U.S. servicemen, but from Japanese reactions to the American reactions to the incident. The *Times* insisted, "The United States forces' day-to-day relations with the Japanese people are among the best that exist between United States servicemen and local populations abroad." The article featured GIs—in uniform—celebrating Christmas with a Japanese family, wearing traditional garb. One of the GIs holds up a little girl to see an ornament on a Christmas tree. See Robert Trumbull, "Japan: A 'Strange' but Cordial Land," *NYT,* 30 December 1957, 5.

66. Klein, 134–135. As Klein points out, Americans who did challenge their nation's global policies—Paul Robeson, W. E. B. Du Bois, and Pearl Buck—were silenced.

67. "Where there is anxiety," anthropologist Alan Dundes has argued, "there will be jokes to express that anxiety." "Remember," Dundes writes, "people joke about only what is most serious. That is why there are so many jokes about death and ethnic stereotypes." Alan

Dundes, *Cracking Jokes: Studies of Sick Humor Cycles and Stereotypes* (Berkeley: Ten Speed Press, 1987), vii–viii.

68. *Geisha Boy*, directed by Frank Tashlin (Paramount Pictures, 1958). The aunt, however, translates the request literally into the type of stilted English that has made the Japanese seem much more polite than they really were: "Would you please do me the honor of becoming my esteemed father?"

69. *Pete-San*, original teleplay by Rudy Makoul, Geisha Boy file #3616, AMPAS.

70. Revised final screenplay, dated 3 June 1958, pp. 82–94, Geisha Boy file #3616, AMPAS.

71. *Geisha Boy* press book, Paramount Press Sheets Releases Season 1958–59 Group A-18, AMPAS.

72. Final screenplay, dated 9 May 1958, Geisha Boy file #3616, AMPAS.

73. Lee Besler, "Geisha Boy Premiere High, Wide and Zany," *LA Mirror-News*, 31 December 1958, clipping in Geisha Boy production file, AMPAS.

74. Lewis seems to have ad-libbed the Brando comment, as it does not appear in the final revised draft of the script. Revised final script, 3 June 1958, p. 45, Geisha Boy file #3616, AMPAS.

75. Geisha Boy, file 5 of 9, Paramount Production and Budget Records, AMPAS. Pleshette earned $500 per week, in contrast to McCarthy's salary of $300 per week.

76. See, for example, a cartoon in John W. Dower, *War Without Mercy: Race and Power in the Pacific War* (New York: Pantheon Books, 1986), 187.

77. Paramount Press Sheets Releases, Season 1958–59 Group A-18, AMPAS.

78. Even the final draft of the screenplay, dated 9 May 1958, reflected this lack of concern for accuracy by continuing to call the Japanese female lead "Sing-Sing Sikota"—a mishmash that must have sounded like a Japanese or an "Oriental" name to American ears during the 1950s. The final revised draft, dated 3 June 1958, made an attempt at a closer approximation of a Japanese name for this character: Kimi Sikita. "Kimi," often short for "Kimiko," is a popular female name, but since the "si" sound is missing from the Japanese lan-

guage, "Sikita" was as bad as the original "Sikota." Geisha Boy file #3616, AMPAS.

79. Frank Krutnik, "Jerry Lewis: The Deformation of the Comic," *Film Quarterly* 48 (Fall 1994): 12–26.

80. Margaret T. McFadden, "America's Boy Friend Who Can't Get a Date: Gender, Race, and the Cultural World of the Jack Benny Program, 1932–1946," *Journal of American History* 80 (June 1993): 118.

81. Another joke about gender confusion, however, does punctuate the film's end, destabilizing once again Wooley's control of a situation. As dozens of bunnies pop out of his top hat during this gala show, Wooley discovers that his trusty sidekick, Harry the Hare, was all along a "Harriet" instead.

Epilogue

1. Orville Prescott, "Books of The Times," *NYT,* 27 April 1960, 35.

2. "A Yen for the Games," *Business Week,* 26 September 1964, 39.

3. *Saturday Review of Literature:* "Hiroshima 1964," 18 April 1964, 24–27; "The Orphans and the Maidens," 25 April 1964, 20–22; "Japan: Of Dynamo and Destiny," 9 May 1964, 24–25.

4. [Luce], "The Unique Era, but What Now?" *Life,* 11 September 1964, 3.

5. Incidentally, the hot spring baths with the very best views such as this one are usually reserved for male customers in most of Japan's famous *onsen* resorts.

6. Luce, "The Unique Era"; Edwin O. Reischauer, "Inevitable Partners," *Life,* 11 September 1964, 27–28.

7. The Nixon policy is described in Michael A. Barnhart, "From Hershey Bars to Motor Cars: America's Economic Policy Toward Japan, 1945–1976," in Akira Iriye and Robert A. Wampler, eds., *Partnership: The United States and Japan, 1951–2001* (Tokyo and New York: Kodansha International, 2001), 201–222.

8. Ezra F. Vogel, *Japan as Number One: Lessons for America* (Cambridge, Mass.: Harvard University Press, 1979); William G. Ouchi, *Theory Z: How American Business Can Meet the Japanese Challenge* (Reading, Mass.: Addison-Wesley, 1981).

9. While planning a trip to the National Archives at College Park, Maryland, I explained my topic—in my American-accented English—to this archivist, and he responded with a startling narrative about how he despised the Japanese. At the end of our conversation, he asked brightly, "So when are you coming in?" I hedged and did not offer my name, nor did I ask for his. This man, a SCAP archivist, probably assisted Japanese scholars on a daily basis since Japanese researchers, after Americans, are the most frequent visitors to NARA-College Park. Telephone conversation with anonymous archivist, early summer 2001.

10. Louis R. Coatney, e-mail to author, 1 August 1995; emphases in the original. Coatney wrote: "Feel free to share this exchange between us with *anyone* you wish." See also his thread on the Enola Gay controversy on H-Asia: *www.h-net.org/~asia/threads/thrdenola.html.*

11. See Ian Buruma, *The Wages of Guilt: Memories of War in Germany and Japan* (New York: Farrar, Straus and Giroux, 1994). He posits that Germans have been more forthcoming about their war crimes because they felt guilt, whereas the Japanese only felt shame.

12. Christopher Shannon, "A World Made Safe for Differences: Ruth Benedict's *The Chrysanthemum and the Sword," American Quarterly* 47:7 (December 1995): 659–680.

13. Bruce Cumings, *Parallax Visions: Making Sense of American–East Asian Relations* (Durham: Duke University Press, 2002).

ACKNOWLEDGMENTS

All historians, I once read somewhere, are looking for their past. Why and how I came to do this book can surely be traced, in part, to being an expatriate Japanese banker's daughter who spent her formative years in an upper-middle-class, almost entirely segregated neighborhood in Houston, Texas, during the 1970s. The Pacific War and its aftermath were ever-present in my childhood. During visits to Japan, I heard my grandparents' stories about the American air raids on Tokyo; back in Houston I learned, as my mother tucked me into bed, that the emperor was a brave man who asked General MacArthur not to hurt his people. On hot, humid Saturday afternoons, I watched strange old movies about Japan on TV. By reading Jeanne Wakatsuki Houston's *Farewell to Manzanar*, I found out about the wartime internment of Japanese who happened to be American, just like me. I knew that "we" were once the enemy to Americans, but now we were friends. This article of faith, however, was unstable—that much was apparent even to a child.

Most historical studies are not as long in the making as this one, and I have incurred many debts. I would first like to thank those who shared their personal stories: Robert Yukimasa Nishiyama, Mitsuya Gotō, Kōya Azumi, Steve Yamamoto, Harumi Ebihara, Chiyoko Yamamoto, Shelley Mydans, Yuri Kochiyama, Haruko Akamatsu, Miyoko Matsubara, Bruce and Betty Johnstone, and Hugh and Yuko O'Reilly.

Second, my thanks go to Michael Sherry, Laura Hein, and the late Robert H. Wiebe. Mike is an ideal mentor, encouraging and exacting at the same time. Laura's perspicacious comments about my project were ones that I kept returning to and thinking about for years. Bob has passed away, but I remain grateful for his consistent, sometimes sharp prodding to finish the project and publish it. I have been able to lean on Andrew J. Rotter for professional and research matters since my graduate school days and am grateful for Andy's continued support and sage advice.

My cohorts at Northwestern University sharpened my thinking, read parts of this work, cheered me, and helped me enjoy life despite grad school. I thank Fritz Fischer, David Futrelle, David Ruth, Lane Fenrich, Kate Lucey, Jennifer Hicks, Mikki Ray, Jacalyn Harden, Leslie Dunlap, and Seth Jacobs. Petra Goedde has been a marvelous friend and collaborator, and Michele Mitchell remains one of the best people I know.

In Hawai'i, George Akita, Robert Perkinson, and Mimi Henriksen also read and critiqued chapters in this book. I miss arguing with Akita-sensei and remain grateful for his encouragement. Robert and I were rookie professors together at the University of Hawai'i, and I don't think he can know how much I have learned and continue to learn from him. I especially want to thank Mimi, who many years ago as my graduate instructor at Berkeley first gave me the idea that I could be a historian.

I'm also grateful to my other UH colleagues who gave me advice about chapters or were helpful in my thinking about Japanese history: Karen Jolly, Marcus Daniel, Paul Varley, John Stephan, and Mark McNally. My work and research at UH would have been impossible were it not for Gwen Agina, Susan Abe, Pauline Sugiura, Margaret Hattori, Ryan Nakagawa, Jodie Mattos, and Tiana Kwan. They have my sincere thanks.

One of my greatest debts is to the women of my interdisciplinary writing group. Monisha DasGupta, Cindy Franklin, Linda Lierheimer, Laura Lyons, Kieko Matteson, and Mari Yoshihara helped me refine my prose and analysis, chapter after chapter, and, as it turned out, year after year. Their sharp insights and constructive criticisms have improved this book in countless ways, from small matters of style to restructuring chapters and strengthening arguments. I thank my lucky stars for being a part of an intellectual community with these amazing women.

Here, I must also mention Lon Kurashige to express appreciation for his critiques, but more important, for his exceptional generosity.

At Brown, I've been blessed with another vibrant and collegial intellectual community. Generous colleagues, including Bob Lee, Jim McClain, Kerry Smith, and Susan Smulyan, read my work carefully, gave me invaluable advice, and saved me from errors. I've benefited from the feedback of graduate students: Jin-Suk Bae, Jane Hong, Jessica Johnson, Danielle Kantor, Jooyoung Lee, Ben Leff, Amy Marshall, Julia McCombs, Ani Mukherji, and Shiri Sandler. And I'm particularly grateful to Dan Kim, my colleague in English, whose attentive reading of the entire manuscript and last-minute interventions have made this, I believe, a stronger and more engaging book.

I could not have researched or finished this book without the assistance of friends, relatives, and others who, over the years, provided me with sources, helped me select images, and gave me a place to stay during my research trips: Donna Alvah, Joe Henning, Richard Minear, Jayson Chun, Brian Niiya, Julie Fry, Minako Saburi, Mieko Saburi, Ken Shibusawa, Chris Wasden, Tomoko Shibusawa, Kevin Turbitt, Yoshiaki and Kieko Shibusawa, and Sheila Martinez-Lemke. Special thanks to Rodney Barker, who shared his research materials on the Hiroshima Maidens. My research assistant, Samantha Schoeller, helped me obtain permissions for the images in this book, and I am thankful for her good cheer in completing this often frustrating task.

A year-long sabbatical from teaching, partly funded by the Andrew W. Mellon/ACLS Fellowship for Junior Faculty, allowed me to finish the book. Assistance from Karen Mota, Cherrie Guerzon, Mary Beth Bryson, Julissa Bautista, and Holly Snyder has eased my transition to Brown, helping me in innumerable ways to bring this project to a close. I am grateful also to Beth Bailey and the other two outside readers for their encouragement, endorsement, and constructive advice—particularly Beth, who took time to discuss her report with me. I have been truly fortunate to work with two excellent editors at Harvard University Press: Joyce Seltzer, a rare editor who still edits with a red pencil, and my copy editor, Mary Ellen Geer.

Finally, I give thanks to the three who are closest to me. Two of them have had to live with this book for their entire lives, and the other, trained as an economic and social historian, has tried to keep this cultural historian honest. With deep gratitude for their patience and with much love, I dedicate this book to my husband, Andy Lohmeier, and our two daughters, Arisa and Miya.

INDEX

Acheson, Dean, 167
Adams, Henry, 23, 24
Adkins, Carl D., 236
Adler, Mortimer, J., 82–84, 320nn60–61
African Americans, 7, 49, 74, 75, 85–86, 168, 169, 197, 199–200, 313n110
Akamatsu, Haruko, 245
Akihito, crown prince, 118–120, 208
Alien Land Laws, 167
Ambrose, Stephen, 138–139, 333n108
American charity initiatives for Japanese, 29, 178. *See also* Hiroshima Maidens; Hiroshima moral adoptions; Johnstone Scholarship; O'Reilly, Hugh; Wolfhounds
American civilization. *See* civilization, western
American Civil Liberties Union, (ACLU), 167, 169, 232
American exceptionalism, 9, 73–74; extending benevolence, 65, 32, 176, 187, 232–234, 242, 252; "manifest destiny," 64, 73
American Indians, 73–74, 197; compared to Japanese, 1, 6, 14

American Jews, 165, 242–243, 257, 363n7
American Magazine, 51–52, 201
American Mercury, 42, 49
American Presbyterian Board of Missions, 187
American prisoners of war. *See* prisoners of war (POWs), American
American Red Cross. *See* Red Cross, American
American Veterans of Foreign Wars (Amvets), 169
American women: flattering depictions of, 39, 40; giving war bride lessons to Japanese, 46–47; privilege over Japanese women, 35; unflattering depictions of, 39, 40, 41–44, 267–268, 283, 311n88; wartime gains and retraction, 6–7, 42. *See also* Japanese women, stereotypes of
Americans as world leaders, 28, 77, 280; Cold War education and, 77–80, 82–84, 320n56; racial tolerance and, 193, 277
Americans, Japanese views of, 53, 46, 136. *See also* Hiroshima Maidens; Hiroshima moral adoptions; hostility

Boyington, Dorothy M., 221
Brando, Marlon, 255, 256, 262, 265–268, 283, 366n18, 372n74
Breen, Joseph I., 257, 363n7
Bridge on the River Kwai, The (1957), 257, 258, 284–285, 364n11. *See also* Japanese in U.S.-released films
Brines, Russell, 72
Bronfenbrenner, Martin, 8, 39, 309n73, 309–310n76, 310n77
Brooklyn College, 83, 84
brothels. *See* sex work
Brown, Margery, 8, 43–44, 53, 311n95
Bruce, William L., 140–141, 142
Brundidge, Harry, 130
Buchanan, Robert C., 193–194
Buck, Pearl, 226, 228, 371n66
bunraku, 258, 275
Burgman, Herbert John. *See* World War II treason cases
Buruma, Ian, 257, 296, 374n11
Busch, Noel, 25, 64–66, 111
bushido, 34
Businessweek, 289
Buttons, Red, 265–266
Byrnes, James, 99

Candler School of Theology, Emory University, 213–214
capitalism: Freud and, 75; maturity and, 57, 89; racial tolerance and, 88
capital punishment, 156–157, 158, 169–170
CARE, 31
Carey, Phil, 263, 366–367n22
Carter, James M., 146, 151, 161, 172
Catholic World, 30
Charlie Chan, 179, 201, 270
Chase, William C., 99
Chaze, Elliott, 8, 40, 52
China, 40, 54, 62, 94, 257, 259; keeping China "open," 193; Manchuria,

102, 122, 332n101, 347n34; Nanjing Massacre, 323–324n89; 357n75
Chinese, 123, 142, 154, 186, 187, 195, 200
Cho-Cho-san. *See Madame Butterfly*
Christian Century, 215, 226, 243, 244
Christianity, 68, 77, 89–90, 93–94, 104, 112, 118, 147, 198, 208, 345n16; Cold War policy and, 187, 192, 215; postwar reconciliation and, 186–187, 191–192, 194, 240. *See also* civilization, western; Green; Johnstones; Methodists; Quakers; Tanimoto; Vining
Chrysanthemum and the Sword, 60–61, 63, 66. *See also* Benedict, Ruth
Chulakongkorn, crown prince of Siam, 119
civilization, Japanese: American views of its backwardness, 126, 330n74; Japanese beliefs of being advanced, 56, 102, 314n2. *See also* Japanese, as an immature people: feudal
civilization, western: Americans responsible for preserving, 76–80, 93; compared to Japanese civilization, 64–65; in crisis, 93–94; and education, 82–84; and manliness, 64–65, 74, 78, 80, 124; as a racialized continuum of evolutionary development, 56, 59, 74–80, 181, 212; test of, 59, 89–92; as universal, 9, 62–63, 68, 74, 83–84, 85, 92, 181, 233, 253. *See also* maturity; racism, scientific
Civil Rights movement, 7, 50, 168, 199–200; and Cold War, 7, 171, 180, 183, 194, 196–197, 209, 271–272, 278–279, 292–293. *See also* racial tolerance
Clark, Mark, 56, 218
Cold War: civil rights and, 7, 8, 76, 171, 180, 183–184, 194, 196–197, 209, 257, 271–272, 278–279, 292–

Life (magazine) *(continued)*
on Japan, 290–292; "Sunday at
Hirohito's," 113–117; using readers'
letters, 193–194,
Linkletter, Jack, 255
Lions Club, 203
Lippmann, Walter, 82
Logan, Joshua, 256, 257, 265, 266–
267, 268, 270–271, 369n42
Los Angeles Times, 147, 158–159, 160
Loti, Pierre, 23, 39–40
Luce, Henry, 2, 26, 76–77, 93, 193,
291, 292
Lucky Dragon, 231, 234, 237, 354n40
Lundberg, Ferdinand, 42

MacArthur, Douglas A., 8, 60, 92, 94,
149, 218; defense of Hirohito, 110;
description of the Japanese as a boy
of twelve, 54–59, 289; initial meeting
with Hirohito, 96–98; retaining
Hirohito, 103–108; shielding
Hirohito, 113, 116; using Hirohito,
112, 137
Madame Butterfly: modern version, 34–
41, 44, 64, 258, 267; Pierre Loti
novel, 23; Puccini opera, 22, 273. *See
also* Baby-san
Malcolm X, 245
Manila Times, 195, 196
Marchetti, Gina, 368n31
marriage. *See* intermarriage
Martin, Dean, 286
Marxism, 89
masculinity, deviant, 124–127, 130–
131, 144–145, 149–150, 160, 174,
258, 330nn71–72
Masugi, Shizue, 227, 228, 246, 354n33
Mathes, William C., 8, 155–159, 169,
172
Matsubara, Miyoko, 228, 359n95
Matsuoka, Yōsuke, 192–193
Mature Mind, The (1949), 85, 89

maturity, 5–6, 9, 10, 25, 55–59, 101,
212, 296, 300n12; capitalism and,
57, 89; gender and, 12, 24, 27–28,
50–51; 57, 73, 86, 117; puppets
and,108–110, 300n12; race and,
124; racial tolerance as, 39, 84–89,
257, 261–266, 276–279; through interracial relationships, 261–268,
280–281, 286–287, 367n26. *See also*
Cold War liberals; Japanese as an
American responsibility; Japanese as
an immature people; masculinity, deviant; Momism; Overstreet
McCarran-Walter Act, 47, 168, 278,
361n110. *See also* immigration laws
McCarthy, Nobu Atsumi, 280, 282,
283
McFayden, John W., 193–194
McNabb, Eula, 276–277
Mears, Helen, 8, 61–63, 84, 315n15
media. *See* shifting enemy to ally *and
individual periodicals*
medieval. *See* Japan, stereotypes of: feudal
Meiji emperor, 105, 328n43
Meiji University, 141, 172
Methodists, 214, 226, 236, 348n37,
354n30
Metro-Goldwyn-Mayer (MGM), 275–
276
Michener, James A., 31, 48; marriage to
Mari Sabusawa, 48, 49; *Sayonara,*
48, 256, 257, 258, 265, 266–267,
367n26, 369n42
Mikado, The (Gilbert and Sullivan), 22,
109–110, 125
Miki, Takeo, 170–171
militarism or militarization: American,
61, 62, 102, 326n16; German, 92;
Japanese, 61, 126, 189; as orientalist
term, 102, 132
militarists, Japanese: to blame for war,
101–102; contrasted with emperor,

Rape of Nanking. *See* China: Nanjing Massacre
Ravensbrueck Lapins, 249–250, 359n91
Ray, Aldo, 263, 366n22
Reader's Digest, 106, 118, 232–233
Red Cross: American, 29, 46–47; Japanese, 46. *See also* Crockett
Red Scare, 143, 165
Reed College, 168, 344n10
Reischauer, Edwin O., 62, 137, 292, 304n16, 325n11
reparations, 4, 181–182, 252
"reverse course." *See* Supreme Command for the Allied Powers (SCAP): "reverse course"
Riggs, Angela, 169–170, 341n82
right-wing dictatorships, 300n12
RKO, 165
Robertson, Walter, 234, 252
Robeson, Paul, 174, 371n66
Robinson, Jackie, 174
Roger Wolcott School, 221
Romulo, Carlos, 91
Roosevelt, Eleanor, 228
Roosevelt, Franklin, D., 171
Rosenberg, Ethel and Julius, 165
Rostow, Eugene, 86–88
Rostow, W. W. (Walter Whitman), 88
Russell, Richard B., 100
Russell, Rosalind, 271
Russia. *See* Soviet Union
Ryan, Cornelius, and Frank Kelley. *See* Kelley, Frank
ryōsai kenbō ("good wife, wise mother"), 46

Saga of Anatahan (1953), 272
Said, Edward W., 11–12
samurai, 294
San Diego Tribune-Sun, 160–161
San Francisco Chronicle, 147, 156
Sands, Franklin, 91

Saturday Evening Post, 29, 47, 71, 77
Saturday Review of Literature, 8, 74, 92, 94, 216, 217–225, 226, 232, 291, 320n56
Savannah News, 241
Sayonara (film, 1957): Gruver's maturity, 265–266, 280; Hana-Ogi's transformation, 267–268; limits on promoting equality, 278–279, 282; marketing, 268–269, 274, 275; premiere, 255–256, 260; production, 257–258, 266–267, 268–271; reviews, 275, 278, 370–371n64. *See also* Japan in U.S.-released films
Sayonara (novel, 1954). *See* Michener, James
scholarship programs. *See* GARIOA *and* Johnstone scholarship
scientific racism. *See* racism, scientific
Seiko, 289
Senior Scholastic, 8, 25, 110
sex work, 38–39, 272
Shaw, Victoria, 271
shifting enemy to ally, 4–12, 47, 51, 223, 288–291; adapting pre-existing frameworks, 25, 110, 137–138, 258–259, 288; cohesive narratives, 10, 123, 192–193, 197, 211, 212, 294–295; complex and uneven, 9, 175; importance of women and children, 19, 26, 51; Japanese participation in, 7, 202, 205–206, 207–208, 218, 238–240; media shaping of public opinion, 307n41; naturalized framework, 4–6, 10, 20, 25, 138, 216–217, 253; not orchestrated, 9–10, 53, 101, 112, 215, 237–238, 259, 261; privatizing reconciliation, 213–217, 224–225, 242, 250–254; repetition of narrative, 64, 105–106, 117, 120, 194, 243, 259. *See also* Hiroshima Maidens; Hiroshima moral adoptions; Hirohito; Japanese in U.S.-re-

shifting enemy to ally *(continued)*
  leased films; Nishiyama; O'Reilly;
  Tōjō; travelogue
Shigemitsu, Mamoru, 324n6
Shinto, 97
Shion-kai, 227, 228
Showell, David, 199, 203
Shriners, 203
Sinatra, Frank, 364n12
Sino-Japanese War, 332n104
Social Darwinism, 78–80
Sorbonne, 208
souvenir shopping and touring, 16, 51–
  52
Soviet Union, 28, 40, 54, 77, 90, 183,
  184, 194, 232, 235, 241, 245, 259
spectacle: Hollywood films on Japan,
  258, 259, 260, 273, 279, 282; Japan
  as, 51–52; refusal to make of Hiro-
  shima Maidens' injuries, 237; *Sayo-
  nara* premiere, 255, 260; Tōjō's sui-
  cide attempt, 128
Stanford University, 188
Stars and Stripes, 31, 42
Star-Spangled Mikado (1947), 108–110
State Department. *See* U.S. Department
  of State
Stephan, John J., 339n56
Stoddard, George D., 71
Strecker, Edward, 42, 80–82
Sugihara, Chiune, 243, 358n82,
  358n83
Supreme Command for the Allied
  Powers (SCAP): aid to atomic bomb
  victims banned, 214; Benedict's influence on, 60; censorship, 63, 184,
  309n73, 365n13; Civil Information
  and Education Section (CIE), 18,
  206; educational reforms, 71–72;
  fraternization policy, 40–41; GHQ
  Labor Division, 62–63; GI philanthropy promoted, 29; Hirohito
  and, 97, 103–105, 110–111, 133,

138; Hirohito publicity, 112–
  118, 120, 122, 328n53; officials,
  8, 11, 17, 75–76, 101, 112, 127,
  181; orientation for GIs, 9, 17–20,
  304n15; policy to reintegrate Japan,
  17, 25, 127; "reverse course," 3–4,
  40, 181–182, 198 313n112; re-colo-
  nizing Asia for Japan, 196–197,
  347n34; sex work policy, 38; shared
  goals and attitudes with other Americans, 10, 112; tourism encouraged,
  20, 313n112; travel restrictions for
  Japanese, 187, 189; undemocratic
  edicts, 40, 69. *See also* GARIOA
  scholarships; O'Reilly, Hugh;
  Wolfhounds
Swarthmore, 220
SWNCC 150/4/A "Initial Post-surrender Policy for Japan," 100, 110

Taira, Kankichi, 200
Taka, Miiko (a.k.a. Bette Ishimoto),
  255, 256, 267, 268–270, 274,
  369nn40–41
Takarazuka Theater, 131
Talmadge, Eugene, 193
Tanimoto, Kiyoshi, 213–214, 217–218;
  creating Hiroshima Maidens, 226–
  229, 232, 233–234, 238–239, 240,
  246, 249, 353n33, 355n46; Cousins
  and, 217, 357n74
Tashlin, Frank, 281, 286
Teahouse of the August Moon (1956),
  256, 262, 279, 286. *See also* Japan in
  U.S.-released films
television, 176–180, 234–235
Thailand, 364n11
Three Stripes in the Sun (1955), 262,
  263–265, 366n20. *See also* Japan in
  U.S.-released films
Thurmond, Strom, 193
Time (magazine), 123, 190, 191, 193
  307n41